Enter through the Image

ENTER THROUGH THE IMAGE

Published by Recluse Pub.
First edition - 2009

Parts of Ch. XII. on visionary art have previously appeared in print in:
The First Draft of A Manifesto of Visionary Art, L. Caruana, Recluse 2001.
Parts of Ch. XII. on Johfra have previously appeared on line at:
The Visionary Revue No. 2, Spring 2003, http://VisionaryRevue.com

About the author:
http://www.LCaruana.com

Library of Congress cataloging-in-publication data
Caruana, Laurence, 1962 -
Enter Through the Image:
The Ancient Image Language of Myth, Art and Dreams
1st edition - Recluse Publishing
ISBN-13: ISBN 978-0-9782637-1-3
ISBN-10: ISBN   0-9782637-1-5
1. Mythology
2. Religion
3. Title

ENTER
The Ancient
THROUGH
Image Language
THE IMAGE
of Myth, Art & Dreams

Caruana

Μαλλον δὲ αὐτή σε ἡ εἴκων ὁδηγήσει...
The image itself will show you the way...
Corpus Hermeticum (IV, 11)

RECLUSE
PUBLISHING
~2009~

IV

CONTENTS

DEDICATED TO THE MEMORY OF

Martin Hodel
1966 - 1995

*Am Karfreitag durch einen Bergunfall in Engadin
hat sein Leben ein allzu frühes Ende gefunden*

*Ah life's midday...
Was it not for you that the glacier today
exchanged its grey for roses?*
- Nietzsche, Upper Engadin 1885

VII

Preface

The idea of an image-language is one I have been pursuing faithfully for many years – attentively recording my dreams, rendering the more remarkable ones in paint, and accumulating a large quantity of remarks over several volumes of my notebooks. Many hours have been spent in pleasant research at the University of Toronto libraries, the *Gasteig* and *Ludwig Maximilians Bibliothek* in Munich, and the *Bibliothèque Nationale de France* in Paris. And so I would like to thank these institutions by acknowledging them here.

But a book such as this cannot be born in solitude. I also have to thank John Davis, Kevin Walters, Martin Hodel, Eric Schumacher, Bremner Duthie, Lisa Pasold, Martin Romberg, Delphine Proner, Romuald Leterrier, Alexandre Lehmann, Juan Gonzalez, Marité Fernández, Pierre Peyrolle, Michel Henricot and Ernst Fuchs for many fruitful discussions lasting late into the night, often in quaint, smoke-filled cafés such as Café May in Toronto.

During my travels, I've had the good fortune to cross paths with artists and thinkers whose conversations have left indelible impressions in my mind. A heart-felt *namaste* to Erik Davis, Benny Shanon, Luis Eduardo Luna, Gyrus, Voke, Amanda Sage, Andrew Gonzalez, Maura Holden, Luke Brown, Delvin Solkinson, Daniel Mirante, Ellen Lórien, De Es, Robert Venosa, Martina Hoffmann, Allyson Grey and Alex Grey. As well, I must thank Florence Ménard for correcting my French translations, just as Steven Toepell rendered similar such aid for my translations from the German.

As a wandering scholar and painter, I have continually sought my inspiration in that strange netherworld where art, myth and dream interfuse. At first, I was content merely to explore the interplay of these three creative forms. But slowly, a door opened onto their underlying logic. The images of ancient art, and even of my own works, strangely became transparent. Unexpectedly, I had learned to *enter through* these images to the *Mysterium* at their source. And so, the time has come for me to organize my research, conversations, intuitions and meditations into a single coherent work. This is done with the hope that others may follow the paths I've laid out here, and so find the same experience at their end as remarkable as I have.

L. Caruana
Paris 2009

INTRODUCTION

Coptic fragment from the Nag Hammadi Library
3rd Century

CHAPTER I

The Ancient Manner of Thinking in Our Modern Era

> *Truth did not come into the world naked,*
> *it came in types and images.*
> *[...One] must enter through the image*
> *into truth.*
> – The Gospel of Philip (67:9)[1]

I. The Lost Fragment

An ancient heretical text buried for seventeen hundred years and resurfacing in the last century bore within its aged pages one short but endlessly intriguing fragment. The text, a Gnostic Christian work of the third century, was discovered in 1945 when two Muslim peasants accidentally unearthed a jar near Nag Hammadi Egypt containing twelve leather-bound books. Although one of the books was burned by their widowed mother for fuel, most of the volumes were brought to Cairo by a one-eyed merchant, where French scholars immediately recognized them as an important cache of Gnostic gospels, preserving a long-forgotten outlook onto the world. Among the fifty-two tractates, a single fragment of text enjoins us, quite mysteriously, to *"...enter through the image."*[2]

If we wish to learn the ancient language of images, then we must first learn, as this fragment of text suggests, to *enter through* the image. We must learn to not only *think in images*, but to combine our vision and thinking into a more meditative gaze that sees the hidden, higher shapes. *"The image itself will show you the way,"* another ancient text reminds us... *"It takes hold of those who have the vision, and draws them upward."*[3]

In all cultural manifestations of the Sacred, from Egyptian hieroglyphs and Sumerian cylinder seals to Buddhist mandalas and Byzantine icons, an ancient mythic outlook is preserved in meaningful arrangements of images. *To enter through the images* of these older cultures is to behold, once again, the Sacred that lies at their source.

Although many relics of art and remnants of their myths have been passed down to us, we have lost the key that, with its gentle turning, would release the mysteries locked within them. To step across their hallowed thresholds requires that we approach the images themselves, think in accord with their constructs, and so regain the ancient manner of image-thinking still contained in their ever-silent forms.

Like art and myth, our dreams each night also create meaningful arrangements of images, improvising narratives that continually evolve into visions of eternal significance. The more ancient manner of image-thinking also manifests itself in *dreamwork* – a style of thought our cultural ancestors echoed in their sacred art and story telling, seeking thus to elevate its unknown workings into our understanding. If we wish to *enter through the images* of ancient culture, we must re-acquire their forgotten image-language, a language which continues its silent monologue still – in our dreams.

The ancient manner of thinking that underlies this image-language is precisely what we shall intend by the term 'iconologic'.

Iconologic, simply put, means *thinking through images*. In dreams, in myths, and in works of art, images are so composed as to bear their own unique message. The recurrence of certain motifs, now here in a dream, now there in a myth, suggests that an inherent order or logic underlies these arrangements. To uncover the forgotten image-language and expose its latent logic – or 'iconologic' – is the journey that awaits us in this work – a threefold journey along the Mythic, Symbolic and Oneiric Paths before a final in depth encounter with Iconologues at the end. For, with this knowledge, we may re-enter our dreams, and recover a view onto our oneiric creations long-since unconsidered. What is more, we may learn to *enter through* the images of more ancient cultures, and regain their long-lost outlook onto life and the Sacred.

Iconologic, then, underlies the ancient image-language, and organizes our images into meaningful arrangements, be they the image-clusters of myth, art or dreams. Those image-clusters which betray a recognizable meaning and arrangement shall be referred to, henceforth, as 'iconologues'. Symbols, mythologems and mythic narratives constitute the most obvious iconologues, though many others exist. For, symbols may be *combined*, myths may *cross* one another, and mythologems may be *displaced* from one culture to another. Hence, these continuous transformations shall also concern us over the course of our inquiry.

The ultimate aim of this work is to uncover an array of such iconologues, and to learn to *think* again *through* their antiquated forms. For, through an understanding of the ancient image-language, we may regain an older, indeed, forgotten view unto life – a more ancient philosophy that sees life itself as a gradual unfolding of the Sacred...

II. The Quest for Iconologic

Our quest for iconologic is not new. Many of our culture's greatest thinkers have betrayed, through certain fragments in their works, the desire to seek out this lost manner of thinking. In each case, they saw image-thinking as *a more ancient style of thought*. For example, after a lifetime of tireless wandering through the dark forests and twisting caverns of his own innermost thinking, Nietzsche realized that:

> *In our sleep and in our dreams, we pass through the whole thought of earlier humanity. I mean, in the same way that man reasons in his dreams, he reasoned when in the waking state many thousands of years ...*
>
> *The dream carries us back into earlier states of human culture, and affords us a means of understanding it better.*[4]

This lone thinker, standing on the mountain's highest peak and staring down into the abyss within himself, came to the important realization that man *'reasons in dreams'* – just as man once reasoned *while awake* thousands of years ago. Presumably, Nietzsche meant in our ancient mythology, for he recognized that *"myth itself is a kind or style of thinking."*[5] But, his insight also bespeaks the possibility of an iconologic, persisting over thousands of years, and sounding silently still, in our own century.

While it has indeed survived and remains with us unconsciously in dreams, this unique style of thinking was gradually forgotten over the course of man's history. It was replaced by a more logic-oriented discourse, based on the predicate logic of our spoken and written language. We live, as Hegel and Goethe lamented, 'in an age of prose'.[6]

But, considering that mankind formulated its 'First Philosophy' through *mythical thinking*, linking things mundane to those transcendent via symbol and metaphor, the loss of this older mode of thought was of profound consequence – for humanity had thus lost the ancient image-language which allowed us *to see* the Sacred and speak of it, as was indeed the case in the distant past. Martin Heidegger, one of Nietzsche's philosophical heirs, has written extensively[7] of the *finis metaphysicae:* how our age has witnessed *the end of metaphysics*, due to modern man's loss of the power to create a mythopoeic philosophy, such as we had done in more ancient times.

III. The 'Archaic Vestiges' &
'Mental Antiquities' of Dreams

Shortly after Nietzsche's plunge into madness, another thinker emerged who also sought his destiny in the darkened world of psychosis and dreams. If Nietzsche's *Zarathustra* unfolds like a dream in some ways symptomatic of his own incipient madness, then Freud's *Interpretation of Dreams,* written twenty years later, reveals an intense striving to find in dreams the way *out* of such madness. Like Nietzsche, Freud suffered traumatically from the occasion of his father's death. He acquired a neurosis which he was only able to cure by journeying into his dreams and re-emerging once more with the key to their decryption.

In the process, Freud made a series of startling discoveries regarding the ways in which images are arranged in dreams. He discovered, first of all, that the images of dreams are *symbols* which, once interpreted in light of the dreamer's free associations, reveal unconscious thoughts, wishes and desires – even the lost memories of earliest childhood – which underlie our forgotten life-conflicts and otherwise hinder life's on-going development.

But, of even greater consequence, Freud came to realize in a chapter entitled 'the Means of Representation in Dreams' that 'symbolization' is not the only way in which images are arranged in dreams. *Condensation, displacement, reversal* and other forms of 'dreamwork' also compose images into dream narratives – sometimes revealing, sometimes obscuring the deeper significance reposing beneath them. This series of 'iconologues' uncovered by Freud is not unique to dreams alone: ancient myths and sacred works of art also betray a tendency to reverse, displace and condense their images, thereby revealing or obscuring their underlying source.

Like Nietzsche, Freud was enamoured of ancient Greek culture, and saw the interpretation of dreams as a new hermeneutic capable of unveiling aspects of archaic culture hitherto lost and forgotten. Indeed, depth psychology could be considered a veiled attempt to recover the ancient manner of thinking at the root of our lost image-language. In *The Interpretation of Dreams,* Freud wrote:

> *We can guess how much to the point is Nietzsche's assertion that in dreams, 'some primæval relic of humanity is at work which we can now scarcely reach any longer by a direct path'; and we may expect that the analysis of dreams will lead us to a knowledge of man's archaic heritage, of what is psychically innate in him.*
>
> *Dreams and neuroses seem to have preserved more mental antiquities than we could have imagined possible; so that psychoanalysis can claim a high place among the sciences which are concerned with the reconstruction of the earliest and most obscure periods of the beginnings of the human race.*[8]

In Sophocles' tragedy of *Oedipus Rex,* Freud found an ancient myth that still functioned dynamically in the psyche of modern man – 'the Oedipus complex'. It followed that, if such an ancient myth could illuminate the dark workings of the modern mind then, *vice versa,* an investigation into our present day-to-day fantasies, dreams and delusions could reveal lost and forgotten fragments of mythologies past. Could, for example, the plot of the second and third parts of Aeschylus' lost *Prometheus* trilogy – which, only fragments thereof have come down to us through time – be recovered by seeking out parallels of its narrative in our dreams? Would the Promethean fire, extinguished in our age, thereby be rekindled?

It was C. G. Jung, Freud's 'adopted son' and designated heir, who extended this journey into darker realms of the unconscious, discovering beneath the personal figures populating dreams a whole host of archetypes from mythologies past. Jung distinguished between the dreamer's 'personal' unconscious, as explored by Freud, and his newly discovered cultural or 'collective' unconscious, which he explored as a result of his traumatic break with Freud, who had always assumed the role of Jewish elder and patriarch.[9]

Jung eventually realized that the figures in dreams were not only personal acquaintances from the dreamer's waking world, but more archaic and universal figures which the analyst was able to recognize through his knowledge of art and myth. These mythic figures arose from the older and darker recesses of the unconscious, *das kollektive Unbewusste,* an ancient fount of archaic memories. Jung described the collective unconscious as *"a fund of unconscious images... a matrix of mythopoetic imagination which has vanished from our rational age."*[10]

A knowledge of mythology thus became the means to orienting us further through dreams and, conversely, dreams could lead us further into the dark origins of our own earliest thinking. Following up Nietzsche and Freud's original inspiration, Jung wrote:

> *Many... mythological motifs... are also found in dreams, often with precisely the same significance... The comparison of dream motifs with those of mythology suggests the idea – already put forward by Nietzsche – that dream thinking should be regarded as a phylogenetically older mode of thought.*[11]

Jung's contribution to the attempt, in our times, to regain this lost and forgotten manner of image-thinking comes with his discovery of *the archetypes.* The archetypes are precisely what myths and dreams share in common. In Jung's own words, they are *"...forms or images of a collective nature which occur practically all over the earth as constituents of myths and, at the same time, as autochthonous, individual products of unconscious origin. "*[12] Thus, figures such as the Child, the Wise Old Man, or the Fool arise in dreams, fantasies and delusions but, as spontaneous products of our imagination, are also to be found in myths, fairy tales and even Tarot cards.

IV. Myth, Narrative & Time

There are other thinkers who, during these darkened times, have journeyed into the chthonic realms of our primordial thinking. But, rather than following the dark forest path of dreams and madness, they travelled instead beside the dried river bed *of ancient myth*. The task was to re-animate the decayed structures and skeletal forms still encrusted like fossils along its banks.

And the world that subsequently revealed itself in myth was not unlike the world of dreams and madness: full of wonder, terror, pity and bliss; an ever-turning wheel of joy and woe, where delight quickly dissolved to darkened illusion and moments of agony broke through to God's revelation.

Especially in the writings of Northrop Frye, Mircea Eliade, Heinrich Zimmer and Joseph Campbell, the attempt was made to bring ancient myths back to the fore of our modern consciousness. In particular, they discovered how myths are an arrangement of images *in time*. This is true both of *Cosmogonic myths*, involving the world's creation or destruction; and *Hero myths*, involving the hero's departure, descent and deed performed at the darkest nadir, followed by his subsequent ascent and return.

Hero myths in particular arrange their images in accord with distinctive *narrative patterns*, which arise in different forms due to differences in the *hero's task*. These three features of myth – *time, narrative* and *the hero's task* – constitute three of the most important iconologues used by our mythologies to arrange images in a meaningful way.

In his final works, Northrop Frye explored the temporal structure and narrative patterns underlying our own cultural myth, realizing that the Christian narrative arranges images over *linear time*, which transpires in a once-only unfoldment of history. Over the course of linear history, certain images from the Creation recur, undergoing modification from the Old Testament to the New, until they finally re-appear and resolve in the Apocalypse. Though Adam falls from paradise at the beginning of time, Noah, Abraham, Moses and other saviours culminating in Christ descend in their myths to a dark nadir, so as to restore that lost paradise. Only at the end of time, during the Apocalypse, will that vision of paradise be fully restored.

Hence, the narratives of Judæo-Christianity transpire in linear-historical time, and acquire, according to Frye, *a U-shaped narrative structure*. The *hero task* of Christianity is to restore, in the end, that paradise which was lost at the beginning. In this way, the Bible has become for our culture 'a Great

Code' which we have followed unerringly in all our mythic arrangements of images in literature, poetry and art. It is also the code which our culture, in its attempts to understand the art and myths of other cultures, inevitably projects upon them.

Meanwhile, Heinrich Zimmer and Joseph Campbell delved into the Sanskrit and Pali canons of Hindu and Buddhist scripture, and discovered differently shaped narrative structures which arrange their images in *ever-recurring cycles of time*. Due to cyclic time, the *narrative structures* of Hindu-Buddism, Campbell claimed, are *O-shaped*. Figures like Brahma, Vishnu and Shiva continually create, destroy and restore the cosmos. And so the Buddha's *task*, in contrast to Christ's, is to find that one stilled point at the centre of time's ever-swirling illusion.

But, these two opposing views on time came to be further augmented by Mircea Eliade. In his book *The Myth of the Eternal Return*, he recognized the existence of another, more ancient mode of time, which he called *mythical time*. Like Zimmer and Campbell, Eliade had begun his studies in Hindu scriptures, but quickly moved beyond them to a broader analysis of all the world's religions. He also delved into the shamanistic practices of Primitive cultures, whose beliefs may constitute the primordial origins of all religions.

His analysis revealed a view on time decidedly different from Judæo-Christianity and Hindu-Buddhism, because ancient narratives arrange their images in a more remote *mythical time* – a sacred and eternal time which transpires *before and after* linear history, and is *closed off* from time's ever-recurring cycles.

The iconologues of time, narrative and the hero-task become keys that unlock the gates of, not only myth – but dreams. For myths and works of art have continually sought their source-imagery *in* dreams. Yet, by giving these fleeting apparitions a more permanent form, art and story-telling have thereby *elevated* the dark mechanisms of dreamwork into the light of consciousness.

In this way, dreams, like myths, must be recognized as arrangements of images *in time*, which unfold according to certain set *narrative* structures. In them, the dreamer is given some *task* to accomplish, and must cross over a dangerous life-threshold to complete it. And so, as Campbell concluded after a lifetime of research into mythology, *"In myth... we enter the sphere of dream awake."*[13]

In this way, Campbell slowly became conscious of the same deep accord which Nietzsche, Freud and Jung had also detected between dreams and myth. For myths, in a more structured way, use the same symbols and narratives which arise, almost spontaneously, in dreams. *"Imagery, especially the imagery of dreams,"* Campbell remarked, *"is the basis of mythology."*[14] And Eliade echoed this sentiment: *"In the oneiric universe, we find again and again the symbols, the images, the figures and events of which mythologies are constituted."*[15]

Returning, then, to myths, we must recognize that myths are also arrangements of images where 'some primæval relic of humanity is still at work'; they too manifest the 'mental antiquities' and 'older modes of thought' characteristic of dreams. Thus, among the discoveries of Nietzsche, Freud and Jung, among the various symbols, archetypes, condensations and displacements which arrange images into dreams, we must also include the mythic structures of time, narrative and the hero's task, as elucidated by Frye, Eliade, Zimmer and Campbell. All constitute various iconologues which underlie the ancient image-language.

In the 20th century, there have also been certain artists and writers who, through the peculiar arrangements of images in their works, have betrayed a secret desire to seek out iconologic's lost manner of thinking. Our inquiry into the ancient image-language would not be complete unless we also considered more modern works of art wherein the ancient tendencies still persist.

Among the painters who have pursued dream imagery in their canvases stand the Surrealist masters Dalí and Magritte, as well as the Visionary artists Ernst Fuchs and Johfra. Among the modern writers who have crossed ancient myths in their narratives stand Nikos Kazantzakis and Hermann Hesse. All have demonstrated in their works a gradual awakening and awareness of the ancient image-language, and the attempt to *enter* once more *through the image...*

V. Surrealist Logic

Through his pioneering journey into the unconscious, Sigmund Freud inspired a generation of Parisian artists in the 1920's to undertake similar such voyages to this realm below consciousness – chronicling in poetry, painting, theatre and film their nightly wanderings into the dark world of dreams.

In the end, Surrealism brought dreams and their peculiar manner of thinking more and more into our waking world, so that their unique oneiro-logic could become immediately apparent. In short: it *elevated* the unconscious *into* consciousness.

In a celebrated passage from the *First Manifesto of Surrealism* (1924), André Breton defined the surrealist image, citing the ideas of Pierre Reverdy:

> *The image is a pure creation of the mind... born from the juxtaposition of two more or less distant realities. The more the relationship is distant and true, the stronger the image will be – the greater its emotional impact and poetic reality.*[16]

The classic example of a surrealist image was taken from Lautréamont: *"Beau comme la rencontre fortuite sur une table de dissection d'une machine à coudre et d'une parapluie."*[*17] In many Surrealist paintings we find evidence

---

*As beautiful as the chance encounter of a sewing machine and an umbrella on a dissecting table.

of these *rencontres fortuites*. In de
Chirico: beside an attic nude torso
lie a bunch of bananas. In Magritte:
bourgeois gentlemen rain from the
sky. And in Dalí: a grasshopper is
pressed to the dreamer's lips.

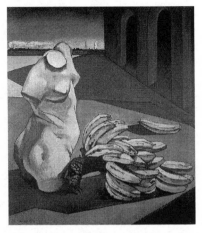

The 'patron saint of Surrealism',
Sigmund Freud, had previously recognized these strange juxtapositions
in dreams and characterized them as
condensations. Through the *strange
juxtaposition of objects* in their
paintings, inspired by an underlying
dream-*condensation*, the Surrealists
raised into consciousness an important
iconologue identified by Freud – a
means of arranging images in accord
with the logic of dreams.

Strange Juxtaposition of Objects
Giorgio de Chirico:
The Uncertainty of the Poet (1913)

In Magritte's *The Ladder of Fire* (1939), we find another example
of iconologic, as well as the iconologue that underlies the image's strange
arrangement. Here, a key, a rock and a crumpled piece of paper are placed
side by side and each is consumed by fire. Within the world of Aristotlean

Displacement of Quality - René Magritte: The Ladder of Fire (1939)

logic it is perfectly acceptable for a crumpled piece of paper to ignite afire. But only in a world ruled by surrealist logic may a rock and key also burst into flames...

To *displace* fire's combustible quality onto a rock and key is the poetic step *par excellance* that suddenly transports the viewer out of the Aristotlean constructs of reality and into *surreality*. In the resulting disorder, the essential defining properties of objects shift. Earth is no longer distinct from water, nor is air from fire. Hence, a rock, which is normally earthen, becomes fiery, such as in Magritte's painted vision. And in the ever-metamorphosing world of dreams momentarily held still by Surrealist painters, liquid becomes solid, and solid, combustible. Thus, a key burns, a statue bleeds, and a bowl of fruit appears to be made of stone. Or, in Dalí's celebrated *Persistence of Memory*, pocket watches soften, melt and turn into images of liquid time. Freud recognized the dream-logic underlying these shifts, and characterized them as *displacements* – another essential iconologue identified by Freud and elevated by Surrealist painters into consciousness.

It is the 'strange juxtaposition' *between objects* (condensation) or *their qualities* (displacement) that ushers us into the realm of dreams, because the relation that holds within the resultant image is more or less unconscious, and hence, in accord with a more ancient, mythopoeic mode of thinking.

But, the more we look at Dalí's or Magritte's work, it becomes apparent that both artists preferred to use modern, day-to-day objects in their juxtapositions: bowler hats, umbrellas, pocket watches and other *petit bourgeois* articles. Through the strange juxtaposition of these *Herrenartikel*, we see symbols of the type often encountered in dreams – dreams which, for Freud, had a hidden, sexual intent.

In his chapter on 'Representation by Symbols' in *The Interpretation of Dreams*, Freud focussed his analysis onto the *petit bourgeois* objects of his day, and saw *Herr Biedermeier's* hats, umbrellas and neckties as phallic in nature: *"All elongated objects, such as ...umbrellas (the opening of the last being comparable to an erection) may stand for the male organ."*[18] *"As regards articles of clothing, woman's hat can very often be interpreted with certainty as a genital organ, and moreover, as a man's... In men's dreams, a necktie often appears as a symbol for the penis."*[19] Meanwhile *gnädige Frau's* sewing machine and other *"complicated machinery and apparatus occurring in dreams stand for the genitals."*[20] Hence, following the tradition initiated by Freud, these artists became preoccupied with 'bourgeois' dreams revealing Herr Biedermeier's hidden and repressed sexual wishes.

Yet, as Jung was able to demonstrate, the source of our dream material is not only the personal unconscious, with its residue from our day-to-day encounters, but also the deeper, cultural strata of our collective unconscious. Dreams contain collective or cultural symbols which reveal, not only hidden and repressed sexual wishes, but more intricate and complex issues of life's

Combination of Sacred Symbols
Ernst Fuchs: Moses Before the Burning Bush (1957)

fulfillment and wholeness. Indeed, the symbols of our dreams may have a higher, more sacred purpose: to awaken man to the presence of the Sacred in his life...

VI. The Visionary Art
of Fantastic Realism

While Freud's philosophy influenced a generation of artists in Paris after the First World War, Jung's philosophy eventually found its influence on a generation of artists after the Second World War in – of all places – Vienna. The 'Vienna School of Fantastic Realism' consisted of five *nachkriegzeit* artists who were initially influenced by Surrealism, but carried their art forward into images of greater cultural and religious significance.

Their works may better be characterized as 'Visionary': using a flawless classical technique, they pursued mythic, dream-like and even hallucinatory imagery in their canvases. These painters – Ernst Fuchs, Rudolf Hausner, Arik Brauer, Anton Lehmden and Wolfgang Hutter – exhibited their work collectively and individually for over thirty years, while also publishing numerous catalogues and books.[21] It is particularly the work of Ernst Fuchs that characterizes 'Visionary Art'[22] as an important emergence from the art of Fantastic Realism.

In Fuchs' *Moses Before the Burning Bush* (1957), we find another fine example where the ancient manner of image-thinking has been preserved in a modern work of art. Here, the Hebrew figure of Moses is depicted in Gothic style, but juxtaposed within the same picture is the face of the Buddha. On the left, within the burning bush, is the figure of Yahweh, and aside from the Jewish symbol of the menorah burning around him, he also possesses the Hindu iconographical feature of 'four-handedness', each hand gesturing as if with a distinctive Indian *mudra*.

The first iconologue to be noted in this work is Fuchs' juxtaposition of *sacred* symbols from *different* cultural traditions. Not only have traditional symbols of the sacred been juxtaposed, but *combined* in new and unexpected ways. Such a combination allows us to think further through their antiquated forms, arriving at a new, more creative and comprehensive view onto the Sacred.

While Surrealist painters began with *petit bourgeois* objects and, through their strange juxtaposition, created dream symbols from the personal unconscious (tinged with sexual associations); Visionary artists began with *sacred* symbols and created, through their strange juxtaposition, dream symbols from the deeper cultural matrix of the collective unconscious (with a halo of more sacred associations). Through his combination of different cultural symbols, Fuchs is able to elevate more ancient strata of the collective unconscious into our modern awareness – in particular, the ancient's greater awareness of the Sacred...

In the case where recognizable religious symbols are combined, a series of more sacred associations arise. Because, sacred symbols remain situated *within* their mythic contexts. As such, when two such symbols are combined, *their associated myths are also evoked* and, indeed, *cross one another.* At the one moment in time that is manifest in this painting, two different mythic narratives meet at their nadir. In Fuchs' painting, we witness that moment of epiphany when Yahweh manifest himself to Moses in the form of a burning bush – while witnessing, simultaneously, the epiphanous moment when the Buddha finally broke through to enlightenment.

Joseph Campbell, in *The Hero with a Thousand Faces*, calls upon and crosses *exactly these two myths* to illustrate the narrative pattern of the hero's 'separation' from the world, his momentary 'initiation' into a sacred revelation, and his subsequent 'return' as he attempts to offer this revelation to the world: *"The whole of the Orient,"* Campbell writes, *"has been blessed by the boon brought back by Gautama Buddha – his wonderful teaching of the Good Law* [the Dharma]– *just as the Occident has by the Decalogue of Moses."*[23] In Fuchs' marvelous painting, we are able to witness how these two narratives meet at that nadir moment of epiphany when the wisdom and the word, the *Dharma* and the *Decalogue*, were finally revealed...

VII. The 'Immutable Face
behind all Religious Symbols'

Through the iconological *combination* of different sacred symbols, Visionary art expands our cultural horizon, so as to manifest a broader yet more unified vision of the Sacred. This higher, more culturally diverse yet singular vision of the Holy also appears in the writings of Nikos Kazantzakis and Hermann Hesse.

For example, in his autobiography, Kazantzakis describes an event in his youth while visiting the Temple of Knossos in his homeland of Crete. While at the temple he had a most fortuitous encounter with an old Parisian *abbé:*

> *We stopped at a square column of glazed plaster, at the top of which was incised the sacred sign: the double-edged axe. The abbé joined his hands together, bent his knee for a moment, and moved his lips as though in prayer.*
>
> *I was astonished. "What – are you praying?" I asked him.*
>
> *"Of course I am praying, my young friend. Every race and every age gives God its own mask. But behind all the masks, in every age and every race, is always the same never-changing God."*
>
> *He fell silent, but after a moment: "We have the cross as our sacred sign; your most ancient ancestors had the double-edged axe. But I push aside the ephemeral symbols and discern the same God behind both the cross and the doubled-edged axe, discern him and do obeisance."*
>
> *I was very young at that time. On that day I did not understand, but years later my mind was able to contain those words and make them bear fruit. Then I too began to discern the eternal immutable face of God behind all religious symbols.*[24]

Meanwhile, in his allegorical novel *The Glass Bead Game,* Herman Hesse also pursued this 'immutable face' behind all the masks of God. Over the course of its narrative unfolding, Hesse invents an age-old imaginary game which becomes an extended metaphor for the quest after bliss.

In the fabled province of Castilia, a symbolic language akin to Chinese pictograms, musical notation and mathematical formulæ was developed, which allowed the artistic, scientific and philosophical ideas from various cultures to be faithfully translated into one universal script. A form of meditation was added to the manipulation of these symbols, creating a kind of quest after ever higher and more encompassing combinations of symbols. This then evolved into the time-honoured 'glass bead game' practiced among various orders and leagues, and *"...represented an elite, symbolic form of seeking for perfection, a sublime alchemy, an approach to that Mind which beyond all images and multiplicities is one within itself – in other words, to God."*[25]

A game might begin with a theme from a Bach fugue, or a sentence from Leibniz or the Upanishads, and from there, depending on the talents of the player, evolve so as to include related themes from various other arts and disciplines – seeking always the underlying unity among this multiplicity. Of particular interest to our quest for iconologic (which resembles the glass bead game in a startling number of ways) is the fact that, at one point in the novel, Hesse's protagonist realizes

> ...*that every symbol and combination of symbols led not hither and yon, not to single examples, experiments and proofs, but into the centre, the mystery and innermost heart of the world, into primal knowledge. ...Every transformation of a myth or religious cult, every classical or artistic formulation was,* [he] *realized in that fleeting moment, if seen with a truly meditative mind, nothing but a direct route into the interior of the cosmic mystery, where... holiness is forever being created.*[26]

As with Kazantzakis' abbé, so here, the glass bead game player recognizes that the multiplicity of sacred symbols, when combined with one another, leads beyond their surface imagery to a much deeper awareness of the *Sacramentum* they all share at their origin.

Our quest for the ancient image-language may be likened to the glass bead game, with the exception that it concerns itself exclusively with *images* of the Divine, and seeks in dreams, art and myth the means by which these images may be arranged and *entered through* so as to lead us ever further inward, into an experience of the Sacred.

The numinous experience of the Holy, as Fuchs, Kazantzakis and Hesse have shown, is characterized by an experience of *unity*. Beyond the multiplicity of ephemeral forms, a sudden awareness dawns – of the deity at the heart of the cosmos' creation, of the sun as the source of all life and light, of 'the One' from which 'the all' have come forth, and to which 'the all' will return. In the mystical traditions of all religions, the Sacred reveals itself, ultimately, as an invisible, ineffable and inscrutable unity...

CHAPTER II

The Sacred Experienced as Unity

Eternal light, that in thyself alone
Dwelling, alone dost know thyself, and smile
On thy self-love, so knowing and so known.
— Dante, Paradiso[1]

I. The Sacred Unity

In the Old Testament, the Lord appeared to Moses as a burning bush. But then, from the midst of its all-consuming flame came the words *"I am what I am,"* expressing that He also possessed a higher, unseen unity (Exodus 3:14).

When we pause briefly to consider some the many mythic images which have manifest the Sacred over time, we come up against a peculiar if not interesting dilemma... When these images, as sacred sculptures or altarpieces, become objects for meditation, they may powerfully evoke a sentiment of divine oneness. And yet, our speech, in the form of reasoned argument or rational discourse, stands mute before such an experience.

Indeed, as our culture progressed from ancient times, with its more mythopoeic manner of thinking, to the *logos*-oriented discourse of modern times, the awareness of this sacred unity was *passed over in silence* — then ignored... and finally forgotten. The history of this forgetting — a veritable *obscurum per obscurius* — is not without clues and traces, which may still be discerned in the philosophical works of ancient Greece.

In his *Republic*, Plato wrote that he would prefer to banish poets and story-tellers from his ideal state, since their mythic imagery evokes nothing more than 'base' emotions... *"We were justified,"* Socrates says, *"in banishing her* [poetry] *from our city. For it was reason which led us on. And lest she condemn us as rather harsh and rough, let us tell her that there is an ancient feud between philosophy and poetry."* (607b)[2]

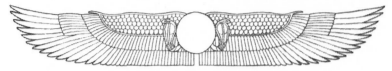

The sun at its zenith: the winged solar disk

The rising and setting sun: Khoprer the scarab and Khnum the ram-headed elder

Soon thereafter, Aristotle contributed to this 'anti-mythic' stance, claiming in his *Metaphysics* that, *"It is not worthwhile to examine carefully the opinions of those who exercise their cleverness in the form of the myths."*[3] And for Plotinus as well, the philosopher is characterized as that contemplative soul who *"...presses onward to the innermost sanctuary, leaving behind him the statues in the outer temple."*[4]

And yet, the emergence of this ratio-critical, *logos*-based attitude caused the poet Euripides to lament, through the blind prophet Tiresias, that *"...the ancestral beliefs which we hold are as old as time, and they cannot be destroyed by any argument or clever subtlety invented by profound minds."*[5]

As philosophical thinking emerged from the depths of myth and progressed from the Pre-Socratics to Plato and Aristotle, our awareness of 'the One' (*to Hen*) was gradually ignored and obscured. Only in Gnosticism and Neo-Platonism did 'the One' briefly re-emerge before being forgotten for the remainder of history. (In the case of Gnosticism, it was condemned as a heresy and literally 'buried' until the Nag Hammadi discovery fifty years ago).

The rationalist tradition inaugurated by Plato and Aristotle played no small role in this obscurification. While the philosophical terminology necessary to describe 'the One' was gradually honed and refined in their writings, the mythic images necessary to evoke its presence were soon avoided and even despised. This, in spite of the fact that Plato and Aristotle themselves often preserved mythic images in their writings.

II. Egyptian Myths of 'the One'

Meanwhile, if we turn to the hieroglyphic texts of the Egyptians, we discover that they did possess a philosophical worldview, which expressed itself through a plethora of refined imagery and an unfortunate paucity of concepts – a situation which Hellenic culture subsequently tried to remedy.

When the Egyptians evoked the Sacred in their myths, they named it *Atum* 'the Complete One'. In the serpentine form of *Amun* 'the Hidden One', the presence of this unity remained locked and hidden away. But 'the One' also manifest itself each day as *Re*, 'the Sun'. This daily epiphany of *Atum-Re* thus consisted of the invisible (*Amun*, the Hidden One) momentarily made visible (*Atum*, the Complete One) in a blaze of light (*Re*, the Sun).

Uræus: "She who rears up"

Meanwhile, the Pyramid Texts reveal that 'in the first time' (*tep zepi*), there were only the primæval waters, a dark and formless abyss. If there were any tenebrous stirrings of life, they lay hidden in the watery depths as *Amun*, the Hidden One in the form of the primæval serpent.

But then, light, life and awareness emerged on the horizon, *for in the beginning the sun rose out of the primæval waters.*[6] It rose like a cobra (the *uræus*: 'she who rears up'); it rose like a phoenix (the *Benu bird*: 'he who created himself' by rising from the Isle of Fire); it rose like a divine child from the folds of the lotus (Horus and the Nile lily: the infant god emerging from the lotus, which eternally surfaces and blossoms at dawn, then closes again and sinks underwater by night).

Bennu bird: "He who rose from the Isle of Fire"

It also rose as if a scarab beetle had pushed its solar disk across the heavens. As the rising sun, the One was called *Khoprer* 'the Becoming One', and was symbolized by the sacred image of the scarab upholding the solar disk. As the sun at its zenith, the One was called *Re*, and was symbolized by the image of the winged solar disk. (Horus, the winged falcon who soars across the heavens, bore Re's solar disk upon his head). And as the setting sun, it was called *Khnum*, symbolized by the image of a ram-headed elder with a staff in his hand.

Horus child emerging from the Nile lily

Nut the Sky Mother
separated by Shu, god of the Air,
from Geb the Earth Father

The *Corpus Hermeticum*, emerging out of Ptolemaic Egypt around 200 A.D., claimed to express in its conceptual Greek terminology the Egyptian philosophical worldview which their images had evoked but their words had otherwise failed to express. In the first discourse, a vision of the creation is recounted wherein the primæval darkness *"coils... like a serpent"* while *"a clear and joyful light"* emerges. This light is called, at one and the same time, *God* and *mind.*[7]

This transcendent source of light, life and awareness is later described in the Hermetica as *"...the One who alone is unbegotten, is also unimagined and invisible, but in presenting images of all things He is seen through all of them and in all of them."*[8] The *Hermetica* also describe a vision of *"God's immortal circle"*[9] in which *"all are one, for they are linked so that they cannot be separated from each other."*[10]

In the mythology of the ancient Greeks, similar images of a transcendent unity appear. *"First of all,"* Hesiod recounts in his *Theogony*, *"was Chaos born"*[11] – a swirling, cloudy abyss. Then *Ouranos* the Heaven was constellated above, and *Gaia* the Earth took shape below. But (we soon understand) Chaos was born from the *separation* of these two (since the Greek word *chaos* means literally 'a gap'). *Gaia* the Mother Earth and *Ouranos* the Father Sky were both, once, *of one form*, indistinguishable from each other. And from that primordial unity, the Sky and Earth came to be, as male and female, above and below.

In the earlier Egyptian rendering of this tale, the primordial unity is also separated into male and female, above and below, except now it is *Geb* the Earth Father and *Nut* the Sky Mother who are separated by *Shu*, god of the Air. (*Shu*, like the ancient Greek *Chaos*, has connotations of emptiness or 'the abyss')

III. The Greek Philosophy of 'the One'

The *Orphicum Fragmenta*, a collection of Orphic writings which date back as far as the 6th century B.C., offer us a glimpse into some of the earliest speculations of Greek philosophy. While many Orphic fragments offer tantalizing pieces of a creation myth, other passages provide some of our first philosophical speculations.

And it is here that we have the earliest explicit mention, in Greek thought, of the vortex (*diné*) and the One (*to Hen*). According to the Orphic doctrine, *"Everything comes to be out of the One and is resolved into the One."*[12] Meanwhile, we learn in another fragment how, in the beginning, this solitary unity *"...began to move in a wondrous circle."* (71b)[13]

This image of *a swirling vortex with the One at its centre* appears repeatedly in early Greek Philosophy. The image shows how the One divides itself into a swirling multiplicity, which may nevertheless be united once more with the One at their centre. To explain this mysterious process of 'separation and union' became the principle task of the early Greek philosophers. As the *Orphicum Fragmenta* phrased it, *"How may I have all things one and each one separate?"* (165)[14]

For the Pre-Socratics, the solution lay in the nature of the One's substance, and the manner in which it passed through separation and union. At various times, this primary substance was seen to be either water (Thales), air (Anaximenes) or fire (Heraclitus), but eventually, it became four – Empedocles' earth, water, air and fire – which 'run through one another' and so remain one.

Beginning with Anaximander (c. 580 B.C.), these *"eternal and ageless"* (2) substances were characterized as a series of opposites which emerged from the One due to its vortex motion: *"The opposites which are present in the One, are separated out from it."* (A9) *"The opposites are the hot, the cold, the dry and the moist."* (A9)[15] These opposites continually combine, separate and re-combine into the multiplicity of things.

Soon after, Heraclitus (c. 500 BC) sought *"the purpose which steers all things through all things."* (41) He discovered that all things are in continuous motion or *flux*, like an ever-flowing river or all-consuming fire. This is due to Strife, which keeps the opposites at war with each other. And yet, beyond this multiplicity, there is a *"hidden harmony"* (54) which keeps things together through the *"balanced tension of opposites."* (51) In fact, *"that which is in opposition is in concert, and from things that differ come the most beautiful harmony."* (8) Hence, behind all opposites lies a deeper unity, which manifests itself through their coming together: *"The way up and the way down are one and the same."* (60)

This union of opposites is manifest in God himself, since *"God is day-night, winter-summer, war-peace..."* (67) What Heraclitus eventually found, beyond ever-changing multiplicity, was the all-unifying One: *"When you have listened, not to me, but to the* logos, *it is wise to agree that all things are one."* (– or, as *"Hen panta"* may also be translated: *"that the One is all."*) (50) Although this higher unity continually manifests itself in the cosmos, it remains hidden. It even remains hidden behind the names of the gods: *"That which alone is wise is One: it is willing and unwilling to be called by the name of Zeus."* (32)[16]

Heraclitus' successor, Parmenides (c. 475 B.C) possessed a similar vision of this transcendent unity. But, contrary to Heraclitus, he saw it as *static:* a timeless, eternal and unifying Being. Hence, for him, the One was *"the way that Is. To this way there are many signposts: that Being has no coming-into-being and no destruction, for it is whole... without motion and without end. And it never was nor will be, because it Is now, a whole all together, One, continuous...Nor is Being divisible, since it is all alike...all is full of Being."* (7,8)[17]

Finally, in the works of Empedocles, the various differences among the Pre-Socratics found their resolution. For him, there is *"a twofold tale. At one time it grew together to be one only out of many; at another, it parted asunder so as to be many instead of one – Fire and Water and Earth and the mighty height of Air."* (17) These four substances, the 'four roots' which are 'one only', variously combine, separate and re-combine to make the multiplicity of all things: *"There are these alone; but, running through one another, they become now this, now that, and like things evermore."* (17)*

The mysterious process of 'separation and union' which, at times makes the One many and, at times, makes the many One, is due to *Love* (the unifying principle, like Parmenides' never-changing Being) and *Strife* (the dividing principle, like Heraclitus' Strife in the ever-changing flux). Empedocles writes: *"There are these* [four substances, earth, water, air and fire]; *but running through one another, they become men and the tribe of beasts. At one time, they are all brought together into one order by Love, at another, they are carried in different directions by the repulsion of Strife... in so far as they never cease changing continually, they are evermore, immovable in the circle."* (26)

Hence, Empedocles gives us a vision of *a swirling vortex (diné)* in which Strife brings about the separation of the One into many, dispersing the multiplicity along the periphery. Meanwhile, Love is able to unite them all, bringing them together once more *into the One in the centre.* This comes out explicitly in a final fragment: *"When Strife was fallen to the lowest depths of*

* For a diagram of fire, water, earth and air as four substances that remain 'one only', see page 117.

the vortex, and Love had reached to the centre of the whirl, in it do all things come together so as to be one only..." (35, 36)[18]

A most important issue, which many of the Pre-Socratics failed to agree upon, is the role of *time* in all this. For Parmenides, the One never changes in time, while for Heraclitus, it experiences periodic alterations (the 'Great Year'). For Empedocles as well, there are alternating periods of unity and multiplicity. But, what is more, *he himself* was once in loving union with the One, but fell from it due to Strife:

> *"There is an oracle of Necessity, an ancient decree of the gods... that whenever one... in strife has sinned... for thrice ten thousand seasons he wanders, far from the blessed gods, being born throughout that period in all kinds of mortal shapes... I, too, now am one of these – a fugitive from the gods and a wanderer – because I put my trust in raging Strife."* (115)[19]

In this fragment, Empedocles gives voice to an ancient tale otherwise lost to obscurity: that we were all, once, in union with the One – existing *at the very centre* of creation, in a more timeless eternity. Yet, at the present time, we are fallen from the One – existing in a more mundane segment or cycle of time *on the periphery of the swirling vortex*. We shall meet again with this ancient tale, since it constitutes 'the eternal Hero journey of the soul'.

Finally, in the writings of Plato, Aristotle and Plotinus, the idea of 'the One' re-appears, but is denuded of all imagery. Questions of the One's substance, whether as earth, water, air or fire, no longer pre-occupy their thoughts. Instead, the One becomes a conceptual affair, related to 'thinking', 'becoming' and 'contemplation'.

In the *Timæus*, Plato accepts Empedocles' doctrine that all things in this world are the product of earth, water, air and fire in differing combinations. But, what is more, all that is created is a 'becoming in time' modelled after the image of the One in eternity. While this One *"rests in unity"* (37d) as eternal and unchanging Being (29a), all things created over time are *"a moving image of eternity."* (37d) Hence, for Plato, the multiplicity of things in this world becomes so many fleeting images of that One which 'rests in unity.'[20]

For Aristotle as well, the idea of God as a unity persists. But this unity manifest its oneness, not so much in images, but conceptually: *through its thinking*. For this reason, Aristotle refers to God as 'Mind' (*nous*) or, more literally, as 'thinking' (*noésis*). Because God is perfect, He does not think upon the world, which is divisible and always changing. Instead, Aristotle decides *"It is of himself then, that He is thinking."* (Meta 1074b) What is more, because God thinks upon himself, there can be no division between thinking and thought: *"the two will be the same, and so both the thinking and the thought will be one."* (Meta 1075a) Thus, for Aristotle, God manifests his inherent unity as *'noésis noéseós noésis'* or *"the thinking a thought of itself thinking."* (Meta 1074a)[21]

It was Plotinus, the 3rd century founder of Neo-Platonism, who took the ancient philosophy of 'the One' to its ultimate conclusion. For Plotinus, as the philosopher withdraws ever deeper into himself, he discovers within, first of all, the Soul, then Intelligence, and finally the One. These are like three modes of thinking which, like three concentric circles, ultimately reveal the same source at their centre. By releasing thought from the multiplicity of its perception, then from the ideal forms of its reason, and finally, from thinking itself, the contemplative may behold the One at the source of all thinking:

> *What then is the One? ...Everywhere things are reduced to unity. For each thing, there is a unity to which it may be reduced* [the perceptible object], *and there is for each unity that which is superior to it but is not unity as such* [the ideal form]. *This continues until one reaches unity as such* [the One]. (III, 8, 10)

> *The man who obtains the vision becomes, as it were, another being... Absorbed in the beyond, he is one with it, like a centre co-incident with another centre. While the centres co-incide, they are one. They become two only when they separate. It is* [only] *in this sense that we can speak of the One as something separate. Therefore, it is so very difficult to describe, this vision, for how can we describe as separate from us what seemed, while we were contemplating it, not other than ourselves, but perfect at-oneness with us?* (VI,9,10)

A little later, Plotinus refers to the ancient Greek Mysteries, in which the neophyte is initiated into a vision of the Divine, but forbidden to speak of it: *"The man who saw* [this vision] *was identical with what he saw. Hence, he did not 'see' but was rather 'oned' with it. If only he could preserve the memory of what he was while thus absorbed into the One, he would possess within himself an image of what it was."* (VI,9,11) Unable to find an adequate image of the One, Plotinus finally decides, *"If you look upon yourself in this state, you find yourself an image of the One."* (VI,9,11)[22]

VI. Conclusion

In the transition to a more *logos*-oriented style of thinking, the conceptual terms necessary to describe the One were gained, but those images which had invoked its presence were gradually lost. Also lost were the myths which evoked its presence, such as the Greeks and Egyptians had achieved in their mythopoeic age.

For, in the Egyptian myth of creation, the eternal One manifests itself each sunrise. At that moment, the beholder and the beheld, the contemplative and his God, become one in a momentary epiphany – yet our conceptual thinking refuses to admit this possibility. We remain mute and speechless, trapped within our rational stance.

Our words, at best, may attempt to *describe* this experience through concepts, but our language lacks the power to *evoke* it. Only the myths and images from the mythopoeic age preserve that power. If we regain the ancient image-language, we may once again 'speak' the One into existence. By combining our vision and thinking into a more meditative gaze, we may *enter,* once more, *through the image* – into that numinous experience promised by all sacred works of art.

As evidenced by the Greeks in their philosophical fragments, one archaic motif has resolutely persisted through time: the mythic image of *the One at the centre of a swirling vortex.* This archetypal form, preserved in so many ancient texts, may very well provide us with the image that we lack – the key which, with its gentle turning, allows us to *enter through the image...*

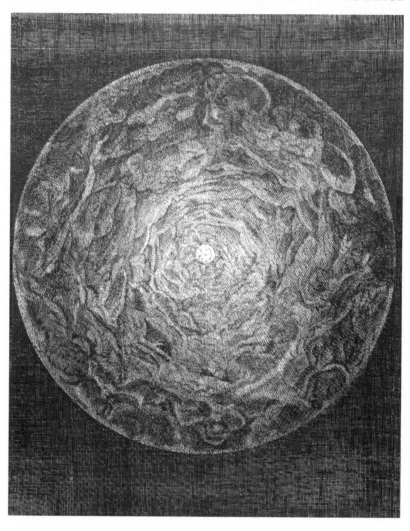

THE ANCIENT TEMPLATE
The One (to Hen) at the centre of a swirling vortex (diné)
Escalier des sages (1689)

CHAPTER III

The Ancient Template

In your mind you have seen
the archetypal form, the pre-principle
that exists before a beginning without end.
– Corpus Hermeticum (I.8)[1]

I. The Sacred Image

Whenever we stand in silent awe before a sacred image, we find ourselves, caught unawares, before a hallowed threshold. How then do we *enter through* the image? Clearly, whatever we need to step through its doorway has already been given to us in this life. For, it is our own life experiences – be that of our birth, of suffering, of our mother's caress or our father's wisdom – which relate us to images of the Christ-child, the Buddha, the *Magna Mater* or *Pater Omnipotens*.

But, the majority of our life experiences seem to be locked away in our memory, and are only called forth in the event of a great life-crisis. And yet, it is precisely our dormant memory-images which, once they are awakened, *animate* those cultural images that otherwise *remain dead* to the world. With these personal memory-images, we engage the cultural memory-images of sacred art *with our own lives*, and so step, in this way, across their hallowed thresholds.

It is worth remembering that both Freud and Jung undertook their first explorations into the imagery of the unconscious as a result of a life-crisis. Finding themselves unable to move forward across life's next threshold, they underwent a sudden 'backward movement' through their personal life-history. In a letter to Fleiss, Freud remarked that *"my father's death has affected me profoundly... inside me, the occasion of his death has re-awakened all my early feelings. Now I feel quite uprooted."*[2]

This sudden backwash of childhood memories and dreams became the 'creative illness'³ necessary for his next step forward: the creation of his breakthrough work, *The Interpretation of Dreams*. In the Preface to the second edition, Freud came to see how *"this book has a further subjective significance for me personally – a significance I grasped only after I had completed it. It was, I found, a portion of my own self-analysis, my reaction to my father's death – that is to say, the most important event, the most poignant loss, of a man's life."*⁴

In a similar way, Jung's reaction to his parting from Freud was *"a period of inner uncertainty... a state of disorientation..."*⁵ culminating in his own 'confrontation with the unconscious.' He withdrew from his position at the university, published almost nothing, and surrendered himself to the stream of dreams, visions, childhood memories and fantasies upwelling from within. Over the course of this 'backward movement' through life, Jung encountered certain distinctive figures which, eventually, he was able to recognize as 'the archetypes.' And so, through this profound process of interiorization, he found the knowledge necessary to move forward across life's next threshold, creating his own 'analytic' psychology.

In *Memories, Dreams, Reflections*, Jung recounts how his creative illness began with a series of bizarre dreams. Then, pursuing these images to their unconscious source, he purposefully began to fantasize. Sitting at his desk, he would imagine a steep descent, and then fall ever further into the images. And, through this technique of 'Active Imagination', he came to realize that the images upwelling from the unconscious could only be confronted by a mixture of *feeling and imagination* – by a controlled release of the feelings which activated the images. Although these feelings exploded like *"one thunderstorm followed by another,"*⁶ increasingly threatening to overwhelm him, he accepted that his task was to gradually release them into consciousness.

For the feelings themselves were generating the images with the aid of the imagination – with, that is to say, the matrix of mythopoeic imagination he later recognized as the collective unconscious. His feeling-toned memory-images of a personal nature soon gave way to more archetypal ones, arising from the deeper, cultural strata of his memory. Through Active Imagination, he pursued a deeper and ever steeper path into the unconscious by first accepting and acknowledging the emergent archetypal images, and then giving them life by filling out their otherwise empty forms with the feelings and experiences that arose from his own life.

Again and again Jung was forced to emphasize while explicating his theory of the archetypes that: *"Archetypes are not determined as regards their content, but only as regards their form... A primordial image is determined as to its content only when it has become conscious and is therefore filled out with the material of conscious experience."*⁷

Although our ultimate aim is to learn how to *think through*, and so *enter through* images, we must keep in mind that *thinking alone* will not transport us across their silent thresholds. Instead, we must learn to combine our seeing and thinking into a more meditative gaze. We must conjure forth from within us a combination of *feeling and imagination*, and then render these onto the image, so as to bring the symbols *to life*. For, ultimately, it is the *feeling for life* flowing through each individual that enlivens these otherwise dead and empty archetypes.

When we are confronted by the mythological image of a god, hero or saviour as portrayed in painting and sculpture, we are, in essence, confronted by an archetype arising from the collective memory of an entire culture. But this collective memory-image will remain *empty*, a mere *form* (perhaps of some curious aesthetic value, but *empty*) unless it is filled out with memories of a more personal nature, bound up with great feeling, and arising from *our own* life history. Hence, it is precisely our more personal memories which, once evoked by the image, will carry us across its silent threshold. So that an image of the Madonna and Child, for example, will conjure forth in us feelings of our own childhood...

II. To Enter Through the Image

In our first attempt to *enter through* the image, we shall take as a suitable example one panel from Van der Weyden's *Miraflores Altarpiece*. It depicts a rather solemn and gentle Madonna with a naked Christ-child on her lap.

To *enter through the image*, we must allow the image to evoke our more personal memories and feelings. We must allow it to draw forth from within us certain recollections of our earliest infancy, and then pursue these memories even further, unto the profound feelings related *to our own birth*. While every one of us will accept the fact that we were born, few will ever have any *recollection* of that event, and many would deny that the associated *feelings* still persist in us.

Yet, the explorations into depth psychology initiated by Freud would suggest otherwise. Certain events in life which are experienced by the adult ego as traumatic are in fact evocations of the feelings which the individual first experienced in the trauma of his birth. As Nietzsche was perhaps the first to observe, *"only that which never ceases to hurt stays in the memory."*[8]

The many traumatic experiences accumulated over a lifetime, from painful moments of falling, feeling lost or abandoned as a child, to difficult breaks in relationships – be that the pain of leaving one's parents, one's lover, or even one's own childhood self – are all memories constellated around the birth trauma and united by their common feeling of *severance* and its profound pain. These memories persist in us, though accessing them in their earliest incarnations seems nigh impossible. All that remains in us from the

Rogier Van der Weyden: Miraflores Altarpiece (detail)

experience of our birth is a series of painful sensations culminating in our first primal scream for life...

Meanwhile, feelings of another nature, also of great importance, are also associated with the event of our birth. This is the feeling of *absolute joy* which the infant also felt within its mother's embrace – feelings associated with earlier 'inter-uterine' memories of being safely ensconced within the womb, or feelings associated with after-birth memories of being held, comforted and breast-fed in a new world full of light...

The visionary poet William Blake, in an attempt to evoke the after-birth experience, resorted to lines of the utmost simplicity and beauty in his poem *'Infant Joy'*:

> *"I have no name:*
> *I am but two days old."*
> *What shall I call thee?*
> *"I happy am,*
> *Joy is my name."*
> *Sweet joy befall thee!*[9]

In these six short lines we have a profoundly simple rendering of a forgotten childhood memory which is similarly expressed in Van der Weyden's simple but profound image of the infant Christ.

As is the case with our traumatic memories, the moments of joy which we are fortunate enough to experience later in our lives are in fact evocations of an earlier 'infant joy'. Each new experience in life thus becomes a memory-image associated positively or negatively around infant feelings of either joy or pain. And though the actual experience of ourselves as a child seems to be forever lost, *it can be regained if we are able to rediscover and relive the memory-images constellated around our feelings, and gradually regress backward through them to their earliest moments.*

Such an inward journey is by no means easy as, with each successful recollection of a forgotten event, feelings of innocent suffering must also be re-experienced *to the full*. Painful as this may be, the regression will eventually culminate in a re-experience of the ecstatic joy which we once felt as a child: the feeling that 'I happy am...'

Jung described his descent into the unconscious as the attempt *"...to find the images which were concealed in the emotions."*[10] Yet, despite the manner in which memories tend to cluster around certain feelings, the core experiences we felt so traumatically or joyfully as a child may be *lost to us* permanently – locked deep in our unconscious, and lacking the associated memory-image which is the only key that, with its gentle turning, could release them. Hence, we may painfully wend our way through the unconscious, not knowing that such a descent may ultimately end in darkness...

This is why the image of the infant Christ depicted by Van der Weyden serves such a profound purpose. It provides us with *the key* that we lack: *the image* of ourselves as a child which was otherwise lost to our memory ...seemingly forever. Our task is to accept this cultural and collective image – the Christ-child – as an image that is also personal and unique – that is, as an image *of ourselves* as a child. By meditating on this image of the Christ-child – by *entering through this image,* we are able to evoke those earliest feelings within ourselves which would otherwise have been lost forever.

But the memory regression is not yet complete, nor have we, as of yet, successfully *entered through* the image. The next step is to behold the image of the Christ-child as it always and ever has been construed in its associated mythology. That is, as a symbol of the Sacred incarnated on this earth in the form of an innocent and helpless child.

Hinduism also possesses such a figure, in the playful form of the divine child Krishna. Buddhism too, in the newly-born figure of the Buddha taking seven steps on lotus blossoms. So too does ancient Egypt, with the head of the Horus Child emerging from the Nile lily, and even Judaism, with Moses in a basket floating down the Nile. Indeed, almost all of the world's mythologies possess this Child archetype – what Jung called the *Puer Æternus* – which, ever and always, symbolizes the Sacred in one of its temporal aspects: in this case, through innocence and joyful wisdom.

To *enter through this image* would be to identify our childhood self with the Christ-child, and then to identify the Christ-child with the Sacred, and so cross its threshold to a sudden moment of illumination. During that brief epiphany, as we *enter through* the image of the Divine Child, we experience 'the source' of all these personal and collective memory-images – that which unites them at their centre. We recognize ourselves as divine in origin – momentarily re-united with 'the One' at the centre of the swirling vortex...

III. To Draw a Circle on the Face of the Deep:
The Ancient Template

At the head of this chapter stands an alchemical design which shall aid us in all our forthcoming contemplations of images. By virtue of its image-inducing design, it will grant us a more meditative gaze, and open thereby new pathways to our mind's interior. By combining our vision and thinking, this 'Ancient Template' shall aid us to focus our gaze each time we, using a mixture of feeling and imagination, attempt to *enter through* images.

The engraving in question is from an alchemical text, *Escalier des sages* of 1689, and its timeless image illustrates the archaic chaos which first arose at the moment of the cosmos' creation. These are the elements of earth, water, air and fire all intermixed and, as yet, un-ordered. But it also illustrates the mind's inner darkness and disorder – the *massa confusa* as it was termed – the random swirl of unconscious thoughts that the alchemist experienced when peering into his *vas hermeticum*. In alchemical terms, this image shows the *prima materia* at the beginning of the *Opus Alchymicum*.

Its archetypal form reminds us of that archaic motif preserved in so many philosophical fragments. Here is *the One (to Hen) at the centre of a swirling vortex (diné)*. Before us stands that unity in which *'all things come together so as to be one only'* (35, 36) as Empedocles phrased it.

The clouds' circular motion also recalls the world's creation as described in the Old Testament *Book of Wisdom*:

> ...*When* [the Lord] *established the heavens,*
> *he drew a circle on the face of the deep* (Prov. 8:22)

And yet, the poet Gérard de Nerval, while on the brink of insanity, peered into his own mind, and wrote:

> *Lying on a cot, I seemed to see the heavens unveiled and opened, revealing a thousand vistas of unparalleled magnificence. It seemed that ... immense circles were traced in the infinite.*[11]

Gazing at this image for an extended moment, we behold how the series of dark clouds spins ever deeper to the circle of light at their centre. What are we to make of the myriad forms spiralling toward the inner circle of light? The beholder is free to associate whatever he wishes with this imagery. He may choose to associate *nothing* whatsoever, and so remain in darkness and confusion...

Or, he may choose to see the circle of light at the centre, like the sun in ancient times, as *the source* of all illuminated things. Such a sacred centre may be understood, as in the more ancient traditions, as 'God' – the One at the source of all things. It may also be understood, as in our more modern traditions, as 'the Self' – the innermost source of all consciousness. Or, it may be understood, uniting these two traditions, as *both:* when the Self, immanent and within, beholds the eternally Sacred and recognizes, as if in a sacred looking-glass, that both, in truth, are *one.*

This figure is called the Ancient Template because it conjures forth in our mind *'the archetypal form, the pre-principle that exists before a beginning without end'* (as the First Discourse of *The Hermetica* phrases it). Its unique shape models both the structure of the cosmos and the structure of the mind. And it brings them all into one accord.

If this is so, then how do we cross the threshold of this most ancient and archetypal image? As with the example of Van der Weyden's Christ-child, we must use a mixture of imagination and feeling to wend our way through a labyrinth of memories personal and cultural. We begin with those figures who have continually appeared to us throughout our life, and altered its course so profoundly.

Firstly, in the cloud formations on the periphery, we imagine all those figures from our personal life who, now and in its history, have continued to influence our feelings in some way. This would include mother and father, lovers and friends, not to mention the image of ourselves. These personal memory-images along the periphery form a ring around the centre, like the constellations of a zodiacal wheel that spins, in truth, round our inner firmament.

Secondly, in the cloud formations in the middle, we imagine all those mythological figures in our cultural memory, now and in its history, which have continued to evoke our feelings in some way. For most people of European descent, this would be Christ, the Madonna, Adam and Eve, *et al*, but could also involve figures from other mythologies. These too form a ring around the centre. But, as more ancient cultural memory-images, they stand closer to the Sacred at the centre of all things.

The task that now confronts us is to isolate a certain feeling, and trace it back through the memories personal and cultural which have constellated around it. One such feeling would be the joy of union; another could be the pain of separation. Each wends its way like a thread through the ancient labyrinth.

As in the case with Van der Weyden's image of the Christ-child, we must be willing to associate a series of personal memories around this feeling, regressing ever further back to the powerful experience at its core. At a certain point in the regression, the personal memory-images may be lacking, and so images from our cultural memory may, indeed *must* be substituted and used. These images from our cultural memory – stone statues, icons and altarpieces – are all inherently designed so as to lead us to an experience of union with the Divine.

As we shall see, these are all Threshold Images – arising at the nadir of myths and preserved in sacred works of art – which are able to induce in us a momentary epiphany. Thus we pass from memory-images of a personal nature to those of a collective nature, and thence, to the Sacred at their source. We *enter through* these evermore ancient images to experience at their core: a brief and fleeting epiphany of the One at the centre of the swirling vortex.

IV. The Mythic Path

In this chapter we shall, for the first time, pursue a series of images through the template's swirling depths. Such images will *still be linked by their associated narrative*, constituting the Mythic Path. In the following chapters, the template will be used once again, but this time to *enter through* a series of images *independently* of their narratives. This shall constitute the Symbolic Path. Finally, during our journey through Dreams in Part III, we shall discover that an Oneiric Path also exists. All of these paths trace their own course through the winding labyrinth to the Sacred at the centre.

Having imagined the figures of Christ, the Madonna, Adam and Eve on the middle ring of clouds, what essentially relates these figures to one another is one of the many myths of Christianity. For our purposes, Christ and the Madonna will be arranged to depict the nadir moment of Christ's sacrifice, when he hung upon the cross while the Madonna suffered her own moment of agony and revelation below him.

Beside this image-cluster, another arrangement may take form in the middle circle of clouds. The figures of Adam and Eve may be composed in the form of the fall, with the serpent and the tree of knowledge between them.

The Fall (1526)
Lucas Cranach the Elder

The Crucifixion (1454)
Rogier Van der Weyden

Each of these compositions depicts a certain moment in Christian myth. Yet the figures themselves, emanating with a symbolic power all their own, may remain independent of these momentary mythic arrangements. Indeed, we are free to imagine them as we wish – even falling into mythic arrangements from other cultures and ages. Our template allows us to envision these symbols as independent of their associated myths, and yet, as also capable of falling into their established mythic patterns.

We are now prepared to journey through the myth of Christianity as envisioned on the Ancient Template. But the Christian myth is not unique. In many other cultures, similar such myths offer their adherents just such a soul-journey to the Eternal. The Mythic Path which the Template displays is, essentially, 'the eternal Hero myth of the soul', regardless of any particular cultural inflection or measure of its time.

According to this eternal myth, the *soul, atman, ba* etc. which was once, at the beginning, one with the Divine in the centre, now finds itself caught in a cycle or segment of time on the periphery. Fallen thus, it seeks that experience which will allow it to return, and so be united again with the One at the centre. This is the task of the sacred hero, which will be accomplished at the nadir of his myth. And his accomplishment of this sacred deed creates a nadir Threshold Image which all may then *enter through* to an experience of union with the Divine.

In the case of the Christian myth, the majority of its images are constellated around the two overwhelming feelings of, firstly, loss and separation from God, and secondly, the unquenchable desire for re-union.

Hence, we begin at the periphery of the swirling vortex, recalling memories of a more personal nature involving painful moments *of loss*, as well as the subsequent, longed-for hope of *re-union*. Such personal memories arise, unfortunately, during moments of greater crisis. Whether it be the death of a family member, the traumatic break with a lover, or even the separation from our own childhood self, we continually come up against one of life's painful threshold crossings.

But, accompanying these experiences is also the hope for re-union. This may be expressed through a spontaneous memory regression: the sudden, unwilled recall of happier moments, when the dead relative was still with us, or the lover still loved us, or the child within still experienced this world with wonder and joy. All express themselves spontaneously in arrangements of images that are tinged by great emotion.

But, as we follow these feelings of separation and re-union ever further backward through our lives, the personal images constellated around them soon become unclear and distorted. In their place, cultural images of a more sacred and archetypal nature arise, to draw more distinctly the lineaments of our own loss and longing. Each image offers us the key that we lack. Christ, through his resurrection, offers the dead relative new life. The Madonna, in her wisdom and compassion, offers the lost lover the consolation of the Goddess' love. And the nativity of the Christ-child offers us anew the miracle of our birth. Each of these sacred images is a key that, with its gentle turning, opens new doors in our memory, possibly revealing a momentary epiphany. And so, wending our way through the Ancient Template, we descend to the circle of sacred figures further down.

Moving to the middle layer of clouds on the Ancient Template, we imagine the scene of the crucifixion and, beside it, the fall from Eden. We remember how, in the beginning, Adam beheld the fullness of God's creation and spoke 'face to face' with the Creator. In Eden we experienced *absolute joy*, as a part of this divine plenitude, since our eternal soul dwelt in total *union* with the One.

But, through Adam's folly and sin at the tree, our soul fell from its sacred state. Banished by angels bearing flaming swords, we endured suffering, shame and the loss of wisdom. Still more difficult to bear was the enduring pain of *separation*, as we fell from the Father. Through Adam's fall at the tree, we cross over the Threshold Image that bodies forth our soul's initial *separation* from God.

Finding itself imprisoned in historical time, our soul seeks, with unbearable longing, to be one with God again. And indeed, through Christ's sacrifice on the cross, we are able to rise, through him, into union with God. We are able to gaze once more into God's willful countenance. Such a moment will be experienced for all time in the Apocalypse at the end of history, when Paradise is regained.

But this momentary epiphany may also be experienced *here and now*, in the middle of history, if Christ's image is successfully *entered through*. Our deepest longing – our soul's loss and its need for reparation – leads us *through* this sacred image. We follow Christ down through the depths of his myth, and there, at the nadir, we *enter through* the Threshold Image of Christ crucified to experience a momentary death and resurrection, a cleansing and perfection of our vision which brings us into God's sacred circle. For a moment, we return to our original state of *union* with the Sacred. This, a stirring moment of epiphany, then expires, and we find ourselves trapped once more in time's more mundane passing.

V. Unravelling the Narrative Thread

Hence, in Adam's *fall*, the soul's first *separation* from God is imaged forth. And, in Christ's *rising* to God, its reparation and momentary *re-union* finds symbolic form. The Christian images of Adam at the tree and Christ on the cross, so arranged, become Threshold Images which we may *enter through* to a momentary experience of divine oneness.

It is a most fortuitous co-incidence that the myth just recounted was created through the *crossing over* of mythic fragments from two *different* cultures: the Hebrew mythologem of Adam's fall, and the Christian mythologem of Christ's rising. Given this, we can see that the myth of Christianity could conceivably cross the mythologems of other cultures. The hero of one mythology could set out, and the hero of another mythology return.

Because, as sacred heros, their movements describe the basic separation and return of the eternal soul to and from its divine source. In Christianity, it is Adam who separates us from God, and Christ who returns us. Yet, it is only by reading these two mythologems as different moments in the 'eternal Hero myth of the soul' that the two narrative fragments – one Hebrew, one Christian – *fuse* in order to become *one* myth.

Myths, fundamentally, are an arrangement of images *in time*. Through the temporal unfolding of their *narratives*, they model our separation and union with the divine. At the same time, their sacred heros struggle to complete *the task* of our fall or redemption, thus dramatizing our own sacred agony and joy.

And so, like ancient codes, the mythic iconologues of narrative, time and the hero's task have been handed down to us, so that we may read images in such a way as to experience their inherent epiphanies. We descend with the sacred hero to the mythic nadir, and experience there with him the divine revelation.

Meanwhile, with the aid of the Ancient Template, we are also free to arrange images in whatever order or combination we need. Once images are liberated from the fixed arrangements demanded by their myths, we are at ease to consider new temporal and narrative orders. Temporally, we may read the images forward *or backward or selectively* along the course of their established narratives. Or, at some point in their progression, they may *cross over* and follow the path of another culture's narrative. Such narrative cross-overs and temporal regressions constitute just a few of the many iconologues at our command. By thinking in a more mythopoeic manner, re-arranging and displacing narrative segments, we begin *to speak* the ancient image-language.

The many different cultural myths which we have recovered from antiquity or encountered through contact with other cultures now appear before us – as *new* paths to follow through the eternal labyrinth. Yet, we must be willing to engage the sacred heros of these cultures *with our own eternal soul*. We must bring *our own lives* to these figures, and allow them to be transformed thereby. If we successfully wend our way through the labyrinth, then we will find at the centre, not this or that culture's particular vision of the Sacred but – *entering through the image* – the ancient One that unites them all.

VI. Cosmogonic Myth

In Cosmogonic myths, a series of images are laid side by side, so as to reveal this world's coming-to-be or conclusion.

In myths of the Apocalypse, the most important images are encountered, naturally enough, 'at the end'. For, it is here that the final Threshold Image appears of, for example, our soul's last judgement, its final salvation or damnation. The narrative of an Apocalyptic myth may thus be laid out on the Ancient Template, and its images be *entered through* in temporal succession to the grand revelation at the end.

Meanwhile, myths of the Creation reveal their most important images 'at the beginning'. But, in order to lay these out on the Ancient Template and re-enter them, we must read the myths *in reverse succession*. We must work our way backwards through the unfolding of the creation, to '*the interior of the cosmic mystery, where... holiness is forever being created*' as Hesse put it. Only in this way may we *enter through* a creation myth to 'the most Ancient of Days'.

By using the Ancient Template to read these myths, we realize that Cosmogonic myths may also be understood as more ancient *models of the mind*. Like Hero myths, Cosmogonic myths have a more life-centred purpose: they reveal aspects of our mind's history which have otherwise descended into darkness. By working our way backwards through images of the creation, we uncover those key-images capable of unlocking new doorways in our memory, and revealing infantile memories otherwise obscured.

On the Ancient Template, the backward movement through the creation may be imagined as a spiral down through the clouds to the circle of light at the centre. Cultural memory-images from the creation would appear in those clouds closest to the centre.

But, for us to *enter through* these images, we need to relate to them in some way, and that would be through our feelings. Hence, we need to situate personal memory-images of certain events in the clouds just above the archetypal forms. Then, the mythic arrangement of images will guide us as we follow a course through our own memories. The course is regressive, a *regressus ad uterum* working our way backward through ever more ancient memory-images.

In the Egyptian myth of the creation, all began as a dark and formless abyss. But then, light, life and awareness emerged on the horizon, *for in the beginning the sun rose out of the primæval waters*. These epic events, unfolding in the depths of the mythic abyss, may also stir our personal memory-images into awakening, since they lie in the clouds just above the archetypal forms.

In a flash, we recall the moment when a unifying source of light, life and awareness first appeared on the horizon *of our own consciousness*. In our infantile memories, this is the moment when we first became aware of ourselves as a creative and self-conscious being, seeing a world separate from ourselves. That is, when our identity emerged *for the first time* on the horizon of our personal awareness.

Such an infantile memory, usually occuring at the ages of three to five, may indeed be remembered later in life (though it is often equally forgotten...). Nevertheless, the Egyptian myth of the creation offers us those collective memory-images which *activate* the personal memory-images. By *entering through* each of these in succession, the greater unity at their source may be experienced *anew*.

In the Greek myth of the creation, a tremendous yawning abyss emerged from the separation of the Sky Father and Earth Mother. And, from the midsts of that swirling chaos, all came into being: time, light, the sun, the lesser gods and the entire cosmos found its place between the heavens and the earth. When we *enter through* the images of this myth *in reverse succession*, time comes to an end, the sun goes black, order is lost and chaos emerges. The horizon disappears: the Earth and Sky mingle, the Mother and Father merge – and all are subsumed once more into their oneness.

Meanwhile, in the spiralling clouds with our own personal images, events are transpiring for which *we have no* memory-images. This is because they transpired at a time *before* the emergence of our ego on the horizon of consciousness. In our personal memory regression, we must erase that horizon, eliminate the ego, and so return to the time *before* mother and father were distinct in our mind. We must return to the time *before* the child knew a world separate from itself, and knew its mother and father to be separate from each other.

Hence, we must return to a time when the child, in mind, was *one* with the mother and father – neither male nor female, but indistinguishably *in union* with the two. Of course, to regress to the memories before these moments is nigh impossible. When we trace our feelings back, the images from our personal memory give way to cultural ones. Myths emerge on the innermost spirals of clouds, and we *enter though* these images to the sacred oneness at their source.

Nevertheless, *such a creation myth has allowed us to model the mind* and predict certain contents which would otherwise have remained unconsidered and unknown. We cannot be certain as to the validity of these contents, but myths at least point the way to their existence. As models of the mind, myths of the creation portray those life-theshold crossings which lie beyond the ken of our present ego.

Many Cosmogonic myths portray the infantile ego's concern with the earlier life-thresholds of thinking through opposites, separating the mother from the father, and acquiring identity. The Greek myth of the Father Sky and Mother Earth reflects these first two concerns, while the Egyptian myth of the creation reflects the third: when the ego emerged *for the first time* on the horizon of our consciousness.

But our attempts to *enter through* these images ends, invariably, with the Sacred at their source. Our imaginary movement through infantile memory-images soon gives way to cultural memory-images, with their halo of more sacred associations. And so we move, for example, from the first emergence of the ego to the first emergence of Atum-Re, and thence, to the more timeless appearance of the sacred unity. Or, we move from the blurred distinction of our own parents, to the original *hieros gamos* of Sumerian times – the union of the archetypal masculine and feminine in the One.

As Eliade notes, many cosmogonic situations are possible:

> *All creation implies a wholeness that precedes it, an* Urgrund. *Hierogamy is only one of the forms of explanation of Creation from a primordial* Urgrund; *there are other cosmogonic myths besides the hierogamic; but they all presuppose the prior existence of an undifferentiated unity.*[12]

Creation myths offer us perhaps the clearest models of the mind's interior history, but Apocalyptic myths could also be read in this manner. With the aid of the Ancient Template, the succession of their images would, of course, *be read forward* to the final images of 'the Last Days'. In a myth such as the Christian apocalypse, many of these images have already been seen: time ends, the sun goes black, and chaos emerges. We are subsumed once more in the undifferentiated unity.

Hence, whether the images in the spiralling clouds be read in a forward movement to our anticipated end, or in a backward movement to our earliest beginnings – either way – time is ultimately transcended. All Cosmogonic myths, be they of the creation or apocalypse, merely use time as a means to arrange images in succession, much like a painter uses perspectival space in his canvas. And just as our task is to look beyond the surface of the canvas, so as to *enter through* the image, so must we transcend the segments of historical time used by myths, so as to *enter through* them into the eternal *mythic time*.

This more ancient, mythopoeic understanding of time shall concern us in Part I, on the Mythic Path. For ultimately, the journey forward through time is the same as the journey back: the two spiral to a timeless moment at the centre, where the One in holiness for eternity dwells.

PART I

THE
MYTHIC
PATH

I will open my mouth in a parable;
I will utter dark sayings of old;
which we have heard and known,
and our fathers have told us.
– Psalm 78

CHAPTER IV

Myth as Narrative and as a Measure of Time

*In myth, as in dream, it is the secret
of the inner world that comes to us...
Out of our own depths arise the forms,
but out of regions where man
is still terrible in wisdom, beauty and bliss*
– Joseph Campbell[1]

I. Time's Measure & the Hero Task

When we peer backward through time, gazing at the remote origins of humanity through the images of myth, what we behold is a dawning awareness of Nature's alternating cycle between death and rebirth. In their earliest myths, the Egyptians saw, in the daily circuit of the sun, Atum-Re's dangerous underworld passage through the land of the dead each night, and his amazing re-emergence into the land of the living each day. Meanwhile, in the moon's monthly waxing and waning with three days' darkness in between, the Sumerians saw the Goddess Inanna's seven step descent to the Underworld, her death before her darker sister Ereshkigal, and her eventual rebirth and return.

Through the timely recitation of such myths, ancient man gradually marked and measured those signs which were constantly recurring in the heavens. Yet, the myths themselves told a more epic tale, based on the heroic patterns recurring in man's own life.

Hence, with the nightly descent of the Evening Star for two hundred and sixty three nights, followed by its re-emergence before dawn as the Morning Star for another two hundred and sixty three nights (with eight nights of darkness in between), the Aztecs saw the feathered serpent Quetzalcoatl plunge into underworld flames, undergo a cleansing and purification, then be reborn as his heart rose heavenward like a flaming star. And again, in the seasonal parching, sterility and death of all vegetation during the hot season, and its miraculous reflowering and new growth with the rains, the Egyptians, Sumerians and Phœnicians saw their shepherd-god Osiris, Damuzi and Baal continually die and rise again.

In this way, nature's ever-recurring cycles created a mythic template for man's heroic journey, portraying his life as an on-going cycle of death and rebirth. When we look at myths from former times to the present, this template continually re-appears. It underlies, first of all, those Cosmogonic myths which describe the world's creation and eventual dissolution. And it underlies those great Hero myths which transpire in the time in-between.

Regarding Cosmogonic myths, Mircea Eliade has noted that:

> *The lunar rhythm regularly presents a 'creation' (the new moon) followed by a growth (to the full moon), a diminution and a 'death' (the three moonless nights). It was very probably the eternal birth and death of the moon which helped to crystallize the earliest human intuitions about the alterations of life and death, and suggested later on the myth of the periodic creation and destruction of the world.*[2]

Hence, while the moon could offer the Sumerians a heroic vision of Inanna continuously alternating between death and rebirth, it also suggested the periodic destruction and re-creation of the entire cosmos.

Meanwhile, Eliade notes elsewhere that:

> *Most heroic mythologies are solar in structure. The hero is assimilated to the sun; like the sun, he fights darkness, descends into the realm of death, and emerges victorious.*[3]

And so, like the Egyptian solar-myth of Atum-Re, it was the sun's circular movement in the heavens which inspired our first tales of the hero's departure, descent and deed performed at the darkest nadir of the underworld, followed by his ascent and re-integration into the overworld full of light – all of which constitutes the basic narrative pattern of the Hero myth.

But, persistent in these cyclic visions alternating between death and rebirth is the undercurrent of time and its measure. Each of these mythic arrangements of images also offers us *a mythic measure of time*. It is now our task to look more closely into the basic narrative patterns which arrange a temporal succession of images into a myth. What are the fundamental, ever-recurring forms that underlie myth? And, most important of all, how may we begin to *think through* a mythic arrangement of images to understand its innate image-language?

For us, a myth is an iconologue – 'an image-cluster which betrays some kind of recognizable meaning and arrangement'. In particular, it is a series of images arranged *over time*, which uses a basic *narrative pattern* to depict the world's creation, the sacred hero's world-saving deed, or the world's end. Within these narrative patterns lies another structuring element, involving *the completion of the hero task:* its acquisition before setting out, its accomplishment at the mythic nadir, and its integration into society upon his return. Our task, over the next few chapters, will be to identify these three particular iconologues as they arise in mythic arrangements of images.

As we have noted, there are basically two types of myth: the Cosmogonic and the Hero myth. First, we shall consider the Hero myth, particularly the myth of the *sacred* hero, such as it appears in Judæo-Christianity, Hindu-Buddhism, and the ancient Near East (Egypt and Mesopotamia). Then, at the end of Part I, we shall consider Cosmogonic myths, using the Gnostic myth of creation as our example.

We shall concentrate on the different ways in which mythic images *measure time.* Any arrangement of images that marks a measure of time – Atum-Re's diurnal and nocturnal boat journey, Inanna's seven-step descent and return – reveals the presence of, what we shall call, *the Iconologue of Time's Measure.*

As well, the narrative structures of myth – whether 'O' or 'U' shaped – arrange a series of images into a definite *Narrative Pattern.* Finally, the sacred hero's task – its acquisition, accomplishment and integration – links one image to the next through, what we shall call, *the Iconologue of Task Completion.* This may be portrayed as follows:

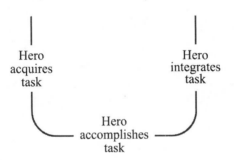

These iconologues are silently at work whenever we read a mythic arrangement of images.

II. The Great Code
& the Monomyth

Over the course of the last century there has been, largely in France, a fury of debate over the semiotics and structure of narrative. But two writers, one a Canadian and the other an American, have remained at a distance from this controversy and so, by consequence, have emerged with a profound grasp of narrative structure that is also profoundly simple.

The Canadian, Northrop Frye, was a literary critic who, over the course of his life, wound his way ever deeper through the poetic maze of imagery in Shakespeare, Milton and Blake. But Frye, ordained an Anglican Minister at the beginning of his life, continued to see echoes of the Bible in the works of English literature's greatest writers. And so, toward the end of his life, he turned the power of his critical gaze onto the Bible, accomplishing a most penetrating analysis of its imagery and narrative structure in his books *The Great Code* and *Words with Power*.

The result was that he came to regard the Bible as 'a Great Code' for understanding the narratives and imagery of, not just English literature, but *all* cultures: *"If we take the Bible as a key to mythology, instead of taking mythology in general as a key to the Bible, we should at least have a definite starting point, wherever we end."*[4] In the end, the Bible encapsulates the entire mythological framework and expectation that we by necessity project onto other mythologies in our attempts to understand them.

Frye recognized that all the Bible's narratives basically portray 'loss and regain', and so are 'U' shaped:

> *We may take* the Book of Job, *perhaps, as the epitome of the narrative of the Bible, just as the* Book of Revelation *is the epitome of its imagery... It is a U-shaped story: Job... falls into a world of suffering and exile, 'repents' (i.e., goes through a* metanoia *or metamorphosis of consciousness), and is restored to his original state, with interest.*[5]

In general, the hero falls from a once-idyllic state, and in his descent undergoes a series of trials and ordeals ending in a profound moment of crisis, realization and transformation, allowing him to finally rise again to his former state. Essentially, what the hero has lost and must regain is a sense of oneness with the creation.

Frye calls this 'the loss and regaining of identity':

> [This is the] *outline of a story that has been told so often, of how man once lived in a golden age or garden of Eden or of the Hesperides, or a happy island kingdom in the Atlantic, how that world was lost, and how we someday may be able to get it back again... This story of the loss and regaining of identity is, I think, the framework of all literature. Inside it comes the story of the hero with a thousand faces, as one critic calls him, whose adventures, death, disappearance and marriage or resurrection are the focal points...*[6]

In essence, the sense of oneness or 'identity' which the hero has lost and must regain is a re-experience of that timeless unity which once existed at this world's beginning and will exist again at its end. In other words, what the hero accomplishes at the nadir of the Hero Myth is a momentary glimpse into that timeless paradise which Cosmogonic myths describe.

The American who told that story of 'the hero with a thousand faces' was Joseph Campbell – who, by interest and by contrast, was born a Roman Catholic. Through the Catholic's intuitive, ingrained and inculcated understanding of symbolism, Campbell eventually recognized that his faith was indeed a mythology, *"a constellation of perfectly traditional mythological symbols arranged in such a way as to bear to us... a message."*[7] And so, he reached beyond the complex of Christian symbols given to him in childhood to, for the remainder of his life, embrace in his writings an ever greater, more collective and cohesive understanding of narrative and imagery from all the world's mythologies.

In his classic book, *The Hero with a Thousand Faces*, he delineates the basic structure of the Hero myth, seeing it as a series of threshold crossings in which the hero, called to adventure and challenged by various threshold guardians, first passes downward, across the Threshold of Separation, into a dark underworld. There, he undergoes a series of trials and ordeals, encountering fabulous forces which he must master through conquest, assimilation, atonement or perhaps even marriage.

At the low point or 'nadir' of his downward journey, the intentions of the hero must alter so profoundly that any former attachment to his life must be released and, possibly through death and sacrifice, possibly through realization and enlightenment, he experiences a profound moment of transformation. Having crossed this fundamentally life-altering Threshold of Initiation, he is free to pass upward again.

But at the entrance to the overworld, he must still cross over the Threshold of Return. To bestow upon his fellow man the boons he has acquired, he must successfully transform those underworld powers into powers of light. Only then may he return with his prize to the land from whence he first set out.

In brief: the *acquisition* of the hero-task, its *accomplishment* at the mythic nadir, and its final *integration* into society underlies the narrative pattern. Following James Joyce, Campbell called his basic narrative pattern, 'the Monomyth' and, inspired by *Finnegan's Wake*, visualized the shape of myth differently from Frye in one most important aspect: closing the upper prongs of Frye's 'U', Campbell delineated the basic structure of myth in the form of an 'O', a perfect circle.

The slight variance revealed by the way these two thinkers visualized their ideas may seem of slight consequence. But it also reveals a fundamental difference in their conceptions *of time.*

Frye rightly saw Christianity as characterized by a historical sense of time suspended between the creation and apocalypse, with Christ's mission transpiring along *a linear segment* bounded by these events on either side. The Cosmogonic myths of Genesis and the Apocalypse form an important prelude and coda to the Bible, as they reveal the timeless eternity which bounds history on either side. Meanwhile, the Old and New Testaments offer us a linked series of Hero myths in which time passes *historically*.

Christ's ministry on earth begins with his divine birth, then descends to his death and resurrection, and culminates finally with his ascension. Hence, the fundamental shape of Christian narrative may be seen as a 'U', with 'the loss and regaining of identity' accomplished along a thread of time suspended between the creation and apocalypse. Much like a tight-rope walker, Christ tread across linear history step by step, slowly bearing the soul of man over the abyss.

Campbell on the other hand was steeped in Heinrich Zimmer's studies on Hindu-Buddhism, and so rendered a much different image of time. The hero of his Monomyth acts within an *ever-recurring Cosmogonic cycle.* Like Frye's lost sense of 'identity with the creation' which the hero, at the nadir of his myth, seeks to regain; for Campbell an undifferentiated unity permeated the cosmos before its creation and will do so again after its end. And, it is into this timeless ground that the hero descends:

> *Briefly formulated, the universal doctrine teaches that all the visible structures of the world – all things and beings – are the effects of a ubiquitous power out of which they rise, which supports and fills them during the period of their manifestation, and back into which they must ultimately resolve... This is the great theme and formula of the cosmogonic cycle, the mythical image of the world's coming to manifestation and subsequent return into the non-manifest condition. Equally, the birth, life, and death of the individual may be regarded as a descent into [it] and return... The adventure of the hero represents the moment in his life when he achieves illumination.*[8]

Once again, the task of the sacred hero is to re-experience, at the nadir of the Hero myth, that timeless ground or 'ubiquitous power' which first manifest itself at the beginning of the cosmogonic cycle and will manifest itself again at the end.

Eliade referred to this 'return to the source' as:

> *'...the nostalgia for paradise'. I mean by this the desire to be always, effortlessly, at the heart of the world, of reality, of the sacred, and briefly, to transcend, by natural means, the human condition and regain a divine state of affairs: what a Christian would call the state of man before the Fall.*[9]

In his description of the Hero myth, Campbell rendered an image of the cosmos which could also account for its cyclic recurrence. According to this image, the cosmos passes through an endless series of cycles – each creation being destroyed, then restored or recreated in an eternal round. In Hindu-Buddhism, these cycles are called *yugas*, and constitute our greatest suffering (*samsara*). Meanwhile, the ancient Greeks also possessed a cyclic view on time, which the Pythagoreans called *anakuklosis* and the Platonists, *apokatastasis*. And so, the fundamental shape of mythic narrative was seen by Campbell to be a circle. And the fundamental aim of Hindu-Buddhism was not, as in Christianity, to successfully cross over to the other side, but to return to the place from whence we originated, so as to find, ultimately, a still point in the midsts of this ever-turning wheel.

III. Inscribing Lines and Circles
in Eternal Mythic Time

Mircea Eliade, in his classic work *The Myth of the Eternal Return* was perhaps the first mythologist to recognize *a more ancient* understanding of time in myth. Eliade was born in Romania but lived most of his life in exile – in France and later in America. This gave him a familiarity with the Orthodox, Catholic and Protestant branches of Christianity. But, as a young man he spent a number of years in India, both as a guest-student in the home of a Sanskrit scholar and as a disciple of yoga in the *ashram* of a swami. This extended his knowledge into the intricacies of orthodox and unorthodox Hinduism. Later, during his first years of exile in Paris, he wrote a major study on Shamanism and its 'archaic techniques of ecstasy' which return the shaman to a more primitive, indeed, primordial state of consciousness. The result of this ever-deepening life-quest into time and the Sacred was Eliade's distinction of *three* different renderings of time in myth,[10] which may be imagined respectively as a circle, a circle repeatedly redrawn, and a line.

The first and most ancient form of time is *mythic time*, and may be imagined as a circle. It is a circle because the flow of time in a Cosmogonic myth, from the beginning to the end, closes in upon itself so as to be complete in itself. Most such myths take place in a time that is distinctly a-historical – *"Once upon a time"*, *"In the beginning"* (Genesis), *"When the skies above were not yet named"* (Enuma Elish[11]). They take place *en archai*, during 'the first time' (what the Egyptians named *tep zepi*), and 'at first', such as *"Darkness there was at first, by darkness hidden"* (Rg Veda[12]). We also hear this in Hebrew myth through the words of *Hokhmah* (Wisdom), whom the Old Testament Prophets regarded as God's helper in Creation: *"...The Lord created me at the beginning of his work, the first of his acts of old."* (Proverbs 8:22)

The time that transpires in these myths is co-incident with eternity, passing without measure. In the words of Northrop Frye, the action of such myths "...*takes place in a world above or prior to ordinary time.*"[13] In this sense, ancient myths take place outside the mundane flow of time and in the more sacred, measureless 'dream-time' familiar to us from our dreams. This sacred and unmeasured eternity was characterized by Eliade as *mythic time*.

Within this ancient circle of sacred time closed off from mundane history there passes a thousand different stories told within any one culture. Such stories are eternally true, and so oft-repeated that they become ever-contemporary. In Hindu-Buddhism, all of these stories became temporally related to one another when, within the closed circle of mythic time, *cyclic* time was born. (This is not to suggest that cyclic time originated in India. Evidence of both linear and cyclic time may be found in ancient Egypt, Greece and Mesopotamia. But, it must be stressed, cyclic time reached its greatest cultural flowering in Hindu-Buddhism).

In cyclic time, time takes on a linear quality, but this line is a circle redrawn continuously so as to make the end of one cycle the beginning of the next. Hence, at the end of each cycling *yuga*, history begins anew. That is why India possesses so many different myths of the creation. Each creation myth describes the world at the beginning of one of its many manifestations and permutations. We are presently living in the last of the four yugas, called the *Kali Yuga*. It is, unfortunately, an age of darkness and decline, but will eventually cycle towards the age of light.

However, it is also possible to identify one segment of time within the eternal circle of mythic time, isolate it and remove it, so as to form the 'U'-shaped narratives so characteristic of Judæo-Christianity. Now, all events take place at some point along a linear segment of time which has a definite beginning and end. As well, it is regarded as *all* of history, encompassing the present moment as well as moments past and to come.

Linear historical time is not closed off from us, like the circle of mythic time: we are caught in its midst. This is true of cyclic time as well: the Hindu or Buddhist is caught within its ever-recurrence. For that reason, linear-historical time and ever-recurring cyclic time may be thought of as mundane. Yet, in all these traditions, tales are told of the sacred hero's world-saving deed – his crucifixion or awakening which, though it transpires in time's very middle – *breaks out of the segments or cycles of the mundane time and becomes, like the creation or apocalypse, an event coincident with the eternal mythic time.*

When we follow the narrative of a myth, we are enjoined to imagine the succession of events in its narrative unfolding. And so, a mythic narrative arranges a succession of images *in time*. This span of time is something we are free to imagine as we will, but it is usually imagined in accord with the version of time determined by the hero in the myth. And so we imagine the events of Christian myth as unfolding within linear-historical time, while those of Buddhist myth transpire in ever-recurring cycles of time.

But, when we remember that ancient myths took place in the unmeasured eternity of *mythic time*, then it becomes clear that the narratives of Hindu-Buddhism and Judæo-Christianity have *created* these measures of time's linear or cyclical unfolding. We must recognize the silent presence of the Iconologue of Time's Measure, which uses the different arrangements of images in these myths to *create different measures of time*. The Christian narrative, transpiring in linear-historical time, offers us one Iconologue of Time's Measure; the Buddhist narrative, transpiring in ever-recurring cyclic time, offers us another. But these stories could, should we wish it, also transpire *in each other's times*. We are responsible for the temporal measures we project upon myths, through the different cultural Iconologues of Time's Measure.

We in the West have been so thoroughly conditioned by the Judæo-Christian iconologue of sacred history that we fail to regard how peculiar it is in our culture to measure time forward from an event that happened 'two thousand years ago and half a world away'. Eliade has noted[14] that this Judæo-Christian idea of a historical theophany, where God reveals himself slowly through the unfolding of events in history, is unique among the religions of the world. We must therefore make an effort to believe that other cultures could conceive of time differently...

"One figure in an amazing multiplicity of guises..."
Rogier Van der Weyden: Christ in The Last Judgement (1451). Detail.

CHAPTER V

Mythic Narrative in Judeo-Christianity and Hindu-Buddhism

For now we see in a mirror darkly
But then we shall see face to face.
1 Corinthians 13:12

I. Mythic Christianity

When we admire the various images of Christ in art, rather than read the myth of his passion in the Bible, we behold one figure in an amazing multiplicity of guises: he is crucified, transfigured, betrayed, anointed, scourged, resurrected, mourned, adored by kings, crowned with thorns, ascended to Heaven, descended to Hell, tempted, doubted, born in a manger and entombed – among other things. Without the narrative of Christ's life, what we behold is a vision worthy only of madness, grandiosity and delusion.

But, when we turn to the Bible to seek some sense of narrative order for this plethora of imagery, we find four somewhat differing accounts of Christ's life in the New Testament gospels, each of which makes no sense whatsoever without some prior knowledge of a hundred or so other stories from the Old Testament and Book of Revelation.

Hence, it would now be of some benefit to unravel the Hero myth of Christianity, using Northrop Frye as our source. The basic structure of this myth and the hero-tasks it creates may then be compared to Hindu-Buddhism, using Campbell as our source, so as to more deeply understand their underlying iconologues of time, narrative and the hero's task.

More importantly, we wish to understand how these iconologues underlie *all* mythic arrangements of images, and are able to offer *one* particular image at the mythic nadir – the sacred hero at his moment of death, rebirth and awakening – which, as a Threshold Image, may eventually be *entered through* to a momentary epiphany.

In *The Great Code*, Northrop Frye identifies several basic narratives that could be considered the archetypal *mythoi* of Christianity. From these, we have isolated three, each of which has Christ as its hero. In these myths, the Iconologue of Task Completion – the task's acquisition, accomplishment and integration – varies in time from three days to thirty-three years to an eternity.

Although these three myths seem to vary widely in their temporal measure, the tasks they present to Christ are basically the same, and so too is their narrative structure. To identify and appreciate the basic structure of Christian myth, it will be necessary first to review a few examples of its precursors in the Hebrew Old Testament.

The most significant of the Old Testament narratives follow the basic 'U' pattern: first, an initial downward movement into disaster and bondage, called by Frye 'apostasy'; then, at the bottom, a moment of realization and understanding, called 'repentance'; finally followed by the returning movement upward led by a saviour figure, and called 'deliverance'.[1]

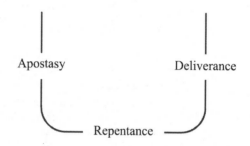

Adam's fall from Eden was the first great downward movement in created history, and remains unremedied throughout the Old Testament. His sin was partially repaired by Noah, who delivered from the flood Adam's only remaining pious descendants. But these too fell into dissolution, and this time it was Abraham, after willing to sacrifice his own son, who delivered the Israelites out of Sodom and Gomorrah and into the Promised Land. But the Israelites again fell into bondage as the slaves of the Egyptians, and it was now Moses, after destroying the tablets of the Ten Commandments, who (with Joshua) delivered the Israelites to a new Promised Land. Then, the Philistines defeated Saul, and the Israelites again fell into bondage until David, and later Solomon, established the kingdom of Israel with its temple in Jerusalem. These were eventually overrun, and the period of the Babylonian captivity began, until the temple was rebuilt.

There are many such narrative movements of loss and regain in the Old Testament, which may be laid side by side to portray the ever downturning, upturning historical journey of the Hebrew people. And it is only Christ, according to the New Testament, who can successfully restore all that Adam lost – forcing the head of this twisting serpent of history upward to a final movement of ascent.[2]

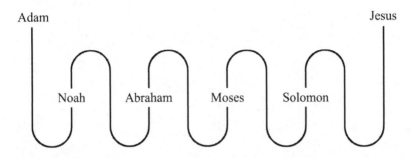

All the previous saviours of the Israelites – Noah, Abraham, Moses and Solomon among them – prefigure the final appearance of the Christian saviour. The traditional hermeneutic method of interpreting this phenomenon is to recognize any Old Testament figure or event prefiguring the appearance of the Christian saviour as a 'type' (*tupos*) of Christ. And so, contrarily, when the New Testament saviour mirrors a figure or event from the Old Testament, he is called their 'anti-type' (*antitupos*). Adam, for example, as 'the fallen one', is a type for Christ; while Christ, as 'the risen one', is the anti-type of Adam. With this method of interpretation, we are able to identify three major 'U'-shaped narratives which constitute the archetypal *mythoi* of Christianity.[3]

II. The Three Christian *Mythoi*:
The World Saviour Myth

The first may be referred to as 'the World Saviour myth', as it describes Christ's earthly incarnation – a life history encompassing some thirty-three years. The narrative begins with Christ's descent into the world through his *incarnation* and virgin birth. Then, it extends through his *ministry* on earth culminating in the crucifixion. Finally, it ends with his *ascent* into Heaven.

From Byzantine iconostases to Gothic altarpieces, the moment of Christ's descent is depicted in the form of the Annunciation and Nativity. The moment the angel Gabriel announced to the Virgin that she was to bear a child, Christ's spirit descended into her in a flash of light. And the moment the Madonna gave birth, Christ's incarnation was made complete: the eternal *Sacramentum* had appeared here on earth in the form of an innocent child. Yeats described his appearance as *"the uncontrollable mystery on the bestial floor."*[4] By incorporating golden-flaked haloes, mandorlas and other effects

"The uncontrollable mystery on the bestial floor."
Hugo Van der Goes: The Nativity, Portinari Altarpiece (1475). Detail.

for the *splendor divinus*, artists have shown that these moments constitute veritable epiphanies. All these *Heiligenbilder* and *pictura sacra* offer us, what we have referred to as, Threshold Images.

The incarnation is followed by Christ's *ministry* on earth, which involves a good number of trials: his baptism, temptation in the desert, moment of doubt in Gethsemane, betrayal, scourging and road to Calvary. Each of these episodes in the life of Christ form their own, smaller 'U'-shaped narratives with Threshold Images at their nadir.

In the Baptism for example, Christ stepped down into the Jordan and experienced a sudden epiphany as John poured water over his head: the heavens opened, a dove appeared, and a voice called out that he was indeed the Son of God. Stepping out of the river, he had undergone a transformation and renewal, a kind of death and rebirth.

Finally there is the Crucifixion. Here, Christ is at the nadir of his suffering and experiences his greatest moment of revelation and transformation. Each of the above moments have achieved deep, heart-felt expression in Christian art, but it is particularly the Crucifixion which has become fixed in our cultural memory as a sacred symbol. It is a Threshold Image which we, if we can bear to meditate upon it, could *enter through* to his momentary revelation and transformation.

After the entombment, harrowing of Hell and resurrection, which form a 'U'-shaped narrative all their own, comes the re-appearance of Christ among the living, where he dwelt for forty days. This is a time of joy and an upward movement in the narrative, culminating with the moment of his *ascension*: a final up-turning and return to the Heaven from whence he came.

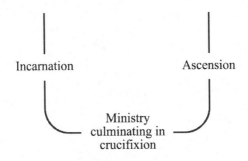

Incarnation   Ascension

Ministry
culminating in
crucifixion

III. The Infernal Saviour Myth

The second archetypal myth of Christianity, also with a 'U'-shaped narrative, may be called the 'Infernal Saviour myth', and covers the span of three days and nights when Christ entered the underworld. It consists of Christ's entombment, harrowing of Hell and resurrection, and is rather apocryphal. The narrative does not receive explicit treatment in the Bible at all.

In the earliest recorded source, the *Gospel of Nicodemus*, Christ descends to Hades' pit, binds Satan, and frees all the souls imprisoned below because they, from Adam to John the Baptist, had died before the gates of salvation were opened by his sacrifice:

> ...*The gates of brass were broken in pieces and the bars of iron were crushed and all the dead who were bound were loosed from their chains... And the King of Glory entered in like a man, and all the dark places of Hades were illumined.* (V. 3)
>
> ...*Then the King of Glory seized the chief ruler Satan by the head and handed him over to the angels saying: Bind with irons fetters his hands and his feet and his neck and his mouth. Then he gave him to Hades and said: Take him and hold him fast until my second coming.* (VI. 2)
>
> ...*The King of Glory stretched out his right hand and took hold of our forefather Adam and raised him up. Then he turned to the rest and said: Come with me all you who have suffered death through the tree which this man touched. For behold, I raise you all up again through the tree of the cross.* (VIII. 1)[5]

"And all the dark places of Hades were illumined."
School of Savoy: The Harrowing of Hell (15th century).

Thus Adam, who fell because of the fruit of the tree, rises again through Christ, whose cross becomes the new tree, offering resurrection and life.

In Christian art, themes such as the Descent from the Cross, the Entombment and the Resurrection portray important moments from the Infernal Saviour narrative. Due to its apocryphal nature, the Harrowing of Hell does not appear as often, but Gothic and Byzantine art offer some fine exemplars of the *'katabasis eis hadou'* or *'descensus ad inferos'*. Adam and Eve are always depicted as the first to emerge from the underworld.

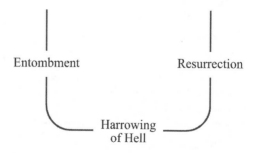

IV. The Celestial Saviour Myth

The third, and perhaps most important of the archetypal Christian *mythoi* – possessing a 'U'-shaped narrative, but extending across recorded time, from the creation to the apocalypse – may be called the 'Celestial Saviour myth'. This is not the story of Jesus but the Christ. We must be willing to see Adam and all other messianic figures from the Old Testament as *types* of Christ: instigating acts, covenants or prophecies which will eventually be fulfilled by Jesus who, as the final incarnation of Christ, constitutes the final appearance of the Celestial Saviour.

Essentially, the Celestial Saviour narrative is a sacred Hero myth which expands to Cosmogonic proportions. The narrative begins with an initial downward movement brought about by Adam's fall. This is followed by a series of trials and ordeals experienced throughout Hebrew history, culminating with their prophecies of the Messiah. Finally, that Messiah appears in the form of Jesus Christ, who is crucified, dies and rises again, then ascends to Heaven. In the final upward movement, the risen Christ will restore, during the apocalypse, all that was lost by Adam during the fall.

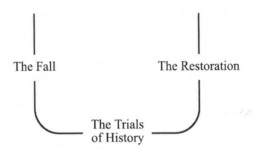

The Fall   The Restoration

The Trials
of History

At the end of the Bible, in the *Book of Revelation*, Christ announces in his final parting words: *"I am the Alpha and Omega, the first and the last, the beginning and the end."*(Rev 22:13) Where was he, then, at the beginning? And at the end?

V. The Four Hidden Narratives

At the end, in *Revelation*, Christ appears to us in several metaphorical guises: as the Judge of the living and the dead, as the Lamb, as the Bridegroom and as the Word of God. That is to say, as the key figure in the drama of, say, a trial, sacrifice, marriage or vision. Frye makes the perspicacious observation that the *Book of Revelation* is *"...an incredible tour de force singlehandedly working out the entire* dianoia *or metaphor cluster of the Bible"*[6] Using this imagery to read our way backwards through the Bible, we can see that the recurrence of certain images creates four distinct dramas or 'hidden narratives'[7] in which Christ's hero-task is revealed: to restore all that Adam lost in the fall.

In the first hidden narrative, of 'the trial', Adam committed a crime by disobeying God's command. Throughout the Old Testament, a series of new covenants, laws and commandments appear which, if followed, could restore this broken link. But only Christ, following God's command to the end through his crucifixion, was able to restore the law of God. This is why, in the future, he will embody that law as Judge of the living and the dead.

In the second hidden narrative, of 'the sacrifice', Adam's fall is not merely a case of disobeying God's command, but of provoking his wrath through impudence. Such a sin may only be purged and expiated through suffering and sacrifice. Throughout history, the Hebrews suffered one ordeal after another, but it was only Christ, through his sacrifice on the cross, who was able to successfully invoke God's love, mercy and forgiveness.

In the case of 'the marriage', the narrative is somewhat obscure. When Adam and Eve fell, they had to toil upon the earth and bring forth children in pain. Their experience of the world, and of each other, was bound up in a series of unfulfilled pains and pleasures. Their bodies aged and decayed unto death. Generation after generation was born to die. The world, over the course of history, declined, appearing as a Garden reduced to toil, a Promised Land corrupted by slavery, or the kingdom of Israel and its holy city Jerusalem overrun and destroyed. Christ, through his death and resurrection, was able to purify the body of its death and decay while also establishing 'the Kingdom' permanently. Hence a dual metaphor appears in *Revelation*, where Christ is seen as the Bridegroom, and the Kingdom, the 'New Jerusalem' appears as the *"bride adorned for her husband"* (Rev. 21:2).

This New Jerusalem is described in detail as a celestial city *"bright as crystal... transparent as glass."* (Rev. 22:1, 21:21) and is symbolic of the world restored to a state of permanence. Since the body too will be restored to perfection, we shall *see* this vision of the celestial city *with our own eyes*. We shall see it as Adam saw Eve and Paradise before the temptation: perfect, untouched, unspoiled – nothing less than *a direct view* unto the timeless mystery of the creation, now unveiled for all eternity.

As such, the end of time is 'a wedding', in which we shall all become wed, in soul, to the Bridegroom. Through Christ's higher love, which the Christians indicated by the distinctive word *agape*, we shall enter the bridal hall and join with him in an endless vision of paradise.

In all three of the above cases, Adam lost something in the fall which could not be remedied through the course of Hebrew history, nor even through the life of Jesus on earth, but which Christ – the 'second Adam' – will restore finally in the apocalypse. The figure of Adam is particularly important in this scheme of things because, without Adam, there would be no fall, no need for restoration, and so no Celestial Saviour. The Christian myth, to be understood, must *cross over* with this ancient Hebrew myth, and at the point where they cross, a new revelation is achieved.

VI. The Word, Wisdom & Eternal Vision

The last of the guises which Christ assumes in *Revelation*, the Word, produces perhaps the most elusive narrative of the Bible, but also its most profound. As the *Logos,* or 'the Word of God', Christ says at the end of time, *"Behold, I make all things anew"*(Rev 21:5). He has this power to re-create the world at the end of time because it was also he who, as the Word of God, created the world in the beginning. John writes of this in his gospel on the life of Christ: *"In the beginning was the Word ...and through him all things were made. ...the word became flesh and dwelt among us."* (Jo 1:2-14) In many Byzantine copulas, we find stunningly beautiful mosaics of Christ as the *Pantocrator*, the *Creator of all.*

But if we look at the myth of the creation in *Genesis*, we find no mention whatsoever of Christ as the creative Word. However, in the Old Testament *Book of Proverbs*, the creation of the world is again described, and this time the figure of *Hokhmah* or Wisdom appears. She introduces herself, saying:

> *...The Lord created me at the beginning of his work,*
> *The first of his acts of old.*
> *...When he established the heavens, I was there*
> *when he drew a circle on the face of the deep*
> *...When he marked out the foundations of the earth,*
> *then I was beside him like a master workman.* (Prov. 8:22)

The figure of Wisdom in the Old Testament became a *type* for the figure of the Word in the New Testament. As such, Jesus – the Word of God – overtook the symbolic role of *Hokhmah* – the Wisdom of God.

Thus, at the end of time, when Jesus appears as the Word to restore all that was lost, he will also restore the wisdom that was manifest in creation but lost when Adam, through his folly, fell from God's favour. But what wisdom, what vision, could Adam have possibly *lost*? For he was supposed to have *gained knowledge* by eating the forbidden fruit...

What he lost when he gained knowledge was wisdom in the sense of *a more timeless way of seeing* the creation, an endless and eternal gaze into all created things, where the *Sacramentum* at their source is revealed. He lost nothing less than the power to gaze upon God *'face to face'* – a direct view into the eternal *Mysterion*.

For the remainder of the Bible, and throughout history, God appears *'in a mirror darkly'* – disguised behind burning bushes, doves, cherubim, angelic messengers, and so on. But, through his moment of suffering and revelation on the cross, Christ was able to behold the Divine *directly* and *'face to face'*.

The fall, understood in this way, was not disobedience to God's law or impudence evoking his wrath, but *the loss of wisdom and vision* – the loss of a timeless and more eternal gaze, a *way of seeing* the creation and meditating upon it, so we may behold the Sacred at its source. Only Christ, through his suffering and awakening, was able to restore that gaze.

At the nadir moment of his narrative, Christ experienced a momentary epiphany which broke him out of historical time as he glimpsed, for one brief and fleeting moment, time's underlying eternity. This singular event in the middle of historical time became co-incident with the measureless eternity that existed before the creation and after the apocalypse. In his own flesh, he became a timeless *symbol* of the Sacred – a *divine doorway* or, we could say ...a Threshold Image.

The four hidden narratives of the Celestial Saviour myth are indeed difficult to grasp, based as they are on images of Christ in *Revelation* read selectively through the Bible. It is only because certain images recur, from one testament to the next, that we are able to see them all in a linear arrangement, roughly falling into a structure of loss and restoration.

They remain 'hidden narratives' because a single forward reading of the Bible would probably not reveal them. It is only when we re-read and select, discarding the vast majority of what we read and highlighting only those images which follow the line of loss and restoration, that the hidden narratives gradually appear before our eyes. In essence, we are selecting a series of related images which, when laid side by side, reveal a hidden 'U'-pattern.

And yet, when all is said and done, it is particularly the Celestial Saviour myth that characterizes Christianity. Of all the archetypal Christian *mythoi*, it is the most profound. The shorter narratives of Christ's life, culminating with his death and resurrection, make very little sense unless situated within the larger context. That is to say, unless the shorter, particularly Christian myths *cross over* with the Hebrew myths, especially the myth of Adam's fall, and also with the apocalyptic visions related in *Revelation*. The books of *Genesis* and *Revelation* thus provide an important prelude and coda to the story of the life of Jesus as told in the synoptic gospels, crossing over with them and altering them profoundly...

As the Celestial Saviour, Christ subsumes under him many messianic figures – Adam, Noah, Moses, Solomon, Jesus – uniting them all into one hero whose spiritual journey traverses a multiplicity of crossed myths

– juxtaposing them all spontaneously and almost at randomn into a single, higher narrative.

And, in the end, it is the Celestial Saviour myth which provides us with the hero-task of Christianity. This hero-task links the images of Christianity, forming a single U-shaped structure extending from the beginning of time to its end. It holds all the narratives of the Bible together as *one myth*.

In essence, Christ's task was to restore all which Adam had lost in the fall. He acquired this task at the beginning, and accomplished it at the nadir point of the narrative through his death and resurrection. At the time of the apocalypse, he will finally integrate that task into the cosmos, through his return and restitution of all things. As we have seen, the *acquisition* of the task, its *accomplishment,* and a return to the place of origin for its final *integration* constitute the three stages of the hero's task.

Through the iconologues of time, narrative and the hero's task, the plethora of imagery in Christian art – the Nazarene's nativity and entombment, his ascent to Heaven and descent to Hell, his suffering and revelation – may all be read and understood as constituents of *one* sacred Hero myth.

In essence, the journey of this saviour-hero through the worldly, infernal and celestial realms constitutes a path *for our eternal soul*. The path is created by Christ, and those souls who choose to follow him must retrace the steps of his mythic movement. In this sense, the myth of Christianity becomes one example of a more fundamental *Ur-myth*, which we have called 'the eternal Hero myth of the soul'.

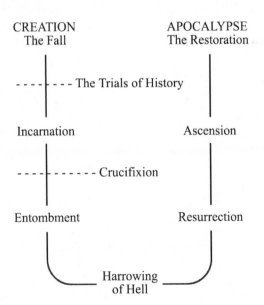

To conclude then, there are three archetypal Christian *mythoi*, each of which possesses a 'U'-shaped narrative created through loss and restoration. The World, Infernal and Celestial Saviour myths may be laid one beneath the other so as to display the one Christian narrative that unites all three as a descent and ascent through Heaven, Earth and Hell. This myth covers a span of, not just three days, or thirty-three years, but extends as far back as the beginning of time, where Christ appeared as the Word *'through whom all things were made'*, and extends as far forward as the end of time, when he will appear again as the Word *'through whom all things will be made anew'*. We call this, quite simply, the myth of Christianity.

VII. At the Nadir of a Myth: the Threshold Image

If we consider the above 'U'-shaped narratives, we shall see that the most important moment, aside from the beginning and the end, is that nadir or low point at the bottom which becomes the 'turning point'. Frye refers to this as a moment of Repentance, and is quick to cite the Greek source, *metanoia*, for this much-abused English word. *Metanoia* means 'to turn around' (*meta*) 'our way of knowing' (*noia*) – a 'transformation of the mind' or, as Frye translates it, a 'metamorphosis of consciousness'.

It is precisely at this moment in the narrative that a realization is made, insight arrives, and wisdom arises. The image of Oedipus blinding himself is perhaps one of the most brutal but profound renderings of this experience of sudden insight. The image of the Buddha beneath the Bodhi tree is another, more typical image of wisdom arising from within. For us, using different aspects from all these myths, it typically takes the form of a death, rebirth and awakening.

Since myths are *a series of images* linked and arranged through narrative, then there is *one image* at the nadir of a narrative which encapsulates that moment of epiphany. Such a nadir-moment arises at the darkest threshold-crossing confronting the hero; a threshold which is – paradoxically – also the most enlightening. And it is precisely these momentary scenes of death, rebirth and awakening that become fixed for all time in our cultural memory through the art of statuary and painting. We refer to them as Threshold Images, because it is precisely these images which possess thresholds that we, in our meditations, may attempt to step across and eventually *enter through* to their momentary revelation of the Sacred.

Now, as we return to Campbell's monomyth, we shall see how the momentary epiphany in Hindu-Buddhism, and later in more ancient mythologies, differs significantly from Christianity. This is because time is understood to be, not a line of history drawn once only, but an ever-recurring cycle and, ultimately, a more timeless circle. And so, the moment of revelation now shifts from the end of time to a point in the midsts of its ever-cycling and, indeed, to its very centre.

VIII. The Thresholds of Myth

Early in his career, Campbell developed a most helpful tool for discerning the basic structure underlying most if not all myths, called the Monomyth.

In its initial, more basic form, it describes the hero journey as a circle moving from Separation to Initiation to Return. In the course of this mythic round, several important thresholds are crossed. At the first initial downward movement, *"a hero ventures forth from the world of common day into a region of supernatural wonder,"* and so crosses the Threshold of Separation into the underworld. Then, progressing to the bottom, he undergoes a series of tests leading to a final Threshold of Initiation where *"fabulous forces are encountered and a decisive victory is won."* Last, for his homecoming, the hero must cross back, over the Threshold of Return, to the overworld, and if successful *"...comes back from this mysterious adventure with the power to bestow boons on his fellow man."*[8]

The basic Monomyth may be expanded through the inclusion of various archetypal deeds accomplished along the way so as to form the following adventure:

THE MONOMYTH

The hero is called to an adventure which he either refuses or accepts.

He acquires a helper, guide or charm to accompany or protect him.

He bestows this boon on others possibly as a restoration or healing

He encounters a Threshold Guardian, often symbolic of the unknown side of himself. He may successfully overcome this figure through a battle won or sacrifice made, and so go alive into the Underworld. Or he may be unsuccessful – crucified or dismembered through trickery or defeat – and so go dead into the Underworld.

As he returns to the Overworld, he must successfully bring across the threshold the boon he acquired below

He loses the aid of protective powers or defeats those pursuing him.

He undergoes a series of trials and ordeals, acquiring Underworld aid in the forms of helpers, guides, protective weapons or charms.

If blessed by the Underworld powers he departs under their protection. But, if not, he flees and is pursued.

At the nadir, he alone experiences the supreme ordeal, which may be a sacred marriage to the all-nurturing Mother Goddess or an atonement with the all-creating Father God or an enlightened transformation leading to his own apotheosis. On the other hand, he may not appease these forces but contest them, and so steal his bride, or fire, or his power (such as an elixir or prize)

Buddha (5th century, Uttar Pradesh)

IX. The Jewel in the Lotus

At the nadir of the mythic round, the Buddha sits beneath the Bodhi tree in meditation, and is presented with numerous manifestations of this world-dream – not only demons to terrorize and torment him, but voluptuous beauties to tempt and entrap him – which he defeats by simply touching his hand to the ground and proclaiming this spot to be an immovable spot at the centre of the swirling flux.

To better understand how this transformation of consciousness was made possible, the story of the Buddha's life is offered at the end, in Appendix I. The gradual narrative unfolding is offered there, and may be summarized here according to Campbell's Monomyth:

The Bodhisattva descends from heaven. As a white elephant, he enters Queen Mayadevi.

Holding the branch of a tree, Mayadevi gives birth from her side. The child takes seven steps. Seers predict he will become a monarch or the Buddha.

Young Siddhartha sees old age, illness and death. Seeking release from suffering, he secretly departs from the palace, and becomes the monk Guatama. Mara tries to tempt him from his path.

He apprentices himself to several masters, then practises extreme asceticism, but abandons it after six years, in favour of the 'middle path'.

Deep in meditation, the Buddha dies.

He acquires disciples; the Order is founded.

The great 'Fire Sermon'; many are converted.

In the Deer Park of Benares, he teaches the Dharma for the first time: the Middle Way and Four Noble Truths, setting the Wheel of the Law in motion.

Out of compassion, the Buddha resolves to teach others the Path.

Alone, Guatama sits in meditation beneath the Bodhi tree. Mara attempts to distract him, but is dispelled. He beholds all prior incarnations, sees the cause of suffering and the path to its cessation, thus achieving Enlightenment.

In traditional tellings of the Buddha myth, Prince Siddhartha journeys four times outside his palace walls, and each day beholds a different vision of suffering: of a man struck down by poverty; of another, by illness; and of a third, by death. Finally, on the fourth day, he beholds a monk, and at that moment the sacred hero-task of Buddhism is *acquired* – to eradicate all forms of suffering, be that old age, illness or death. In order to accomplish this task, the Bodhisattva secretly leaves the palace at night, thus crossing the Threshold of Separation.

Meditating Buddha
opening "a door of salvation
in the closed circle of Eternal Recurrence."

He undergoes a series of ordeals: first acquiring masters and eventually abandoning them, then mastering and abandoning his own ascetic extremes. Finally, at the mythic nadir, he crosses the Threshold of Initiation to confront his ultimate task. At dawn, the Buddha *accomplishes* a transformation of consciousness (*bodhi*) which breaks him out of time's eternal round and its attendant illusory suffering. With eyelids half-raised, he beholds the spectacle of this world, but with its endless cycle of pleasures and pains finally brought to a standstill. In the words of Nikos Kazantzakis, he opened *"a door of salvation in the closed circle of Eternal Recurrence."*[9]

But, the path of release must still be taught to others. Only when others have attained release through his teachings will the myth of the Buddha be made complete. Hence, he crosses back over the Threshold of Return and teaches others 'the Way', setting the Wheel of Dharma in motion. In this way, his task – to offer others release from suffering – is *integrated* into society.

It is the *acquisition, accomplishment* and *integration* of the task that holds all these images together into *one myth*, transpiring over a finite segment of time. But, if the myth of the Buddha is properly understood, then that segment must *cycle round* – and will continue cycling round until *we ourselves* enact the Buddha's myth, and so transcend it. In this way, the iconologues of time, narrative and the hero's task combine in Buddhist myth to show us the way *through images* to their ultimate transcendence.

Over the course of his life, from its early abundance and eventual asceticism to his final stillful repose beneath the Bodhi tree, the Buddha traced out a path which each of us may follow, through the gradual unfolding of his own life-journey. Though perhaps not in this life, the *atman* of each individual, wandering through time over a multitude of incarnations, may eventually find that path which the Buddha trod. In this sense, the mythic life-path of the Buddha is yet one more variation of, what we have called, 'the eternal Hero myth of the soul'.

At the nadir of the Buddha myth lies the image of the Awakened One, sitting in calm meditation beneath the Bodhi tree. This timeless image slows and indeed holds still the moment of awakening as it transpired in his myth. As such, his momentary epiphany has become fixed for all time in our cultural memory through Buddhist statuary and *thangka* paintings. And it stands, to this day, as a kind of sacred doorway, a Threshold Image which may be *entered through*, resulting in a profound moment of awakening for he who can successfully meditate upon it.

While many of the events in the Buddha's life have been rendered into sacred symbols, it is particularly the moment of his awakening which is encountered at the heart of a Buddhist temple. Sometimes, his right hand is raised in the *Abhaya* gesture reminding us to overcome fear of death and attachment

Buddha with his right hand   *Buddha touching the ground*
raised in the Abhaya gesture   *in the Bhumisparsa gesture*

to this life. Other times, he touches his right hand to the ground in the *Bhumisparsa* gesture, reminding us of the awakening that can be achieved through meditation and concentration onto a single stilled spot. And so, in a variety of ways, this contemplative image becomes a kind of mirror in which we may see reflected our own interior oneness, stillness and perfection.

X. The Cross & the Bodhi Tree

The images of Christ on the cross and the Buddha beneath the Bodhi tree thus constitute mythic moments of *epiphany*. And, as nadir Threshold Images, they may be *entered through* to effect a most profound transformation *in us* – in our *way of seeing* the world. Both unveil the inscrutable visage of the Sacred, which lies hidden behind them, as if behind one of the many different 'masks of God'.

But, as we have seen, narratives usually present a series of threshold-crossings, a series of episodes before culminating in a moment of total realization and transformation. At the nadir of each of these more minor episodes, other important Threshold Images occur: Christ's baptism or his transfiguration, the Buddha's confrontation with Mara or his first Fire Sermon. These also constitute important symbols of transformation. But the profound moment of death, rebirth and awakening at the nadir-threshold of a sacred Hero myth becomes, for each culture, its most powerful Threshold Image.

Over the course of a lifetime, each of us, in his own way, must attempt to *enter through* these images to their interior unity. But, the Iconologue of Time's Measure continually holds us back. The linear-history of Christian myth, combined with the endless cycling of Buddhist myth, continually postpones our momentary awakening. Only through a study of archaic myth may we transcend these temporal measures and regain *the more ancient mythopoeic understanding of time...*

CHAPTER VI

The More Ancient Mythopoeic Understanding of Time

Drawn across the plainland to the place that is higher,
Drawn into the circle that dances round the fire,
We spit into our hands, and breathe across the palms.
Raising them up, held open to the sun...
– Peter Gabriel 'Rhythm of the Heat'[1]

I. The Daily Epiphany

During his travels in Africa, C. G. Jung came across a tribe who woke before dawn every morning, then spit into their hands and blew across the palms before holding them upward to the newly rising sun. When he asked for the meaning of this ritual and why they performed it, the Elgonyi replied that they did not know – they had always just done so.[2]

Yet, in the earliest myths that have come down to us, carved in the tombs of the Egyptian kings, an understanding of time arises which may explain the mysterious portents of these ritual gestures. In particular, the Egyptian *Books of the Afterlife*[3] relate how the sun rode upon a solar barque each day across the heavens, but then descended at night into the Underworld. During the course of this perilous night-journey, the solar barque had to pass through twelve gates, encountering the primæval serpent Apopis at the end, who threatened to swallow, extinguish, and so, annihilate it completely.

Only if the sun-god could successfully overcome this ancient serpent would it dawn in the heavens the next morning. The appearance of the sun each morning was therefore *a victory and an epiphany* – the god Atum-Re's wondrous return to the heavens. We can now divine the forgotten meaning of the gestures performed by the Elgonyi tribe, for they were ritually greeting, welcoming and praising the sun for its heroic re-appearance that day.

*The Egyptian Solar Barque
overcoming Primæval Serpent Apopis*

But what is perhaps more wondrous is the mythopoeic understanding of time created through this myth. The sun's rising in the morning was, for the Egyptians, nothing less than *the creation of the world*, just as its setting at eventide forebode the world's end.

The *Pyramid Texts* recount how, at the beginning of time, *Atum* 'the Complete One' *rose like the sun out of the Primæval Waters.* And, in the form of the scarabæus *Khoprer* 'the Becoming One', the sun then moved across the heavens.[4]

These images of the creation re-appear toward the end of *The Egyptian Book of the Dead* (the *Am Duat*), emphasizing that the sun's dawning at the end of its night-journey was nothing less than the creation of the world. As one visionary passage explains:

> *I have seen the sun born from yesterday... What is that?
> It is an image of the morning sun as it is born everyday.*[5]

In his study of Egyptian mythology, Mircea Eliade recognized that *"the cosmology is repeated every morning, when the solar god 'repels' the serpent Apophis..."*[6] and the Egyptologist R. T. Rundle Clark confirmed: *"All showings of force, whether natural or human, were re-enactments of some myth. The sun rose at the beginning of the world, but this great drama of creation is repeated every morning."*[7]

The sun's first rising 'at the dawn of time' is an event *outside* of history. It transpires 'in the beginning', in the unmeasured eternity which Eliade characterized as *mythic time*, and which the Egyptians themselves called *tep zepi:* 'the first time'.[8] Yet, in the *Book of Am Duat*, the sun's rising *each morning* is understood as a re-enactment of that primordial event. Through this myth and its attendant ritual gestures, the sun's daily rising becomes

The sun's rising as the dawn of time:
In the solar barque upheld by Shu, god
of the air, the scarabæus Khoprer
upholds the rising sun.

a divine epiphany, a momentary intrusion of 'the first time' into our mundane passage of history.

And through his mythic and ritualistic recognition of the sun as Atum-Re, the worshipper is, himself, momentarily transported into an experience of the eternal *mythic time*. He witnesses a primordial event. Each time the sunrise evokes the sacred image of his myth and he performs his ritual gesture, the devotee returns to the primordial time 'of the beginning'. It is his myth and its recurring arrangement of images that is able to repeatedly return him to 'the first time'. This ancient, more mythopoeic understanding of time arises from, what Eliade calls, 'the myth of the eternal return':

> ...*a periodical return of the same primordial situations, and hence, a re-actualization of the same sacred time. For religious man, re-actualization of the same mythical events constitutes his greatest hope; for with each re-actualization he again has the opportunity to transfigure his existence. In short, for religious man of the primitive and archaic societies,* [the eternal return is accomplished through] *the eternal repetition of paradigmatic gestures and the eternal recovery of the same mythical time of origin sanctified by the Gods.*[9]

There are three mythic events which constitute most divine epiphanies: the creation of the world, the apocalypse, and the triumphant, world-saving deed of the sacred hero which transpires in its very midsts. In each case, an event transpiring within the circle of the eternal *mythic time* momentarily breaks through into the mundane passage of linear or cyclic time, altering it profoundly. These sacred epiphanies break apart time's linear or cyclic aspects, and reveal for one brief and fleeting moment the sacred eternity behind it:

> *To transcend profane time* Eliade writes, *and re-enter into the mythical Great Time is equivalent to a revelation of ultimate reality – reality that is strictly metaphysical, and can be approached in no other way than through myths and symbols.*[10]

II. The God of the
Ever-Rising & Setting Sun

In ancient Egypt, the sun's daily rising was mythologized into two timeless events: the creation of the world, and the sacred hero's world-saving deed which transpired in its very midsts. Two different types of myth – one Cosmogonic, the other a Hero myth – crossed and eventually fused, thus creating the unusual feat of time's transcendence.

Nevertheless, the sun's repeated disappearance and re-appearance in the sky continued to measure the span of a day. We have called an arrangement of images which marks a measure of time an Iconologue of Time's Measure. But the effect of this particular Egyptian iconologue was to *sanctify* mundane time – to 'give us this day our daily epiphany'. Through the mythic arrangement of images recurring on the horizon, *that day* was rendered sacred. The sun's rising, for the Egyptians, became a specific iconologue which not only *measured* a span of time but, by virtue of the Atum-Re's momentary epiphany, *rendered it sacred.*

This ancient myth and its Iconologue of Time's Measure may be laid out in a manner similar to its Christian and Buddhist variants, as follows:

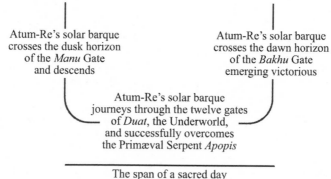

Atum-Re's solar barque
crosses the dusk horizon
of the *Manu* Gate
and descends

Atum-Re's solar barque
crosses the dawn horizon
of the *Bakhu* Gate
emerging victorious

Atum-Re's solar barque
journeys through the twelve gates
of *Duat*, the Underworld,
and successfully overcomes
the Primæval Serpent *Apopis*

The span of a sacred day

If we look at the imagery used in ancient myth, it soon becomes clear that new arrangements of images were created which, as Iconologues of Time's Measure, continually extended the span of sacred time to ever greater lengths – from a day to a month to a year and so on. But, the unfortunate result was that the moment of epiphany was also delayed for ever greater lengths of time. Eventually, the moment of epiphany passed beyond the witness of a single life-time. And ultimately, with Christianity and Buddhism, the moment of epiphany was delayed over the entire course of time's linear or cyclic measure.

In each case, a wondrous event in the heavens was awaited, a momentary epiphany from the eternal mythic time. Then, through our mythic and ritual recognition of that event, mundane time was momentarily transcended, and the devotee participated in its more timeless revelation. That wondrous event, and the new mythic arrangement of images it inspired, became *a new measure* of time. A series of examples, drawn from more ancient cultures, shall demonstrate this wondrous phenomenon.

By understanding myth as an arrangement of images over time and, more than that, as capable of offering different Iconologues of Time's Measure, we may begin to think about time in a more ancient manner. Indeed, we may begin to experience time as it was first understood and expressed in the ancient image-language.

III. The Goddess of
the Waxing/Waning Moon

Over the course of man's earliest epochs, the moon became mythologized as an Iconologue of Time's Measure: its twenty-eight day cycle of waxing and waning with three days of darkness in between became a mythic motif preserved in numerous early mythologies.

Perhaps the oldest myth to come down to us, recorded in cuneiform script on clay tablets, is *Inanna's Journey to the Underworld*. As was told in this ancient tale, Inanna the Sumerian goddess of fertility sought her destiny in 'the dark below', passing through the seven gates of the seven walls surrounding 'the Great City' of the desolate Underworld. At each of the seven gates, she had to surrender one insignia of her power. Finally, in

Venus of Laussel
c. 20,000 BC
holding a crescent
horn or moon

Inanna, the winged and horned Goddess standing on her lion mount

the innermost of hall of hell, she encountered her darker sister Ereshkigal. Naked, Inanna fell to her knees and, before the barren queen's throne, *"she instantly sickened to death. Her body was a corpse that hung on a spike."*[11]

But, while Inanna withered away and died in the presence of her dark sister, Ereshkigal's womb suddenly swelled with a child and the pangs of its birth. From the overworld, spirits were sent to offer Ereshkigal relief and, as payment for the comfort rendered, they asked for the corpse of Inanna. *"Over the corpse hanging on a spike, they scattered the bread of life, they sprinkled the living water, and Inanna stood up alive."*[12] And so, *"after three days and nights,"*[13] Inanna, 'the Great Lady of Heaven' rose up, appearing again in the night heavens. (Later, she betrayed her shepherd lover Damuzi, who had to descend to the Underworld in her place).

The fertile Inanna and the barren Ereshkigal, like the waxing and the waning of the moon, are two aspects of the same thing, of the same goddess in fact. This ancient *Magna Mater*, like the moon, cycles through periods of fertility and sterility; life and death. In ancient times, the serpent also, due to the shedding of its skin, became a symbol of death and rebirth. Together, the Great Goddess, the moon and the serpent formed an ever-recurring constellation of mythic imagery which marked time's renewal (through, what we shall later investigate as, the Mythologem of Death and Rebirth).

Hence this new Iconologue of Time's Measure marked a longer segment of time. The lunar cycle symbolized *the span of the sacred month*. One month would pass before the moon re-enacted the myth's primordial event, and the ancient goddess would re-appear in the heavens. Such a re-appearance, it must not be forgotten, was a sacred epiphany. The Holy One appeared in the heavens, fertile, full, blissful and bountiful.

The ancient myth of Inanna's descent, and the Iconologue of Time's Measure that it engenders, may be laid out in the following manner:

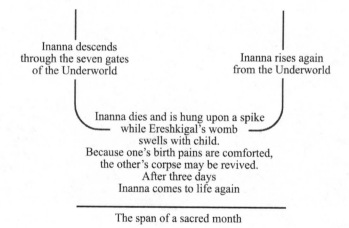

Inanna descends
through the seven gates
of the Underworld

Inanna rises again
from the Underworld

Inanna dies and is hung upon a spike
while Ereshkigal's womb
swells with child.
Because one's birth pains are comforted,
the other's corpse may be revived.
After three days
Inanna comes to life again

The span of a sacred month

Damuzi, god of fertility, amidst fresh sprouts.
He stands between two rams and two hay bails which are signs of Inanna

IV. The Zodiac &
the Dying/Rising God

While the daily rising and setting of the sun told the tale of Atum-Re's deadly boat journey, the moon's monthly crescendo and diminuendo portrayed the myth of Inanna's death and rebirth. But, after she rose from the Underworld, the goddess Inanna was warned that, if she hoped *"to escape the pit alive, she must leave another who shall wait in her place."*[14]

Henceforth, it was Damuzi, her shepherd-king and consort that descended into the dark Underworld. Though he passed through the same Mythologem of Death and Rebirth as Inanna, Damuzi descended, died and and rose again *yearly*, with the seasonal cycle of rain and drought. Like Osiris in Egypt, Attis in Syria, and Baal in Canaan, the 'Son of the Abyss' became a new Iconologue of Time's Measure, marking *the span of the sacred year*.

The dying/rising god marked the passage of a year by mythologizing the signs that recurred in the earth's fertile cycle. Like the fertile seed at the time of the harvest, Damuzi was seized, thrashed and cut to pieces: *"They flew at his face with hooks, bits, and bodkins; they slashed his body with a heavy axe."*[15] And, like the seed buried under the earth so as to gestate and sprout again, he was dragged into the Underworld, where he remained – until the re-emergence of the crops themselves embodied his resurrection: *"It is echoed in the wilderness... the grass will shoot from the land ...the waters rise."*[16]

Each time the fields manifest new growth, the god of vegetation also became manifest. Through the image of the dying/rising god, the intervals of the fertile year were measured and, through his earthly epiphany, that span was rendered sacred. The myth of the ever-dying/rising Son of the Abyss, may be laid out as follows:

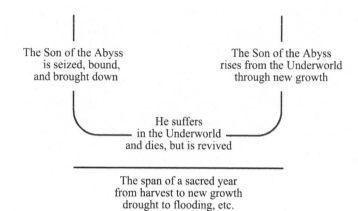

The Son of the Abyss
is seized, bound,
and brought down

The Son of the Abyss
rises from the Underworld
through new growth

He suffers
in the Underworld
and dies, but is revived

The span of a sacred year
from harvest to new growth
drought to flooding, etc.

Meanwhile, a fascinating series of images have come down to us from Sumerian culture which were never arranged in accord with a myth. This array of images, when taken together, also symbolizes the yearly cycle. From the vantage point of their spiralling *ziggurats*, the Sumerian priesthood were able to discern a multitude of ancient images in the night-sky.

Eventually, they learned to read the heavens like a book – which is what they called astrology, *Shitir Shame*, 'the Book of Heaven'. By following the path of *Sin*, the moon, over the course of a year, they recognized twelve celestial figures: *Luhunga* 'the Hired Man' (Aries), *Guanna* 'the Bull of Heaven' (Taurus), *Mastabbagalgal* 'the Great Twins' (Gemini), *Allul* 'the Crab' (Cancer), *Urgula* 'the Lion' (Leo), *Absin* 'the Furrow' (Virgo), *Zibanitum* 'the Scales' (Libra), *Girtab* 'the Scorpion' (Scorpio), *Pabilsag* 'the Centaur' (Sagittarius), *Sahurmasku* 'the Fish-tailed Mountain Goat' (Capricorn), *Gula* 'the Great' (Aquarius) and *Kummes* 'the Tails' (Pisces). Together, these twelve images formed, what the Greeks called, 'the wheel of the *Zodiac*' (from *zôé*, life, *zôidion*, small figure, and *kyklos*, circle or wheel, giving us *zodiakos* 'the wheel of life'.)[17]

Thus, in Mesopotamia, there were two iconologues to measure the passage of a year, one celestial and one terrestrial. This fertile crescent, lying between the Tigris and Euphrates rivers, created the first city-states of Sumer and Akkad. From this cradle of civilization, such powerful images as the Zodiac and the dying/rising god spread eastward into India, China and Japan, and westward into Canaan, Palestine and Greece. During their assimilation into other cultures, these images underwent some interesting and noteworthy transformations – and so too did the measures of time which their iconologues rendered sacred.

V. The Kali Yuga
& the Platonic Year

As the more ancient Iconologues of Time's Measure moved eastward and westward, their mythopoeic understanding of time was lost and its epiphanies were eventually forgotten. In particular, linear or cyclic time lost those divine interventions which appeared with each passing day, month and year.

In the West, greater emphasis was placed upon time's linear-historical measure while, in the East, it fell upon time's cyclic recurrence. New Iconologues of Time's Measure began to appear in the heavens – displacing the older images, and rendering their measures 'minute' by comparison. Meanwhile, each of these new images contributed a novel, time-altering symbol to the ancient image-language.

For example, in ancient Greece, a new Iconologue of Time's Measure arose in the form of 'the Great Year'. Over the course of many generations, the Greeks noticed how the constellation behind the sun at the time of the spring equinox had gradually shifted. After approximately two thousand years, the sun of the spring equinox shifted from Aries to Pisces to Aquarius (due to a phenomenon later discovered as 'equinoctial precession', because the earth tilts slightly on its axis with each orbit around the sun).

This ancient Greek discovery created a new Iconologue of Time's Measure, marking the longest linear duration of time known to the West. Since the constellation appearing at the spring equinox shifted every two thousand years, the passage of the sun through the twelve signs of this Millennial Zodiac constituted a new image of time's measure – attributed to Plato and subsequently called the Platonic Year – lasting 25,920 years.

Despite the emphasis which the West placed on linear-historical time, this iconologue was actually cyclic. For, at the end of this extremely long segment of linear time, the world's demiurge (Plato claimed) would appear so as to turn the great wheel in motion again, and all that occurred in history would repeat itself. The re-appearance of the Platonic demiurge thus constituted a kind of epiphany.

Meanwhile, in India, new Iconologues of Time's Measure had arisen, creating measures of linear time considerably longer than any imagined by the Occident. In the Hindu mythologies preserved in the *Puranas* ('ancient' or 'legendary' books), the present age is called the *Kali Yuga* and is believed to last 432,000 years. It is a dark age, a period of decline, the last of the four yugas. The previous age, called the *Treta Yuga*, was twice as long, and not so full of strife, battle and quarrel as our own, but still a period of darkness. Before that came the *Dvapara Yuga*, three times as long as our own, when the balance between dark and light first shifted in favour of darkness. And before that was the *Krita Yuga*, a golden age full of light – and an age to which we shall eventually return once all four yugas, forming the *Maha-Yuga* or Great cycle, have passed.

Of these *Maha-Yugas*, cycling round from interminably long ages of darkness to even longer ages of light, one thousand must pass to make a single *Kalpa* or Day of Brahma. This, a period of 4,320,000,000 years (or one hundred and sixty-seven *thousand* Platonic Years) is the longest linear segment of time known in India.[18]

Despite the thousands upon thousands of years which must pass before a Kalpa comes to an end, the myths of India place greater emphasis upon time's ever-recurrence – the cosmos' coming-to-be, continuance and consummation ever cycling round. The cause for this shift in emphasis lies in the Hindu view of life itself.

Though the present Kali Yuga is extremely long, the soul (*atman*) of each person is trapped in *samsara*, a never-ending succession of deaths and rebirths. Hence, the soul, at present, is cycling through the linear span of the Kali Yuga which, itself, is cycling through the linear span of the *Maha-Yuga*, which itself is cycling round. Thus, all is seen to be cycles within cycles within cycles. From this magnificent but fundamentally negative vision of the cosmos arose several powerful symbols of the soul's entrapment (*samsara*) and ultimate release (*moksa*).

During one Day of Brahma, according to the *Puranas*, the earth is flooded by a great deluge fourteen times. Each time a Noah-like figure manages to escape the flood and re-establish the human race. He is called Manu, and so there are fourteen Manu intervals in each Day of Brahman.

The importance of this lies in the fact that the god Vishnu incarnated himself on the earth once in each of these Manu intervals, appearing as an *avatar* or world saviour. Once, Vishnu descended as the Boar *Varahavatara*, and saved the world by diving deep into the cosmic flood and bringing the goddess of the earth up from the depths. Another time he descended as *Vamana*, the Dwarf, and saved the world from *Bali's* evil rule by an exquisite ruse: after *Bali* consented to grant *Vamana* all the land he could encompass in three steps, the dwarf transformed into a giant and stepped across the earth and heavens in just two steps. Most interesting is his incarnation as the Buddha, who saved the world from the flood of its *maya* (illusion) by rising up from time's ever-swirling round.

The heroic world-saving deed of each *avatar* is movingly portrayed in myth and rendered into powerful symbols through the complex iconography of Hindu art. Each of these symbols celebrates the sacred moment when Vishnu's heroic deed breaks through into this world, marking the measure of cyclic time into one of its ever-repeating Manu intervals.

And, as such, each of these unique arrangements of images – the Boar, the Dwarf – is an Iconologue of Time's Measure. But, what is more, Vishnu's world-preserving deeds also constitute *divine epiphanies*. Each time one of his *avatars* descends, the eternal *mythic time* may be re-experienced for an instant. As such, each depiction of Vishnu's *avatars* constitutes a Threshold Image which we could attempt to momentarily *enter through...*

VI . The Christian & Buddhist Iconologues of Time's Measure

Through their *yugas*, *kalpas* and Days of Brahma, the Hindus created the longest measures of time known to world mythology. Despite the emphasis which the Hindus themselves placed on time's ever-recurrence, their iconologues achieved time's longest ever linear extension. Uncountable eons must pass before Shiva's dance will destroy this present Kali yuga.

As a result of these ever-lengthening Iconologues of Time's Measure, the divine epiphany at the end of each measure was postponed for greater and greater lengths of time. Indeed, it was delayed for such unbearably long lengths of time, that new symbols of the Sacred emerged, offering some form of salvation or release.

In the Hebrew books of history and prophecy, a succession of covenants over many generations extended linear time ever further forward as they patiently awaited the coming of their Messiah. And in the course of this awaiting, a heretical branch arose which witnessed his death and resurrection in the person of Jesus Christ.

In the Hindu books of the *Vedas* and *Upanishads*, the transmigration of souls created a cyclic view on time which appeared to cycle round endlessly and without reprieve. But, in the midsts of these ever-cycling æons a saviour emerged in the person of Guatama Buddha.

Each of these world saviours broke through the bounds of linear or cyclic time and became, in this way, a new sacred symbol. Their images also became *new Iconologues of Time's Measure* – images which have been used to *measure time* from that moment to this very day.

While the world-saving deeds of Christ and the Buddha transpire, ultimately, in the eternal *mythic time*, their great accomplishments are set against the backdrop of Hebrew history and the cycling æons of Hinduism. Christ's crucifixion and the Buddha's awakening are not described as taking place 'in the first time', but as the culmination of Judæism's messianic expectations and Hinduism's hopes for release from *samsara*.

Nevertheless, their world-saving deeds had the effect of profoundly altering the historical time in which they were situated. Because, for one moment, Christ and the Buddha *broke out* of time's linear or cyclic bound, and *into* a more timeless eternity. Henceforth, those events became fixed as the new epiphanies.

But the effect of these epiphanies was also to measure time *anew*. In the myth of Christianity as portrayed in the last chapter, the event of Christ's crucifixion takes place at the very nadir of the 'U'-shaped narrative. That point is *in the very middle* of the 'U'-shaped segment and, from the Christian standpoint, takes place *at the very centre of linear-historical time.*

By the same token, the image of the Buddha's awakening is imagined at the nadir of time's ever-turning circle. When the Buddha touched his hand to the ground to claim his place beneath the Bodhi tree as 'the immovable spot', this point became fixed not only in space, but in time. It became *a fixed point in the middle of time's endless cycling.*

Hence, Christ and the Buddha's iconologues extended themselves across time's entire duration, marking *all* its moments from creation to apocalypse. And their myths, through their temporal unfolding, determined the span of time in which we saw ourselves as existing: the linear-historical segment or ever-recurring cycle in which we are caught, and which we may, through them, ultimately be liberated.

Although they are Threshold Images promising time's transcendence, as Iconologues of Time's Measure, Christ and the Buddha have continued to extend the duration of the cosmos unto ever greater lengths of time. So far, Christ's awaited epiphany has co-incided with the entire measure of time's linear history, and the Buddha's, with the whole of its endless cycling.

In the retelling of their myths and the rituals celebrating their deeds, the lives of these figures have repeated themselves forward through recorded history, becoming patterns which generations have followed. Their U- and O-shaped narratives have been recited, lived and passed on from the time of their awakening through all the generations to our own. And in this way, the lives of these figures have become the measure for our lives. Their immortal images have been rendered in precious metals or time-resistant stone, enshrined in temples and venerated yearly, monthly and daily. Rituals have been carefully observed which, by their repeated enactment, have continued to mark the ever-increasing measure of time they created, while still anticipating the final moment of epiphany they promised.

VII. Ruptures in Eternal Time: Karma & Sin

Particularly through the belief in *sin* which Christians inherited from Judæism, and through the similar belief in *karma* which Buddhists inherited from Hinduism, an action performed here and now acquires an other-worldly significance, counting as 'evil' or 'negative'. The accumulation of sins in a Christian's life will eventually tip the scales of the archangel Michael's balance at the end of linear time. And so too does the accumulation of negative *karma* in the earthly life of a Buddhist bear consequences in cyclic time, since it will result in his re-incarnation.

In this way, life became a dreaded awaiting of *eternal* damnation for the Christian, or of *eternal* re-incarnation for the Buddhist. The fear that the Christian felt for a spiralling Inferno of vast and endless depths was felt by the Buddhist for the endless repetition of suffering (*samsara*) in cyclic time.

Hence, by this strange reversal, the eternal time of the ancients took on the divided qualities of Hell or Heaven in the West, and entrapment or release in the East.

Meanwhile, the more ancient mythopoeic view on time had gradually been forgotten. The moment of the sacred epiphany had shifted from its daily, monthly or yearly occurrence *over the course of life* to the rare and long-awaited moment that could only come *at its end.*

VIII. The Sacred & Eternal Moment

In the mysterious markings of their hieroglyphs, the people of the Nile had unintentionally hid an ancient philosophy that, though forgotten over the coming millennia, had been secretted and so was preserved. What the arrangements of their holy images and sacred myths revealed, once they were recovered and interpreted, was the more ancient mythopoeic understanding of time which our culture had otherwise lost. Only by unearthing the ancient images and *thinking through them* could we became aware of that loss.

For, in the Nile valley, when Atum-Re appeared on the horizon during the sunrise, *time was transfigured and its measure transcended.* And, through a ritual turning of his palms to the heavens, the devotee could participate in that momentary burst of eternity.

Time was transcended because an event from the eternal *mythic time* – Atum-Re's emergence on the horizon – had broken through into mundane time and manifest itself in the heavens *at that moment.* In their recognition of Atum-Re as the rising sun, Inanna as the waxing moon, or Damuzi as the new growth, the ancients created myths and performed rituals which celebrated the divine epiphany as it continued to manifest itself *within their own lifetimes* – each sacred year, each sacred month, each sacred day – indeed, *each moment.*

If we look once more at the myths of Christ and the Buddha – thinking through their images in light of the ancient image-language – we can see that their images may also alter our outlook onto time. Both commit a deed that, in one moment of time, transforms the closed cycle or segment of mundane time into an endless vision of eternal time. It is that moment of wisdom and awakening which became, for our culture, the divine epiphany.

Hence, images of Christ and the Buddha not only *extend* time's measure – they are capable of *obliterating* that measure completely. They not only offer us Iconologues of Time's Measure, but more timeless Threshold Images. And such images may be *entered through* to achieve, *hic et nunc*, a union of the eternal and the now – a vision of the essential oneness of time. For their images offer us a transformation of consciousness – a repentance (*metanoia*) or awakening (*bodhi*) – which may, in one sacred moment, transform our vision of the world, with its linear or cyclic flow of time, into one that is endless and *without measure.*

Hence, our continued longing for a renewed Paradise, where time will transpire as it once did *at the beginning*. As Eliade notes:

> *What may be called the 'nostalgia for eternity' proves that man longs for a concrete paradise, and believes that such a paradise can be won* here, *on earth, and* now, *in the present moment. In this sense, it would seem that the ancient myths and rites connected with sacred time and space may be traceable back to so many memories of an 'earthly paradise', some sort of 'realizable' eternity to which man still thinks he may have access.*[19]

This creates the disturbing insight that all the sacred symbols of the world's mythologies are doorways, yet the vast majority remain closed to us because, while we believe they once altered the lives of their ancient devotees, they can no longer do so for us today. These divine doorways were opened once, but are now closed to us – as they lack the life or experiences therein which only we can bring to them.

In ancient cultures, a ritual gesture such as 'spitting into one's hands and breathing across the palms' allowed the devotee to participate in an event from the forgotten mythic time. Such a rite, properly performed, broke the initiate out of his experience of mundane time and into the sacred and eternal time manifest in myths.

> *Through the paradox of rite,* Eliade noted, *the time of any ritual coincides with the mythical time of the 'beginning'... a 'sacred time', 'once upon a time' (in illo tempore, ab origine), that is, when the ritual was performed for the first time by a god, an ancestor, or a hero.*
>
> *There is an implicit abolition of profane time, of duration, of 'history'; and he who reproduces the exemplary gesture thus finds himself transported into the mythical epoch in which its revelation took place.*[20]

It must be remembered that the great Christian and Buddhist works of art which we see today in museums once had a more sacramental purpose. As altarpieces, works of Christian art visualized the mysteries conjured forth during the ritual of the mass. And as images depicting Christ's moment of transformation, they still have the power to transform *us* – even transform a mundane moment into one forever sacred. This experience of a symbol, *this way of seeing,* is one that has gradually been lost in the Christian tradition.

And yet, its remnants, the discarded images, remain with us. Our task then is to re-animate these images, so that they may accomplish their repentance and awakening, not only through the transcendence of time and its measure at some past or future moment, but *now*. At that moment, they become Threshold Images, and effect the transformation of consciousness they promised. We realize this, once we begin to *enter through* images...

CHAPTER VII

The Sacred Moment in Art

The painter's products stand before us as if they were alive,
but if you question them, they maintain a most majestic silence.
– Plato, Phaedrus 275d[1]

I. The Stilled Moment

With amazing perspicacity Heinrich Zimmer describes the effect that the sacred sculptures of India have upon us as we gaze into their eternal calm. A distance full of tension is created between us and these figures, for, in beholding them *"we stand, as it were, at the image's threshold, yet lack the ability to cross it."*[2] Without any clear remembrance of the ancient image-language, we stand in mute incomprehension before these silent stones. The only way to cross their sacred thresholds is to regain their mythic outlook onto the world and onto time.

Through his world-saving deed, the sacred hero fixes one stilled moment at the centre of time's linear segment or repeating cycle. That deed, once it is depicted in a work of art, is as it were *held still* for all time – frozen into a Threshold Image. But how can we, as Christians existing in linear historical time, experience that stilled moment as we gaze upon Christ's tortured visage? And how can a Buddhist, existing in cyclic time, experience that same stilled moment as he gazes upon the more serene visage of the Buddha?

According to the Hindu-Buddhist outlook, all that we behold in thought and vision, from the world to our placement in it, is *maya,* an illusion due to the ever-cycling eons of time. One means of transcending this illusion is named *ekagrata* in the Yoga tradition, a 'one-pointed' meditation on sacred images.

When he places himself before a sacred image, the task of the Hindu devotee is to recognize *the illusory division* between worshipper and the worshipped, himself and his god – and so transcend it. This is achieved in a moment of 'samadhi': *"When the image and the beholding consciousness unite,"* Zimmer writes, *"the goal of sacred ritual is reached: the believer experiences himself as divine."*[3] Since, at the moment of *samadhi,* the identity of Self and God is realized, the sculpted image is finally transcended as illusion. It no longer stands between the two, but has dissolved in their embrace. We may say that its stone threshold has been overstepped, and the image *entered through.*

In India, sacred images are called *yantras,* which is to say, instruments or devices which may rent Maya's illusory veil to reveal our innermost Divinity. Some *yantras* are abstract, such as the holy circle of the *mandala* fixed within its four directional points, or the geometrical lotus-form of the *chakra,* inscribed with its sacred syllables. Others, called *pratimas,* are figurative: statues of the gods standing with their hands in a variety of gesturing *mudras,* or holding their particular attributes of bells, thunderbolts, clubs or conch shells.

But the most peculiar feature of Hindu and even Buddhist sculptures is their air of stillness and tranquility. It is this, the *stilled moment,* that exists simultaneously in the ongoing cycle of mundane time experienced by the devotee and in the eternal circle of mythic time experienced by the god. The task of the devotee, who lives in mundane time, is to – in one moment – become one with the Sacred in eternal time, and so experience 'the eternal moment'. According, once more, to Zimmer:

> *The two hands of the Buddha image exist as gestures in a sphere beyond time – one hand extending forward, palm upward, offering protection* [the Abhaya mudra], *the other opened downward in the act of bestowal* [the Varada mudra]. *In these hands, the virtuous act of giving and the compassionate power of protecting all living things ...are timeless.*[4]

Even a figure in motion, such as the dancing Shiva, or an event from a myth, such as the *Varaha* avatar of Vishnu resurfacing with the goddess of the earth between his boar tusks, exist in a moment of time that is closed off, remote and eternal. The devotee brings his transitory moment of existence to these eternal figures, and the moment he *enters through* it, his finitude expands to embrace eternal existence.

Leonardo Da Vinci: The Last Supper (detail). "One of you will betray me."
Judas, on the far left, pulls back while still reaching for a piece of bread

Meanwhile, for the Christian devotee passing through linear-historical time, the sacred image is more a commemoration of a past event. If we contrast the Buddha's timeless gestures with the hands of Christ in Da Vinci's *Last Supper*, we see that Christ's gestures express an event that transpired for one brief moment in history, and will never be experienced again. Although Christ's left hand is held outward in a 'virtuous act of giving' not dissimilar to the Buddha's *varada* mudra, the other hand is engaged in the momentary task of reaching for a piece of bread.

It is clear that Da Vinci sought to capture in this fresco the fleetingly profound moment in history when Christ announced to his disciples, *"One of you will betray me."* In the wave of momentary reactions in their hands and faces – only Judas betrays himself by not reacting; instead he too reaches for a piece of bread – we witness the sudden outburst of questioning and denial. We also know that in the next moment, Judas will dip his bread in the dish just as Christ, also dipping his bread, reveals to all that his betrayer is *"the one who is dipping bread in the same dish as me."* (Mk 14:20) The right hand of Christ is thus engaged in an act that, though symbolic, is situated within a historical moment in time. The left hand of Christ however, in a gesture of self-offering, may be seen as symbolizing *for all time* his act of sacrifice.

There are other gestures in Christian art which seem to exist in a moment outside of historical time and participate in the eternal time co-incident with the Buddha's gestures. For example, when Christ upholds his hand in the unique Christian 'mudra' of blessing. And what are we to understand by images of Christ as Judge in the apocalypse,* with one hand held up, beseeching us to rise with him, and the other hand lowered, condemning us to fall for all time? This gesture seems to exist *at the very threshold* between the end of historical time and its renewal in eternal time...

* For an image of Christ as Judge, see page 265.

II. The Forward & Backward Movement in Time

The difference in the aims and intentions of Christ and the Buddha brings out an important difference between that moment of revelation or awakening as it is experienced in the East and the West.

Certain events in Christ's Passion, such as the moment of doubt in the garden of Gethsemane, or of accusing God of forsaking him as he hung on the cross, reveal that Christ, through faith rather than foreknowledge, freely committed those deeds which realized God's will. This is why, in most of the Christian tradition, each person is believed to possess a unique, individual and *free-willing* soul which commits those acts that ultimately determine his own salvation or damnation.

In contrast, over the course of the night's three watches as he fell deeper into meditation, the Buddha let go of all individual will and desire, so as to detach himself from illusion. In most of the Buddhist tradition then, one must attempt to *forego* acts characteristic of a unique and individual will.

If we now relate these intentions to their enactment in time, we can see that, for the follower of Christ, *time is a succession of individual moments in which one attempts to bend one's will to an ever higher spiritual purpose.* Time is filled with increasingly meaningful and unique moments, and life consists of an accumulation of such moments which will, when taken successively or as a whole, ultimately render his soul as worthy of salvation or damnation. All is, primarily, a *forward* movement through time.

Meanwhile, for the follower of the Buddha, time *is a cycle of ever-repeating moments in which one attempts to surrender the will* that, always and ever there, was responsible for those deeds committed throughout its long history, creating its *karma.* Furthermore, as the Buddha ceased to will, he slowly broke through the illusory cycles of time and, during those moments, came to know all his past deeds in previous re-incarnations. Then, contrary to Christianity, all is primarily a *backward* movement through time.

For the Christian, the ongoing movement of time is real, actual and necessary for achieving redemption and salvation. One passes forward through time, attempting to commit the deed that will finally open the gates outward, to paradise. For the Buddhist, the ongoing cycles of time are an illusion and unreal, but time nevertheless remains equally necessary for achieving enlightenment. In meditation, one passes backward through it, attempting to achieve the state that will finally open the gates inward, to illumination.

For the Buddhist, the figure of the Buddha has the power to enter into our lives and, *out of compassion*, work backwards through them, eradicating all the *karma* acquired at various points in our past lifetimes. This is because the Buddha, through his Awakening, moved backward through time, passing through various incarnations to the very creation and then realized that it too was an illusion. He exists in eternity.

Christ, by his sacrifice, also committed a deed that had the effect of a backward movement through time, restoring all that was lost by Adam in the fall at the beginning of time. He too exists in eternity. That is why he is also able to enter into our lives and, *through forgiveness,* work backwards through our lives, eradicating those sinful deeds we committed at some point in the past.

III. Wisdom and Awakening

Over the course of the last century, two novelists laboured hard to revive certain ancient myths and make them relevant to our contemporary outlook. In particular, Nikos Kazantzakis did for the Christian myth what Hermann Hesse accomplished for the Buddhist one: to write a narrative so moving, that the modern reader could identify his own life struggles with the ordeals and awakenings of these sacred heroes.

In his novel *Siddhartha*, Hesse portrays the life of a youth who, like the Buddha, seeks liberation and enlightenment. In this way, the novel becomes a kind of allegory which the Westerner may use to 'journey to the east'. As Hesse himself noted: *"Siddhartha is a very European book, despite its setting. The message of Siddhartha begins with the individual, which it takes much more seriously than any other Asian teaching."*[5]

In its dramatic portrayal of a single monk's awakening, the novel expresses some very western sentiments. Such a *mélange* of occidental and oriental teachings reveals Hesse's aspiration *"to grasp,"* as he admitted in the Preface to the Persian edition, *"what all religions and all human forms of piety have in common, what rises above all national difference, what can be believed by every race and every individual."*[6]

At the conclusion of the novel, the author eloquently describes the experience of gazing, for one timeless moment, into the visage of the Enlightened One. Siddhartha's life-long companion and fellow seeker into lucidity, Govinda by name, is only able to forego his rational approach after the awakened Siddhartha, praising the necessity of love, urges Govinda to instead kiss him on the forehead. At that moment:

> *He no longer saw the face of his friend Siddhartha. Instead he saw other faces, many faces, a long series, a continuous stream of faces – hundreds, thousands, which all came and disappeared and yet all seemed to be there at the same time, which all continually changed and renewed themselves and which were yet all Siddhartha...*
>
> *He saw the face of a newly born child, red and full of wrinkles, ready to cry. He saw the face of a murderer, saw him plunge a knife into the body of a man; at the same moment he saw this criminal kneeling down, bound, and his head cut off by an executioner. He saw the naked bodies of men and women in the postures and transports of passionate love. He saw corpses stretched out, still, cold, empty...*

He saw all these forms and faces in a thousand relationships, all helping each other, loving, hating and destroying each other and become newly born. Each one was mortal, a passionate painful example of all that was transitory. Yet none of them died, they only changed, were always reborn, continually had a new face: only time stood between one face and another.

And all these forms and faces rested, flowed, reproduced, swam past and merged into each other, and over them all was continually something thin, unreal, and yet existing, stretched across like thin glass or ice, like a transparent skin, shell, form or mask of water – and this mask was Siddhartha's smiling face...

And Govinda saw... this smile of unity over the flowing forms, this smile of simultaneousness over the thousands of deaths and births... the calm, delicate, impenetrable, perhaps gracious, perhaps mocking, wise, thousand-fold smile of Gotama, the Buddha...

No longer knowing whether time existed, whether this display lasted a second or a hundred years... Govinda stood yet a while bending over Siddhartha's peaceful face... whose smile reminded him of everything he had ever loved in his life, of everything that had ever been of value and holy in his life.[7]

In contrast to the Buddha's calm forehead and quiescent smile, wherein suffering is stilled and tranquility attained with the whispering of a single-syllabled 'aum'; Christ's visage expresses, at the moment of his greatest realization, an enthorned brow with blood, vinegar and tears streaming over his tortured gaze as he utters one final cry of triumphant suffering unto death. Christ's supreme accomplishment, contrary to the Buddha's, was not to regress backwards in meditation but to move progressively forward through life, and finally, at its end, to perform that deed which, at one moment in time, realized God's will: he knowingly, out of love, sacrificed himself.

Christ did not so much renounce his will, as act in such a way as to knowingly surrender it to God. *"Not as I will, but as thou wilt,"* (Mt 26:39) he realized, with some resignation, at Gethsemane. That is why, at the end, he bowed his head and said, *"It is finished."* He did this in full awareness because, at the very end he, *"...crying with a loud voice, said, 'Father, into thy hands I commit my spirit!'"* (Luke 23:44) These words, voicing his will, was his final triumphant, knowing and loving act of sacrifice.

IV. The Vision Uprising
Unbidden from within

But what was his final aim and intention? To *"..utter a loud cry"* before breathing his last? (Mk 15:37) To bow his head in death? He had willfully endured the flogging and thorns, the humiliation, and had surmounted the cross. Now, as he hung upon it, transfixed, *to what further end could he turn his will?* We know that Christ's will and intentions no longer directed themselves to events on this earth, *but turned fully inwards*. They become disjointed and confused, as when he called upon Elijah. His will even turned against itself, expressing doubt, such as when he accused God, *"Why hast thou forsaken me?"* (Mt 27:46).

The figure of Christ at this point – fixed upon the cross, immobile in his solitude – is not that different from the Buddha beneath the Bodhi tree. For both were confronted, before their final moment of awakening, by delusory visions uprising unbidden from within. Although Christ accomplished his spiritual deed in a forward movement through life, it could be argued that he, in those terrible moments of suffering transfixed, also went backward in thought through his life's previous moments. He undoubtedly experienced a moment of doubt and confusion which eventually gave way to understanding and awareness.

Nikos Kazantzakis, in his novel *The Last Temptation* – a fascinating treatment of the Christ myth, mixing it variously with motifs from Odysseus and the Buddha legend – performs an extended exegesis on just this theme. Like Kama-Mara, who appeared at the threshold of both the Buddha's first setting out and at the final threshold of his awakening, in Kazantzakis' novel Satan appears to Christ both at the moment of his first setting out – crossing the desert alone – and, at the final threshold of his sacrifice.

Christ's visions on the cross are full of longing and regret for the joys of this world. He imagines Magdalene as his bride, he fathers children, and he even lives unto old age. But then:

> *He tried with all his might to discover where he was, who he was and why he felt pain. He wanted to complete his cry, to shout LAMA SABACTHANI... He attempted to move his lips, but could not. He grew dizzy and was ready to faint. He seemed to be hurling downward and perishing...*
>
> *But suddenly, while he was falling and perishing, someone down on the ground must have pitied him, for a reed was held out in front of him, and he felt a sponge soaked in vinegar rest against his lips and nostrils. He breathed in deeply the bitter smell, revived, swelled his breast, looked at the heavens and uttered a heart-rending cry: LAMA SABACTHANI!*
>
> *Then he immediately inclined his head exhausted.*
>
> *He felt terrible pain in his hands, feet, and heart. His sight cleared; he saw the crown of thorns, the blood, the cross. Two golden earrings and two rows of sharp, brilliantly white teeth flashed in the darkened sun.* He heard a cool, mocking laugh, and rings and teeth vanished. Jesus remained hanging in the air alone.*

*An allusion to the novel's earlier description of, not only Satan, but Mary Magdalene

His head quivered. Suddenly he remembered where he was, who he was and why he felt pain... Temptation had captured him for a split second and led him astray. The joys, marriages and children were all lies... All were illusions sent by the devil... Everything had turned out as it should, glory be to God!
    He uttered a loud, triumphant cry: IT IS ACCOMPLISHED![8]

Although Kazantzakis' novel provoked an outrage when it first appeared, and was even blacklisted by the Vatican, his version of the gospel remains faithful to the Bible in many respects. For, in two of the four gospel narratives (Mark and Matthew), Christ perishes in a state of utter confusion: his will turned against itself, his aims and intentions distorted and delirious. Only the unwilled act of dying redeems him. Hence, this is the painterly image of the crucifixion in which the dead Christ hangs with his head fallen forward and eyes closed.

Meanwhile, in the other two gospels (Luke and John), he cries aloud, *"Father, into your hands I commend my spirit!"* and *"It is accomplished!"* This is to say that, at the final moment of willfully committing his sacrifice, he was lucid and fully aware of the implications of his deed. This is the image of Christ, not with head bowed in death, but with eyes open and gazing heavenward in wonder.[9]

V. Images of Inner Tranquility & Passion Stilled

The profound moment of breaking through to eternal wisdom may be depicted in Christian art as that one terribly brief but uniquely historical moment before his death when Christ, hanging on the cross, *opened his eyes* to the full, terrible and wondrous implications of his deed.

That same moment is depicted in Buddhist art as the eternal moment *in the middle of his life* when the Buddha, sitting beneath the Bodhi tree, half-closed his eyes, falling ever deeper in his meditations. He passed backward through countless incarnations until, breaking through the illusions of this world, he effortlessly attained enlightenment. And so, *with eyes half-open*, he beheld the spectacle of this world once more, but now fully transformed. No longer was suffering integral to existence, for its source had been found out. Time's endless cycling, in that moment of awakening, had been transcended. And now, this world was beheld as a more timeless work of art.

That is why, when we look upon a statue of the Buddha, his features and gestures seem to exist for all eternity. The image, when so beheld, creates an aura around it of suffering calmed, and of time eternally stilled. The image itself evokes this world's more timeless and sacred aspect: how each and every thing may, through its beholding, become a timeless work of art. And so the sculpture itself becomes a timeless image which we may *enter through* to eternity.

"A timeless moment of inner tranquility."   *"A profound moment of stilled passion."*
Mucalinda Buddha, Cambodia, 12th c.   *Matthias Grünewald: Isenheim Altar, 1516*

By contrast, the moment of breaking through, according to Christianity, is as brief and unique as the moment of death. Indeed, it is *that moment* at the end of life, when we bow down our heads in surrender – such as images of the crucified Christ depict.

The time surrounding Christian works of art is so sudden and soul-shattering that, if the images were *entered through* and truly experienced in the time determined by them, we could hardly bear it in this life. And is that not the actual case when we gaze upon a scene of the crucifixion? If we were to enter as deeply into the image of Christ as a Buddhist in meditation enters into the Buddha, we would suffer inexorably for that moment. Our natural response, once those feelings had been evoked, would be to turn away in horror and fear. Calm meditation upon the image of a crucified Christ is impossible. For we are gazing upon nothing less than an image of our own death – a symbol that, if we were to experience it fully, would lead to the overwhelming feeling of our own death at that very moment. And so, for this reason, the moment manifest in a Christian work of art is preferably relegated to history and the past, where it can no longer disturb us.

The significant difference between the images of these two traditions is that the Buddha's features and gestures express a timeless tranquility and calm to quieten, still and dispel our ever fleeting and confused passions, while the image of Christ evokes precisely those fleeting and confused passions for an unbearable and torturous moment in time which, if we can bear to extend it, would amount to a spiritually exquisite suffering culminating in our own singular and unique annihilation. Before an image of the Buddha, our eyes gaze with unwavering concentration, and are held half open in meditation and gradual awakening. Before an image of Christ, they spread wide in fear and realization. Then, averting their glance, with a fearful shudder they are pressed shut. Hence, the Christian tradition's greatest works of art achieve their deeply moving spiritual expression by manifesting a profound moment *of stilled passion*. This same tendency expresses itself in Buddhism's greatest works of art by manifesting a timeless moment *of inner tranquility.*

VI. Across the Threshold
of the Ancient Image

Thutmosis III
Karnak, 1450 BC

Whenever we stare into the timeless gaze of statues from more ancient cultures, we feel ourselves at a great remove from these more epic beings. The distance these works of art create is not only cultural, but temporal. For, not only have we forgotten the cultural outlook in which they were once worshipped, but the more mundane passing of our lifetimes, some seventy years in all, causes us to feel inconsequential and indeed 'minute' compared to these stone fragments, whose sacred presence extends across the æons.

But more than that, when we stare into their unmoving features, as if, into a mirror, it is our own understanding of time that bars us from seeing our own timeless visage reflected in their stone countenance. For we have lost the ancient, more mythopoeic understanding of time that is immanent yet manifest still in their more timeless gaze. If we think once more in accord with their archaic outlook, than our own visage may appear, once more, in that antiquated mirror.

For the eyeless stare of Osiris transcends an individual lifetime, and reflects to us our eternal aspect. What he mirrors is our eternal soul. Just as the sun rises and falls in the Nile Valley, not just each day, but also for all eternity, so does Osiris eternally die and rise again. And so do we, eternally ensouled, die and rise again with him. As one *Hymn to Osiris* from the Middle Kingdom expresses it: *"Whether I live or die, I am Osiris. I enter in and disappear through you. I decay in you, I grow in you."*[10]

In the New Kingdom *Books of the Afterlife*, the solar myth of Atum-Re's underworld journey crossed over and fused with Osiris' death and resurrection, resulting in a most important underworld myth. According to this myth,[11] when Atum-Re descends into the underworld, his life-giving light awakens Osiris from the sleep of death. Each person who has died and descended to the underworld shall, like Osiris, rise again from the dead. Then, his eternal soul will accompany the solar barque during its passage through the Underworld. At the fifth gate, the souls of the departed disembark and stand before Osiris, who now sits enthroned as Judge of the Dead.* Those whose heart balances with Maat's feather of truth shall live forever in the sun's radiant eternity: with Atum-Re they shall sail *for all time* over the sky in his barque, which is called 'the Boat of Millions of Years'.[12]

This myth is the Egyptian version of 'the eternal Hero myth of the soul'. Through the proper rites, the devotee will able to *enter*, finally, *through* the myth – *through* the endless rise and fall of the sun, and *into its eternity.* For, the sun's daily rise and fall, co-incident with its first rising in the creation, continually participates in eternity. As Plato phrased it, citing the ancient Egyptians as his source, the sun rises and falls *"as a moving image of eternity,"* while *"eternity itself rests in unity."* (Timæus 37d)[13] Which is to say, the ever-rising and setting sun is a moving image of 'the One' which, itself, dwells in eternity.

Hence, each time an Egyptian beheld Osiris' black basalt statue, and stared deeply into the god's eternal gaze, he saw the image of his own soul (*ba*) or life-force (*ka*) in eternity. *"Whoever gazes on the deceased Osiris cannot die,"*[14] one of the Coffin Texts states. At that moment, he 'enters into the cyclical course of the cosmos'.[15]

As everlasting Threshold Images, Christ and the Buddha also reflect, like Osiris, the timeless image of our soul in eternity. They too possess the power to transform our experience of time into a moment that may pass without measure – only the measures of time determined by these two figures in their myths seems to forbid it.

Nevertheless, a sacred work of art – which by its nature stills the moment of transformation into a more timeless image, which then stands before us throughout time – such a sacred image invites us to contemplate their timeless gaze again and again. And through extended contemplation, entering ever deeper into their unwavering stare, these sacred symbols may deliver us finally into an experience of eternity *now and at this moment* – with the further possibility of then returning to mundane time some time later.

* For an image of Osiris as Judge of the Dead, see page 264.

Once the stare is broken, we re-emerge from our soul's innermost eternity to the transitory spectacle of the outer world...

But the potentiality of transformation exists ever and always in these images, and it is only we who view them, seemingly pressed for time, who lack the patience to cross their thresholds. These images therefore stand before us as doorways which we are free to pass in and out of, if we can but regain the more ancient, mythopoeic manner of thinking that was possessed by those who created them in the first place. In short, we must learn to *enter, once more, through the images* left behind by our more ancient cultures.

Gazing into an image of the Buddha as if, into a more timeless mirror, our eternal aspect is momentarily revealed. In a moment of *samadhi*, we come to experience how, in the words of the Chhandogya Upanishad, *"tat tvam asi"– thou art that.*[16] The image before us (*that*) renders an a-temporal reflection of ourselves (*thou*). And so, sinking deeper, we come to experience how, in the words of The Tibetan Book of Golden Precepts, *"thou art Buddha."*[17] Through this timeless being, our own eternal soul is made visible to us.

Images of Christ also possess this power. The longer we gaze at his visage, the more it becomes a reflection of something deeper in ourselves. We recognize how, in the words of Galatians 2:20, *"I live, yet not I, but Christ liveth in me."* His suffering unto awakening is indeed our own. And, in this way, the veiled face of God is momentarily revealed.

But all ancient statuary and works of art, from a vast array of mythologies, stand before us as doorways. What is required of us is an enduring sense of awe. We must regain their lost gaze, recall their long forgotten way of seeing, and step, with awe, across their ancient thresholds. By bringing our own lives to these statues, we may bring their images once more *to life.*

CHAPTER VIII

Cosmogonic Myth as Model of the Mind

The disciples said to Jesus,
"Tell us how our end will come to pass."
Jesus said,
"Then have you laid bare the beginning?
So that now you seek the end?
For the end will be where the beginning is."
– Gospel of Thomas[1]

All is within you;
all comes from you.
– Corpus Hermeticum[2]

I. The Hidden & Forgotten
Revelation to John

The traditional Bible ends with the *Revelation to John*, in which Christ's most beloved disciple beholds a tremendous and awe-inspiring vision of the Final Days. The work which follows is also a Revelation to John, but is an *Apocryphon* (Hidden Teaching) rather than an *Apocalypse* (Revealed Teaching).

And indeed, the Gnostic *Apocryphon of John* remained hidden, as well as forgotten, for over a millennia and a half. Though its existence was known to the Early Church Fathers, it was condemned (possibly by Athanasius), and remained buried in a cave near the Upper Nile city of Nag Hammadi until 1945, when it was discovered by chance in a large red jar with a collection of other Gnostic codices.[3]

The story that unfolds encompasses the creation and the saviour's descent. In true Gnostic style, it uses many traditional symbols from Judaism and Christianity, often inverting them and altering them profoundly, so as to deliver its own unique message of the *gnosis* (revelatory knowledge).

For the sake of brevity, the myth shall be summarized to its essentials, while still attempting to preserve the style of language particular to a Gnostic revelation. The tale begins:

I, John, son of Zebedee, turned away from the temple to a deserted place, to learn why the saviour was sent into the world, and to which Aeon he said we shall go. Straightaway, while I was contemplating these things, behold the heavens opened and the whole of creation shone. I was afraid but, behold, I saw in the light a child. While I looked at the child, it became like an elder. And it changed its form again, becoming like a youth. In the light, the three forms appeared through each other.

The figure said to me, 'John, John, why are you afraid? I am the one who is with you always: the Father, the Mother, and the Child. Lift up your face that you may know the things which have not been revealed: of what is, and what was, and what will come to pass'.

And when I asked to know, it said to me, '*The Parent* of the All is invisible, one, above everything, existing as pure light. It stands alone, perfect, lacking nothing. Time was not apportioned to it. For, being prior to everything, nothing could complete it. The One is illimitable, eternal, immeasureable and ineffable. It is the aeon-giving Aeon, life-giving Life, and knowledge-giving Knowledge. Everything exists in it.

'As *the Father*, the One is the well-spring of pure, luminous water which pours out its light and life-giving water to all the Aeons. In the surrounding water, the One sees images of itself, and reflects upon itself through its images in the watery light.

'And his Thought came forth, appearing as his image in the luminous water around him. This is *Barbelo, the Mother*, who "*became the womb of everything."*[4] And she 'stood at rest' before the Father, and asked him for a fellow worker, and He consented. In the watery light, there appeared *Foreknowledge* and *Indestructibility* and *Eternal Life* and *Truth*. With the Mother, these became five Aeons, surrounding the One in the watery light.

'And the Father looked at his image in the luminous water, and released a spark of his light. And from this spark, Barbelo the Mother conceived, and brought forth *the Child*. This is the only Child of the Mother-Father.

'The Father gazed upon the Child, and poured his watery light upon it, and anointed it, so that it became the Anointed one, the *Christ*. Then Christ 'stood at rest' before the Father, and asked him for a fellow worker, and He consented. In the watery light there appeared *Mind* and *Will* and *Word*. "*Because of the Word, Christ ...created everything."*[5]

'And from the will of the Father and the Son, through the Mind and the *Gnosis*, the *Anthropos* came into being. Revealing their will as perfect and true, the Father named him *Geradamas*. And Geradamas, the *Holy Adam* spoke, saying *"It is thanks to thee that everything has come into being, and everything will return to thee."*[6] And he praised the Father, the Mother, and the Child.

'The Parent then placed Christ over all things, stationing each of them by him. Looking out over the glowing water, He saw beside Christ, the four Luminaries, who are the angels *Armozel, Oriel, Daveithai and Eleleth*. And each of these four angels was in charge of three powers. Armozel stood over *Grace, Truth* and *Form*; Oriel over *Afterthought, Perception* and *Memory*; Daveithai over *Intelligence, Love* and *Idea*; and Eleleth over *Perfection, Peace* and *Wisdom*. And Wisdom, who is last of all, is named *Sophia*. These are the *Twelve Aeons* that 'stand at rest' with the Christ as images of the One in the watery light.

'And *Sophia* looked up in the luminous water. Without the contemplation or consent of the Father, she conceived an image within herself. Alone, without her consort and without his knowledge or consent, she brought forth. And the thing which came out of her was imperfect and misshapen. It was not like the image of its mother, but serpentine, with a lion's face. Its eyes were like the flashes of a lightning's fire.

'When she saw the consequence of her desire, she hid it in a cloud and cast it into the depths, so that the others would not see what she had brought forth in ignorance. This is *Yaltabaoth*, the first of the Archons.

'Through the power taken from his mother, Yaltabaoth increased in strength and glory. Struck mad by his power, he brought forth *the Archons* and placed them in each of the succeeding Aeons. He placed seven kings over the seven firmaments of the heavens, and five kings over the depths of the abyss. The names of the seven heavenly Archons are *Athoth, Harmas, Kalila-Oumbri, Yabel, Adonaiou-Sabaoth, Cain,* and *Abel*. The names of the five Archons of the abyss are *Abrisene, Yobel, Armoupieel, Melcheir-Adonein,* and last of all *Belias,* who sits in the depths of the underworld.

'And each of the seven Archons created seven powers for themselves. These are the seven days of the week. And each of their seven powers created six demons for himself, until they became three hundred and sixty-five in all. These are the days of the year.

'On account of the light he possessed from his mother, the lion-headed serpent blazed like a luminous fire. He became lord of all the Archons and powers and demons who dwelt in the darkness. His light mixed with this darkness, making the light dim and the darkness shine. But he remained ignorant of the true and divine nature of the light within him. Instead, its fire made him vainglorious and mad. For he said, *'I am God, and there is no other God beside me.'*

'And a voice from the Aeons above him came forth, and it said, *'Behold, man exists!'* All the Aeons of the Archons trembled, and all the foundations of the abyss shook. For the image of the Anthropos, Geradamas, had appeared in the luminescent waters above them. *"And through the light they saw the form of the image in the water."*[7]

'Seeing this, Yaltabaoth said to his attendants, *'Come, let us create a man in accord with this image, and according to our own likeness.'* And all the Archons and powers and demons worked together to create the *psychic body* of the Anthropos. Seven powers created the bones of the psychic body, its sinews, flesh and marrow, its blood, skin and hair. Each of the three hundred and sixty-five demons formed a part, gaining rulership over it.

'Four demons made the passions of the soul: *Ephememphi* made pleasure, *Yoko* made desire, *Nenentophni* made grief, and *Blaomen* made fear. From pleasure came pride, wickedness and envy; from desire came anger, wrath and bitterness; from grief came mourning, distress and pain; and from fear came dread, agony and shame. And each of the demons was given rule over the passion it had created.

'In this way, there appeared a being in the likeness of the heavenly Anthropos, whose image they had seen in the phosphorescent waters above them. The lion-headed serpent beheld the psychic body of the Anthropos and said, *'Let us call him Adam.'* But this Adam lay motionless and still, without life.

'And Sophia spoke to the Mother-Father, through whom everything came into being. She asked that the light, which she had lost to her son, be returned to her. The Mother-Father consented, and sent Christ and the four Luminaries into the depths. They hid themselves in the Aeons of the Archons, and advised Yaltabaoth, saying, *'Blow into the face of Adam, and he will arise.'* Yaltabaoth blew his light into Adam's face. He blew into Adam's face the *pneuma*, which is the spirit or breath that had come from his mother. Adam moved, awoke, and began to glow with great luminosity.

"And when the Archons recognized he was luminous, and that he could think better than they, and that he was free from wickedness, they took him and threw him into the lowest regions."[8] With four fiery winds they mixed earth, water and fire, to form his *material body*. They bound him in matter, they made him mortal, they trapped him in dark ignorance, forgetfulness and desire. They hid his spark in that body which is like a shadowy cave and a tomb.

'The Archons took Adam and placed him in Paradise. They bid him to enjoy the garden, and eat freely from the tree of their life, which they had placed in the middle. But of the tree of knowledge, they forbid him to eat. For the *gnosis* was hidden in its fruit.

'And Yaltabaoth wanted to retrieve the part of the light which he had breathed into Adam. So he brought a deep sleep and forgetfulness over his progeny. This sleep, as the Prophet Isaiah said, *'will enshroud your perception, and hinder it like a veil.'*

'But the beneficent and merciful Parent had planted a feminine image within Adam, and named it *Zoe*, which is Life. She is his hidden consort, who awakens him with knowledge of the ascent and the remembrance of the way.

'When Yaltabaoth saw the feminine image of Zoe aglow in Adam, he wanted to bring her out of him, through his rib, but he could not grasp her light. Instead, he made a likeness of her image, a creature in the form of a woman.

'Then *Zoe* hid herself inside the woman, who began to glow with great light. She lifted the veil which enshrouded Adam's perception. He awoke from his deep sleep and rejoiced, saying, *'This, at last, is my consort.'* For he had recognized his counter-image.

'Then Sophia came down to rectify her fault. And I too came down, for it was I who brought about that they ate from the tree of knowledge.'

And I, John, said to the saviour, 'Lord, was it not the serpent that taught Adam to eat?' The saviour smiled and said, 'The serpent taught them desire, that in their begetting they would sow their seed in a corruptible body. For that serpent is Yaltabaoth. But I appeared on the tree of knowledge as an eagle, and bid them eat. And Sophia as well, through Zoe, bid them eat. And when they ate of the fruit in which the *gnosis* was hidden, they remembered their true origin.

'When the chief Archon realized that the man and woman had withdrawn from him, he cast them out of Paradise, and clothed them in gloomy darkness. He planted the seed of desire in her who belongs to Adam, so that, through intercourse, they would bring forth more copies of their bodies. And he made them drink the water of forgetfulness, so they would forget from whence they came.

'And Sophia, who had come down, was seized by the Archons, and they all committed adultery with her, so that the *Heimarmene*, bitter Fate, was begotten through her. This is the last of the terrible bonds. For from that Fate, ignorance and fear and the chain of forgetfulness came forth. By Fate, all are bound by time and by measure. Thus the whole of creation became enslaved forever, from the foundation of the world until now, by the *Heimarmene* of the Archons.

'I, therefore, the light which exists in the Light, descended into the realm of darkness. I entered into the middle of their prison, which is the prison of the body. And I said 'He who hears, let him get up from the deep sleep. Arise and remember that it is you who are called. Follow your root, which is I, the compassionate one. Guard against the Archons and all those who ensnare you. Beware of the deep sleep and enclosure of the underworld. For you are from the immovable race, who will be saved and become perfect. By meditating on these things with neither anger nor envy, nor desire nor greed, you shall not be restrained. Through me, you shall be raised up, and sealed in the luminous water.'

'And behold, now I shall ascend. I have completed everything for you so that, in hearing it, you may write it down and give it secretly to your fellow spirits. For this is the mystery.'

Jesus Christ, Amen

The
Apocryphon
According to John

II. 'Arise and Remember!'
To Return to the One

Once the Gnostic creation is studied and understood, it reveals itself as an elaborate and intricate image of, not only the exterior cosmos, but the interior of the mind. For the entire cosmology, once it has emanated outward from 'the One' in a succession of Aeons, is drawn back into it through the interior of the mind, where the final passage back through the Aeons actually occurs.

The dual nature of this image is betrayed by the names of the Twelve Aeons surrounding Christ, as well as the passions of the soul created by the lesser demons and powers. For the Twelve Aeons, while headed by angels with elaborate names such as *Eleleth* and *Armozel*, consist of the very human faculties of Perception, Memory, Intelligence *et al.* Likewise, demons such as *Blaomen* and *Ephememphi* rule over the passions of the soul, which consist of the very human feelings of desire, pleasure, grief and fear.

The *Gospel of Thomas* (which was discovered alongside the *Apocryphon of John*) is a collection of sayings, proverbs and prophecies attributed to the Gnostic saviour. Among them, Christ says to his disciples:

> *"The Kingdom of the Father is spread out upon the earth, and men do not see it." (113) "For the Kingdom is inside of you."(3) "When you make the two one, and when you make the inside like the outside, and the outside like the inside, and the above like the below, and when you make the male and the female one and the same... then you will enter the Kingdom."(22)*[9]

The *Apocryphon of John* requires that we similarly see the promised Kingdom as, not above and outside, but below and within (and eventually, beyond all such dualities). In our exposition, we shall follow the unfolding of the Gnostic cosmos, noting its parallel structure to the mind. And subsequently, we shall contemplate the journey back, which is a return through the interior of the mind to the source of the creation.

Beginning with the Parent of the All, who is 'above everything' – time, space, thinking – and who stands alone as 'one', we have here the unified source of creation which appears at the centre of the spiralling cosmos and the interior of the mind. In accord with the Gnostic tradition, we shall refer to this unified source of creation as 'the One' (*Monas*). And, like 'the One' (*to Hen*) of the Pre-Socratic and Neo-Platonic philosophers, it may be imagined as a circle of light at the centre of a swirling vortex (*diné*), such as portrayed by the Ancient Template.

In the *Apocryphon*, all the figures emanating outward from 'the One' become *images in the luminous water, in which the One sees itself reflected.* This is a beautiful metaphor, simultaneously showing and explaining how everything that exists, exists 'in the One'. Everything that exists, *reflects* the creator to itself in some way. By virtue of their life, light and consciousness, they reflect the One back to itself as the ultimate source of 'life-giving Life' and 'knowledge-giving Knowledge'.

For each image is an aspect or particle of its life, light and consciousness, whose emanation outward and return inward constitute the grand movement of its reflection. 'The Aeons' measure this movement outward and back to the Divine, as it reflects upon itself through the succession of images arising in its watery light. Meanwhile, 'the pneuma' or 'divine spark' is that particle of life and light which illuminates each image, making it a part of the living and luminous whole.

The first to emanate outward from the One is the Father. The Father comes to exist the moment the One *thinks*. As this *thinking*, the Father has *a thought*, which becomes the Mother, Barbelo. But these two, the Father and the Mother, are masculine and feminine reflections of a more androgynous unity, which is referred to by the genderless term 'the Parent' (or as the dyad, the two-in-one 'Mother-Father').

In the next moment of the creation, the Father releases a spark of its light, through which the Mother conceives *the Child*. Through this Child, the dyad becomes the divine trinity. This trinity, the three-in-one, remains a unity because the One is not just the dyad of *thinking* and *thought* (the Father and the Mother), but *"the thinking a thought of itself thinking"* as Aristotle expressed it in his *Metaphysics* (*'noésis noéseós noésis'*).[10]

The One's unity is made complete when, through the divine trinity, it *reflects upon itself*. For the One does not only possess consciousness (the dyad of 'thinking a thought'), but *self-consciousness* (the trinity of 'thinking a thought *of itself* thinking'). In this way, the reflective nature of the One's unity is preserved.

In the next step, the Father pours his watery light upon the Child and anoints it, so that it becomes the 'Anointed one' which is to say, the *Christ* (since Christ means, literally, 'the anointed one'). Pouring a watery light upon the Child is a prefiguration of Christ's later baptism in the Jordan.

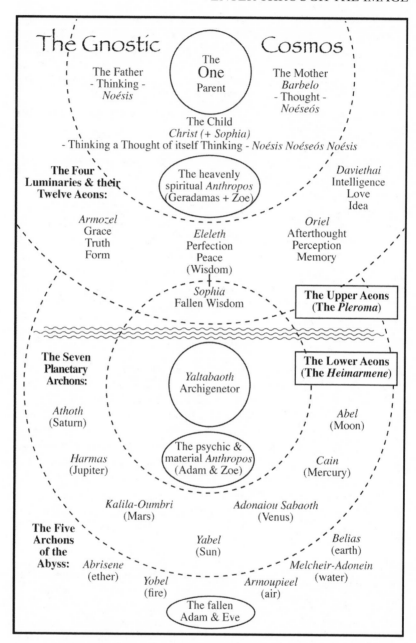

Cosmogonic myth as model of the mind: the Gnostic cosmos

Christ asks for helpers, and receives the Twelve Aeons of which Wisdom – Sophia – is the last. As other Gnostic texts, such as the *Valentinian Exposition,* make clear: Sophia is *the consort* of Christ. Just as the One divides into masculine and feminine opposites, in the form of the Father and Mother, so does the Child divide into the masculine and feminine opposites of Christ and Sophia.

In the Gnostic text, *Eugnostos the Blessed,* we learn how *"the Child... produced a bright androgynous light. The masculine name of that light is Saviour... and the feminine name is Sophia... Then the Saviour consented with his consort Sophia."*(81:21)[11] Hence, the dyad of Christ and Sophia are the masculine and feminine aspects of the Child. While the Father and Mother are images of the One's consciousness, Christ and Sophia form an image of the One's self-consciousness – its first reflective movement back to itself.

Then the Anthropos is created. This too becomes masculine and feminine, as Geradamas and Zoe – which becomes clear when Yaltabaoth separates Eve from Adam: *"When Eve was in Adam,"* the Gnostic *Gospel of Philip* says, *"there was no death. When she was separated from him, death came about. If she enters into him again and he embraces her, death will cease to be."* (68:23)[12]

The creation of the androgynous Anthropos is the last step in the creation of the Upper Aeons. All of these images – the Parent as Father and Mother, the Child as Christ and Sophia, the Anthropos as Geradamas and Zoe – are various reflections of the One in its watery light. In fact, they are two-fold reflections, one masculine, one feminine, which always betray a greater unity. Together with the four angels and twelve powers, they constitute the Upper Aeons, all of which *reflect* the One's unity *to itself* in luminous images.

After his creation in the Upper Aeons, the Anthropos says, *"It is thanks to thee that everything has come into being, and everything will return to thee."* In voice and in word, the Anthropos emphasizes the reflective nature of the divine creation: everything that came to be from the One will return to it.

Then Sophia commits her tragic mistake. *"The world came about by mistake,"* the *Gospel of Philip* (75:3)[13] proclaims. While each extension of the One's unity had been accomplished 'with the consent' of the Parent, by joining with one's consort (one's masculine or feminine counterpart), Sophia creates an image 'without the Parent's consent' and 'without her consort'. The result is her bastardized offspring Yaltabaoth, the lion-headed serpent.

With a particle of light taken from his mother, Yaltabaoth creates the Lower Aeons, a dark and material reflection of the Upper Aeons. While the Upper Aeons are light, spiritual, eternal, boundless and unified; the Lower Aeons are dark, material, temporal, spatial and multiple – lacking the One's primal unity. Though twelve in number, like the Upper Aeons, the Lower Aeons do not reflect the One's light, life or consciousness. Although the One 'knows itself' (*gnothi seauton*) through the Upper Aeons, the Lower Aeons are characterized by ignorance (*agnosia* – a lack of knowledge). Simply put: the Lower Aeons lack the *gnosis*.

Yaltabaoth himself remains ignorant of the divine spark in him. With it, he arrogantly creates the Lower Aeons, until he unwittingly blows his *pneuma* into Adam. In his ignorance, Yaltabaoth also creates Eve, and is outwitted when Zoe enters her, making Eve luminous. Last of all, Adam and Eve acquire the *gnosis* from the tree of knowledge, so Yaltabaoth throws them out of paradise and clothes them in gloomy darkness. He makes them forget their true origin.

Through Yaltabaoth, the Lower Aeons become a distorted, many-layered reflection of the One, in which most of the mirror is obscured in darkness. Though we 'see in a mirror darkly', we have inherited from Adam and Eve that *pneuma, gnosis* and 'divine spark' through which we may *remember* the true creation, and *see* it as an undivided whole. Through our particle of life and light, we may momentarily *reflect* the One to itself, in a rare moment of illumination. Recognizing ourselves as images of the One, we can return to it, becoming one with it in a moment of revelation (the *gnosis*).

But, of what nature precisely is this *pneuma* or divine spark? We know that it is a particle of divine light. And that the divine light contains within it the Twelve Aeons, which are *grace, truth* and *form; afterthought, perception* and *memory; intelligence, love* and *idea; perfection, peace* and *wisdom*. We know also that the light contains the Father and the Mother, which is to say *consciousness* ('thinking a thought'). And the light contains the union of Christ and Sophia in the Child, which is to say *self-consciousness* ('thinking a thought *of itself* thinking').

But all of these Aeons of creation, all of these images in the light surrounding the One are, in the end, things which humanity has had planted within, in the mind illuminated by the divine spark. And this is why all of these Aeons *are also* faculties and powers in our own mind. According to the Gnostic scheme of things, the myth of the creation, with its unfolding of the Aeons, *is* the creation of the mind, where the infolding of the Aeons shall ultimately take place...

Humanity has the unique potential to mirror the One to itself because, through our higher faculties, through our consciousness and self-consciousness, we are able to *know ourselves*, and hence, *know* God as the source of the divine spark in us.

What the *Apocryphon* further reveals is that a part of the creation becomes trapped in darkness, flesh, ignorance and desire. The Aeons continue to emanate further outward from the One, but lack its self-reflective knowledge, its light, life and consciousness. Hence, they are incapable of reflecting its unity. Yaltabaoth becomes the new source of these dark emanations moving deeper into the abyss. He also claims himself to be the centre of its chaotic swirling. And so, just as the Upper Aeons became an elaborate model of the mind, so do the Lower Aeons embody the lower passions of the soul and the desires of the flesh.

Yaltabaoth creates seven Archons in the heavens, which correspond to the seven planets visible in the night-sky (Saturn, Jupiter, Mars, the Sun, Venus, Mercury and the Moon). And he creates five Archons of the abyss, which correspond to the sublunary realm of the four elements in the quintessence (ether, fire, air, water, earth). Together, these constitute the *Heimarmene*: the heavenly movements of the planetary Archons, who influence all bodily compositions in the sublunar realm – thus determining their fate.

The seven Archons also create seven powers, which are the days of the week, and these create three hundred and sixty-five demons, which are the days of the year. That is to say, the Archons, along with their powers and demons, rule over *all space and time* as traditionally conceived in the ancient cosmology.

But our divine spark, which comes from the Upper Aeons, is actually *free* of space, time and determinism – only, we forget this, once we become *trapped* in ignorance...

To further entrap this particle of light, the Archons, powers and demons create Adam's psychic and material bodies. The passions of the soul – pleasure, desire, grief, fear – continually distract our higher faculties. Where these faculties include inner peace, love and perfection, the lower passions are manifold. A demon rules over each base emotion – giving form to these dark and otherwise formless feelings. They mix and amalgamate in the mind's swirling chaos, occasionally rising to the surface, like images in darkened dreams, distracting our peace of mind.

Our particle of light is also trapped in the material body. This corruptible piece of flesh binds us in ignorance, forgetfulness and desire. The body, according to the Gnostics, is a prison, a shadowy cave and a tomb. All that we see are dark and dismal images, ill-formed, unclear...

It was Yaltabaoth who brought this deep sleep over our eyes 'enshrouding our perception and hindering it like a veil'. Hence, the somnambulistic nature of our existence. And hence also, our amnesia and unknowing, due to the huge abyss that separates us from the One.

...Darkness, flesh, ignorance and desire – these all become so many entrapments for our divine spark. But this darkness, for the Gnostics, exists more in *innerness* than the outer world. The Archons and demons characterize *our own mind's* darker depths.

Hence our task, according to the Gnostics, is to liberate ourselves, *here and now*, from the midsts of this elaborate prison. By 'standing at rest' and 'guarding against the Archons' we may remember our origin in the light. By 'meditating with neither anger nor envy, nor desire nor greed' we shall rise up in our thinking, to be 'sealed in the luminous water' as images of the One.

The Gnostic saviour's greatest deed is not his act of sacrifice. What the Gnostic saviour does is *descend*, and this becomes the Father's furthest outreach into the darkness, the greatest expansion of his mind, will and word into the depths. Christ descends to redeem Man in the sense of *awaken* him from the deep sleep and remind him of the light from whence he came. *'Arise and remember'* the saviour says at the end of the *Apocryphon*.

If Christ did indeed suffer on the cross (and not all the Gnostics are agreed on this point), then the aim of his sacrifice was not forgiveness – for Adam and Eve had committed no sin. Rather, Christ sought to show us the way to *transcend* suffering – through revelation and awakening.

III. The Interior Apocalypse

The myth of the Creation created in the *Apocryphon of John* reveals a model of the mind where man may come to *know God* and, in that process, *know the Self*. For man's consciousness *is a particle of divine consciousness*. And it is through the light planted in him that he may *know* God. This *knowing* (the fundamental *gnosis* of Gnosticism) occurs when the Gnostic has, in his meditations, transcended his mind's darkness and multiplicity to behold the Divine within himself, in the oneness of its light. At that moment, he reflects the One to itself, just as the One now reflects, by its wholeness, him to himself. But that is to say, he has become, in his innermost Self, *one with* the Sacred at the source of all creation.

In terms of the Gnostic cosmos, he has freed himself from the bonds of the Archons and ascended upward through the Aeons to the highest One. This means he has freed himself from the Archons' distractions of desire, their impositions of matter, space and time, and even ascended beyond the Twelve Aeons of consciousness, past the dualism of thinking and thought, into re-union with the One, who lies in his deepest Self.

The *Apocryphon of John* offers us a more ancient image of the mind, and if we begin to think within in its constructs, then we may begin to think mythically and *in images* again. We have, as a result of our analysis of this Cosmogonic myth, regained some very intriguing notions concerning the ancient philosophy of unity. We have come to see the cosmos and the mind as mirror reflections, in which man and God seek one another. The One at the source of creation seeks its own reflection in its created cosmos. And it finds its own image in those aspects of the creation which, each in its own unique manner, reflect the One back to itself.

Essentially, it is *humanity*, through *self-consciousness*, that most ably reflects the One. We do this when we become aware, for a brief but revelatory moment, of the unity within ourselves. And yet, to begin, we seek that image of our own interior unity in the images of creation. Indeed, all of creation becomes a mirror in which we seek our own reflection. As in the case of the Ancient Template, we seek, amid the myriad of mythic images in its spiralling mists, that unity which shines as the circle of light at the centre.

When the creation is interpreted *through myth*, it becomes a series of symbols which mirror the mind's own innermost unity. Ultimately, passing through the mind's images to its interior source of unity, to the innermost Self, we find there our own interior reflection of the One. We come *to see* the Sacred 'face to face'.

But this awareness is only achieved through the ancient image-language. When we begin to *think in images* and finally *enter through the image*, we regain a greater awareness of the Sacred as the source of all light, life and consciousness.

IV. The Mythic Path: a Summary

In our next chapter, we shall embark on a new journey through images – exploring examples in Art, following the Symbolic Path.

A myth, to summarize Part I, is an arrangement of images *in time*. Cosmogonic myths relate tales of our world's coming-into-being and falling-away, while Hero myths relate the world-saving deed that transpires in between. Through the *hero's task* – its acquisition, accomplishment and integration – one image is linked to the next, and the whole falls into a *narrative arrangement* of descent, nadir-moment and re-ascent, creating either O- or U-shaped narrative patterns.

At the nadir of a myth, a most important threshold is crossed as the hero accomplishes his task. The event occuring that moment is a revelation or awakening, frozen for all time in works of art as a Threshold Image. But other Threshold Images also appear in art, in particular, during the hero's initial separation and return, and at the nadir of at each, more minor episode.

Threshold Images also appear during the first few moments of the world's Creation and during the last few moments of its Apocalypse. But, it is the sacred hero's momentary death, rebirth and awakening which has become, for each culture, their greatest symbol of the Sacred. All of these Threshold Images, once they have been *entered through,* offer us their momentary epiphanies.

We have also discovered three basic forms of time. The myths of Judæo-Christianity and Hindu-Buddhism are imagined to transpire along linear segments or ever-recurring cycles, which create different *iconologues of time's measure.* But more ancient myths remind us of a much older mythopoeic understanding of time.

Through their heroic accomplishments, Christ and the Buddha broke out of the closed segments or cycles of mundane time, to a momentary experience of the eternal *mythic time*. Their experience of the eternally Sacred can be re-experienced by us the moment we *enter through* their images. For their Threshold Images have stood throughout history as doorways momentarily leading us out of the bounding segments or cycles of time.

These doorways may also be seen to stand both at life's end and it's beginning. For Christ followed his will forward through life to the eternal doorway that opened at the moment of his death. Meanwhile, the Buddha renounced his will to move backward through life, past his birth in this and all previous lives, to finally experience a more timeless existence.

Attempting to follow the dictum that 'the image itself will show you the way', we have learned, fundamentally, that the time created by different cultural myths may be transcended. Our myths not only gather moments together into one narrative, they impose their own measures of time upon them. Ultimately, each cultural myth is *a variation on the theme of time*. But, these measures may be transcended and the myth itself may be *entered through* to its original timelessness.

Several times in Part I, we have followed the Mythic Path into the swirling depths of the Ancient Template. This means that we have followed certain O or U shaped narratives as they traced out a line of descent and re-ascent through the Ancient Template. At the nadir of each myth, we momentarily beheld the Sacred which lies at the very centre of the template.

This sacred unity, we have just learned, creates images in the surrounding mists through which it may reflect upon itself. Viewed in this manner, each myth must also be understood as the One's attempt *to reflect upon itself*. In the surroundings mists, the Sacred creates, not only *singular* images of itself, but entire series of images linked to one another *through myth*. Each myth, viewed in this manner, is also an imaginary creation of the One as it attempts to reflect upon itself in the unfoldment of time.

When this series of images takes the form of Cosmogonic myths, then the One's grand reflection consists of 'the Creation' (unfoldment from the centre) and 'the Apocalypse' (infoldment and return to the centre). Through these myths, the One sees itself reflected in the entire creation and dissolution of the cosmos.

But, in the time in between, a different series of images appears in the mists, in the form of the sacred Hero myth. Now, the One's grand reflection consists of the hero's descent, nadir-moment of epiphany, and return. The One sees itself reflected in the hero's mythic journey, particularly in his 'world saving deed' which occurs at the very nadir. At that moment, the hero himself becomes an image or reflection of the One. The world saviour becomes a sacred symbol, while his world-saving deed becomes a sacred mythologem.

Thus, through this hero, the Sacred sees itself as *acting* within its own created cosmos.

In this sense, the Mythic Path is nothing less than a grand temporal reflection of the One as it creates, periodically saves, and finally destroys that cosmos which mirrors its own movements ...in eternity.

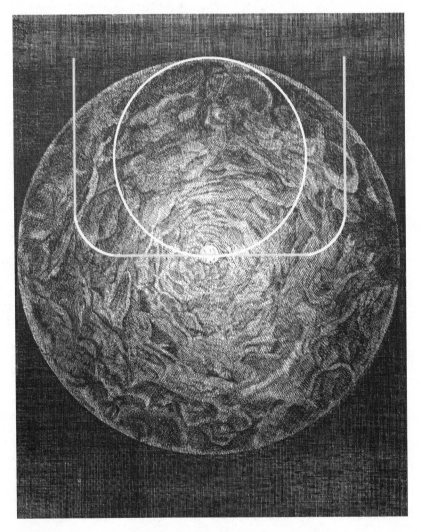

O and U shaped mythic narratives
tracing a line of descent and ascent
through the Ancient Template

PART II

THE SYMBOLIC PATH

Truth did not come into the world naked,
it came in images.
One will not receive truth in any other way.
– The Gospel of Philip (67:10)[1]

CHAPTER IX

Symbols of the Sacred

The images are manifest to man,
but the light within them remains concealed...
– The Gospel of Thomas 47:20[2]

I. The Sacred & Mundane

Symbols throw us across a spiritual abyss. When contemplating a sacred work of art, it may feel as if *a great divide* separates us from the Holy hidden in images. Then, our vision expands, and the image becomes transparent to its transcendent source. We are *thrown together* with the Sacred in a fleeting moment of epiphany...

The expressions just used were not ill-chosen. If we take the time to trace the etymology of the word 'symbol' through its Attic Greek antecedent, *symbolé*, we discover that it means literally *to throw* (*balló*) two things *together* (*sym*).[3]

What symbols throw together, essentially, are sacred and mundane experiences, making them one. Thus, the mundane experience of bringing one's fingertips together combines with the sacred experience of beseeching the Holy, to become 'hands in prayer'. A cup, combined with a momentary awareness of God's indwelling presence, becomes 'the chalice'. And by a similar token, the man bound to a stake and cross-piece, when combined with a sudden realization of release from suffering, becomes 'the saviour'.

Ultimately a symbol reveals, not just a mundane object but, transcending that, a more sacred epiphany. The experience of the mundane object is combined with a more sacred experience of its indwelling holiness. It is this aspect of a symbol which interests us, and ultimately forces us to recognize its arrangement of images as an iconologue. The singular image or image-cluster 'betrays some kind of recognizable meaning and arrangement', and so becomes 'the Iconologue of the Sacred Symbol'.

But symbols may be combined. Indeed, several symbols of different cultural origins may be combined in a single work of art. To think through the symbols of such a work, to read them in accord with their ancient image-language, requires that we regain the forgotten manner of 'symbolic thinking'. Then, the symbols may be read independently of their mythic context, and in relation to each other.

With the symbols encountered thus far, their narrative context has determined to a greater or lesser extent their associated meaning. And yet, it is possible to recognize a symbol independently of its mythic context. Indeed, there are sacred symbols completely isolated or removed from their associated narratives, such as the sculptures of the ancient Goddess which have come down to us from a time before recorded myth. As well, *the Water Bearer, Twins, Virgin, et al.* create a cycle of twelve images arranged, not according to any myth, but the wheel of the Zodiac. The Greater Arcana of the Tarot pack – *The Hanged Man, The Wheel of Fortune, The Fool* – offer us a series of twenty-two emblematic and, indeed, enigmatic images. These Arcana, which first emerged in the ducal courts of Northern Italy around 1415, reflect the Mediæval world's pre-occupation with death, romance and the end of the world. And yet, they are devoid of any narrative association. What ancient manner of 'symbolic thinking' will allow us to read such images?

II. The Golden Chain of Being

To begin, we must regain a more ancient view onto the world, a mythic and symbolic view which links all things together *through images*. It was Macrobius, a fifth century follower of the Neo-Platonic school, who preserved into our times much of the ancient philosophy that would otherwise have perished forever. He recognized the presence of a higher unity from which *'all things proceed, and up to him return.'*[4] In his *Commentary on the Dream of Scipio*, Macrobius described this ancient outlook as follows:

> *Since... the supreme God... forms and suffuses all below with life, and since this is the one splendor lighting up everything and visible in all, like a countenance reflected in many mirrors arranged in a row, and since all follow on in a continuous succession, degenerating step by step in their downward course, the close observer will find that from the supreme God to the bottommost dregs of the universe there is one tie, binding at every link, and never broken. This is the golden chain...*[5]

In this antiquated view onto the world, the Divine and the mundane form one long 'Chain of Being', each intermediary forming a link, one in succession with the other. And each link in creation becomes *like a mirror, reflecting the divine source back to itself, each in its own unique way.* Clearly, we have here the same vision of unity as manifest in the *Apocryphon of John*.

Gustave Doré: Dante's Vision of Paradise

There, God is 'the well-spring of pure, luminous water' which 'seeks its reflection in the series of images in its watery light.' Here, God is, 'the one splendor lighting up everything' and 'is visible in all of them, like so many mirrors arranged in a row.' As in the *Apocryphon*, so here the solitary outpouring of all creation grants its unity to all things while seeking those images among the many-layered multiplicity which reflect its unity back to itself.

In this archaic scheme of things, man plays a most important role, as the highest of all animals, and yet, the lowest of intelligent beings. And so he is, as it were, the link between angel and beast, spirit and matter, the Sacred and the mundane...

Hildegarde Von Bingen:
The Nine Orders of Angels (12th c.)

Another fifth century Neo-Platonist (under the assumed name of Dionysus Aeropagite) described a ninefold division in the order of angels, who link the chain of intelligent beings downward from God to man. The heavenly hierarchy surrounding God are like celestial circles of light emanating outward in a threefold trinity. (And, as a trinity of trinities, all are regarded as essentially *one...*).

First come the contemplative *Seraphs, Cherubs* and *Thrones;* then the less contemplative and more active *Dominations, Virtues* and *Powers;* and finally the most active *Principalities, Archangels* and *Angels.* Because Man is blessed with a soul and with reason, he is linked to the lowest order of angels, who are able to appear before him, and turn his attention back to the Higher.

But, like the lower beasts, man is also an admixture of appetites, humours and baser elements. The cold & dry in him combine to form his earth-

The Four Humours:
Phlegm (Flegmat), Blood (Sanguin),
Choler (Coleric) & Melancholy (Melanc)

en *Melancholy*; the cold & moist, his watery *Phlegm*; the hot & moist, his airy *Blood*; and the hot & dry, his fiery *Choler*. Although he is blessed with 'the god-like faculty of reason', his beastly passions and appetites turn his attention away from the Divine.

Nonetheless, man is still 'the paragon of animals' (*Animalia*), standing above the eagle who is 'chief of birds', the lion as 'king of beasts', and the whale as 'lord of fish'. And these, according to the Mediæval *Bestiaries*, stand above all *Vegetabilia*, where the oak is 'the forest's king' and the rose its 'queen of flowers'. These, in turn, stand above all *Mineralia*, where the diamond is 'the most valuable of stones' and gold, 'the most precious of metals'.

In this way, the *Catena Aurea* or Golden Chain of Being descends 'from the supreme God to the bottommost dregs of the universe'.[6] But, since each has 'the divine seal' imprinted on it, mirroring the creator back to itself, this chain could also become *a ladder of vision*, with each rung mirroring its maker. Or, it was *a celestial stair*, each turning in the steps like a fragmented shard of the divine glass, but all reflecting the spiral upward to the creator. Finally, all of creation could be seen as *a celestial rose*, each object a different petal in the spiral, but all as petals *of one rose,* and all leading in their spiral *to the same centre.*

If man was but able to turn his gaze away from the *Theatrum Orbi* with all its earthly distractions, he could behold once more the Higher in himself, and so *see* God. For let us not forget that man was, in part, divine. That divine part of himself was revealed when he successfully ascended the spiral staircase, through his meditations. What he had to do, in essence, was realize the perennial truth *gnothi seauton* – 'know thyself'. For, according to Plotinus, *"The man who has learned to know himself will at the same time discover whence he comes."*[7]

The key for working one's way back through the creation was to recognize that everything is, as Macrobius put it, *"distinguished by a difference and associated by a similarity."*[8]

III. The Lineaments
of a More Antiquated Logic

The idea of the 'unbreakable chain', or Golden Chain of Being, allows us to see all things as linked together into one creation. 'Associating through similarity' and 'distinguishing by difference' allows us to think through the chain of being, linking one thing to the other through the logic of 'similarity and difference'. And, by imagining the creation as *a swirling vortex* (*diné*) with the One (*to Hen*) as a circle of light at its centre, we are able to see how all things on the periphery may be linked, and indeed, united with the greater unity in their midsts.

To picture 'the unbreakable chain that bounds the elements together', Macrobius used a cosmogonic model (see right) offered first by Empedocles and established later by Plato and Aristotle (yet, its circular form allows us to identify it with the swirling vortex of our Ancient Template). According to this model, all things are created as a compound of four *elements:* water, earth, air and fire. As well, there are four different *qualities* which underlie these four elements: hot and cold; moist and dry. Each element is a mixture of two of them: water is cold and moist; earth is cold and dry; air is hot and moist; and fire is hot and dry.

Hence, as Macrobius notes, each element is thus *differentiated* from the other, due to the *difference* in one of their underlying qualities. Water is cold *and moist*, for example, while earth is cold *and dry*. But, since each also shares a common quality, an important *similarity* also underlies these elements, allowing one to be *assimilated* with the other. Now, we see that *both* water *and* earth are *cold*, though water is moist and earth is dry. Through these similarities and differences, all four elements are linked together into the 'unbreakable chain'. The whole forms one continuous circle,[9] which is illustrated on the page opposite.

Drawing from the Clavis Sapientiae of Artephilius (15th c.), illustrating 'the Philosopher's Wheel'.

The wheel divides the four qualities into pairs: (top left:) cold & dry, (top right:) cold & moist, (bottom right:) hot & moist, (bottom left:) hot & dry.

The qualities are referred to by their Latin names: cold (frigiditas), moist (humiditas), dry (siccitas), hot (caliditas).

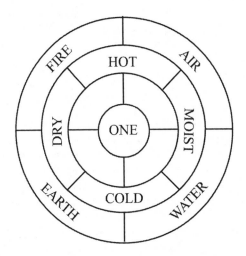

The Four Elements (outer circle) and their Pairs of Qualities (inner circle):
Fire = dry & hot; Air = hot & moist; Earth = dry & cold; Water = cold & moist
All these similarities and differences come to unity in the centre.

In this way, Macrobius says, the divine creator

> *...wove air and water into fire and earth, and thus a mutual attraction*
> *ran through the universe, linking together unlike elements by the*
> *similarities underlying their differences.*[10]

The differences are equally necessary in this scheme of things, as they force the whole to be constellated into its four parts. Each element is opposed to the other, because it possesses two qualities *contrary* to those of the other. Earth, for example, is constellated opposite air, because it is cold and dry, while air, on the contrary, is warm and moist. And the same is true of water and fire: *"Not only are adjacent adhering qualities compatible, but the same unity is preserved in the elements* that are separated: *as earth is* [opposite] *to air, so is water* [opposite] *to fire; and wherever you begin, you will find the same mutual attraction. Thus they are linked together by that very feature which makes them uniformly different from each other."*[11]

We have here the same 'balanced tension of opposites' as already described by Heraclitus* – including his idea of a deeper, 'hidden harmony'. Through this explanation of the 'unbreakable chain', Macrobius preserves into modern times a more antiquated logic – the logic of 'similarity and difference'.

* See page 19.

Hence, according to this more ancient view of the creation, all things are differentiated from each other, due to their differing proportions of elements. And the elements themselves are differentiated from each other, due to the differences in their qualities. In this way, the One divides into the many, forming a vast array of multiplicity.

And yet, a counter-movement may also occur, through similarity. All things hold together because they share the four elements, of which they are variously composed. And the elements themselves form a continuous circle, because they are assimilated to each other through their common underlying qualities. In this way, the many find their origin, once more, in the One.

Ultimately, a more fundamental unity underlies all these similarities and differences. For, when the One at the source of creation *"...poured itself forth to animate the immense universe, it did not,"* Macrobius says, *"permit any division of its singleness."*[12] All things, composed variously of elements and qualities, betray in their fundamental constitution a deeper unity, which is derived ultimately from the One.

This is the antiquated logic that lies at the root of iconologic. In order to think through images, we must learn to think in a logic that sees things in light of the unity at their origin. And hence, we must learn to think in terms of a logic that is more ancient than the traditional Aristotlean one, which places greater emphasis on *'difference'* and the series of classifications it *'defines'* thereby. Such a creative, more unified way of thinking is achieved when we place equal emphasis on *'similarity and difference'*.

IV. Of Angels & Scarabs

As an example, we take Aristotle's definition of a man as 'a rational animal', and of a bird as 'a flying animal'. A *similarity* between the two exists, in so far as both are animals (they share the same *genus*). But there is also a *difference*, because the man thinks while the bird flies (and hence, each may be defined in terms of their *differentia*).

Meanwhile, according to the more ancient philosophy, a *hidden unity* underlies all these similarities and differences.

If we recall that all of creation has the One as its source, and variously reflects that One back to itself, then we learn to see the similarities and differences in the context of their greater unity. Man is that aspect of creation which reflects the One back to itself *through thinking*, while the bird reflects the One back to itself *through flying*.

In our visions and dreams, we may experience these two forms *in combination:* the manner of a man and a bird may combine in *visions of flight*, offering us a more sacred, indeed, *elevated* vision of the divine creation. The Egyptian image of Horus the falcon (whose name means 'he who is above'), the winged guardians of ancient Babylon, and even our Christian angels manifest such miraculous flights of thought. By combining thinking and flying, they reflect the One back to itself through *'winged thought'*.

While this combined image reveals the greater unity underlying certain *differences*, other image-clusters reveal the greater unity that underlies their *similarities*. For example, if we pause to admire the Egyptian symbol of the scarab upholding the solar disk,* we see two different forms in combination. Yet, to *enter through* this combined image, we must attempt to think through their *similarities*.

The scarab beetle *rolls* a ball of dung; the sun-disc *rolls* across the heavens. What is more, the ball of dung which the beetle rolls is that same ball from which (it was thought) it died and was reborn. Meanwhile, the sun rolling across the heavens is that same sun through which (it was thought) we shall all die and be reborn. The two forms reflect the One back to itself in similar ways. And, by thinking through these similarities in the awareness of their greater unity, the combined image is *entered through* to the One.

Hence, the images of dreams, art and myth betray, through their various arrangements, the presence of a more ancient manner of thinking. As we think through images in terms of similarity and difference, this underlying iconologic gradually emerges. This more ancient manner of 'symbolic thinking' allows us to see arrangements of images in light of their higher unity; it reveals, behind images, the ancient One at their shared source...

When the creation is viewed as 'a ladder of vision', we attempt this visionary ascent by climbing the hierarchy of minerals, plants and animals 'rung by rung'. Yet, the Golden Chain of being need not be ascended and transcended 'link by link'. Instead, the various *combinations*, even the *displacements* among the different links allow us to create different arrangements of images, each offering us its own unique path back to the source. Each arrangement offers a different route, though they all lead to the same destination.

Thus, an angel is an arrangement of images that *combines* various differences (a man thinks while a bird flies). A scarab is an arrangement that *combines* various similarities (both the beetle and the sun die and are reborn). But *all* of these figures – man, bird, beetle, sun – may be composed and recomposed into different divine messengers through their underlying similarities and differences. The possibilities are endless, once we begin to think again through images.

In Macrobius, we have rediscovered the antiquated logic of 'similarity and difference' which underlies the more-unifying manner of 'symbolic thinking'. This logic allows us to think our way through the Ancient Template while arranging images independently of their myths. Instead, we learn to think in accord with the ancient image-language. Each time an object becomes a sacred symbol, it becomes a *mirror* offering a momentary reflection of the

---

* For an image of the Egyptian scarab, see page 71.

Sacred at its source. And the moment man gazes at this object in a certain state of mind, he himself beholds the Sacred *as it is reflected* through this unique aspect of the creation.

This is possible because man himself is also a mirror, a unique aspect of the creation. He possesses qualities common to *animalia* (movement, appetite, humours), even *vegetabilia* (growth) and *mineralia* (existence, substance: a compound of water, earth, air and fire). Yet, he also possesses a God-like awareness, linking him to the angels and higher beings – even to the One itself. In this sense, he is, in his mind, a *microcosm* (lit. 'a little world') mirroring the greater world around him, but with the awareness of a higher unity.

Each time he gazes at an eagle, a rose, or a diamond, its unique quality – to soar, to blossom, to sparkle – combines with man's unique quality – to contemplate each in the awareness of the One – so as to become a momentary reflection of the Sacred. The moment the two become one in their reflection of the Sacred, man experiences a sacred symbol. At that moment, he 'thinks symbolically'.

V. Symbolic Thinking

We have developed the Ancient Template to aid us each time we attempt to *enter through* the image. Through its unique form, the template continually draws our attention back to the One at the centre of the cosmos and at the centre of our own mind. Hence, whenever we contemplate an object with the aid of the Ancient Template, we seek to *enter through* the series of images it conjures, passing step by step, to the greater unity at their source. This visionary descent through a series of images constitutes 'the Symbolic Path' through the endless labyrinth.

First, we must remove the object from its particular context, so as to focus more on the uniquity of its existence. The object, be it an eagle, a rose or a diamond, conjures up certain, more personal ruminations and memory-images in us. We recall that, to fulfill its appetite, the eagle moves across the heavens on outspread wings; to grow, the rose blossoms open in a crimson spiral; merely to be, the diamond sparkles with refracted light. Each, in its own way, reflects the creator at its source. And so we place an image of each on the outer mists spiralling towards the centre.

But, when we reflect upon ourselves, when we focus on the uniquity of our own existence, we realize that we, in our own way, reflect the creator *through our consciousness*. And *through our self-consciousness* – through the awareness of our own innermost Self, we are able to mirror the presence of that higher unity. Hence, when we combine this awareness with the eagle's soaring, the rose's blossom or the diamond's sparkle, we spiral down through their images in the mists. We *enter through* these images which, illuminated by our vision, have now become symbols of the Sacred.

We now find ourselves in the middle layers of the mists. For, we have associated these objects with a much broader category of being: with the word, symbol or cultural image arising from our collective memory. Each is now a cultural memory-image. The eagle has become the mighty *Thunderbird* of Native Indian mythology; the rose, the *Mystical Rose* of Christianity; and the diamond, the Buddhist *vajra*, its diamond-tipped thunderbolt a manifestation of our newly-crystallized vision.

Each of these is now a sacred symbol, because it brings the sacred and mundane together; it 'throws' our mundane experience 'together' with a more sacred vision of the One. The object's unique quality combines with our higher awareness to become a shared reflection of the One at their source.

Finally, in a moment of revelation and awakening, we *enter through* each of these images to a more sacred and unique Presence. In our vision, we become one with the circle of light at the centre.

VI. The *Mysterium Tremendum et Fascinans*

Although the resulting epiphany is beyond verbal description, the presence of this ineffable *Mysterium* is nevertheless evoked *through images,* and particularly through the iconologue of the sacred symbol. Many attempts have been made to describe this ultimately ecstatic experience of the Sacred, though each attempt, from the very outset, was doomed to failure. Like Icarus, we fly ever higher to that which, in the end, destroys the very wings we forged.

Eliade has described the experience of the Sacred as a 'hierophany': *"Life springs from an* over-fullness, *from a* wholeness. *To men of the traditional cultures... all life was a* hierophany, *a manifestation of the sacred."*[13] He goes on to add that this mystical vision *"...resists time, its reality is coupled with perenniality."*[14] Aldous Huxley, under the influence of mescaline, described it as *"...a perpetual present made up of one continually changing apocalypse,"* and finally summarized it as *"the sacramental vision of reality."*[15]

Rudolf Otto, in the 1917 publication of his book on *Das Heilige* (The Holy), described a two-fold feeling of, firstly, *fear* before an overwhelmingly superior power – the *mysterium tremendum* – and secondly, of *wondrous awe* before a majesty radiating a perfect plenitude of being – the *mysterium fascinans*. In the end, he described any experience of this *Mysterium tremendum et fascinans* as *numinous*.[16]

Whatever it is – this feeling of epiphany, enlightenment, absolute understanding and ecstasy – it alters man's outlook onto the world so that all objects now possess the potentiality of metamorphosing into a sudden manifestation of the Sacred. That is to say, each object now expresses not only a mundane, but also a higher, more sacred purpose: a chair becomes 'the throne of the holy'; a table, 'the sacrificial altar'; a cup, 'the libation'. Take up a book in your hand – it is 'the Word', 'the Holy Writ'. Look at a building – it becomes 'a temple' whose architecture manifests the sacred structure of the cosmos: its pillars uphold the vault of the heavens, and its four corners stand at the limits of the four directions. To step through its doorway is to enter the sacred centre of all time and space. Smoke, incense, fire, and water – in a moment these all transform into in-dwellings of the Holy. The transcendent becomes immanent through them.

Hence, this momentary revelation flashes through our minds like a *vajra* thunderbolt, forcing us to treat each object in the field of our vision as a manifestation of the Sacred. As Nietzsche said of his inspiration while writing his highly symbolic work *Thus Spoke Zarathustra*: *"The things themselves approached and offered themselves as metaphors."*[17]

The inherent structure of mundane things therefore becomes of great importance, for the Sacred will henceforth manifest its presence through the particular qualities of *that* object: this thing, and no other, shall momentarily contain the Divine, and so, serve as the mundane aspect of the sacred symbol. *"Any object whatever may paradoxically become a hierophany,"* Eliade writes, *"[and] a receptacle of the sacred, while still participating in its cosmic environment (a sacred stone, e.g., remains nevertheless a stone.)"*[18]

But not only stones – plants, animals and persons too may, through their distinct qualities, mirror the Divine. This also extends to types of persons with whom we have developed a very strong relationship, based upon a certain type of *feeling*. And in this case, it is now the person and our relationship to them, be that mother, father or lover, and the resultant longing for reconciliation, reunion or embrace, which leads us to a union with the Sacred – now envisioned as the *Magna Mater* or *Pater Omnipotens*. Each of these symbols offers us 'a mirror various and divine'...

VII. The Symbolic Path

The two most ancient and universal forms which the Sacred has achieved has been that of either 'Sky Father' or 'Earth Mother'. In this case, the Sacred revealed itself through those *feelings* which were experienced *in relation to* the archetypal mother – 'the *all-giving* Goddess'; or father – 'the *all-powerful* God'.

Individually, we feel ourselves to be separated from our mother or father, and so seek union with them once more. Collectively, as a whole culture, we feel ourselves to be 'fallen' from the God or Goddess, and so seek re-union or reconciliation with them.

According to our most ancient traditions, what we seek is the plentiful, all-fecundating source of creation, symbolized by *embrace* with the *Magna Mater*. Or, we seek to be in accord once more with the wise, just and all-forgiving Word of creation, symbolized by *atonement* with the *Pater Omnipotens*.

Freud, in his *Totem and Taboo*, describes in detail how the child's infantile experiences of its mother or father determined, during the infancy of our culture, the nature and quality of our deities. According to him, our infantile traumas sufficiently expanded through religion to become the sacred formative experiences for the entire race.

In particular, Freud saw the patricidal Oedipus myth as the hidden *Urmyth* at the basis of all religions. So that, in the case of Christianity, its emphasis on the blood sacrifice of the son reveals a deeply repressed guilt-feeling for the murder of the father. Christ's sacrifice was not merely an attempt to atone for Adam's sin, but a more desperate attempt to expiate the forgotten Oedipal murder of the Father. To obtain his thesis, Freud crossed the myth of Christ's crucifixion, not with the myth of Adam's fall, but with Oedipus' murder of his father.[19]

A more balanced view sees a number of infantile traumas as formative to our development – leaving their various marks in our minds – thus causing these forgotten events to be eventually modelled by the events of myth. In particular, feelings of loss and longing may lead us through images of the Mother and Father – from whom we feel separated, and with whom we seek reunion – into the lost experience of union with the Sacred, now imagined as the *Magna Mater* or *Pater Omnipotens*.

Through such feelings, images in our personal and collective memory may suddenly be re-activated, and their symbols be brought back *to life*. This is particularly true during moments of crises in life. Although Western culture is characterized by its exercise of the will, and its attempts to move *forward* through time, a momentary life-crisis has the effect of paralyzing our will, and sending us on an unexpected journey *backward* through time. When we come up against a life-threshold that cannot be crossed, the sudden eruption of feeling re-activates those long-forgotten memory images.

And so, even against our own will, we undertake a backward journey through them. By virtue of the powerful feeling-tone accompanying them, these symbols may extend that journey further backward, from personal memory-images to the collective memory-images of an entire culture. And so we find that, through symbols, a unique path may be pursued through the Ancient Template, which we shall pursue here as the Symbolic Path.

VIII. The *Magna Mater*

Turning once more to the Ancient Template, we may see how feeling-toned symbols function as a series of doorways to the Divine. We have, for example, ancient stone images of the Great Goddess which, by virtue of their antiquity, exist independently of any accompanying liturgy or myth. Such an image of the ancient Goddess may be envisioned on one of the innermost circles of the spiralling mists. Meanwhile, our more familiar cultural images

- Christian Madonna - Ancient Goddess - Hebrew Eve -
Left: Hans Memling: Madonna and Child, detail (1472)
Centre: Venus of Willendorf (c. 18,000 BC)
Right: Jan Van Eyck: Eve, detail of the Ghent Altarpiece (1432)

of the Hebrew Eve and Christian Madonna may be imagined on the spiralling clouds in the middle. On the outermost ring, we find the more personal image of our own mother, as well as any other woman who may influence our feelings in some way. All of these images and the associated feelings create the Symbolic Path through the eternal labyrinth. The path moves from personal and cultural memory-images of the *Magna Mater* to the *Mysterium* beyond them.

All these images of 'the Goddess' are related to one another, not only by virtue of the similarity that obtains in their external appearance, but by the related feeling-response they invoke in us. The Goddess is the fertile source of creation, the mistress of all love and life, from whom we all feel separated, and with whom we desire re-union once more. We have become separated from her, in our own life, through those childhood experiences felt in regard to our own mother: the traumatic separation from her at the moment of our birth, and the countless times we cried ourselves to sleep at night, in fear that she had abandoned us forever.

Yet, the first time she held us close to her body after birth, and each time she appeared to us the next morning, offering us caresses on a new day full of light, we felt ourselves to be once more in the comforting embrace of the Goddess. But, due to the passage of time, that feeling of union which we once felt as a child in our mother's arms has been lost to us forever – buried over in our memory by countless other experiences.

It is this *feeling* for the Goddess – a feeling of loss and a longing for re-union – that allows us to *imagine* a deeper and ever steeper path through the spiralling mists.

During our descent, cultural memory-images rise up which, empowered by our longing, replace the personal images we lack. By virtue of their form, these cultural images offer us the imagined fulfillment of our long-desired re-union; they model contents of the mind otherwise repressed or forgotten. What is more, they become keys that, with their gentle turning, extend our path ever further through the swirling mists of the Ancient Template.

As we spiral through the middle mists, we behold a vision of Eve. She – naked, fallen, ashamed – conjures forth unexpected memories in our mind: some painful, others more repressed. What forbidden act has she committed – she, who is 'the Mother of all'? And what does Eve reveal about our own mother? – the faults she committed, which harmed us so deeply, and seemed to tear us away from the infantile source of all maternal love. Although we accessed the love of the all-giving Goddess *through* her – did we recognize that *she herself* was only human? – with her fair share of faults, failures and shortcomings... By *entering through* this image of the Hebrew Goddess, we extend our passage through the spiralling mists of our memory.

And, as we *enter through* the image of the Christian Madonna, her image fulfills one aspect of our longing: she, the virgin mother, embraces the innocent child with infinite compassion. Like our own lost mother, she offers us once more the feeling of infant joy in her all-nurturing embrace. We begin to feel ourselves, once more, in union with the Goddess.

...And finally, we behold the image of the ancient Goddess, pointing with one hand to her nurturing breast and the other to her all-accommodating womb. By *entering through* this ancient image of the Great Goddess, our feelings of loss and longing are finally fulfilled. We feel ourselves to be one with her, ensconced, as it were, within the nurturing waters of her all-generating womb.

Through these feelings, we may *enter through* various images of the Goddess to that which unites them *all* at their source: the One at the centre of the swirling vortex. Then, the feelings themselves are elevated and transformed into an overpowering experience of divine *union and epiphany* – a final movement into the inner circle of light, wherein 'the One' for eternity dwells. In this way, it is built into the very structure of these images which, depicting the One as Great Mother – full, plentiful, all-nurturing and embracing – is able to re-awaken in us the feeling of return and eternal union.

IX. The *Pater Omnipotens*

Atonement with 'the God of our fathers' is accomplished when the rift that separates us from him is repaired. This is accomplished, typically, through a difficult, dangerous, even painful contest that finally gains his recognition and approval. For, through this contest of the will, we prove ourselves to be worthy of his higher powers. And indeed, we become the embodiment of those powers, making ourselves 'at-one' with the archetypal Father.*

Essentially, it is through feelings of *accomplishment* that we become at-one with 'the Father'. According to the Hero myths of many Patriarchal cultures, we must demonstrate skill, courage and overcoming during a battle or contest. Typically, this contest occurs in mythic images of the hero battling a primæval monster, or of the warrior overcoming his more human foe.

But, moving beyond this, we must also demonstrate a sense of justice and order, even a wisdom worthy of the Father. This appears through mythic images of the hero or warrior now seated upon the throne as wise ruler and judge. These powers, which the Father himself acquired in ancient times, are our worthy inheritance.

In the battle with a primæval monster, the creature from the depths symbolizes the primordial chaos which the god had to master at the beginning of time and bring into order. This primordial event may also occur at the middle or end of time, creating the recurring Threshold Image of the hero's battle with a winged, seven-headed serpent or dragon.

In the Babylonian epic of creation for example, Marduk defeats numerous monsters created by the evil Tiamat, including a seven-headed snake called *Musmahhu*. In ancient Greece, Zeus rose to supremacy through his defeat of Typhon – *"from the shoulders of this frightening dragon, a hundred snake heads grew."*[20] Meanwhile, in the middle of time, Heracles defeated the nine-headed hydra, 'which grew back two heads for each that

---

* The English word 'atone', while meaning 'to reconcile, expiate, or make reparation', is derived from the obsolete English verb 'to one', i.e. 'to [make] one' or 'unite'.

Left: Marduk defeating Tiamat (Sumerian cylinder seal c. 900 BC)
Right: Zeus defeating Typhon (Greek vase c. 500 BC)

Left: Victory Stele of Naram-Sin (Akkadian c. 2200 BC)
Right: Palette of King Narmer (Egyptian c. 3200 BC)

was severed'. He became thereby the only Greek mortal to be apotheosized. Finally, at the end of time, in *The Book of Revelation*, the Archangel Michael battles with the great beast of the Apocalypse, an 'ancient serpent' with seven heads and ten horns.*

This image is foreshadowed in the Old Testament, where both *The Psalms* and *The Book of Job* make allusions to Yahweh's victory over Leviathan – *'the dragon of the waters with many heads.'* (Psalm 74:13) This Old Testament myth was probably drawn from the *Ras Shamra* tablets of the Phœnicians (discovered in 1929), where Baal *"didst smite Lotan the primæval serpent... the close-coiling one with seven heads."*[21] Again and again, the same symbolic Threshold Image emerges, of the god's great moment of *conquest* over the seven-headed serpent.

Meanwhile, in ancient Egypt and Mesopotamia, other myths told the heroic tale of their fore-fathers' *first* conquest over their more human enemies. In the *Victory Stele of Naram-Sin* or the *Palette of King Narmer*, we find the same symbolic image: 'the first of all kings' is depicted in the stance of victory, upholding his mighty weapon while stepping down on his fallen foe.

Brutal as it may seem, the hero has manifest himself in this manner, 'trampling his enemy underfoot', to evoke our associated feelings of victory, conquest and accomplishment. By vanquishing the monster or more human enemy, the archetypal Father has used courage, strength and skill to eventually establish his rule and order over the land. Now, forgoing his warrior aspect, he must rule wisely as king, decree sage laws and render fair judgement.

* For an image of the seven-headed serpent, see page 257.

Hence, the only way for us to be reconciled with 'the God of our fore-fathers' is to discover those same traits within ourselves. In our day-to-day contests with others, we must demonstrate similar such powers.

Each time we fail in our attempt, our fall from the Father is repeated. We fail to demonstrate the courage, strength and skill first manifest in our father and forefathers, and which the God Father demonstrated so admirably in the age of myth. But, the moment we succeed, the accompanying feelings of *accomplishment* allow us to *enter through* all of these images of conquest. We become reconciled to the Father, winning his recognition. Indeed, we ourselves become an embodiment of the Father, wielding the same timeless power as him.

And yet, it must not be forgotten that all these images are, in the end, illusory symbols. Behind the face of the hero, king and all-powerful Father lies 'the One'. On the Ancient Template, we would have to *traverse* all these images and eventually *transcend* them. Only then would we reach the circle of light that gives the *Pater Omnipotens* ...his power.

X. Conclusion

The process of symbolization occurs *by overwhelming necessity:* the mind, over-awed and frightened by a profound and soul-shattering experience of the Sacred, desperately seeks those objects which can, by virtue of their structure, contain such a momentous outpouring of the Divine – which is threatening otherwise to blast apart the very vessel into which it is being poured. At such a moment, an object is sought for its power to appropriately contain the awesome appearance of the *Numinosum*, and so, a symbol is created.

In the earliest ages of mankind, the Sacred was experienced in this way – as a thunderous epiphany that led *per force* to the creation of a symbol. Then, a series of symbols were strung together by ancient myth, with certain Threshold Images at their nadir, to become our hieratic works of art. And, as we survey the many masterpieces of *ars sacrum* created over the course of history, we find that most offer us symbolic doorways, constructed by the visionary artists of old, as images to *enter through*, and then left behind for succeeding generations to attempt in crossing.

The symbols of the past are not totally outdated, antiquated and useless; they resonate still with unseen powers. Yet, it is only by bringing our own lives, preoccupied with its present conflicts and needs, to these eternal symbols, that the forms forgotten by time may thus be enlivened, and our own lives may be transformed thereby – informed once more by their ancient inhering power.

CHAPTER X

The Mythologem of 'the Coniunctio'

What I tell you
Let the singer weave into song.
What I tell you
Let it flow from ear to mouth,
Let it pass from old to young
- The goddess INANNA
speaking to her consort DAMUZI
in a Sumerian poem[1]

I. The Word & Womb of Creation:
Ptah & Isis

Last century, a fascinating text was found inscribed on a battered old tablet christened 'the Shabaka stone'. A hole cut into the centre of the monolith with lines radiating outward gave it a most unusual appearance. Meanwhile, the priesthood of Memphis had chiselled onto its surface a series of hieroglyphs which announced that their god Ptah had created the entire cosmos, *"according to commands thought by the heart and issuing from the tongue."*

Shabaka stone (Egypt c.715 BC)

Although this in itself is unique – a god who *spoke* the cosmos into being – Ptah also created the entire pantheon of Egyptian gods, from Atum-Re to Osiris, in a similar manner. This is not to say they descended from him, inheriting a share of his divine essence. Rather:

It is said of Ptah... he had fashioned the gods, made the cities, founded the names, installed the gods in their shrines, established their offerings and equipped their holy places.

...Thus it was he who made every work, every craft, the action of the arms and the movement of the legs and the activity of each member, according to commands thought by the heart and issuing from the tongue.

...And in this way, all the gods and their kas (life-force) *are at one with him, content and united with the Lord of the Two Lands.*[2]

What is singularly unique about this religious text is that it intimates a view onto the world resplendent with a wisdom rarely expressed by other mythologies: it acknowledges and accepts the other deities, each in his or her own shrine, and then goes on to suggest that *their mere presence, by its variety and multiplicity, betrays a higher, solitary and unitary source.*

As such, the idea here exists, perhaps in its most rudimentary form, of 'the One' to which the deities of all mythologies ultimately refer.

"He who made every work."
The Egyptian god Ptah
(New Kingdom c. 1350 BC)

Roman statue of the
Egyptian goddess Isis (c.120 AD)

An Egyptian deity similar to Ptah arose several hundred years later, and was eventually incorporated into Roman mythology. The sacred text describing this deity is not a battered millstone but a ribald though religious novel from the second century A.D. called *The Golden Ass.*

Its author, Lucius Apuleius, was a well-travelled, philosophically educated opportunist and bohemian who, during his travels, was initiated into the mysteries of the Egyptian goddess Isis. He convincingly records in his novel his own transformation into an ass who, after a series of adventures and owners, prays to the Goddess for release ...and is finally granted his request.

Near the end of the novel Lucius, as the ass, beseeches the Goddess with the following prayer:

> *Blessed Queen of Heaven, whether you be pleased to be known as Ceres, ...or whether as celestial Venus, ...as Artemis ...or as Proserpine... I beseech you, by whatever name, in whatever aspect, with whatever ceremonies you deign to be invoked, have mercy on me in my extreme distress.*[3]

And the Goddess responds:

I am Nature, the universal Mother, mistress of all the elements, primordial child of time, sovereign of all things spiritual, queen of the dead, queen also of the immortals, the single manifestation of all gods and goddesses that are...Though I am worshipped in many aspects, known by countless names, and propitiated with all manner of different rites, yet the whole round earth venerates me...[4]

Here, the Goddess is manifest in all the multifarious expressions of her being: all forms of worship, all the rituals that are celebrated and the names invoked – invoke her. Once more, we bear witness to a unique spiritual outlook, as similarly expressed by the priests of Ptah. For, the Goddess manifests the solitary unity at the source of all sacred symbols.

While Ptah creates the world through his Word, or *logos*, Isis sustains it through her fertile Womb, or *eros*. Each of these divinities unites and *almost* transcends a multiplicity of aspects, but remains decidedly masculine or feminine: the *Pater Omnipotens* and *Magna Mater*.

II. *Hieros Gamos:*
The Sacred Marriage

Throughout history, myths and works of sacred art have attempted to portray the *Pater Omnipotens* and the *Magna Mater*, not only separately, but *in union*. This is true especially of the 'World Parent' myth and its view of the creation as the initial separation of the God-and-Goddess-in-union. We have seen this already in Hesiod's *Theogony*, where *Gaia*, the Earth Mother, separated from *Ouranos*, the Sky Father. In Egypt as well, *Geb* the Earth Father was separated from *Nut* the Sky Mother. But what of their primordial union?

Through the mythologem of the *Coniunctio*, that moment of creation has magically been made present, and their primordial unity ritually re-lived. Throughout the Near East, including Egypt, Phœnicia, Syria, and Sumeria, the *hieros gamos* or 'sacred marriage' was ritually celebrated each year: in 'the bridal chamber' high atop the holy temple, the king or high-priest united sexually with the temple *'hierodule'* (sacred prostitute or priestess), so as to imitate the union of the Goddess of Fertility with her consort and lover.

This Goddess of Fertility – wise, loving, erotic and plentiful – was known variously as Isis, Astarte, Cybele or Inanna, depending on the land in which she was worshipped. She united sexually with her divine lover, the ever-dying-and-rising 'Son of the Abyss', Osiris, Baal, Attis or Damuzi, so as to bring forth from her fertile womb the plentiful bounty of next season's crops.

In Sumeria, the rite of sacred marriage was performed *"on the day of the disappearance of the moon,"*[5] and this constituted *"the New Year's Day, the day of rites."*[6] As such, the ritual act of intercourse constituted a momentary *epiphany*: the original union of God and Goddess in the eternal *mythic time* appeared momentarily, here in mundane time, to effect through its fertilizing act of creation, the yearly renewal. As such, the mythologem of the *Coniunctio* constituted a momentary epiphany, resulting in both the sanctification and the renewal of time.

From the fragments and shards of cuneiform tablets, certain passages from the Sumerian ritual have been preserved to our own day. The original act of love between Damuzi and Inanna took place in a garden paradise much like Eden. Damuzi begins:

> *My sister, I would go with you into my garden,*
> *Inanna, I would go with you into my garden.*
> *...I would go with you to my apple tree.*
> *There I would plant the sweet, honey-covered seed.*

And Inanna replies:

> *He brought me into his garden,*
> *My brother Damuzi brought me into his garden,*
> *...By an apple tree I knelt as is proper,*
> *Before my brother coming in song,*
> *Who rose to me out of the poplar leaves,*
> *Who came to me in the mid-day heat.*

The fragment ends:

> *Before my lord Damuzi,*
> *I poured out plants from my womb*
> *...I poured out grain from my womb.*[7]

Unlike the garden of Eden, the act of love celebrated here ends, not in death and the fall from paradise, but in birth and paradise's new creation. Time began *anew*.

In their ritual re-enactment of this myth, the high priest and hierodule *enter through* the mythologem of sexual embrace to its original experience of *divine union*. Another litany sung or recited by the priestess reveals:

> *I bathed for the wild bull,*
> *I bathed for the shepherd Damuzi,*
> *I perfumed my sides with ointment,*
> *I coated my mouth with sweet-smelling amber,*
> *I painted my eyes with kohl.*

> *He shaped my loins with his fair hands,*
> *The shepherd Damuzi filled my lap with cream and milk,*
> *He stroked my pubic hair,*
> *He watered my womb*
> *He laid his hands on my holy vulva*
> *...He caressed me on the bed.*

Now I will caress my high priest on the bed,
I will caress the faithful shepherd Damuzi,
I will caress his loins, the shepherdship of all the land,
I will decree a sweet fate for him.[8]

For thousands of years, through this ancient celebration of the *hieros gamos*, king and priestess, man and woman ritually re-enacted the sacred union of God and Goddess, and participated thereby in the fertile act at the source of all creation. The act of union with one another led, thence, to union with the Divine.

The mythologem of the *Coniunctio* diffused both eastward into India and Tibet, and westward, through Phœnicia and Judæa, to Greece. And yet, while it would seem that such a rich, natural and universal image of divine union would receive widespread acceptance, instead it went underground, and became a secret hermetic tradition associated with various 'mystery' religions.

In the East, the image persisted in the rich mythological imagery of Tantrism. In the West, it survived, hidden and forbidden, in the symbolism of Gnosticism.

III: The Heretic & the Whore:
The Gnostic Revelation

Simon Magus was a wandering magician in Judæa who became the first important 'Gnostic saviour'. Although no trace of him is found in the Nag Hammadi texts, the early Church Fathers considered him to be a founding figure of the Gnostic movement: 'the father of all heresies', they said, from whom *"all heresies took their origin."*[9]

According to Irenæus (*Contra Hæreses* 1. 23. 1-4), Clement (*Stromateis* 2. 2. 7) and Hippolytus (*Refutatio Omnium Hæresium 6. 2-15*),[10] Simon was a Samarian, a contemporary of the apostles, who is even mentioned once in the Bible (Acts 8:10). He revealed himself to his disciples as the Messiah *'who hath stood, standeth, and shall stand'* (*o estós, stas, stésomenos*).[11]

Accompanying him, ever and always, was a singularly beautiful woman named Helena, whom he first came upon in Tyre. When he met her, she was 'standing upon a rooftop' (meaning that she was either a prostitute or *hierodule*). He 'ransomed' her, that is, he paid the nominal fee demanded by Astarte for celebrating the hierogamy just outside her temple and, from that day forward, she accompanied him. He eventually gathered about him thirty disciples and quite a number of followers, to whom he preached the following account of the creation – in which Helena played a most significant role.

Simon preached that, in the beginning, there was one God, hidden and transcendent, called 'The Boundless Power'. This god was described as:

> One Power divided into above and below, generating itself, making itself grow, seeking itself, finding itself, being... mother, father, one, being a root of the entire circle of existence.[12]

Although this singular Power is one-in-itself, it manifests itself as two:

> There are two offshoots, having neither beginning nor end, from one root... One of these offshoots appears from above, which is the creative Nous (thinking), who orders all things, and is male. The other offshoot is from below, Ennoia (thought), who generates all things, and is female. From whence, as consorts (syzygies), they undergo conjugal union, and manifest [the Upper Aeons], which have neither beginning nor end.[13]

We have here a vision of the creation similar to that recounted in the *Apocryphon of John*. And indeed, when Irenæus summarized the *Apocryphon of John* in his *Contra Hæreses*, he attributed the myth to the followers of Simon Magus.[14] As in the *Apocryphon*, so here, the One manifests its unity through the male and female consorts (*syzygies*) of *Nous* and *Ennoia*. By 'thinking (*Nous*) a thought (*Ennoia*) of itself thinking', the One's unity is made complete.

According to Simon, he himself was descended from the male principle, *Nous*. He roamed about the earth in search of the lost female principle, *Ennoia*, until he finally found her in the form of the ransomed prostitute Helena. And it was she who, as *Ennoia*, had separated from her consort in the beginning to generate the Lower Aeons:

> Having redeemed from slavery at Tyre, a city of Phoenicia, a certain woman named Helena, he [Simon Magus] was in the habit of carrying her about with him, declaring that this woman was the first thought (Ennoia) of his mind (Nous)... For this Ennoia, leaping forth from him... descended to the lower regions, and generated the angels and powers [i.e. the Archons] by whom he also declared this world was made.[15]

Ennoia's fall resembles in many ways the fall of *Sophia* in the *Apocryphon of John*. There, Sophia mistakenly created the Chief Archon Yaltabaoth. Here, Ennoia generated the Archons and powers 'by whom this world was made'. But Ennoia's tale reveals an important piece of information, about which the Nag Hammadi texts remain silent:

> *Ennoia was detained by those powers and angels* [i.e. Archons] *who had been produced by her. She suffered all kinds of contumely from them, so that she could not return upwards, but was even shut up in a human body, and for ages passed in succession from one female body to another... suffering insults in every one of them until, at last, she became a common prostitute; and she it was that was meant by the lost sheep.*[16]

In the Nag Hammadi texts, the fate of Sophia is left unclear. What *is* clear is that Christ came to manifest himself on earth in the form of Jesus the Nazarene. *But what of Sophia?* The conclusion to be drawn from the tale of Simon and Helena is that Sophia manifest herself on earth 'as a common prostitute' who was called 'the lost sheep'. In the Christian tradition, that prostitute, also called 'the lost sheep' ...was Mary Magdalene.

One Gnostic text from Nag Hammadi makes an important, though oblique, connection between Sophia and Mary Magdalene:

> *As for Wisdom* [Sophia] *...she is the mother of the angels* [i.e. Archons]. *And the companion of the saviour is Mary Magdalene. The saviour loved her more than all the disciples, and used to kiss her often on her mouth. The rest of the disciples... said to him "Why do you love her more than all of us?"* (63:30)[17]

The implication here is that the divine Sophia had come to exist *in* Mary Magdalene, and that the saviour 'kissed her often on the mouth' to manifest that Jesus and Magdalene, like Christ and Sophia, possessed a higher, unseen unity.

In the case of Simon Magus, he taught that sexual union was one means of re-entering into our primordial state before the fall – when each of us was still a part of that One Power whom, *"being both male and female, existed in unity."*[18] Thus, each man sought out his consort (*syzygy*), his feminine image (*Ennoia*, Helena) with whom he could re-unite in the One. And so did each woman seek out her masculine image (*Nous*, Simon) with whom she could likewise enter into union with the One. In the moment when the two experienced this union, the *gnosis* was achieved, for the divine *unity* had been *made known.*

Gnosticism was able to use sexual union as a means of achieving oneness with the Divine by virtue of the symbolic structure it gave to the Sacred. By portraying the Divine as, not just masculine (the *Pater Omnipotens*) or feminine (the *Magna Mater*) but as *a union of the two* (the 'One Power'), two devotees could experience the Divine *through their own union.*

IV. Shiva & Shakti:
The Tantric Revelation

Shiva is the Great Destroyer of this world's illusion, and he destroys it variously: by a furious cosmo-cataclismic dance or else in silent ascetic meditation. In his Tantric image, we behold him in sexual embrace with his consort Shakti, who sits upon his lap. The two gaze deeply into each other's eyes, their unbroken stare sustaining a form of meditation upon each other. But Shiva is alone.

For *shakti* is nothing more than the feminine personification of the god's own divine energy. Indeed, she is the very embodiment of that *maya* which, ever and always, creates this world in its multiplicity of forms. As such, she is also the all-giving Mother Goddess who, in her positive aspect, manifest herself in India as Shiva's beautiful consort, *Parvati*. What is more, she is also *Kali*, Shiva's darker consort, who manifests the negative aspect of the Mother Goddess: indiscriminately cruel, merciless in her killing and, by a higher necessity, all-devouring. Whether as Parvati or as Kali, *shakti* embodies the creative-destructive play of Shiva's own divine energy.

The task awaiting the devotee is to meditate upon this image, as upon the play of forces operating in his own soul. In Shiva lies the desire to destroy this world's illusion. And in Shakti lies the desire to create it. The image portrays the two, and the desire they feel for each other, as playfully entwined and erotically engaged. Having thus embraced each other deeply, they now exist as one.

Heinrich Zimmer, who has furnished us with this understanding of Tantra, expresses the powerful and poetic quality of the Tantric image thus:

> *From the eyes of these calm countenances, completely trans-figured from within, their gaze steadfastly interlocked,* [we can see] *a complete merging of two figures, who totally permeate each other.*[19] *...They are imbued with the secret knowledge that, though seemingly two, they are fundamentally one.*[20]

This, in essence, is the task that awaits the devotee as he sits before a sacred Tantric image. He must learn to see that the sacred image, like the world, is an image which he has created through his own desire – through the creative power of his own inner *shakti*. And then he must learn, through Shiva's destructive power, to annihilate this very image which exists, in truth, deep in himself: destroy it, so as to transcend it, and so to become one with the Divine in it. He must, in essence, *enter through the image*, so as to become one with the Sacred at its source.

In Buddhism, this same image is encountered in *yuganaddha* figures (Tibetan *yab-yum*) depicting the Bodhisattva in the embrace of his female *shakti*. He sits in a calm, meditative posture while she, in his lap, holds a skull-cup to his lips, inviting him thus to drink of desire and death.

Bodhisattva with Shakti
(Tibet c. 1750)

The Buddhist *shakti* may also take the form of a *dakini* – an alluring, nude female figure with swelling breasts and long flowing hair, whose sinuous dance manifests the ever-changing movement of thought-in-flux. One of her most dramatic representations occurs in statues of Chakrasamvara embracing his consort Vajravarahi. He stands with his legs apart, his blue body is powerfully arched, and two of his twelve arms enfold his small *dakini* in a sexual embrace that symbolizes the union of compassion and illumination.

In this manner, the mythologem of the *Coniunctio* reveals a hidden, higher purpose. Through ritual, the masculine and feminine powers may join once more in their primordial unity. We have seen many such pairings: the high priest and hierodule, Inanna and Damuzi, Gaia and Ouranos, Geb and Nut, Simon and Helena, Nous and Ennoia, Jesus and Magdalene, Christ and Sophia, Shiva and Shakti, Bodhisattva and Dakini, or Chakrasamvara and Vajravarahi. The variations on this theme are endless, and as numerous as the deities and their chosen devotees. In the moment of their joining, all are united once more in the ecstasy of oneness.

CHAPTER XI

Combining Symbols and Crossing Myths

*Christ is not a person, as far as I am concerned, but a hero,
a myth, a vast shadow picture in which humanity sees itself
projected on the walls of eternity.*
– Hermann Hesse[1]

I. The Image behind images

In one of his more illuminating novels, Hermann Hesse illustrates the peculiar way in which we, in our inner visions, pursue the Symbolic Path from personal to collective memory-images. But, beyond even these personal and collective images lies something deeper, hidden and unseen: 'the Image behind images'. This theme is pursued in dialectical fashion over the course of his novel *Narziss and Goldmund*, complements of its two main characters.

The elder of the two, Narciss, is a mediæval monk cast from the same mold as Abelard or Augustine: worldly wise, yet sacrificing that knowledge for a more ascetic, elevated, and logically rigorous outlook onto the world. The younger, Goldmund, is a one-time scholar and novitiate of Narciss' who escaped the life of the cloister to become a tireless vagabond, and who ultimately found adequate expression for his view onto the world by carving those simple, wooden, pious yet profoundly moving sculptures so characteristic of the mediaeval imagination.

The novel uses these two protagonists to give us the contrasting outlooks of the philosopher and the artist. At one point in the story, the artist Goldmund says:

I have made many drawings and lost them all. And yet I can tell you why I would learn [the sculptor's] *craft. I have watched many faces and shapes, and afterwards thought of them. Some of my thoughts have never ceased to plague me, and still they give me no peace. I have seen always, in every shape, a certain form, a certain line, repeats itself; how a forehead seems to tally with a knee, a hip with a shoulder, or forehead. And this too, I have noted, which I saw one night as I helped a woman bear her child: that the sharpest pain and sweetest pleasure seem to have almost one expression.*[2]

Later it is Goldmund's fate, after a life-long pursuit of women, wine and wandering, to meet up again with Narciss. The two, who have not seen each other since Goldmund disappeared from the cloister in his youth, engage in a dialogue on the sculptor's craft. Narciss asks, *"What comfort did your carving bring you? What did it mean?"* And Goldmund replies:

'It meant the conquest of all that perishes. I saw that in this zanies'-tumble and death-dance, something can remain of our lives, and survive us – our images. Yet they too perish in the end. They are buried, or they rot, or are broken again. And yet their lives are longer than any human life, so that, behind the instant that passes, we have in images a quiet land of shrines and precious shapes. To work at these seemed good and comforting to me, since it is almost a fixing of time forever.'

And Narciss, ever the philosopher, replies:

'Your words delight me Goldmund... Yet I think that by your definition you have not exhausted all the wonders of art. ... I have seen many works of painters and carvers, many saints and madonnas, of which I do not believe they are true copies of the shape of any single person, who lived once, and whose form and colour were caught and preserved by the maker.'

'You are right,' cried Goldmund, *'...The pattern of any good image is no real, living form, or shape, although such shapes may have prompted the maker to it. Such images have their home in the craftsman's soul.'*

'I am very glad. But see, amice, *how, without knowing it, you have strayed into the midst of philosophy, and given words to one of her secrets.'*

'You should not mock me.'

'And I do not. You have spoken of "first patterns" [Urbilder] *– of images without existence save in the soul of the carver, but which he transmutes into matter, making them visible. So that, long before such a carver's shapes can be seen, and so obtain their formal reality, they are there already, as forms within his soul. And this same "first pattern" – this shape – is, to a hair, what old philosophers called "the idea".*

...Once you have wandered into ideas, you have wandered into the realm of intellect, into our world of theologians and philosophers, and so you admit that, in all this confusion, ...this endless, weary dance of death of our living and corporeal substance, there is a spirit which fashions for eternity.'[3]

As the artist, Goldmund says that, in the beginning, a series of personal experiences prompted him to the creation of his works. He formed an image in his memory that encapsulated the vast variety of his experience within the simple lineaments and flowing contours of its form: 'how a forehead seemed to tally with a knee...' so that 'in every shape, a certain form, a certain line, repeats itself.' This, then, became his personal memory-image.

But, through his skill and craftsmanship, the sculptor carves those images which transcend an individual lifetime, and become cultural icons. Though they too 'perish in the end, are buried, broken, or rot', they preserve, as much as possible, the shared vision of an entire culture. They become collective memory-images.

Yet, as Narciss observes, beyond each personal or cultural memory-image lies something much deeper: those 'images without existence' which the craftsman 'transmutes into matter, making them visible'. This is 'the first pattern', what Jung called the Archetype and Hesse chose to call instead *'das Urbild'* – the Image behind images. And it is through such images that we ultimately behold, what Narciss calls, 'the spirit which fashions for all eternity.'

We must not forget Jung's cautionary words regarding the Archetypes: primordial images, though universal in form, have no existence whatsoever unless they are filled out with the contents of personal experience. That is to say, they can never be divorced from particular circumstance; they can never exist on their own. As such, an archetypal image will always be particular, individual and unique, depending on the singular soul who beholds it in that particular moment in place and time.

And the same holds true of Archetypes as they become manifest in different cultures. The Archetype itself has no existence whatsoever until it is reduced down to a definite period in history and cultural locale, where it now bears a more potent message to the culture in question. As their cultural symbol of the Sacred, it expresses their collective experience of awe and fear in the face of the eternal *Mysterium*.

According to Jung,

No archetype can be reduced down to a simple forumula. It is a vessel which we can never empty and never fill. It has a potential existence only, and when it takes shape in matter, it is no longer what it was. It persists throughout the ages and requires interpreting ever anew. The archetypes are the imperishable elements of the unconscious, but they change their shape continually.[4]

This image often, indeed always, varies from culture to culture, because the time, locale and circumstance, the language with its peculiar variety of images and metaphors, the very rocks and stones from which the symbols are hewn, differ. But, as Eliade has noted in his study on *Images and Symbols*, these cultures are still able to communicate with each other because each mythology, though unique, is based on the same timeless and eternal Images – images which refer, ultimately, to an inscrutable *Sacramentum:*

> *It is the presence of* [these archetypal] *images and symbols that keeps cultures 'open'... If the Images were not at the same time an 'opening out' into the transcendent, one would ultimately become suffocated in any culture, however great and admirable one might believe it to be... Images provide 'openings' into the trans-historical world. ...Thanks to them, the different 'histories' can inter-communicate.*[5]

Beyond each personal or cultural inflection of a symbol lies the universal *Mysterium* to which it refers. And yet, although this *Numinosum* manifests itself in all cultures and for all to see, no one culture can make exclusive claims to its symbolic representation. Each cultural symbol of the Sacred, while being unique, constitutes only one such epiphany. By necessity, the hierophany will always be reduced down to a certain time and place. And, what is more, the epiphany contained in each culture's symbolic work of art will, by necessity, be reduced once more, since it only reveals itself to individuals. It is only *we*, born in a particular time and place, who bring our feelings to these works of art – feelings borne from *this* life as lived *uniquely* – who are then able to *enter through* those images to their interior unity. We may do this, in our times, by thinking once more in accord with the ancient image-language.

II. The Symbol that Conceals

Truth *"as was primordially surmised in the* oldest *tradition of ancient philosophy,"*[6] Heidegger says, is *a-létheia*, the *'un-concealing'* of something's existence. That is to say, the etymology of the Greek word for 'truth', *alétheia*, derives from the privation *a-* ('un-') of the Greek word *lanthanei* ('to conceal'). Hence, a *true* work of art *un-conceals* its subject.

By this same token, a work of art may also *conceal* (*lanthanei*) that which it seeks to reveal. Yet, such *"entities have not been completely hidden,"* Heidegger says. *"They are precisely the sort of thing which has been uncovered* [by images], *but at the same time, they have been disguised..."*[7]

'Truth', in the more archaic sense of *a-létheia*, is a two-edged sword: not only may a mythic image *unconceal* whatever is holy; unfortunately, it may also *conceal – cover over, disguise*, even *bury* it ...until it is quite forgotten. As such, the fixed paths in our image-thinking – due to the cultural images we've inherited from our past – have resulted in our own cultural myth covering over, disguising, even burying over 'the One'.[8]

In his exposition on *Ancient Greek Thinking*, Heidegger cites a fragment from Heraclitus which we have already encountered above: *"The One... is willing and unwilling to be called by the name of Zeus."** In Heidegger's interpretation, this fragment would be better translated as: *"The unique, unifying One is not ready to be assembled under the name of Zeus."*[9] That is to say, the image of Zeus thunder-hurler may evoke a particular aspect of 'the One' but, simultaneously, it disguises other aspects, which thus remain undisclosed.

In this regard, Nietzsche realized all-too-presciently (in a fragment of writing published post-humously) how certain mythic images in our culture have become fixed as *the only* metaphors for truth:

> *Only through forgetfulness can man ever achieve the illusion of possessing a "truth"... What is truth? A mobile army of metaphors, metonyms and anthropomorphisms...which have been enhanced, transposed and embellished poetically and rhetorically, and which after long use seem firm, canonical and obligatory to a people; truths are ...metaphors which are worn out and without sensuous power; coins which have lost their pictures and now matter only as metal, no longer as coins. ...To be truthful means using the customary metaphors.*[10]

Hence, any attempt to fix 'the One' through a single form or metaphor is genuinely misguided. Although these designations, such as 'Thunder-hurling Zeus', 'Thinking a thought of itself thinking', or *'Pater Omnipotens'* may disclose *one* aspect of the Sacred – and that, at a certain time in history – they fail to disclose *all* aspects of the Sacred for *all* time. They become symbols that not only disclose, but disguise...

And so, what Nietzsche criticizes so passionately in this passage is, to be precise, the human-all-too-human tendency *to forget* the source of our metaphysical thinking: to forget that the words, symbols, and even the 'truths' which we now accept in our culture as canonical and firm were once, in truth, fluid images and metaphors. That is to say, symbols as various, vibrant and alive as the mysterious Being which they once named.

III. The Symbol Opening Outward

In his studies into Hindu mythology, Heinrich Zimmer had seen evidence of this historical situation in India. Then, in 1942, he delivered a lecture on this theme, expressing the concern that our age was pressing toward some revelation because we are at the crossroads of so many cultures:

*See page 20.

> *We of the Occident are about to arrive at a crossroads that was reached by the thinkers of India some seven hundred years before Christ. This is the real reason why we become both vexed and stimulated, uneasy yet interested, when confronted by the concepts and images of oriental wisdom. This crossing is one to which the people of all civilizations come in the typical course of the development of their capacity and requirement for religious experience, and India's teachings force us to realize what its problems are. But we cannot take over the Indian solutions. We must enter the new period our own way, and solve its questions for ourselves, because though truth, the radiance of reality, is universally one and the same, it is mirrored variously according to the mediums in which it is reflected. Truth appears differently in different lands and ages according to the living materials out of which its symbols are hewn.*[11]

To escape the Aryan aspirations of Germany during the *Nazi-zeit*, Zimmer fled his homeland and eventually settled in New York. And it was there, in that multi-cultural city, that Zimmer delivered these words before his untimely death two years later. Joseph Campbell happened to be one of the auditors of that lecture, and undertook the task of editing the remaining five volumes of Zimmer's writings before commencing work on his own four volume opus, *The Masks of God.* The title of that work reflected Campbell's own fundamental belief that the mythologies of different cultures were each, in their own unique manner, carefully crafted masks over the inscrutable and unattainable visage of God.

Upon completion of the fourth and final volume, Campbell wrote:

> *Looking back today over the twelve delightful years that I spent on this richly rewarding enterprise, I find that its main result for me has been its confirmation of a thought I have long and faithfully entertained: of the unity of the race of man, not only in its biology, but also in its spiritual history, which has everywhere unfolded in the manner of a single symphony, with its themes announced, developed, amplified and turned about, distorted, reasserted, and, today, in a grand* fortissimo *of all sections sounding together, irresistibly advancing to some kind of mighty climax, out of which the next great movement will emerge. And I can see no reason why anyone should suppose that in the future the same motifs already heard will not be sounding still – in new relationships indeed, but ever the same motifs.*[12]

The key expression in this passage is Campbell's belief that the same mythological motifs will, in the future, be sounding still but *in new relationships.* It evokes the idea of mythic narratives from different cultures crossing into one another, so as to reveal a fundamental unity at their source.

But what is this climactic moment of 'crossing' to which Zimmer and Campbell refer? The 20th century was so preoccupied with war, catastrophe and economic upheaval, forcing people to flee, seek refuge or emigrate to so many other lands, that we may perhaps fail to notice that the cultural crossroads of that century were not only geographical but *historical.*

The 20th century could perhaps be best compared to the Renaissance, in the sense that both times were confronted by the discovery of a previous epoch of profound cultural depth. Artists and philosophers of the Renaissance adapted ancient Greek and Roman models to their own Christian needs, altering their outlook in the process, and thus enhancing and enriching their sacred worldview.

We today have discovered a plethora of cultural epochs of amazing complexity and depth, and are confronted by them at this instant, yet have so far failed to successfully assimilate them into our sacred art and mythology.

To give a few examples, in the early 19th century, Champollion successfully translated the Egyptian hieroglyphs inscribed on the Rossetta Stone, opening up for us the entire mytho-philosophy of the ancient Egyptians. That same century, Grotefend achieved a similar accomplishment with cuneiform script, exposing the ancient Mesopotamian worldview.

Then came a series of archæological discoveries: in Mycenæ: Troy; in Egypt: the Valley of the Kings and Tutankhamun's tomb; in Mesopotamia: Nineveh, Nimrud and Ur; and in Minoan Crete: the temple of Knossos mentioned in Kazantzakis' narrative.

But it was not only the buildings and sculptures of these previous cultures that came to light, revealing a horde of ancient and fantastic imagery. Also of profound significance were the cuneiform tablets, cylinder seals, hieroglyphic texts and papyri which were discovered, deciphered, then translated and published, revealing the metaphors and myths of entire cultural complexes.

Such discoveries continued apace with the *Ras Shamra* texts, unearthed in 1946, and revealing to us Phœnician and Canaanite mythology. Soon thereafter, the first of the *Dead Sea* scrolls to came to light, exposing new aspects of Judaism. And at the same time, the fifty-two codices of the *Nag Hammadi* library were unearthed. These seminal texts, coming only gradually into the public domain, cast a new light onto Gnosticism and the darker side of early Christianity.

It is for this reason that Campbell concluded the last volume of his study on mythology, in the domain of our modern *Creative Mythology*, with the incitation:

> *The norms of myth... through an intelligent 'making use' not of one mythology only, but of all the dead and set-fast symbologies of the past, will enable the individual to anticipate and activate in himself the centres of his own creative imagination, out of which his own myth ...may then unfold.*[13]

IV. The Sacred Life Quest

The resulting vision has already manifest itself in many poetic works. T.S Eliot's *The Wasteland* is a conglomeration of diverse sources, varying from Tarot cards and the Grail legend to the Upanishads and the Buddha's Fire Sermon. The imagery in Leonard Cohen's work moves freely between various mythologies. For example: his *Last Year's Man*, which crosses the Christian *Song of Songs* with the Sumerian *heiros gamos* to arrive at a more ancient image of unity at their source.

> *I came upon a wedding that old families had contrived,*
> *Bethlehem the bridegroom, Babylon the bride.*
> *...And when we fell together, all our flesh was like a veil*
> *That I had to draw aside to see the serpent eats its tail.*[14]

And Yeats, mixing Christianity with eternal recurrence, could ask in *The Second Coming:*

> *...but now I know*
> *That twenty centuries of stony sleep*
> *Were vexed to nightmare by a rocking cradle,*
> *And what rough beast, its hour come round at last,*
> *Slouches towards Bethlehem to be born.*[15]

Anyone who has read the works of these poets may be simultaneously mesmerized and dismayed by the beauty, depth and scope of these creations. Their beauty is manifest for all to see, but understanding and interpreting them seems a daunting task. In this regard, one of Hermann Hesse's characters could rightly declaim:

> *And all at once I felt a repugnance against the whole business, this cult of mythologies, this mosaic game...playing with fragments of traditional religious beliefs.*[16]

Zimmer and Campbell were also wary of this tendency, and each in his own turn appended the above passages with the following injunctions. First, Zimmer:

> *Through all of these* [symbols], *a transcendent reality is mirrored. They are so many metaphors reflecting and implying something which, though thus variously expressed, is ineffable, though thus rendered multiform, remains inscrutable. Symbols hold the mind to truth but are not themselves the truth, hence it is delusory to borrow them. Each civilization, every age, must bring forth its own. ...We cannot borrow God. We must affect his new incarnation from within ourselves.*[17]

And Campbell:

> *In this life-creative adventure the criterion of achievement will be, as in every one of the tales here reviewed, the courage to let go the past... to die to the world, and to come to birth from within.*[18]

At present, the mythology of the Occident lacks the necessary 'catholicism' (i.e., universality and wholeness – from the Latin *catholicus* – universal; and the Greek *kata* – completely, and *holis* – whole) to embrace our contemporary experience of the world. This does not mean that our Christian tradition should be dismissed out of hand as outmoded and old-fashioned. After two thousand years, it is our culture's only true inheritence. And its figures remain a rich source of inspiration, as is evidenced by the masterpieces of art and music to which it gave rise over the course of its history, and which may still be experienced today as a momentary awakening.

Our task, then, is to *revive* the symbols of Christianity, which have been placed in museums side by side with the reliques of other forgotten cultures. To revive these symbols means, in part, to overcome the reluctance to engage them imaginatively and, in part, to juxtapose them in relationships with figures from *other* mythologies – necessarily expanding their qualities, and opening them outward to 'pagan' and other more ancient influences.

V. Combining Symbols
& Crossing Myths

An invitation has been given to us. In the words of the reclusive Canadian poet and mystic, Leonard Cohen: *"Let us compare mythologies."*

In Fantastic and Visionary Art, we meet with examples where sacred symbols are juxtaposed, causing their associated myths to coalesce. Particularly in the works of Ernst Fuchs, many instances of 'crossed myths' occur, as has already been demonstrated by his work *Moses Before the Burning Bush*. A similar such event occurs in an earlier canvas called *The Veil of Veronica*. Here, the symbol of the veil evokes two different mythic contexts, and so two different narratives – both of them Christian – cross one another, causing two sacred moments to coalesce.

While describing his work, Fuchs mentions both narratives explicitly:

> *The painting* The Veil of Veronica, *wiping blood and perspiration from Christ's brow, becomes a veritable icon of suffering. The great curtain of the Temple tears at the moment of death on the cross.*[19]

Hence, on the one hand, we have Nicodemus' fifth century legend of Veronica bathing the blood and sweat from Christ's brow as he fell on the path to Golgotha, and thus receiving an image of Christ's face on the veil; a *vera icona* (true image) which, though acquired that moment, was to remain for all eternity. On the other hand, Luke reveals that, at the terrible moment of Christ's death, *"the curtain of the temple was torn in two."* (Lk 23:45)

What we see in this painting is Veronica's veil but, like the veil of the temple, it is rent from top to bottom – thus evoking the two different myths simultaneously. The message here is that Christ is an eternal image, a symbol of suffering and awakening, and yet we shall only see through the veil, and rent it from top to bottom, when we *enter through his image.*

While *Veronica's Veil* mixes two Christian myths, other works such as *Moses before the Burning Bush* and *Job and the Judgement of Paris* (which we shall examine next chapter) mix the myths of *different* cultures. It is particularly in combinations of this type that our horizon expands beyond our own cultural symbols to embrace a broader yet more unified vision of the Sacred. What are we now to make of such images?

Since a painting freezes one moment in time seemingly forever, this moment can now be seen to exist simultaneously in two different mythic narratives. Though myths themselves, through the unfolding of their narratives, arrange events in linear or cyclic time, certain events can be freed from their temporal flow and then combined in a work of art, so that they transpire *simultaneously* in the one moment of time frozen still in the painting. That moment, since it is held still seemingly forever, becomes a doorway into the eternal *mythic time.* As such, two different cultural myths, each with its series of images arranged in linear or cyclic time, can be seen to meet at that one timeless moment *where the entire series of images coalesce.*

Such a point would obviously not be just anywhere, but more likely at the nadir of a narrative, where a Threshold Image arises. While Cosmogonic myths offer us Threshold Images at 'the Beginning' or 'the End', Hero myths offer us Threshold Images at the moment of the hero's departure (separation), return (re-union), and – most importantly – at the moment of his nadir-initiation (epiphany).

Particularly at the nadir of sacred Hero myths, the saviour breaks out of the bounding course of linear or cyclic time and *momentarily* experiences the eternal *mythic time.* In the example given earlier, Adam falling and Christ rising are two different Threshold Images which were combined, so that the

Ernst Fuchs: The Veil of Veronica (1953)

series of events in their different myths *coalesced into one myth,* which is now commonly accepted as our cultural myth (the Celestial Saviour myth).

However, a painting could similarly envision a moment in time where the entire series of events in Christ and the Buddha's myth would cross over and coalesce. But this attempt to cross figures from different mythologies must not be undertaken merely as an intellectual exercise, *'a mosaic game ...playing with fragments of traditional religious beliefs,'* as Hesse has said.

It arises rather out of a necessity that is both personal and cultural. In the case of the former, the figures of Christianity are not in themselves sufficient for encapsulating the plethora of feelings arising from personal experience. They fail to reflect our present circumstances, and lack modern, more timely metaphors.

In such times of dire need, as we come up against one of life's thresholds, a figure from another mythology may be sought as that key-image capable of unlocking the otherwise unreleased flow of feeling. Such key-images may not only borrow *figures* from other mythologies, but may even depict a recognizable figure from Christianity now enacting the *event* of another myth – a different cultural mythologem.

And so, on the middlemost spirals of our own memory, not just Christian symbols, but those of other cultures and mythologies may offer us new pathways to tread in the resolution of our conflicts. As we *enter through* new combinations of images, 'the eternal Hero myth of the soul' is, for a fleeting moment, made complete. We come to behold a more ancient image of the Sacred – and, a more sacred unfolding of life itself.

This step from personal memory-images to the collective icons of other cultures is undertaken, not only by Visionary artists, but by *all of us*. Due to a certain life-conflict, the spontaneous recollection of personal memories throws us, almost against our will, onto the Symbolic Path. Dreams and fantasies spring up of their own accord, and we have no choice but to follow their spiralling paths into the depths of our memory. As such, each of us pursues the Symbolic Path ever further through the endless labyrinth. But it is particularly the vocation of the Visionary artist to leave behind, for the succeeding generations, the outward signs of his inward journey.

In the case of cultural necessity, which may indeed be the historical moment in which we find ourselves situated, the figures of Christianity are not sufficient unto themselves to deliver our culture from its current situation. For we find ourselves, after two thousand years, still awaiting the moment of the Apocalypse, when a Virgin shall finally appear in the heavens bearing a child, and the dragon with seven heads will arise threateningly from the depths. Do we still, as a culture, believe that time will end in this manner, and that Christ will return thus 'to make all things anew'? Are we still, in this way, marking time with our cultural images, while ignoring their inherent epiphanies?

Despite their ancient inhering wisdom, our inherited forms have failed to deliver us from our present spiritual predicament. As Jung noted, *"Christianity slumbers and has neglected to develop its myth further in the course of the centuries."*[20] Symbols from other cultures have been sought instead, and substituted as more timely, relevant and meaningful.

Hence, out of a need that is both personal and cultural, we combine existing symbols in new and ever more creative ways. In order to rediscover the ancient significance reposing still in *all* cultural symbols, we seek out, not just one, but any and all symbols from the past that offer us new paths to our own life-fulfillment. In the Visionary works of art that have emerged over the past century, this tendency will become abundantly clear...

CHAPTER XII

Symbols in Modern Visionary Art

The artist looks beneath the flux of everyday reality,
and sees eternal, unchanging symbols.
– Nikos Kazantzakis[1]

I. What is Visionary Art?

Where the Surrealists tried to elevate the dream-state into a higher reality (and opposed the use of narcotics), Visionary artists use all means at their disposal – even at great risk to themselves – to access different states of consciousness and expose the resulting vision. Visionary Art attempts to show what lies *beyond* the boundary of sight. Through dream, meditation, entheogens, trance and other altered states, these artists attempt to *see the unseen* – attaining a visionary state that transcends our regular modes of perception. The task awaiting them, thereafter, is to communicate their vision in a form recognizable to 'everyday sight'.

All Visionary artists are united by this spirit of on-going experimentation. And their works bear testimony to those mind-altering, soul-shattering but potentially enlightening experiences which may transpire over the course of each creative experiment in painting.

Among the eldest of the Visionaries still alive and practising his art today is Ernst Fuchs. *"I have always been drawn towards things which man cannot see from the exterior,"* he has written. *"And I have always practised a kind of art which depicts things that, otherwise, man only sees in his dreams or hallucinations. For me, the threshold has to be crossed from inner images to their expression in wakeful being – the transformation of dreams and fantasy into the world of reality and its plane of visual imagery."*[2]

Many of Fuchs' students have gone on to pursue visionary themes in their works. This is particularly true of Mati Klarwein, De Es Schwertberger and Robert Venosa. In the company of other artists such as Johfra, H. R. Giger, Alex Grey, Martina Hoffmann and Maura Holden, a veritable movement in Visionary art has gradually emerged, characterized by the pursuit of nightmares, visions and dreams in painstaking techniques of classical precision.

II. Circuitous Paths of Imagery

While each sacred symbol, when viewed in isolation, offers us a doorway to the Divine; a series of such symbols, when arranged into a work of art, offers us instead a labyrinth with many possible turnings and unexpected passages. Especially in modern works of Visionary art, the symbols of old are encountered in new and unexpected combinations, creating their own Symbolic Path to the Sacred. This is particularly true of the Visionary works of Fuchs and Johfra, whose circuitous paths of imagery we shall pursue in depth over the following pages.

By combining two symbols into a singular work of art, an image-cluster is created which 'betrays some kind of recognizable meaning and arrangement'. Hence, it betrays the hidden presence of an underlying iconologue which, in this case, we may call the Combination Iconologue.

But, it is not enough to bring the two symbols together in a work of art; we must also learn how to *think through their combination* in light of their ultimate origin in 'the One'. Especially in Visionary works of art, many symbols of different cultural origin are combined into a single and unified vision of the Sacred.

This occurs in two possible ways, depending on the symbols' context or lack of context in a myth.

In the first case, the two symbols may be combined, yet they would remain impossible to read because they still require their associated myths. Hence, we must locate each symbol in the context of its own myth, and see whether it arises as a Threshold Image at the beginning, nadir, or end. Then, the symbols and their associated narratives may be combined in light of 'the eternal Hero journey of the soul'.

Does one symbol offer us a fall, departure or separation from the One, while the other offers instead a re-union or return? Then, they may be combined if we *cross* their myths: we set out on one narrative fragment, and return along the other.

Or, do both symbols offer us a moment of awakening at the mythic nadir? Then, the two myths may cross when they meet each other at *that* point – at the mythic nadir where a Threshold Image arises.

In any case, all these combinations of symbols and the crossing of their myths offer us the same thing: a series of variations on 'the eternal Hero myth of the soul'. And, as such, they all follow the Mythic Path to the centre of the spiralling labyrinth. We shall follow this path while elucidating Fuchs' work, *Job and the Judgement of Paris.*

In the second case, the two symbols combined in a work of art may be read *independently* of their mythic narratives, because they resonate with a symbolic power all their own. Now, it is the symbols themselves and their Symbolic Path which we may trace through the eternal labyrinth. We use the more ancient manner of 'symbolic thinking' to transcend the similarities and differences in light of their higher unity. After Fuchs, we shall follow this Symbolic Path through Johfra's *Gemini* painting from his Zodiac series.

III. Job and the Judgement of Paris

Fuchs' *Job and the Judgement of Paris*, despite its ornate architectural programme and plethora of figures, depicts the Hebrew hero Job as judge in the contest for feminine beauty between three Greek goddesses. Upon first viewing, this may not be immediately apparent. Indeed, it is only the title and a knowledge of the myths to which it refers which orient the viewer through this work. Hence, the symbols must be situated in their mythic contexts to be understood.

In his book *Architectura Cælestis*[3] Fuchs describes his early years in Paris, when the painter was poor and struggling. His various marriages and affairs did not help his situation, since he fathered children in each of his relationships. Meanwhile, his artistic and spiritual aspirations remained unfulfilled. In 1957 he fled to Israel and, for six months, lived in the benedictine Monastery of the Dormition on Mount Zion (where, incidentally, he painted *Moses Before the Burning Bush*). The abbot accepted him as a 'brother painter' but, due to his obligations to his families (four children from three women), Fuchs' requests to become a monk were denied. He returned to Vienna, founded a new family, and subsequently became a painter of world-renown.

The figure of Job thus became for him a personal as well as cultural symbol of spiritual suffering. But this painting offers us the Judaic hero in a very different cultural context. In his quest to behold the supreme God through suffering and awakening, Job encounters instead three very voluptuous images of the Eternal Feminine. In his own spiritual quest, the artist, like the Greek hero Paris, had to confront the Goddess in three of her aspects before he could successfully embrace the Sacred. Through personal experience, different symbols from Judaic and Greek myth came alive and, through life's greater awakening, these symbols combined to reveal a broader vision of the Sacred.

As such, if we were to envision this painting on the Ancient Template, we would follow their Mythic Path through the spiralling clouds to 'the One' at the centre. That path, it may be recalled, uses 'the eternal Hero myth of the soul' to cross different narrative fragments. In this case, the soul's fall from 'the One' would be imagined through the Judaic myth of Job: his fall from God's favour, and the many tests (both of the spirit and the flesh) he had to undergo before beholding God at the nadir.

And yet, that nadir-moment of revelation crosses over, in this painting, with the nadir moment of the Greek myth, where Paris had to decide which, among the three goddesses, was the most beautiful. As such, he came face to face, not only with the Hebrew God, but the Greek Goddess in the tripartite form of her beauty. And it was only then, after the Sacred had revealed itself as both God and Goddess in combination, that the hero could re-ascend; that the soul of man could continue on its spiritual quest for union with the Divine.

IV. The Hidden Prime of Styles

While beholding the eternally Sacred in a vision, the Visionary artist frees himself momentarily from his inherited spiritual tradition, with its particular cultural symbols and styles of expression. During that momentary epiphany, his vision partakes of the universal, *sans* cultural perspective: it acquires a stilled, more timeless, even eternal way of seeing. This extraordinary way of seeing is also manifest in the strange stare on the faces of Babylonian and Greek sculptures: their elongated eyes, opened wide, absorbing a vision without horizon. They are beholding the eternal.

But, the moment the artist attempts to render this expanded vision, he is caught once more in the currents of his own time, its style of rendering bound by perspective and finite perception. The resulting image betrays his age's fashion, its preference for a certain line, form and proportion, while still revealing – above and beyond it – the timeless shape, the divine symmetry briefly glimpsed from a higher world.

Ernst Fuchs realized that, behind the temporal and cultural styles of different epochs, there lies *'ein verschollener Stil'* – a 'hidden prime of styles': *"A secret art whose traces I have discovered with almost all people and cultures, but also in nature itself – there where the primæval world appears... like a notion, a memory of the submersed culture of a long passed, unmeasured time which preceded history."*[4]

As such, while Visionary works of art have emerged throughout history in different lands, epochs and cultures, a more ancient, primordial, indeed *eternal* style of rendering silently underlies all the historical periods of its development. Visionary art seeks to return us, in our visions, to the primordial world *that preceded history* – like hieroglyphs leading us back to a paradise of lost imagery and forgotten symbols.

Ernst Fuchs: Job and the Judgement of Paris, detail (1966)

Where 'the ancient prime of styles' left its greatest traces in the West, first of all, in the 'pure' or clearly-defined styles of the Egyptians, Babylonians and Greeks, it also re-appeared later in the personal styles of certain Visionary artists – except the 'pure' cultural styles of the past now re-appear inextricably *mixed* with one another.

It is particularly true of the greatest Visionary artists of the Occident – Michelangelo, Blake, Moreau – that the ancient cultural styles *resurface* – subtly invoked, turned about, re-asserted, and then merging harmoniously with one another into a single, personal style which, though shared, remains unique. In many of his works, Fuchs also demonstrates an uncanny ability to combine *different cultural styles of representation*. His broad figures with constant profiles evoke the more monumental style of the Babylonians. Meanwhile, his slender figures with their tortured expressions evoke the Gothic.

This combination of different cultural styles betrays a more culturally diverse and temporally expanded vision of the Sacred. Such a vision may also lead to the combination of different cultural images and symbols. And such is certainly the case with the Dutch Visionary painter Franciscus Johannnes Gijsbertus van den Berg, who was known, more simply, as Johfra.

V. The Gemini

In his series of twelve Zodiac paintings, Johfra reveals a marked tendency to combine different cultural symbols, but now from various Hermetic traditions. Since these symbols resonate with a sacred power all their own, they create their own course through the spiralling labyrinth: the Symbolic Path.

From Johfra's writings, it becomes clear that the painter combined these symbols in an attempt to think further through them:

> *The sphere of influence of symbols broadens and deepens into infinite Being when they enter* into combination with one another. *Then they have a decisive influence upon one another in a most illuminating way. In brief: a symbol, for those who can meditate upon it and lose themselves in it,* is like a door *offering entrance into a new spaces and dimensions of consciousness.*[5]

In his *Gemini* painting, numerous symbols from different Hermetic traditions combine into a single totality. The Twins, for example, are taken from astrology (and, as such, lack any associated narrative). Yet their stance, holding between them Mercury's *caduceus*, recalls an image from alchemy: the *Mysterium Coniunctionis*, in which the male and female principles shall, like the entwining serpents, be combined.

But, with the serpents between them, the twins also evoke the Hebrew image of Adam and Eve – the fall they wrought upon themselves, and the long-awaited hope to rise again. Adam's gesture of pointing heavenward and Eve's of pointing earthward invokes not only this myth, but also recalls the alchemical expression 'As above so below'.*

*Johfra explains their gestures in light of this expression, which is to be found in *The Emerald Tablet of Hermes*: "*What is above is like what is below. What is below is like what is above... Everything is formed from the contemplation of unity, and all things come from unity.*"[6]

Johfra: The Gemini (1975)
From the Zodiac Series

Below them sits the God Thoth in his baboon form (the *cynoscephalus*), which is the Egyptian equivalent of Mercury (a god of knowledge and initiation). And beside them stand the male and female figures of the Fool and Temperance from the Tarot's Major Arcana (images which, once again, lack any associated myth). Meanwhile, the red and blue pillars are a reference to the Chokmah and Binah pillars of the Kabbala, as masculine and feminine principles. They are crowned with the baton and the cup (each a suit from the Tarot's Minor Arcana) and, above them, the sun and moon – symbols once more of the masculine and feminine.

Arranged along the left and right of the canvas, all of these images symbolize *opposite* aspects of the Sacred, as its male and female principles. As such, they place greater emphasis on 'difference', and describe the cosmos as so many differing, indeed, opposite expressions of 'the One' at its centre.

Meanwhile, the series of images along the middle axis place greater emphasis on 'similarity', as they are all symbols of the male and female *opposites-in-union*. This begins with the entwining snakes of the *caduceus*, and ascends to the entwining dragons. Then, in that same constellation of images, we behold the alchemical symbols of the two-headed eagle and the *hermaphroditus*. All of these symbols, arising from a variety of Hermetic traditions, unite opposites into a singular expression of the Sacred.

The hidden presence of this ancient unity may be imagined in the circular mirror atop the *caduceus*. Situated at the centre of the composition, it *reflects* all the different forms, containing them all in its circle and hence, unifying them at their centre. In our consciousness, we must attempt a similar reflection of the totality of images. By thinking symbolically, considering them in light of their similarities and differences, the greater unity underlying their diversity may gradually emerge.

Hence, if we now envision these arrangements of images on the Ancient Template, the Symbolic Path they create slowly becomes clear. By looking to the left and right of the painting, we behold 'the One' as divided into its unique, male and female aspects. And yet, by turning our glance to the middle, we behold *combinatory* images of those male and female aspects in union. Essentially, it is the *differences* that separate 'the One' into its multiple aspects, while the *similarities* combine them once more into the unity at their source.

Beginning a meditation on the symbols located on the periphery of the painting, we see the arrangement in terms of its difference: male is separate from female, (as is left from right and above from below). And so, through these images a kind of creation myth occurs, in which the One divides into the many along the Chain of Being. This transpires, first of all, in the cosmos as a whole – the division of the sun and moon; the heavens and the earth (as indicated 'above and below'). This is followed by its division into human forms – the male and female figures from the Tarot; the celestial Twins of astrology; and the fall they undergo in the form of Adam and Eve.

As it continues to divide into gender opposites, the One descends further into primæval creatures and principles: the two dragons with their tails wrapped around the Chokmah and Binah pillars. And finally, simple objects also reflect this division: the phallic baton and womb-like cup of the Tarot. All reflect the One, the circular mirror at the centre, as it has divided itself along the entire chain of being into male and female opposites. As such, they emphasize difference, while still manifesting the unity underlying the multiplicity.

But, as we concentrate on the images along the central axis, a new path is offered us in our thinking. For, all these central images stress the similarities, offering more combinatory symbols of the masculine and feminine *opposites-in-union*. And as we *enter through* them in succession, we follow their Symbolic Path up the Chain of Being to the ultimate source of creation.

The entwined serpents, dragons and eagles offer us more primordial and animalistic images of unity. Moving from crawling to winged beings, these figures slowly ascend the evolutionary ladder of vision. The entwining serpents – instinctually, in darkness and unknowing – reflect the One. As such, they offer a more primordial vision of unity. Still, as we *enter through* their image, the serpents transform, acquire wings, and become like the two dragons. As 'serpents with wings', the two dragons offer us a 'higher' vision of unity.

Then, as their wings expand, the dragons merge into the two-headed eagle. Soaring freely across the heavens, seeing all 'from above', the two-headed eagle reflects the One from an even higher plane. Finally, as the highest link in the evolutionary chain stands man and woman, each reflecting an aspect of the Sacred in their own unique way.

But here, they are presented in the form of the alchemical *hermaphroditus*. Their union symbolizes the *Mysterium Coniuntionis,* the alchemical attainment of highest knowledge. As such, they consciously and knowingly reflect the One's unity. And so, as we *enter through* this image into a 'knowing' union with the Sacred, it is now understood as the *Unio Oppositorum,* as the union of God and Goddess in the One.

As Johfra himself made explicit in his description of this work:

> *In the representation of the Gemini sign, I have especially stressed duality, and used the problem of duality as its main motif... The task is to find their Unity. Therefore, the painting is built up symmetrically. Everything positive is right; everything negative is left, and arranged on various levels... The two poles come together when duality finds its solution in Unity.*[7]

VI. The Unio Mystica

Without a doubt, Johfra's *chef d'œuvre* is a triptych entitled *Unio Mystica*.
This work is an amazing amalgamation of sacred images, all betokening the
inexplicable One that lies at their innermost centre. The whole emerges as
a *monas hieroglyphica* – a 'sacred sign' (*heiroglyph*) of 'the One' (*monad*).
To express this interior unity, Johfra had recourse to Christian, Buddhist,
Egyptian, Taoist, even Nordic iconographies. Though viewed separately, like
so many vignettes in stained glass, these figures may also coalesce into one
image, and then be *entered through* to the single light shining behind them.

A prolonged meditation upon the *Unio Mystica* would reveal to the
beholder, ultimately, the ancient One underlying all these images from their
disparate traditions. It would also offer him a vision of the unity from whence
the contemplative himself first emerged and to which he will ultimately
return. This, in any case, is the ancient worldview mentioned by Johfra as the
inspiration for his work:

> The emergence of all things from the unchanging, absolute
> and divine One is the essence of Neo-Platonic teachings. All things
> emanated from this One, appearing in their multiplicity in the lower
> levels of emanation...
> The things of nature are thus imperfect and incomplete. But
> each does have within it the slumbering remembrance of the original
> archetype after which it was created. And through the beauty of its form,
> a thing reflects this perfect form. The aspiration in each created thing is
> to rise to a higher level. This is manifest in the attempt to release itself
> from space and time, and so, enclose its original essence within the safe
> shelter of that divine One from which it first emanated.[8]

In his *Unio Mystica*, we have a series of images through which we, in
our meditations, may rise up, remember, and ultimately enclose ourselves in
the Divine. Were we to meditate upon this composition, our task would be
to *enter through* its various symbols to their transcendent unity. The circular
composition becomes our first clue: it brings together the many disparate
parts and unites them onto a common centre. The multiplicity of images have
thus been arranged into so many co-centric circles moving inward to the
centre. Our meditation would end, thus, with a vision of the unified whole,
seeing the unity within the totality.

VII. The Vision of Paradise

The Book of Revelation tells us that we shall see the world transformed
at the end of time – see it with our own eyes, but in a more permanent state
of vision. This world 'made anew' is compared to a heavenly city, the
New Jerusalem: *"Its radiance like a most rare jewel, like a jasper clear as
crystal."*(Rev 20:11) Its twelve gates are of sapphire, agate, emerald, onyx,
topaz, and amethyst. They shine with the radiance of pearls, pure gold, and

Johfra: Unio Mystica, detail of central panel (1973)

are *"transparent as glass."* (Rev 21:21) A river *"bright as crystal"* (Rev 22:1) flows through it, and at its centre stands the tree of life, its twelve fruits, each ripening a different month, offering a balm and a healing.

This is the higher world – visible to all of us once (before the creation), and to be witnessed again (after the apocalypse) – a paradise presently hidden, a world which Visionary artists have sought and seen – if only in stolen glances...

In his books *The Doors of Perception* and *Heaven and Hell*, Aldous Huxley has described his visions of paradise which emerged after taking mescaline. He relates that *"Everything... is brilliantly illuminated and seems to shine from within."*[9] In a similar way, Fuchs has commented at length how, after the ingestion of hashish, he marvelled at *"mountains of shining gorgeous stones with a shimmering light on them. Everything was translucent and seemed to glow from within."*[10]

As a rapid flow of eidetic imagery passed before him, Huxley reported, *"...vast and complicated buildings in the midsts of landscapes which change continuously, passing from richness to more intensely coloured richness, from grandeur to deepening grandeur. Heroic figures... fabulous animals..."*[11] The author also mentioned heavenly architecture composed of precious stones, gem-like pigments, glowing gold, swirling marble and remarked upon *"the beauty of curved reflections, of softly lustrous glazes, of sleek and smooth surfaces."*[12]

In Fuchs' *Job and the Judgement of Paris*, we have seen, not only this architectural complexity, but also 'the beauty of curved reflections, of sleek and smooth surfaces' just mentioned by Huxley...

Bosch too delighted in polished stone and metal, and moreover, in their strange, hybrid forms, such as appears in his fountain from *The Garden of Earthly Delights*. Here *mineralia*, *vegetalia* and *animalia* – their various textures and surfaces – are strangely *displaced* from one to the other. Plants seem made of stone, while architectural devices acquire an organic quality.

Bosch's triptych may be understood as three visions of the same garden: in its highest form, it is a paradise – offering a perfect and timeless way of seeing which, alas, we have lost due to the fall. In the middle, this way of seeing visibly degenerates into a garden of fleeting, earthly delights, pleasing to the eye but lacking in timeless perfection. And finally, in its lowest form, the garden becomes a hell of endless torment, where vision is shrouded forever in darkness and continually distracted by infinite demonic inventions.

In Bosch's Visionary opus, and in Fuchs and Johfra's more modern masterpieces, the world we share behind the eyes is momentarily made visible. By fixing our gaze onto these works, meditating upon them with a focussed regard and concentrated vision, our restless eye and distracted mind may finally *come to rest*, and a more perfect, indeed timeless way of seeing may momentarily be regained...

Hieronymus Bosch:
Detail of fountain
from The Garden
of Earthly Delights

CHAPTER XIII

The Mythologem of Death and Rebirth

There is rebirth, and an image of rebirth.
It is certainly necessary that one should be
reborn through the image.
– Gospel of Philip (67:12)[1]

Be not yet born, be in the womb,
be young, old, dead, beyond death.
And when you have understood these
all at once,
...then you can understand God.
– Corpus Hermeticum (XI, 20)[2]

I. The Hero Suffering in Transfixion:
A Sample Mythologem

Our cultural icon of Christ crucified finds its symbolic equivalent in many other cultures, such as the Greek god Prometheus bound to the cliff-rock, or Ixion tied to an ever-turning wheel, or Odysseus lashed to the mast of his ship as it rows past the sirens.

But Nordic mythology also offers us images of the sacred hero 'suffering in transfixion' with Odin hanging from the world ash *'for nights full nine'* to learn the secret of the runes. Nor should we forget the Tarot card of *The Hanged Man*. And, more ancient than these, Sumerian myth offers us the surprising image of the goddess Inanna, trapped in the underworld as a corpse 'hung upon a spike'.

A distinct similarity exists among these images, be it of crucifixion, binding or hanging. All betoken the notion of self-sacrifice, though the meaning of this sacrifice may vary from culture to culture. Nevertheless, the presence of such deeds in a multitude of mythologies suggests that it is the *symbolic action or event*, and not the particular hero who enacts it, which manifests the Sacred in some way.

We shall call such symbolic actions 'Mythologems', meaning that a certain action or event, regardless of its particular place, time or hero, is seen to recur in a variety of contexts, be they myths, works of art or even dreams. Any arrangement of images manifesting this symbolic action or event manifests the hidden presence of 'the Mythologem Iconologue'.

The Greek word *mythologéma* means literally 'a mythical narrative'. Kerényi used the word 'mythologem' to mean the basic mythic motifs (i.e. narrative fragments) which undergo transformations as they pass from the mythology of one culture to another. Such motifs involve

> *...a particular kind of material contained in tales about gods and god-like beings, heroic battles and journeys to the underworld – 'mythologem' is the best Greek word for them – tales already well-known but not unamenable to further reshaping. Mythology is the movement of this material...capable of transformation.*[3]

For us, a mythologem has this adaptable quality, but refers specifically to mythic actions or deeds. There are many kinds of mythologems – *coniunctio*, baptism, *descensus ad inferos*, battling a monster, heavenly ascent – to name but a few. Typically, the most important mythologem occurs at the nadir of a myth. The resulting Threshold Image manifests, not only a *symbol* (the hero himself), but also a *mythologem* (the hero-deed).

Sacred art preserves this event in cultural memory, while the deed itself is repeated forward through time by sacred rituals. While the first enactment of this deed transpired in the eternal *mythic time*, all later ritual re-enactments in mundane time will be used either to repeatedly measure time forward to its end, or to transport their actor back to that more timeless moment which first transpired 'in the beginning'.

II. The Mythologem of Death & Rebirth

Death is not an experience in life. But it is precisely this experience that the Visionary artist tries, with all the skill and powers of his artistry, to portray. He depicts death in its terrifying, ego-shattering forms, as images for us to *enter through*. Such indeed is the case with many of the deeply moving depictions of Christ's crucifixion accumulated throughout the Christian tradition.

Quetzalcoatl as The Lord of Life and Death (front - Huaxtec c. 1100)

Each of these passionately rendered symbols, were we to succeed in passing through them, would result in the momentary evocation of our own death.

In Meso-American art and mythology, a symbol similar to the crucified Christ appears in Quetzalcoatl, 'the lord of life and death'. In one rendering, a free-standing statue reveals his life-giving aspect on the front, while on the back his deathly aspect appears in the form of a skeleton. The image of the skull or skeleton is particularly pervasive in Aztec art, and reveals itself thereby as an archetypal image of death. So too is the skeletal figure of the Buddha in the extremes of his asceticism, and the mummified form of Osiris in the Egyptian tradition. All these 'Images of Death' are, ultimately, symbolic doorways. Yet, *to enter through such an image*, and successfully cross its threshold, requires that we experience within ourselves *the feeling of our own death.*

When we situate each of these images of death in the context of their narratives, a most important shift in their meaning occurs. In all these cases – Christ, Quetzalcoatl, Osiris – we see that their deaths were later followed by an experience of resurrection or rebirth. Adonis, Dionysis, Damuzi – these and many others were all 'dying and rising Sons of the Abyss'.

The myth of the dying/rising god is found in a fascinating variety of cultures, and so arranges its succession of images that no 'Image of Death' is left to stand without being immediately followed upon by an 'Image of Resurrection and Rebirth'. This creates one of the most interesting of all mythologems: *the mythologem of death and rebirth.*

We have already felt its presence in more ancient cultures. Whether it be the rising and setting sun, the waxing and waning moon, or the morning and the evening star, the mythologem remains the same. Its presence allowed the Near-Eastern myth of 'the ever-dying/rising Son of the Abyss' to cross over with the Hebrew myth of 'the Messiah' to eventually become the Christian saviour. The mythologem of death and rebirth recurs in almost all mythologies in all times.[4]

So, according to the most ancient of our myths, there is no death unless later accompanied by some form of resurrection or rebirth. To be more specific, in linear-historical time, death is followed by resurrection while, in ever-repeating

Quetzalcoatl as
The Lord of Life and Death
(back - Huaxtec c. 1100)

cycles of time, it is followed by rebirth. (For the sake of convenience, we shall henceforth include 'resurrection' under the term of 'rebirth'). Never is death seen to be the ultimate end of things.

Bearing this in mind, the mythologem of death and rebirth is of particular importance because each of its images constitutes a Threshold Image – a unique doorway for us to *enter through* in our meditations. As a mythologem, it describes that symbolic movement from death to rebirth which occurs repeatedly, regardless of any particular hero, place or time. As such, it is open to *anyone* who would attempt to *enter through* its mythic movement to a momentary revelation of the Sacred.

For this reason, the mythologem of death and rebirth is used in the rites of many cultures to initiate the neophyte into an ego-shattering epiphany. In Christianity, for example, the ritual of baptism was inaugurated by John the Baptist when he plunged Jesus into the Jordan. Contrary to traditional Christian renderings, this baptism may have been, as it was and is in more primordial cultures, a ritual experience of near-drowning. Through the panic-stricken feeling of death-by-drowning, followed by a sharp intake of breath, a re-experience of one's own birth is evoked. The intense feelings of fear and panic thus return us, in our memory, to the trauma of life's *first* threshold crossing.

In our journey through the Ancient Template, we have used the researches of depth psychology to trace a particular feeling *backward* through our personal and collective memory-images – resulting, finally, in a rare moment of epiphany as we *entered through* symbolic images of the divine child to our life's earliest moments.

But is it possible to trace a particular feeling, such as *fear*, all the way back *into the darkest depths* of our memory? Can we recall, not just the earliest moments of infancy, but even our own birth?

III. The Paths of Light & Darkness

When we look through the variety of symbols left to us in religious works throughout the ages, it immediately becomes apparent that, for each work of beauty and bliss, there is another, equal work of agony and terror. The most visionary of artists in our European heritage did not hesitate to record images of exquisite torment among their other works so ecstatic with joy.

Hence, although Bosch could paint the amazingly mystical image of a soul passing through a tunnel of light, he also depicted, in amazing detail, all the darknesses of Hell. Grünewald's resurrected saviour is a floating figure enhaloed by a blazing aura. Yet, never has there been a more contorted, enthorned, plague-bound figure of death than his crucified Christ.*

*For the image of Grünewald's Christ, see page 91.

Hieronymus Bosch: The Last Judgement (c. 1500)
Left: Visions of Darkness (Detail from the central panel)
Right: Visions of Light (Detail from the right wing)

It is not only the afterworld dualism of Heaven and Hell that separates Christian art into works of light and darkness. *During* his life, Christ experienced forty days' deprivation in the desert, and was tempted and tormented thereby with visions of the devil. Also, his flagellation – stripped bare, crowned with thorns and mocked – as well as his crucifixion – impaled by nail in knowing innocence; hung in humiliation before a jeering, unthinking mob – reveal a darker side to Christ's spiritual awakening. Finally, in the Apocalypse, terrible visions of 'the End of Things' await – plagues, wars, the rule of the false prophet, the emergence of the great whore of Babylon and the seven-headed beast. All of these must be endured before the final cleansing of our vision in the New Jerusalem.

When we turn to other mythologies, the *compendium maleficarum* is no less inventive. Mayan and Aztec imagery is overrun with visions of death and the underworld: bloodsports, beheadings, vision-serpents and plunges into all-devouring flames. So too is Tibetan Buddhism, with its court of Yama Raja and the dead condemned to different domains of demons, where each is a master in his own torturous craft.

When the Buddha left the safe enclosure of his father's palace, the first things he encountered were old age, illness and death. These appeared as a mystery to him: one whose riddle he sought to solve. And so, after leaving his father's palace, he did not hesitate to plunge himself into hunger and suffering, even onto death. And beneath the Bodhi tree, he experienced a terrifying onslaught of demonic tormentors, which he finally endured and dispelled with one upward movement of his open palm.

In classical antiquity, Odysseus, Heracles and Aeneas all had to descend to the underworld (*katabasis eis hadou, descensus ad inferos*) before their own apotheosis or return. Christ also had his 'harrowing of Hell', encountering the horrors of Hades and coming face to face with his darker twin, the Devil. In all of these different traditions, the sacred hero – be he Christ, Quetzalcoatl, Odysseus or the Buddha – has to encounter the horrors of the underworld before his final apotheosis.

These images of horror in their ever-more ingenious contrivances evoke one singular and over-powering emotion – fear. And like joy or pain, *fear* is a feeling which may be traced back ever further in our life, through images that open outward from individual to cultural symbols. The poetry of Rimbaud and the art of Salvador Dalí betray this tendency to seek images that contain ever-greater experiences of horror and revulsion. Dalí's autobiographical writings reveal that many of his images – ant-infested grasshoppers, smears of blood and feces – arose from his earliest childhood memories. These images are the personal and more individual symbols of his infantile fears. But a regression through such individual images of anxiety would ultimately arrive at cultural icons of darkness – expanding outward to embrace the monsters and demons dreamt by entire cultures. This strange but natural tendency in man, following pain and fear ever deeper through his spiralling depths, is what may be referred to as 'the Dark Path'.

In the labyrinth of our own innermost Hell, our fears reveal to us evermore creative images of torment and horror. But what encounter finally awaits us *at the end* of this journey through those images evoked by our greatest fears? Whether it be the West or the East, the mythologies of both cultures render the same timeless message, which we may offer here through the examples of Dante's Divine Comedy and the Kundalini Path of Yoga.

If the three *cantica* of Dante's *Commedia* are taken as a whole, we see that the final aim of the descent (*Inferno*) is a spiritual cleansing (*Purgatorio*) in preparation for the final celestial vision (*Paradiso*). Dante's Beatrice steers the poet, with Virgil's aid, through his soul's innermost depths before lifting him upward to a vision of 'the eternal fountain', leaving Dante to extoll Beatrice with the words:

> *O thou in whom my hopes securely dwell,*
> *And who, to bring my soul to Paradise,*
> *Didst leave the imprint of thy steps in Hell.*[5]

The Commedia is perhaps the finest exemplar in the West of 'the Dark Path', and its final turning towards the light. Gradually penetrating into *a bright expansiveness'*, Dante finally beheld a spiralling vision of the Divine *'in the aureole of the eternal rose'*.

Meanwhile, in the East, a similar vision was obtained by passing through the centre of four-, six-, ten-, and ultimately a thousand-petalled lotus blossom to the divine vision at its centre. According to the Kundalini system of Tantric yoga, the seven stages of release from suffering involve a consciousness of the seven centres of energy in the body, referred to as *'chakras'* (circles) *or 'padmas'* (lotus flowers).

By concentrating on these different 'lotus centres', one experiences the sensation of a serpent rising through the lowest chakra (*Muladhara*) to the highest (*Sahasrara*), and therewith, to an experience of oneness with the all. At the seventh chakra, one's consciousness of one's self, of the world, and of the Sacred, is no longer divided: it is a totality and one, beyond all divisions of form or thought. It is also, according to Tantra, beyond all means of representation in images.

Of greater interest to us, therefore, are the experiences felt at the fifth and sixth chakras. Campbell writes:

> Indian art, I would say, is concerned to suggest and render experiences akin to those of the [different] lotus centres... at [chakra] five, the terrifying, devastating aspects of the cosmic powers in their ego-shattering roles, personified as wrathful, odious, and horrific demons [are represented; and at chakra] six, their bliss-bestowing, fear-dispelling, wondrous, peaceful, and heroic forms.[6]

The Commedia and the Kundalini both reveal that the Dark Path is an independent stage on the way to union with the eternally Sacred. Along the dangerous and dimly-lit meanderings of this path, we encounter the Divine as manifest to us in a darker light. And God manifests himself to us in this manner, so that we may learn to see, in him, the source of all our horror, evil, terror and fear.

If God truly is the source of all creation, then this means pain, suffering and death are necessarily a part of his creation. But more so, if God, the world, and our placement in it are all to be witnessed and experienced *as one*, then evil in its many forms – death, disease and innocent suffering – must also be witnessed and experienced as a part of that oneness.

The result of such a revelation, ultimately, is an overwhelming experience of *awe* that blasts apart any attempts to hold onto our former (more ego-centred) consciousness and participation in the world. The odious and horrific demons are nothing less than that aspect of the Sacred which, by virtue of their horrific deeds, accomplish the devastation and utter annihilation of our 'selfishness' or ego-consciousness. And though the names, forms and features of the Devil may seem vast and unencompassing, all these appearances of evil, ultimately, find their source in the Divine.

When the Sacred is finally experienced through feelings of both *fear* and *wondrous awe* – as a *Mysterium tremendum et fascinans* – then, in the presence of that majestic unity, all fears and fear-born forms will mercifully fall away. The Path of Darkness, in the final turnings of our innermost Hell, transforms to an upward-spiralling stairway – what Yeats called, *"the winding ancient stair."*[7] This, then, is the *Path of Light.*

Such an understanding is evident in the structure of the myths themselves. Whether through Frye's U-shaped narrative of 'apostasy, repentance and deliverance', or Campbell's O-shaped narrative of 'separation, initiation, and return', the hero must first descend to a moment of death, rebirth and awakening before making his final ascent.

In his book *Heaven and Hell*, Aldous Huxley has admirably described the different qualities possessed by Visionary works of art following either of these two paths. Art arising from 'the negative visionary experience' or Dark Path exists in a smoky light, and all bodies grow to dimensions that are *"progressively more dense,"* so that there is an overall feeling *"of pressure and constriction."*[8] This is why images of Hell's tortures, from Dante's *Inferno* to the Tibetan *Bardo Thödol*, include figures shut up in trees, frozen in ice, or crushed beneath stones. *"Every event is charged with a hateful significance; every object manifests the presence of an Indwelling Horror, infinite, all-powerful, eternal."*[9]

Meanwhile, visions of Heaven and Paradise are populated by heroic figures which possess 'a profound stillness.' This calm repose is particularly apparent in Egyptian or Buddhist statuary, though the works of Byzantine Christianity also possess this stilled quality. In such visions, Paradise, whether as a garden (the Garden of the Hesperides) or an island (the Island of the Blessed) is populated by fabulous animals, and in their midsts stands a marvelous tower covered by intricate patterns of ornately sculpted figures inset with precious gems – jasper, diamond, emerald and sapphire – all aglow with an inner light. Such are the images of Heaven that await the Visionary after emerging from the torments of his or her innermost Hell.

IV. Visions & Hallucinations

In the depth psychology initiated by Sigmund Freud at the outset of the 20th century, the attempt was made to trace the symptomatic expression of certain traumas back to their source, even though the memory of that initial experience may have been buried deep in the unconscious. This regressive tendency in psychoanalysis – a veritable *recherche du temps perdu* – was later amplified by Jung. While he granted that the unconscious produces images in fantasies and dreams that harken back to our more personal memories, he also recognized a deeper strata of collective memory-images, comparable to many cultural symbols.

In the last thirty years, research into depth psychology has taken some dramatic steps forward due to the discovery of certain psycho-active substances, particularly LSD. In the controlled environment of clinical therapy, Dr. Stanislav Grof and his colleagues administered set doses of LSD as an aid to their psycho-therapeutic sessions. The subjects reclined on a couch and were told to keep their eyes closed, so as to internalize the experience. After years of clinical research involving both healthy and psychologically disturbed subjects, Grof was able to determine some of the psychological properties of this powerful entheogen, first discovered by Albert Hofmann in 1943.

One, most interesting property is *"the tendency of LSD to selectively activate unconscious material that has the strongest emotional charge,"* Grof reported.[10] This involves a form of visually *"reliving events from the past, and vivid re-enactments of traumatic or unusually pleasant memories from infancy, childhood, or later periods of life."*[11] Hence, *"traumatic or positive memories with a strong emotional charge are activated, brought forth from the unconscious, and relived."*[12] After repeated administrations of the drug on a weekly or bi-weekly basis, patients demonstrated a tendency to regress selectively through a series of biographical memories, constellated around either traumatic or joyful feelings *"until the oldest memory, or core experience,* [was] *completely relived and integrated."*[13]

To the surprise of Grof and his associates, the vast majority of patients began regressing to memories of their own biological birth, and experienced all the anxiety and trauma associated with it. Unwillingly, they had begun to follow the feeling of fear into the darkest depths of their memory. Their regression to the birth process culminated, surprisingly, in an authentic experience *of death*, followed upon by a sensation *of rebirth*. This allowed the patients to feel themselves as momentarily released from their former personality, and enabled them to participate joyfully in their life as if it were *starting anew*.

Patients who completely regressed through the most significant biographical material and eventually re-experienced their biological birth as a form of 'death and rebirth', actually continued their memory regression in later sessions. They went on to report the emergence of image-clusters which pertained, not to biographical memories, but to collective or cultural ones, accompanied by complex symbolic patterns of the most archaic and mythological sort: *"LSD subjects also reported numerous visions of archetypal forms, individual deities and demons, and complex mythological sequences. An intuitive understanding of universal symbols, or the arousal of the Kundalini and activation of various chakras are additional examples."*[14]

The memory regression appeared to extend backward, beyond the individual personality, to the collective or 'transpersonal' level. This included the sensation of regressing backward through the ancestors and even the evolution of the species. Others reported a vivid recollection of past lives, including the traumatic reliving of past deaths. These regressions also culminated in a final and difficult death experience, followed upon by a joyous sensation of *spiritual* rebirth.

Grof described the stages of this spiritual 'death and rebirth experience' as follows:

> *The symbolic counterpart of this final stage... is the death-rebirth experience. ...Physical and emotional agony culminates in a feeling of utter and total annihilation on all imaginable levels. ...This experience is usually described as 'ego death'; it seems to entail an instantaneous and merciless destruction of all the previous reference points in the life of the individual.*
>
> *After the patient has experienced the limits of total annihilation ... he or she is struck by visions of blinding white or golden light. ...The general atmosphere is one of liberation, salvation, redemption, love, and forgiveness. Typical symbolism of the moment of rebirth involves fantastic visions of radiant sources of light experienced as divine... God can appear in the Christian form of an archetypal wise old man, sitting on a throne surrounded by cherubim and seraphim in radiant splendor. Also quite common in this context is the experience of union with the Great Mother, such as the Divine Isis of the Egyptians, Cybele or the Virgin Mary.*
>
> *The symbolism associated with the experience of death and rebirth can be drawn from many different cultural frameworks. The element of ego death can be associated with visions of various destructive deities, such as Moloch, Shiva the Destroyer, Huitzilopochtli, and the terrible Goddess Kali and Coatlicue, or experienced in full identification with the death of Christ, Osiris, Adonis, or Dionysus.*[15]

The result of LSD-activated regression is a seemingly complete review of all personal memory-images clustered around feelings of anxiety, trauma and fear, culminating in the re-experience of one's birth. This *regressus ad uterum* is experienced, interestingly enough, *as a process of dying.* The patient suffers all the associated traumas until, suddenly (and blissfully), the mythologem of death and rebirth enters into the regression, transforming it completely into an experience of unbounded joy.

In other sessions, the regression appears to review collective memory-images and trace them back to their source, culminating in a another activation of the death-rebirth mythologem. Now, after an experience of ego-death, *a spiritual rebirth* and revelation occurs, experienced as a 'transformation of consciousness' (*metanoia*) or awakening (*bodhi*); as an atonement with the *Pater Omnipotens* or embrace with the *Magna Mater*, and finally, as a return to 'the One'.

It is, simultaneously, intriguing and disturbing how the observed effects of LSD-activated memory regression tally with the spiritual awakenings described in traditional Buddhist and Christian mythologies. The mythologem of death and rebirth, which spontaneously appears at the nadir of Christ's and the Buddha's myth, also makes its appearance at the nadir of the LSD experience – transforming a seemingly authentic experience of one's death, or a seemingly authentic memory recollection of one's birth, into a profoundly spiritual experience of *death and rebirth*. Thus, it would seem that the mythologem of death and rebirth, which is preserved in our most ancient of mythologies, may also spontaneously appear in our more modern visionary journeys...

Once again, the contents of various mythologies have modelled memories and contents of the mind which would otherwise have been lost to us. By reading this imagery in accord with the ancient image-language, we may come to see how many forgotten life-threshold crossings – particularly those of earliest infancy and even our own birth – may be made present once more through the images of myth.

V. The First Life-Threshold

Having established the role of the mythologem of death and rebirth in our ancient mythologies and our more modern visions, we may now return to the Ancient Template in the attempt to trace certain feelings *into the darkest depths* of our memory. The two primary feelings we have been able to identify which, aside from fear, lead us ever further backward in our memory regressions are *trauma* and *joy*. In our meditations on the template, we have been able to trace these feelings backward only so far along the path of our memories, from adulthood to infancy.

In its general outlines, this has been imagined as follows. We, as we exist at present, are portrayed on the periphery of the outer circle, along with all the other people in our lives who continue to influence our feelings in some way. By tracing certain feelings to their source, we are able to pass backward through life, recollecting past memories. We move through the various layers of memories as if through the various layers of images in the spiralling clouds.

Gradually, we have realized that the upper layers of the spiralling mists consist of personal memory-images, arranged in a slow descent from the most recent to the most distant. Those personal memories tend to constellate around our feelings of joy, fear and pain.

But, as we attempt to descend through the darkest depths of our memory, we lack the personal memory-images of our *earliest* life-threshold crossings. And so, the collective memory images of art and myth provide us with precisely those images which we lack. With these cultural symbols, we may continue to pursue feelings ever further through our memory. As we bring our lives to these collective memory-images, engaging them as if they were our personal memories, they too become constellated around our feelings of fear, trauma, and joy.

The moment we *enter through* a Threshold Image, we successfully spiral down through the mists of both personal and collective memory-images; we pursue the thread of a certain feeling all the way through the eternal labyrinth. In other words, we trace a feeling of trauma, fear, or joy backward *into the darkest depths* of our memory – and behold there a luminous vision of the Sacred at the source.

The question then arises: are we able to cross back, in our memory, to the experience *of our own birth?* Are there images from art and myth which model this event? Such images would arise if we successfully traced a feeling of fear, trauma, or joy *as far back as possible* through our lives. For there, at life's beginning, we would encounter the memory that was lost, seemingly forever.

Hence, let us now attempt to follow the path of a feeling *as far back as possible* through the spiralling labyrinth of our own memories. To avoid the Dark Path, we shall begin with the feeling of ecstasy and *joy* first experienced in our mother's embrace. This creates its own path to the centre, the Path of Light. Constellated around this particular feeling are a series of recent memories, such as the pleasure felt in the embrace of a present lover. As we trace this feeling backward, we may recollect a series of other pleasant memories – receiving attention, winning awards, being given something we wished for as a child – leading to ever more infantile and yet powerful feelings of joy. But, the supreme joy we once felt as a new-born child, cradled in our mother's arms, is unfortunately lost to us. The very image of it, which we long *to enter through* and so experience in feeling, is lacking...

And so, this feeling of joy is transfered instead to a cultural image. This may be the image of the Madonna and child, or simply of the child itself. This cultural image, like Jung's *Puer Aeternus,* depicts the eternal child in a variety of manifestations, whether as the playful Krishna, the Alchemical *Filius*, the Hellenic *Koré*, the Horus child or the infant Christ as *salvator mundi*. And so, through this cultural symbol of the Divine Child, our passage through the spiralling clouds may be extended further. Looking into this image of the eternal child as if into a mirror of ourselves as a child, we attempt to *enter through* that image to a lost experience of infant joy – that 'I happy am'.

In this regard, Jung has written:

> *Any introversion occurring in later life regresses back to infantile reminiscences which, though derived from the individual's past, generally have a slight archaic tinge. With stronger introversion and regression, the archaic features become more pronounced.*[16]

Horus Child as Pharaoh
Egyptian (c. 1330 BC)

Christ Child as Salvator Mundi
Martin Schongauer (c. 1480)

By following the feeling of joy ever further backward, *entering through* a series of personal and collective memory-images, we re-experience that lost moment of joy when, after our birth, we were first re-united with our mother: held and comforted in her loving embrace. But, we have not, as a result of this regression, returned to the dark threshold-crossing *of our birth*. We have only pursued the Path of Light, and so have failed to re-experience, in our darkest depths, the fear and trauma associated with life's *first* threshold-crossing.

But the journey along the Dark Path, which is motivated by feelings of both fear and pain, ends in quite a different manner...

If we now trace the particularly traumatic feeling of 'separation from one we love' *ever further* back, we shall soon find ourselves in a very dark place in our soul. For, the events constellated around this feeling are both *fearful* and extremely *painful*, insofar as they involve great traumas. Such events may begin on the periphery of our memory, with images of love relationships recently broken, causing their own unique and heart-rending suffering. Also included here would be the pain of separation caused by the sudden death of one close to us.

Earlier childhood images of loss and separation would need be encountered on this painful spiral downward: the ridicule, punishment, shame and abuse inflicted by elders upon the innocent, so as to enforce him to abandon his earlier childlike ways; the tragic loss of a favourite toy companion; even the infant experience of crying, in fear of abandonment, for hours on end in the crib. Finally, the pain and separation which we felt at the very moment of our birth would have to be confronted.

Though the memory-image of that experience may be lost to us, the feelings do remain. For, throughout our lives, we strangely persist in giving the *same* expression to that feeling as it was *first* expressed during our birth – each time we suffer some separation later in life, *we cry,* just as we did *at the moment of our birth.* (By that same token, the smile we use to express feelings of joy was first experienced and expressed by the child in its mother's embrace).

While the personal memory-image of our birth has been lost to us, many cultural images have emerged over time, to express the agony and anguish we first suffered in separation from our mother. Among these images, we may now see, are all of those encountered earlier in our explication of the Dark Path. For, a descent into the dark underworld awakens in us tremendous feelings of *fear.* And, as Freud was the first to note, all feelings of fear experienced later in life are, in fact, an evocation of that anxiety which we first felt during our birth. According to Freud, *"the act of birth is the source and prototype of the affect of anxiety."* [17] And he elaborates:

> In the act of birth... there comes about the combination of unpleasurable feelings... and bodily sensations which has become the prototype of the effects of a mortal danger, and has ever since been repeated by us as a state of anxiety. ...It is highly relevant that this first state of anxiety arose out of separation from the mother. [18]

The myth of the hero's descent into the dark underworld is, in fact, a model for the journey through our own forgotten memories. And the feelings of fear and mortal danger experienced during the descent are nothing less than the evocation of our *earliest fears*, experienced in approach to our birth. All the figures in Hell which the hero encounters during his descent (as described by Huxley in his exposition on 'the Dark Path') model, in a variety of ways, the forgotten memories of our own birth traumas: the dark, smokey, and oppressive atmosphere of the underworld may be compared to the womb; the sensation that all bodies in Hell grow to dimensions 'progressively more dense', may be compared to the pressures increasingly felt by the foetus growing in the womb; and finally, the countless demons with their tortures of binding and constricting may be compared to the first contractions felt in the womb.*

*The pervasive presence of hellish imagery, such as being bound, probed, strangled, and tortured, in the re-activation of the birth experience is confirmed by Grof[19] in his studies on LSD-activated regression.

As we descend ever further through the spiralling mists of our own lost memories, we come to that nadir image which evokes our greatest agony and our own worst fear: the symbol of the sacred hero *suffering unto death*. This Image of Death, be it of Christ, Osiris, Quetzalcoatl or the Buddha, appears to us here to express, paradoxically, the painful experience *of our birth*. In fact, this cultural image models the memory-image we have lost – of our life's first threshold crossing. For the birth experience is nothing less than the agony we suffered in an utter and complete *severance* from our former more pleasant existence. To *enter through* such an Image of Death, evoking thereby all the agony and pain of separation first felt during our birth, is to trace the feelings of fear and trauma *to the very end* of the Dark Path.

As we cross over this Threshold Image, we experience the fear and trauma of separation *to the full*. We suffer a *total* annihilation of ourselves from the world as we know it. But, immediately after that dark and final moment, a light appears. Images of new life appear. At the nadir of our journey, *the mythologem of death and rebirth spontaneously appears.* The sun rises on the horizon; the three-days-darkened moon re-emerges; and the entombed saviour rises again. The Dark Path, in its final downturning, spins round to become a staircase spiralling upward into the light.

Through cultural images of the dying/rising saviour, we momentarily experience our own death, rebirth and awakening. Once all the pain and fear has been overcome, we experience anew the miracle of our birth, but now as a *spiritual re-birth*: the awe of emerging into a new world filled with light...

VI. The Symbolic Doorways
of Birth & Death

The Ancient Template has offered us a series of visionary journeys. By evoking feelings of joy, fear and pain, and reliving the ever more ancient memory-images constellated round them, we have moved backward through time, regressing through the entire course of our lives. Finally, at the end of that regression we encountered a Threshold Image which we *entered through* to its momentary epiphany. We have already discovered that the Buddha embodies this *backward movement* through life to its more sacred awakening.

But the images arising in our visions and dreams sometimes point forward in life, suggesting new experiences and ways of acting. And so, our meditative journey through the Ancient Template may also be undertaken to envision a resolution to the conflicts presently awaiting us in the *forward movement* through life. As we have already discovered, it is Christ who embodies this forward movement through life.

As we live our lives, following the sacred patterns manifest in the myths of these two saviours, we find that Christ and the Buddha embody two very different encounters with the mythologem of death and rebirth, which spontaneously emerges at the nadir of both their myths. Christ, who passed *forward* through life, experienced finally, on the threshold of his own death, the thunderous epiphany of God's revelation. The Christ myth, then, uses the mythologem of death and rebirth as a doorway onto the Sacred *at the end of one's forward progression through life.* The experience of *death* becomes a sudden suffering and awakening, leading to a more sacred vision of the world.

On the other hand, the Buddha beneath the Bodhi tree passed *backward* through life, recollecting memories from this and all previous lives, until he ultimately regressed to his birth and earliest origins. This too became a form of ego-death, followed by his spiritual rebirth and awakening. Hence the Buddha myth, in contrast, uses the mythologem of death and rebirth as a doorway to the Sacred *at the end of one's backward regression through life.* That is, at birth. The re-experience of one's *birth* becomes a *spiritual* rebirth, leading to a new life-awakening.

VII. The Thresholds of Life

Because the serpent sloughs its skin, it has been used from time immemorial as a symbol of death and rebirth. Like the ancient serpent, each of us has had to continually die and be reborn *unto himself* so as to grow from a child to a youth, from a youth to a parent, and so on. Each threshold crossing involves a profound life-transformation that may be likened unto death and rebirth.

Campbell recognized this when he wrote:

> *The birth trauma, as an archetype of transformation, floods with considerable emotional affect the brief moment of loss of security and threat of death that accompanies any crisis of radical change. In the imagery of mythology and religion, this birth (or more often rebirth) theme is very prominent; in fact, every threshold passage – not only this from the darkness of the womb to the light of the sun, but also those from childhood to adult life and from the light of the world to whatever mystery of darkness may lie beyond the portal of death – is comparable to a birth, and has been ritually represented, practically everywhere, through an imagery of re-entry into the womb.*[20]

Since the trauma of life's *final* threshold crossing evokes the trauma of life's *first* – since, that is, death is to be ultimately experienced as birth or rebirth – the mythologem of death and rebirth has been continually evoked in the crossing of *all* life's thresholds. This mythologem arises and is re-lived whenever we cross a life-threshold to a new stage in our lives.

While more ancient societies, such as the Australian Aborigines, have put greater ritual emphasis on adolescent life-threshold crossings – the initiation to adulthood involves elaborate, frightening, and at times, intensely painful rites involving deep subcision and scarring – our more modern religions give this transition lesser ritual emphasis – through the tamer Jewish ritual of the *bar mitzvah* or the Catholic sacrament of confirmation.

These *rites d'entrée* lack the profound initiatory experience of their more ancient equivalents: the body's fearful scarring and tattooing, the intense shock and traumatization inflicted on the initiate, blasting his psyche apart and recasting it into a new and reborn image. It is nigh impossible for the victim of such an experience to go back and reclaim his former childhood ways.

While our modern religions lack these transformative rituals, each of life's threshold-crossings nevertheless leaves its mark upon us. This is not only in evidence through gradual changes in the body's outward appearance but, as we shall see in the next chapters, through the internal metamorphoses that are announced to us, by *dreams*, from *within*.

It is impossible to say precisely how many life-stages there are. It is also impossible to decide the distinct moment of passage from one stage to the next. This is why rituals have arisen from without, and dreams from within, to mark the utterly mysterious phenomenon of sloughing off the older (and now dead) layer of the personality, to emerge as reborn in the newer – like a winged soul or *psyché* emerging transformed from its cocoon.

VIII. Infant Life-thresholds

The new-born child has to focus on crawling, walking and so forth, and mastering each of these tasks constitutes a major threshold of growth. The 'I' that existed at the centre of these activities was not the more mature 'I' of later life, but what we might call the 'infantile I'. All our conscious efforts were directed towards mastering these tasks, and the infantile ego came to exist at the centre of each of them.

These infantile forms of the ego have since submerged into the depths of the unconscious. And so, our present 'I' cannot easily return to these earlier incarnations. Before the acquisition of language, the child thought in terms of images rather than verbally, logically and conceptually. And so we must learn to think in a more infantile manner, and *to think in images*. With an understanding of the ancient image-language, we may regain this forgotten manner of thinking.

Though these infantile ways of thinking are difficult to recover, one of the most obvious iconologues that presents itself in childhood is that of 'the Opposites'. Early on, the child learned to divide the world into such contraries as longing and fulfillment, abandonment and embrace, the comfort of light and a fear of the dark. Using pleasure and pain or shame and reward, the parents later enforced a series of other opposites, such as dirty and clean, naked and clothed, even good and evil.

Then, between the ages of three and five, the child gained a degree of autonomy from its parents. At some point, it crossed a most important threshold in its thinking, and learned to verbalize itself as 'I' rather than through the name given to it by its parents. Henceforth, the world with its myriad forms was arranged perspectively, with this 'I' at the centre.

The world became 'my world'.

At this moment, the 'I' emerged at the centre of consciousness and also at the centre of all opposites. And so, this more mature and conscious 'I' will survive intact through the many forthcoming life-threshold crossings.

It follows that, the attempt to think our way back through earlier ego-incarnations will end, typically, with the memory of when we first became 'conscious': of when the mature ego or 'I' first emerged on the horizon of our awareness. And indeed, many an autobiography has been written with this experience in mind.

The Canadian author Robertson Davies, for example, has left several accounts of that moment for, time and again, the childhood motif of a red peony appears in his novels. In *What's Bred in the Bone*, he writes of the main character's early childhood: *"It was in a garden that Francis Cornish first became truly aware of himself as a creature observing a world apart from himself. He was almost three years old, and he was looking deep into a splendid red peony..."*[21] In *The Manticore*, which delves into Jungian analysis, a Swiss analyst sets the main character's *anamnesis* in motion with the question, *"What is the earliest recollection you can honestly vouch for?"* The analysand responds: *"Oh, that's easy. I was standing in my grandmother's garden, in warm sunlight, looking into a deep red peony. As I recall, I wasn't much taller than the peony."*[22] In a revealing autobiographical piece, Davies wrote: *"I can recall, at a very early age, standing transfixed before a peony, feeling myself drawn into its gorgeous colour; I know I was very young at the time, for the peony and I were about the same height..."*[23]

It is no mere co-incidence that the image which awakens this infant to the newly-found centre of his existence is also a traditional image of the Sacred: the sacred flower, lotus-blossom or celestial rose that symbolizes the Divine as the source and centre of all creation. Such an image, by its very structure, evokes the idea of a stilled point to which all spiralling forms on the periphery may be related at their centre. In effect, this is a Threshold Image standing at the moment of awakening to our own interior unity. The Egyptian image of the sun's first rising on the horizon, or of the infant Horus rising up from the Nile lily, constitute other such Threshold Images. Each models a forgotten memory in our mind.

Thus, the memory of the ego's first awakening – when 'we first became truly aware of ourself as a creature observing a world apart' – marks a most important life-threshold. From it, a series of verbal, logical and conceptual constructs describing the external world can be developed. Before that event, a different form of logic reigned: one more in keeping with dreams: at times poetic, at times utterly chaotic... The world of the child, on the other side of that threshold, is nothing but confusion: a continuous alteration between screaming agony and smiling joy; painful falls and comforting caresses; abandonment unto sleep and a welcome into wakingness. It is both a forgotten hell and a forgotten paradise where, in Shelley's words, *"all is wonder to unpracticed sense..."*[24]

IX. The Stages of Life

Traditionally, the West has seen six or seven stages in life. In the Middle Ages, their images appeared on the facades of cathedrals, and were numbered six: *infantia, pueritia, adolescentia, juventus, virilitas, & senectus.*[25] During the Renaissance, Shakespeare counted them as seven:

> *...One man in his time plays many parts,*
> *His acts being seven ages. At first the infant...*
> *And then the whining school-boy, ...the lover,*
> *...soldier,* [and the] *justice. ...The sixth age shifts*
> *Into the lean and slipper'd pantaloon...*
> *Last scene of all... is second childishness and mere oblivion,*
> *Sans teeth, sans eyes, sans taste, sans everything.*[26]

For a new-born child, the thresholds to cross are indeed numerous and difficult: some involve the co-ordination of bodily movements – focusing vision, grasping, crawling, walking – while others involve the mastery of bodily functions – breast-feeding, eating, toilet-training – all of which are initially tended to by the parents, and which the child must gradually master autonomously. Also included would be the organization of our thoughts and experiences around a conscious 'I' or ego, and the division of these thoughts into opposites of the sort: 'mother and father', 'boy and girl'.

Later, as a youth, we are confronted by the body's own maturing, by an expansion of thinking and feeling, and by our parents' expectation that we channel these new energies into a series of societal roles so as to become self-sufficient. The young adult must find a suitable partner in marriage, a suitable vocation in life, and so on. After crossing these difficult thresholds of marriage and profession, we are confronted by home-building, the birth of our children, the loss of our parents, the gradual decay of our own bodily powers and a possible decrease or increase in our own mental state of awareness until, finally, we are confronted by death, as the *last* of our life-threshold crossings.

Our innermost Self, like the ancient serpent, thus passes through *a series of deaths and rebirths* in life. Using Hindu mythology, we may refer to these stages of life, metaphorically, as 'ego-incarnations' of the Self. In order to progress through life, the ego must repeatedly die and be reborn to the Self. Each time the ego successfully performs the deed that carries it across a certain life-threshold, a new ego-incarnation is born. This new ego-incarnation becomes the latest and 'best' incarnation of the Self. Due to its powerful exercise of the will, that ego is primarily concerned with life's *forward* movement, successfully traversing the next threshold.

However, this forward movement through life may be foregone in favour of the backward one. Sometimes, the trauma of an impassible life-threshold makes it necessary to pursue a path backward through our forgotten memories. Other times, in meditation, we may willingly pursue this regressive path to spiritual enlightenment.

Either way, we encounter at the end of that journey a Threshold Image of death, rebirth and awakening. Threshold Images such as Christ and the Buddha reveal that life, whether lived forward to its end or backward to its beginning, is bounded round on either side by a momentary epiphany.

X. Life's Sacred Unfolding

But such an epiphany also occurs over the course of life. For, with the crossing of *each* life-threshold, we experience a momentary death, rebirth and awakening. And the mythologem of death and rebirth has been used since time immemorial to initiate the individual across *all* the thresholds of life. To grow from a child to a youth, from a youth to a parent, and so on, each of us has had to continually die and be reborn unto himself. Such profound life-transformations are, in effect, momentary epiphanies.

This is made clear by 'the ever-dying/rising Sons of the Abyss' of more ancient culture. Unlike Christ and the Buddha, these gods did not die *once only* at a certain point in linear or cyclic time; and they do not appear to us *once only* at the end of a regression or progression through life. Rather, they appear to die and rise again *continuously* over the course of life; and their death and rebirth *repeatedly* manifests life's momentary epiphanies.

For this reason, the ancient religions evoked the mythologem of their ever-dying/rising god in all initatory rites. For them, the crossing of each life-threshold involved a similar such descent into the dark underworld, a nadir-moment of death, rebirth and awakening, and an eventual return to the overworld with this prize in his grasp.

Take, for example, James Frazer's account in *The Golden Bough* of an ancient rite of initiation used by worshippers of Attis, a dying and rising god of fertility from ancient antiquity:

In the baptism, the devotee, crowned with gold and wreathed with fillets, descended into a pit, the mouth of which was covered with a wooden grating. A bull, adorned with garlands of flowers, its forehead glittering with gold leaf, was then driven onto the grating and there stabbed to death with a consecrated spear. Its hot, reeking blood poured in torrents through the apertures, and was received... by the worshipper on every part of his person and garments, till he emerged from the pit, drenched, dripping, and scarlet from head to foot, to receive the homage, nay the adoration of his fellows as one who had been born again to eternal life.[27]

Each life-threshold crossing is, in truth, a mundane event. But through the images of art and myth, the events of life are ennobled and become sacred. The mundane experiences of life – acquiring a profession, building a home, bringing a child into the world – lead us through symbols to the Sacred. And, as a result of a life-threshold crossing experienced *here and now*, the ancient images *come to life*. As Threshold Images, they offer us a vision of life *as a series* of sacred epiphanies.

The Threshold Image depicting the mythologem of the *Coniunctio* not only reveals to us the marriage of the God and Goddess, but also our own possible experience of marriage. The two are related to each other because they *share the same mythologem*. Our own marriage becomes, through this sacred symbol, a *heiros gamos* – a *sacred* marriage.

Hence, each time we cross a life-threshold, life's sacred aspect is momentarily revealed. And when all of these life-thresholds are crossed *in succession*, life becomes *an ever-increasing* epiphany of the Sacred...

XI. Conclusion

In our explorations of ancient and modern art, we have learned how to *enter through the image* following the Symbolic Path through the Ancient Template. The cosmos is nothing less than a series of mirrors arranged in a row, and each unique aspect of creation reflects its creator. Over time, the eternally Sacred has manifest itself in a variety of symbolic guises, yet all are fundamentally *one* at their source. The manifold aspects of this unity are also linked through the logic of similarity or difference, which variously displaces or combines images along the Chain of Being.

In traditional works of art, sacred images and metaphors have become fixed into canonical forms. Meanwhile, in Visionary works of art, different cultural icons have been freely combined and creatively *entered through* to their underlying oneness.

Our subsequent investigation of Dreams will explore the spontaneous manner in which dreams arrange images. But, most dreams are more concerned with life's *imminent* threshold crossings. Since these may be elevated through the images of art and myth into momentary epiphanies, our dreams will also reveal how life, when lived in its fullness, becomes a more sacred unveiling...

PART III

THE ONEIRIC PATH

Is not every dream
...a significant rent
in the mysterious curtain
that hangs a thousandfold
about our inner life?
– Novalis[1]

CHAPTER XIV

Life-threshold Crossings in Dreams

As the time is equally divided in which we are asleep or awake,
in either sphere of existence the soul contends that the thoughts
which are present to our minds at the time are true;
and during one half of our lives we affirm the truth of the one,
and during the other half, of the other...
Socrates,
in Plato's Theaetetus (158d)[2]

I. Myths, Dreams, & the Thresholds of Life

Dreams, like myths, are a temporal unfolding of imagery that reflect, ultimately, the temporal unfolding of life itself. In myths, the hero acquires a certain task, then crosses over several important thresholds to complete it. At the nadir of a myth he crosses the darkest threshold, undergoing a life-altering experience of death and rebirth that results in a sudden awakening.

The same iconologues of time, narrative and the hero task which underlie our cultural myths also appear each night in our dreams. At night, the dreamer also acquires a certain task, and must cross over several important thresholds to complete it. But, at the nadir of a dream he undergoes a life-altering experience which involves his own, more personal *life*-threshold crossings of abandoning childhood, acquiring a profession and a partner in marriage, or confronting old age and even death. The life-thresholds that arise in dreams are examined in detail at the end of this work, in Appendix II.

Although the dream's nadir-initiation of, for example, 'marriage' may be compared to Campbell's 'meeting with the Goddess', just as 'profession' may be compared to his 'atonement with the Father', it is the unique and individual *life*-thresholds, rather than their more heroic equivalents, which arise in dreams. And, rather than cultural Threshold Images of the *Magna Mater* or *Pater Omnipotens*, it is the more personal *life*-threshold images of our marriage or profession that appear by the dream's end. We shall refer to these life-altering images as *oneiric* Threshold Images.

Over the course of life, an individual must make a series of fearful, traumatic, even joyful threshold-crossings, each involving the death of his former, more infantile self and its rebirth as a later, more mature version of the same. Like the ancient serpent, he must slough off the older personality in favour of the newer. Or, like the ancient 'dying and rising Son of the Abyss', he must die and be reborn *unto himself.* Dreams reveal these transformative life-threshold crossings.

In our more primordial societies, powerful *rites d'entrée* were used to initiate the individual, via an intense experience of death and rebirth, into each new stage of existence. We have already seen this in Frazer's account of the neophyte's frightening yet joyful initiation into the cult of Attis. Meanwhile, our more modern society has foregone such rites (or practises only paltry imitations of them). And yet, as Campbell has noted:

> Apparently there is something in these initiatory images so necessary to the psyche that, if they are not supplied from without by myth and ritual, they will have to be announced again, through dreams, from within.[3]

As the source of our more ancient myths and rituals, dreams preserve these transformative threshold-crossings. Through the oneiric Threshold Images that arise in dreams, these life-altering thresholds are 'announced' and made conscious.

But a dream may also regress, so as to evoke *earlier* threshold-crossings, or even progress, so as to anticipate *future* crossings. Essentially, dreams reflect our ongoing attempts to accomplish *a complete movement through life*, so that it is experienced *as a whole.* In essence, they are concerned with the stages in life that must be necessarily encountered and overcome before finally transcending life as a whole.

II. The 'I' of Waking and Dreaming

Each time we wake in the morning and recollect a dream, we enter into a brief *backward* movement through life: we recall those moments that passed before us in linear succession last night. And it often happens that, as we recollect this mythic unfolding of a dream, it comes to a sudden, disturbing, and strangely *unresolved* end: the very threshold that confronted us at the dream's middle remains uncrossed by its end. Indeed, those nadir-images arising at the dream's middle suddenly *become* the dream's end. This incomplete movement through the dream is precisely what offers us the impetus, and even the means, to tread new paths *forward* through life. We must, in deed, resolve what was left unresolved, in dreams.

Our conscious ego, with its 'forward-looking' attitude, attempts to move us across future life-thresholds through its exercise of the will. Such a forward movement, if it really is successful, causes the older personality to be sacrificed in favour of the newer. Like the Buddha over the course of his many 'bodhisattva' incarnations, in life we each must undergo many deaths and rebirths in order to gradually perfect ourselves. Hence, life itself, over the course of its mythic unfolding, is constituted by a series of successive threshold-crossings, and between these appear the progressive stages of life. We have referred to these stages as various 'ego-incarnations' of our Self. Our conscious ego, as it now stands, is the latest and best of these incarnations.

But the previous ego-incarnations, though dead to the conscious ego, live on unconsciously in us, and re-appear in our dreams each night. The 'I' of our dreams preserves infantile feelings, thoughts, and modes of behaviour which the 'I' of wakingness has outgrown. A most important distinction must be made between this 'waking-I', which exists at the centre of our day-consciousness, and the 'dream-I', which exists at the centre of our nightly sojourns. Gérard de Nerval no doubt had this dream-I in mind when he wrote: "[Dans] *le Rêve ...le* moi, *sous une autre forme, continue l'œuvre de l'existence.*"*[4]

Both the waking-I and the dream-I are a reflection of the innermost Self, but display different aspects of it. While the waking-I is the latest and best incarnation of ourselves, the dream-I preserves feelings, thoughts and modes of behaviour from *all* of our earlier incarnations. Due to these more infantile feelings, Threshold Images related to earlier life-thresholds are constantly evoked in dreams. Hence, the dream-I not only reflects the dreamer as he is at this point in life, but reveals him as he existed at all its various stages.

At the source of the dream, and hence, at the source of all the images swirling in the mind's shadowy mists, lies 'the innermost Self'. The dream-I, no matter which incarnation it momentarily reflects, always reflects the innermost Self. Because, that Self extends over the whole course of life, bringing it into one wholeness. (Since this innermost Self lies at the source of all our dreaming, we may also refer to it as 'the Dreamsource').

When we approach dreams through the ancient image-language, we see that they, like myths, model the interior of the mind. More particularly, they arrange their images so as to model the mind's history: the many life-thresholds that had to be encountered and overcome before arriving at our present state of awareness. Sometimes, the dream-I's actions reflect our earlier life-threshold crossings. Other times, it anticipates future ones. Most importantly, it acts in such a way as to announce our present life-threshold crossings from within.

*"[In] *dreams ...the 'I', under another form, carries on the task of existence.*"

III. To Bring Consciousness
into the Dream

Since the publication of Freud's *Interpretation of Dreams* in 1900, various techniques have been developed to aid us in the task of interpreting our dreams. But the entire task of *interpretation* itself remains a questionable endeavour. For, in order to be interpreted, the arrangement of dream-images must first be translated into words and concepts more palateable to consciousness. And, in this fashion, the dream symbols are presented to consciousness as 'interpreted', and thus 'understood'.

Meanwhile, our task over the entire course of this work has been to recover 'the more ancient manner of thinking' behind myths and art. And now, our present task is to think, in this more ancient manner, through the images of dreams. Thinking through dreams in accord with their ancient image-language may reveal aspects of ourselves and our lives which the conceptual logic of our wakingness has otherwise obscured.

Hence, our approach to dreams will require, not so much an interpretation, but rather a meditation and *elucidation* of the dream's imagery. Rather than bringing the dream into consciousness, our task now is to bring consciousness into the dream – *'to enter the dream awake'* as Campbell put it. Or, in the language we have used thus far, to *enter through the dream.* With the aid of our Ancient Template, we may learn to enter through the dream's narrative, its symbols and symbolic events, so as to reveal the *Mysterium* that lies at the centre of our mind's swirling mists.

But, this is not to say that all dreams are concerned with life's unfolding, and reveal the Sacred at its source. Some dreams, like some myths, are more immediately concerned with life's lesser tasks. Other dreams, it must be admitted, are entirely nonsensical, overly preoccupied with the most trivial of concerns. In anxiety dreams, the dream-I is presented with a task that, in itself, seems trivial to the extreme, yet it is overwrought with the greatest significance. And who has not awoken at least once, wondering if they had not just dreamt someone else's nightmare? But the nonsense in dreams must not mislead us into thinking that the entire enterprise is worthless and misguided...

We shall, for the greater part, concentrate on *somnia* – those archetypal, life-altering dreams that are of such great importance to the dreamer (even though their meaning may remain an enigma). Over the next two chapters, we shall seek out the parallels between myths and dreams. How do dreams arrange images in a manner similar to myths? How are their images linked one to the next through the hero's task and its accomplishment? How are dreams an arrangement of images over time? What Threshold Images arise at their nadir?

After seeking out the oneiric Threshold Images that arise in dreams, we may begin to compare them to sacred symbols and mythologems. We shall seek out, in this manner, their symbolic significance and, more importantly, their sacred aspect. For such dreams may ultimately present a more ancient, indeed sacred view unto life...

IV. The Dream of Baudelaire

We are about to embark on a journey through a number of fascinating dreams. In all cases, the dreams have been taken from recognized figures in history, particularly artists, writers and philosophers.*

The following dream illustrates how various life-thresholds, when crossed more or less successfully in the waking world, are also announced by the dream from within. It was dreamt by Charles Baudelaire, a symbolist poet of the mid-1800's who, despite the dark, intoxicated and visionary imagery of his poems, confessed that dreams, due to *"the fact that they are generally quite alien to my personal pursuits and adventures, always lead me to believe that they form an almost hieroglyphic language to which I have no key."*[5]

He dreamt it while living in Paris, on the night of March 12th, 1856, and immediately upon waking at five o'clock in the morning, wrote it down in a letter to a friend.[6]

> *It was two or three o'clock in the morning (in my dream), and I was walking alone in the streets. I ran into* Castille, *who I think had several errands to attend to, and I told him I would accompany him and take advantage of the carriage to run an errand of my own. So we took a carriage.*
>
> *I felt it a* duty *of sorts to present the madam of a large whorehouse with a book of mine which had just come out. When I looked at the book in my hand,* it turned out *to be an obscene one, which explained* the necessity *of presenting the book to that woman. Moreover, in the back of my mind, this necessity was really a pretext, a chance to screw one of the tarts in passing – which suggests that if I hadn't had to present the book, I wouldn't have dared go into such a house.*
>
> *I said nothing of this to Castille, but stopped the carriage at the door of the house, and left Castille in it, fully intending not to leave him waiting too long. No sooner had I rung and entered than I noticed my cock was hanging out of my unbuttoned fly, and I couldn't help feeling it was improper to appear in such a state, even in a place like that.*
>
> *What is more, noticing that my feet felt very wet, I looked down and found that they were bare, and that I had stepped into a pool of liquid at the bottom of the stairs. Too bad, I thought, I'll wash them before I screw and before I leave the house. I went upstairs. After that, there was nothing more about the book.*

---

* Although the author has recorded thousands of his dreams, comprising seven volumes over a period of thirty years, he has made the decision to use established dreams as source material.

I found myself in vast adjoining galleries, ill-lit and dingy, with the faded look of old cafés, old reading-rooms or seedy gaming-houses. The tarts were scattered around these great galleries, chatting with men, among whom I noticed some schoolboys. I felt very sad and very uneasy; I was afraid someone might see my feet. Looking down, I noticed that one of them had a shoe on it. Shortly after, I noticed that there were shoes on both.

What struck me was that the walls of these vast galleries were decorated with all kinds of drawings in frames. Not all were obscene. There were even architectural drawings and Egyptian figures. As I was feeling more and more nervous and didn't dare approach any of the girls, I amused myself by making a thorough examination of all the drawings.

In a remote corner of one of the galleries, I found a very peculiar series. There was a whole array of little frames containing drawings, miniatures, and photographic prints. Some depicted coloured birds with very brilliant plumage and with eyes that were alive. *Sometimes,* there was only half a bird. *Others depicted bizarre, monstrous, almost* amorphous *beings, not unlike meteorites. In the corner of each picture was a note:* 'Such and such a tart, age.....', gave birth to this fœtus in the year such and such', *and other notes of that kind. It occurred to me that this sort of drawing was not really very conducive to thoughts of lovemaking.*

Another thought I had was this: Only one newspaper in the world, namely, Le Siècle, *would possibly be stupid enough to open a brothel and set up a sort of medical museum in it at the same time. Indeed, I suddenly realized, it was* Le Siècle *that had put up the funds for this brothel enterprise, and the medical museum was explained by its mania for progress, science, and the spreading of enlightenment. So, I reflected, the folly and stupidity of the modern age are useful in their mysterious way, and what has been done for evil can often turn to the good, through the workings of some perverse providence. I admired the accuracy of my philosophical reasoning.*

But among all these creatures was one that lived. It was a monster born in the house, and which sat all day on a pedestal. Although it was alive, it was actually part of the museum. It was not ugly. Its face was even pretty, very swarthy, of an oriental colour, and it had a lot of pink and green in it.

It sat crouched, but in a strange, contorted position. There was also something blackish twisted several times round it and round its limbs, like a big snake. I asked the creature what it was, and he told me it was a monstrous appendage that grew out of his head, an elastic thing rather like rubber, and so very long that if he were to coil it round his head like a braid of hair, it would be much too heavy too support; and so he had no choice but to wear it wrapped around his limbs – but this in any case looked much nicer.

I had a long chat with the monster, and he confided to me all his troubles and woes. For several years now, they had made him sit in this room, up on this pedestal, to satisfy the public's curiosity. But his main worry came at supper time. Since he was a living being, he was expected to eat with the ladies of the house – to stagger with his rubber appendage to the dining room, where he had to keep it wrapped around him, or leave it on a chair, like a bundle of rope; for if he let it trail to the ground, it would pull his head over backwards. To make matters worse, he was obliged, squat little thing that he was, to sit at table next to a big, shapely girl. All this, though, he explained to me without any bitterness. I didn't dare touch him, but I was interested in him.

At this point (this is no longer part of the dream), my wife made a noise in her room with a piece of furniture, and woke me up. I woke up tired, absolutely worn out and aching in my back, legs, and hips. I must have been sleeping in the same contorted position as the monster. I don't know if you will find all this as funny as I do.

V. The Life Thresholds of Marriage & Profession

We know that Baudelaire was thirty-four years' old at the time of this dream. Although his fourteen-year relationship with his mulatto mistress Jeanne Duvall was stormy at the best of times, the two of them had more or less settled down (he refers to her above as 'his wife'), and he was on the point of gaining recognition as a writer.

While he had written articles and poems for the press over the last fourteen years, no book bearing his name had yet been published. The first volume of his translation of Edgar Allan Poe's tales of the macabre (*Histoires Extraordinaires*) would come out that year – as a matter of fact, *on the day before this dream*.[7] One year later, the first edition of his own poetic masterpiece, *Les Fleurs du mal* ('The Flowers of Evil') appeared, to much acclaim as well as condemnation, eventually garnering the author a trial of obscenity and a ban on six of the poems.

Baudelaire was thus, at this stage in his life, still crossing the life-threshold of profession (establishing himself as a writer) while having, more or less successfully, crossed the previous threshold of marriage. Since his first published book came out on the day before this dream, it appears that, in the waking world, he had crossed an important life-threshold: becoming a recognized writer. Yet, he had passed through no established ritual to acknowledge this fact. Instead, this important threshold-crossing was 'announced from within' that night – apparently, through this very dream. And indeed, at the beginning of the dream he is holding '*a book of mine which had just come out*'. Yet, crossing this threshold, of profession, would also have its consequence on the other uncelebrated threshold-crossing, of marriage.

As we shall see, his dream alternates between these two concerns, which we may call *logos* and *eros*. Here, *logos* means using thinking, intelligence, and 'the word' to successfully engage the world, such as in one's profession. This is, normally, the inheritance of the Father world. *Eros* means that feeling, pleasure, pain, and 'the womb' become one's experience of the world, such as in marriage. This is, traditionally, the inheritance of the Mother world. Many images in the dream are arranged around these two themes, and their accompanying life-thresholds of profession and marriage.

Just as the hero of a myth is presented with *a task* at the outset of his adventure, so do dreams often possess one very significant moment near their beginning, when a task is given to the dream-I. At the beginning of this particular dream-narrative, a task is given to the dream-I, and it possesses a two-fold nature.

First, he must *present a copy of his book, which turns out to be obscene, to the madam of a whorehouse. To present a copy of his book:* that is to say, his task is to bring the *logos*, the inheritance of the Father, into the world. To accomplish this would be the crossing of a major life-threshold: establishing himself as a writer. But *the book turns out to be obscene*, meaning that the *logos* is, somehow, seeped in *eros*. Furthermore, he must present this obscene book *to the madam of a whorehouse*, meaning that his task is to bring the *logos*, seeped in *eros*, into the world of the Mother. By accomplishing this task, he will have crossed the profession threshold, but this will possibly have consequences on the marriage threshold as well.

Meanwhile, a hidden intention, revealing a second, very different task is revealed: he wants to use the occasion of presenting the book as a pretext *'to screw one of the house tarts in passing'*. To accomplish this involves the crossing of a quite different life-threshold: expressing his *eros* in an adult manner, by engaging a women sexually.

At this point, it appears that the dreamer's motivation, from beginning to end, was the expression of his *eros* rather than his *logos*. Rather than struggle to engage the world, through the word, why not simply experience it, pleasureably, through the womb? And he does indeed forget about his book, about his task of 'bringing the word into the world', and so, of crossing the life-threshold of profession.

But the second, hidden task – 'screwing one of the tarts' – is also not fulfilled. It is gradually deflected along a series of other more infantile courses: he finds himself *with his cock hanging out, standing barefoot in a puddle, having only one shoe,* and so on, causing him to feel *sad, uneasy, and nervous*. He has not accomplished the first task, has not yet crossed the first threshold, of acquiring a profession, and so remains a child. Hence, as the dream reveals, his expression of *eros* will also remain an infantile one until he does so.

The second task is further deflected along a series of distracting images and drawings, which display the consequences of his desire. And, in this way, the forgotten *logos* appears once more, in the form of *the despised newspaper that runs the bordello* and is responsible for this display of pictures. Each image shows, and *the crouching gnome* actually embodies, the monstrous consequence of the expression of his *eros*. The newspaper accomplishes the task that the dreamer himself could not: bringing the *logos* into the world of *eros*.

The *logos* of the Father world (the book, the newspaper), when it is successfully brought into the *eros* of the Mother world (the madam, the whorehouse), illuminates that darkened world, revealing the full consequences of their union. By having his book published, the dreamer is about to acquire a profession. But, having acquired a wife, the world he now experiences will be altered. The expression of his desire will no longer be deflected along its infantile course, but will also express itself in an adult way: in the creation of a child. And so the full – and monstrous – consequences of the adult expression of his desire are revealed.

At the nadir of the dream, which is also the dream's end, the image of the gnome appears. This image appears at that point in the narrative when the two dream tasks meet, and are partly resolved (the *logos* is brought into the *eros* of Mother world.) At that point, an oneiric Threshold Image appears – an image that, were he to *enter through* it, would transform his life entirely.

Baudelaire displays a respectful curiosity towards the misshapen gnome, a fear and fascination combined: *'I didn't dare touch him, but I was interested in him.'* It is, at one and the same time, an image of the child he will have, as a consequence of his desire for his wife, and of the child he himself was, as a consequence of his parents' desire. It is also an image that stands at two important thresholds in his life. In the backward movement, it is an image of himself as a child, and so it stands at the threshold of his infancy. In the forward movement, it is an image of the child he will have, and so stands at a further threshold which, after the thresholds of marriage and profession, will have to be crossed.

We have sought out these images that stand at certain life-thresholds because, by *entering through* them, the dreamer can begin to approach his life as a greater whole. He may *enter through* these images by meditating upon them, or by living his life such that they are encountered in its forward movement. To *enter*, in meditation, *through* the image of the gnome, for example, would require that the dreamer trace his own feelings backward in relation to this image. By confronting his own fears of himself as a child, he would also confront his fears of the child he will engender. Or, he may *enter*, in life, *through* the image of the gnome, by engendering that child, together with his wife. Then he would be confronting his fears as they appear before him in his waking world, and in the forward journey through life.

VI. Infantile Life-Thresholds

Having identified the dream's nadir-Threshold Image, we may now examine some of the other curious arrangements of images that are constellated around the dream-I, so as to demonstrate how the dream-I passes forward and back over many of our earlier life-thresholds. These images are so composed as to betray something puzzling or enigmatic to our more rational, and hence, more mature ways of thinking. For, dormant in their arrangements are the dream-I's more archaic and at times infantile manner of thinking.

The first unusual incident is that, no sooner had he rung and entered, then he *'noticed that his cock was hanging out'*. Also, that his feet *were bare*, and that he *'had stepped into a pool of liquid at the bottom of the stairs'*. These have already been identified as 'infantile' rather than adult expressions of the dreamer's *eros*. But in what way are they infantile? They reveal the child's disposition towards nakedness, as something natural and enjoyable, as opposed to the adult's acquired attitude of shame and embarrassment.

If we were to *enter through* these images, we would find that they stand at the threshold between the child's natural daring and inclination to be naked, and the adult-imposed strictures upon it as something wrong and forbidden. They are comparable, in Christian mythology, to the fall: when Adam and Eve *'knew that they were naked'*. Although the dreamer, as an adult, feels embarrassed by his infantile behaviour, that child lives on in him, and takes pleasure in expressing its *eros* in infantile ways.

The 'I' journeying through this dream is not the 'waking-I' of the thirty-four year old Baudelaire, but the 'dream-I', which moves freely through all the various thresholds of his life. The brothel appears *'vast'*, because it is seen through the eyes of a small child. This is why *school-boys* are also present among the men. He finds the brothel to be *'ill-lit and dingy'*, and he himself is bare-footed, *though one shoe strangely appears on his foot and, a little later, another.* The dinginess of the place is related to taboo's of 'dirty and clean' acquired as a child. Like 'naked and clothed' or 'wrong and right', learning the difference between 'dirty and clean' constitutes an important life-threshold for a child, and many memories may be constellated around this theme. In this case, the brothel is associated with 'something dirty'.

The bare feet are another matter. At the beginning, his bare feet, because they are naked, are an infantile expression of *eros*. 'Standing in a puddle' also expresses this: a childish sense of joy at being wet. But, to the adult, these bare and wet feet are deemed 'improper'. Thinking he will express his *eros* in an adult manner by 'screwing one of the tarts', the dreamer rationalizes, *'I'll wash them before I screw and before I leave the house'*. This seems like a reasonable, adult solution to the child's improper expression of *eros*.

But the more he walks, the more he is afraid *'someone might see my feet'* that is, recognize his improper and infantile expression of *eros*. Another solution gradually appears: not to wash away the dirty expression of the child's *eros* 'before and after screwing', but to avoid it altogether. And that is what he does subsequently: he turns his attention away from the prostitutes, and begins to focus on the drawings and pictures around the vast galleries. As the dream rather ingeniously shows, it was when he no longer attempted to express his *eros*, either as a child or as an adult, that *the shoes miraculously appeared on his feet*, first one, then the other.

Then come the series of pictures, each with a note in the corner saying, *'such and such a tart, age... , gave birth to this fœtus in the year such and such'*. These are followed by a living example: the squat little monster, oddly crouched on a pedestal, with a black serpentine appendage growing out of its head and coiled round his body. How do we approach such an image?

VII. To Enter Through the Oneiric Threshold Image

We have established that this image is related to the next life-threshold awaiting Baudelaire. Once he has successfully crossed the thresholds of marriage and profession, the threshold of fathering a child awaits. But this image is not only *related* to that life-threshold. Located at the very nadir of his dream-myth, it becomes the oneiric Threshold Image he must *enter through*. The image symbolizes the child which the dreamer will engender to become a father.

And yet, how could he even begin to *enter through* such an image in his meditations? Clearly, the image must also become a symbol of *the child he himself once was*. It is only by recollecting memories of *his own* childhood that the dreamer would begin to *enter through* this image of the child he could engender. And so, to successfully step across that future life-threshold in a forward movement through life, he must first begin with a more backward movement, regressing to the past life-thresholds of his own infancy.

With the aid of the Ancient Template, we may imagine the dreamer's attempt of *entering through* this oneiric Threshold Image. Such an elucidation constitutes the Oneiric Path through the Ancient Template. Starting on the outermost edge of the spiralling mists, we begin by constellating a series of childhood memory-images around this image. Feelings of fear, embarrassment and ridicule may arise, and so be traced ever further backward to their source.

We ask ourselves – why has the child taken on the monstrous appearance of a gnome? Why this *fear*? And why did the gnome 'squat little things that he was' feel *embarrassed* 'to sit at table next to a big shapely girl'. Such feelings may be used to descend ever deeper through the memory-images floating in the mists.

But our attempts to follow feelings back through the personal memories constellated around this peculiar dream image only take us back so far, and soon come to an incomplete and frustrating end.

Nevertheless, this dream-image remains the key which, with its gentle turning, unlocks further memories – but now through collective memory-images rather than personal ones. These cultural arrangements of images may model contents of the mind otherwise unavailable to consciousness. And so, we descend further downward in the spiralling mists of our own memory.

We note that the child in Baudelaire's dream has a certain peculiarity of form. Due to the serpentine appendage wrapped

Serpent-entwined Gnome
Detail from Ernst Fuchs:
Job and the Judgement of Paris (1966)

around it, this figure has *combined* two different symbols into one composite image: the child and the serpent.

As the child, he is like Jung's *Puer Æternus:* 'the eternal child'. Like the infant Krishna, Christ, Moses or Gilgamesh, he is a child abandoned at birth, and one of his divine parents remains unknown.[8] He is the blinding epiphany concealed in an infant's guise. Meanwhile, other cultural images may attach themselves to his serpentine appendage: the ancient serpent that uncoils at the moment of creation. The eternal death-and-rebirth of the serpent sloughing its skin.

But the gnome *combines* these two ancient images. To *enter through* this combination of symbols, we must think through them in the more ancient manner of 'symbolic thinking', seeking out their deeper differences and similarities. The serpent has its abode underground: it lives in the depths of darkness. The child too lives in darkness: in the depths of the unconscious. The ancient serpent, in many Cosmogonic myths, symbolizes those dark and formless powers at the source of creation. The eternal child, meanwhile, symbolizes those same dark and formless powers at the beginning of life. To *enter through* this image is to experience these two in combination: to return to the source of creation and the source of life. We undergo *a momentary return to the source of all light and life:* to 'the Beginning'.

By *entering through* the image of the child, we may come to birth once more 'from within'. And the serpent, with its ever-recurring rebirth, reminds us how we must *continually* return to that ancient fount – *"to die to the world, and to come to birth from within,"*[9] as Campbell has said. By *entering through* this oneiric Threshold Image, we also return to *the dream's* source: a glimpse into our own innermost Self. We enter into the circle of light at the centre of the Ancient Template.

Pertinent to this theme is Eliade's remark that: *"The man of the archaic society is trying to transport himself back to the beginning of the world in order to re-absorb the initial plenitude and to recover, intact, the reserves of energy in the new-born babe."*[10]

As a result of this primordial experience, all our fears of fathering the child, due to our own traumatic feelings of childhood abandonment, embarrassment or ridicule, fall away in favour of a more innocent joy. By moving backward over the thresholds of life, and discovering there this infant epiphany, we are now prepared for the next step forward in life, by fathering that child.

VII. The Dreamsource

We have *entered through* a Threshold Image into the centre of the oneiric cosmos, into the very source of the dream. But, whenever we pursue the Oneiric Path through a dream, *what is that centre to which we have come?*

It is our innermost Self which has lived through each past stage of our growth, and will continue to live through the following ones. It holds together all the various disparate moments of our life, and reflects them to us as one 'wholeness'. Meanwhile, the I of our dreams is very much like the hero of myths: a timeless figure engaged in an endless quest for life's greater wholeness. As it crosses back and forth over previous life-thresholds, or approaches our next life-threshold, it reveals our life in the context of the greater whole: it intimates to us its deeper unity. Thus, the more thresholds it crosses, the more the dream-I reveals the innermost Self.

Like myths of the creation, dreams offer us models of the mind. Their images indicate the existence of certain contents of the mind which consciousness is otherwise unable to access. Thus, these images are *les clés du mystère,* capable of unlocking certain memories which otherwise remain closed off to us.

For we are caught in our present ego-incarnation, and quite incapable of extending our memory as far back as earliest infancy (nor can we extend our awareness into the far future, beyond future life-thresholds and even beyond death). But, the images of our dreams open up new pathways for us to pursue in memory regression – which is, by definition, a memory *extension.* And an extended movement through our memory reveals our life to us in the context of its greater wholeness.

If we recall that all created things, by uniquely mirroring their creator, may become symbols of the Sacred at their source, then our view onto the things we encounter in dreams must also be altered radically. For it follows that, not only the dream-I, but *all* the things surrounding it – other persons, actions, and events – reflect some aspect the Dreamsource. Our innermost Self lies at their very centre, and unifies them all as one plenitude, just as the Divine unifies the cosmos as its centre and source.

And so, through the Oneiric Path, *all the images* we encounter in dreams may be *entered through* to the unity at their source. But, it must not be forgotten that, during dreaming, all of these faces, figures and events are usually constellated around the dream-I. In effect, we enter through the dream-I, *in combination with* its many associated images, to the mystery at their shared source: the Dreamsource.

IX. The Sacred Life Journey

On the Oneiric Path, all the figures recognizable to us from the waking world – mother and father, friend or foe, and indeed, our own ego – may expand in their roles to the *Magna Mater* and *Pater Omnipotens*, the heavenly Helper or dark Opposer, and even the eternal hero – to-initiate us from within into an awareness of life's greater plenitude.

It is no mere co-incidence that all these dream-figures whose thresholds must be crossed in the rites of passage through life – mother, father, marriage, childbearing – are also archetypal symbols from our sacred mythologies, whose thresholds are crossed over into an experience of the Sacred. All the mythologies of this world use the images of life *to give their gods life* – to enliven what would otherwise be empty idols.

And yet, as a result, *they render life itself as sacred*, so that our inner dream-life becomes the sacred path to recognizing our innermost divinity. To live our lives wholly and completely means to live it in the full awareness of all its stages, which are reflected to us in our mythology as initiatory steps leading to the Sacred.

Most dreams symbolize the *attempt* to cross one or more life-thresholds. However, there are indeed dreams where a life-threshold is indeed *crossed*. Such dreams, though rare, are extremely mythic and symbolic in character. This is because our ancient ancestors, the shamans, myth-makers and epic poets of antiquity, have elevated the unconscious imagery of these dreams into our culture and consciousness. Through their artistry and myth-making, they have transformed the fleeting imagery of dreams into timeless Threshold Images.

And now we, through our sacred art and mythology, may return to these primæval dreams, to recognize their hidden marks and read their secret characters. To read a dream's oracles and enigmas requires that we open our minds to the inspiration and experience of the Sacred in them. And we will only do this once we have learned, through dreams, *to see life itself as a many-staged epiphany.*

CHAPTER XV

Narrative and the Hero Task in Dreams

When I say 'my bed will comfort me
my couch will ease my complaint'
then thou dost scare me with dreams
and terrify me with visions.
- Book of Job 7:13

I. The Dream of Descartes

On the night of November 10th, 1619, the French philosopher René Descartes had a most peculiar dream.

Although he was only twenty-three years of age and still learning the art of soldiering under the Bavarian duke Maximilian I, 1619 was a decisive year for him. Shortly before, he had met the Dutch mathematician Beeckman, who had challenged him to stop *"wandering here and there in the world,"*[1] and commence with his philosophical studies in earnest. That night, before he went to sleep, Descartes felt that he had discovered the foundations of his philosophy, which he subsequently published eighteen years later as *The Discourse on Method.*

The dream – or rather, series of three dreams, including Descartes' own interpretation – were recorded in a notebook called *Olympica*, subsequently lost. Fortunately for us, one of Descartes early biographers, A. Baillet, had access to this notebook, and transcribed the dream from Latin to French for his *Vie de Monsieur Des Cartes* (1691). In the process, the dream was also rendered into the third person, but otherwise appears accurate and authentic. As a dream loses its immediacy in that voice, we have rendered it back into the first person, while following Baillet's account[2] faithfully.

On the 10th of November 1619, having gone to bed full of inspiration and engrossed in the thought that he had, that day, discovered the foundations of his science, [Descartes] had three consecutive dreams, which could only, he surmised, have come from above:

Once I had fallen asleep, several phantoms appeared before my mind's eye, terrifying me so greatly that, as I walked through the streets, I was obliged to lean over onto my left side in order to go where I wanted, for my right side felt so weak that I could not hold myself up. Ashamed to be walking in this manner, I made an effort to straighten myself; but just then a great gust of wind carried me up in a sort of whirlwind [tourbillon] and spun me around three or four times on my left foot.

But that was not the most frightening part. I had such difficulty dragging myself along, that I seemed to fall at every step, until finally, noticing a college open along the way, I went inside in search of shelter and a remedy for my pain.

I tried to find the college chapel, my first thought being to go there and pray. But I realized that I had just passed a man I knew without greeting him. I was about to turn back to pay my compliments, when I was violently knocked backwards by a wind blowing toward the chapel.

Then, I noticed another person standing in the middle of the courtyard, who called me by name most amiably and politely, and suggested I go and see Monsieur N., who had something to give me. I assumed that it must be a melon brought from some foreign land.

Meanwhile, I was surprised to see that a crowd had gathered around Monsieur N. and myself to join in the conversation, and all were standing upright and steady on their feet, while I was still hunched and wobbling about, even though we were standing on the same ground, and the wind, which had tried several times to turn me around, had greatly diminished.

With this image in my mind, I awoke, and immediately felt a real pain in my side, which made me fear some evil spirit [mauvais génie] might be at work, leading me astray. I immediately turned onto my right side, as it was on my left side that I had fallen asleep and had the dream.

I prayed to God to protect me from the evil consequences of my dream, and to preserve me from the woes that might befall me as a punishment for my sins. For, although I had led, up to now, a life quite irreproachable in the eyes of men, my sins might still be grave enough to bring the bolts of heaven's vengeance crashing on my head.

After nearly two hours sunk in diverse thoughts on the good and evil that attend us in this world, I again fell asleep. Immediately, another dream came in which I heard a loud, explosive noise, which I took to be a thunderclap. Instantly I awoke from fright and, opening my eyes, saw that the room was filled with fiery sparks scattered all around.

This had happened to me previously on other occasions, and it was not so unusual for me to awaken in the middle of the night with my eyes so sparkling that I could see the objects closest to me. But on this occasion, I decided to look to Philosophy for an explanation. After opening and closing my eyes alternately and in succession, I drew a conclusion as to the nature of the phenomena, which put my mind at rest. And in this way, my terror thus vanished, and I went back to sleep in a reasonably calm state.

A moment later, I had a third dream, which had nothing in it so frightening as the first two. In this one, I found a book on the table, although I had no idea who had put it there. Opening it, I was delighted to find that it was a Dictionary, which I hoped to find rather useful.

At the same moment, I noticed another book at hand, which had appeared from nowhere, and was also new to me. It turned out to be a collection of poems by various authors, entitled Corpus omnium veterum poetarum Latinorum. I was curious to read some of it and, opening the book, came upon the line: Quod vitae sectabor iter? [What road shall I follow in life?]

At that moment, I saw a man I did not know, who handed me a piece of verse beginning with the words Est & Non, [Yes & No] which he recommended as excellent. I told him that I knew the poem, one of the Idylls of Ausonius included in the thick Anthology of Poets on the table. Wishing to show it to the man, I began leafing through the book, whose order and arrangement I prided myself on knowing perfectly.

While I was searching for it, the man asked me where I had come upon the book, and I replied that I could not say but, the moment before I had handled yet another book, which had recently disappeared, and I didn't know who had brought it either, or taken it away again. No sooner had I said this than I saw the book reappear at the other end of the table, but less complete as it had been when I first saw it.

Finally, I found the poems of Ausonius in the collection I was leafing through, but was not able to find the piece which began Est & Non. Nevertheless, I told the man I knew an even finer poem by the same poet, which began Quod vitae sectabor iter? [What road shall I follow in life?]

The man asked me to show it to him, and I began looking for it when I came upon several small portraits in copper engraving. I had to admit that the book was very fine indeed, but certainly not the edition that I knew. Before I could say any more, books and man vanished completely from my imagination, without, however, awakening me.

Doubting whether what I had just seen was a dream or a vision, I actually decided, while sleeping, that it was a dream, and even interpreted it before waking. The Dictionary, I decided, signified nothing other than all the sciences gathered together, while the collection of

*poetry signified in particular, and in a more distinct manner, Philosophy
and Wisdom combined.*

*For it was not surprising to me that poets, even the witless
rhymers among them, should be full of maxims more serious, sensible,
and better expressed, than those of the philosophers. This is due to
Divine Inspiration and the power of the Imagination, which bring out
the seeds of wisdom (that exists in the minds of all men, like fiery sparks
in pebbles) much more easily and even more brilliantly than Reason
can in philosophers.*

*Continuing to interpret the dream in my sleep, I concluded that
the piece of poetry beginning* Quod vitae sectabor iter [What road shall
I follow in life?], *about the uncertainty of the kind of life one should
choose, showed the good counsel of a wise person, or even of moral
theology. Thereupon, doubting whether I was dreaming or meditating,
I woke up.*

*With eyes open, I continued the interpretation of the dream along
the same lines. I understood the poets assembled in the Anthology to
signify Revelation and Inspiration, which I hoped would continue to
favour me.*

The piece Est et Non, *which was the Yes and No of Pythagorus,
was thus the Truth and Falsity of all human knowledge and the profane
sciences. This tallied well with my own inclinations. So that it seemed
to me the Spirit of Truth had, in this dream, opened the treasures of all
the sciences to me.*

Descartes' later remarks[3] on the dream's interpretation may be rendered
as follows:

*The following day, an Italian painter came to visit me. This
explains the copper engravings.*

*The third dream refers to my future, the two preceding ones to my
past.*

*The melon signifies the charms of solitude offered by purely
human enticements.*

An Evil Spirit [mauvais génie] *propelled me towards the chapel.*

*The Spirit of God that had made me take the first steps towards
the chapel did not permit me to be carried off by the evil spirit.* [mauvais
génie]

*The thunder I heard signaled the descent of the Spirit of Truth,
taking possession of me.*

*I was perfectly sober that day, and had not drunk wine for three
months.*

The genius *that aroused my Inspiration had pre-dicted the dreams
before I went to bed. The human mind had no part in them.*

What road shall I follow in life? This phrase occurs no less than three times in his dream. Without a doubt, the dream of that night 'announced from within' the life-altering nature of the discovery he had made that day: the Method of his philosophy. It marks the crossing of an important life-threshold.

But, more than that, his dream shows how the dream-I may regress in its behaviour to earlier life-thresholds, or even advance in its behaviour towards anticipated ones (since the dream-I is capable of moving back and forth across all of the thresholds of life). As a result of these movements, an oneiric Threshold Image appears at the nadir of the dream, encapsulating the present life-threshold awaiting the waking-I in waking life. For Descartes, this present life-threshold was his philosophical discovery, and the dream itself posed several life-questions which his philosophy subsequently attempted to answer.

II. The Meditations
& The Method of Descartes

The dream of November 10th, 1619 was dreamt in response to the thought that, on that very day, he had 'discovered the foundations of his science'. That science, known as Descartes 'Method', was utilized subsequently in all his philosophical works. In the publication of his *Discourse on Method,* Descartes explained that the original inspiration for his Method came to him at the age of twenty-three, while

> *...in Germany, whither the wars, which have not yet finished there, had called me. And as I was returning from the coronation of the Emperor to join the army, the onset of winter held me up in quarters which, finding no company to distract me, and having, fortunately, no cares or passions to disturb me, I spent the whole day shut up in a room heated by an enclosed stove, where I had complete leisure to meditate on my own thoughts.*[4]

The substance of his Method, discovered that day through an undisturbed meditation and subsequent inspiration, was to *"never accept anything as true that I did not know to be evidently so."*[5] This is a radical departure from the method of knowledge acquired from the Jesuits, who acknowledged the authority of certain teachings, and developed instead methods of debate to contest one authority against another.

Descartes preserved the idea of *method* from his Jesuit masters, but altered it in light of his studies of geometry to include the idea of *self-evidence.* He thought the truths of philosophy should demonstrate themselves, just as self-evidently as the truths of geometry – that, for example, 'the three angles of a triangle must always equal 180°'.

Then, on the day of his dream, a further 'revelation and inspiration' came to him. As an essential component of his Method, Descartes resolved to *doubt* all his former beliefs. As he reveals in the first chapter of his *Meditations on the First Philosophy*, he had begun by doubting the existence of his mind, his body, the world, and God.

Then, as each Meditation recounts, he set about investigating which of these thoughts were indubitable. For, he would only accept as *true* those ideas which presented themselves *clearly and distinctly* to his mind. By their *clarity and distinctness*, the truth of these ideas would thus become *self-evident:*

> *I shall suppose, therefore, that there is not a true God, who is the supreme sovereign of truth, but some evil demon* [mauvais génie], *no less cunning and deceiving than powerful, who has used all his artifice to deceive me. I will suppose that the heavens, the air, the earth, colours, shapes, sounds and all external things that we see are only illusions and deceptions which he uses to take me in. I will consider myself as having no hands, eyes, flesh, blood or senses... I shall cling obstinately to this notion.*[6]

Descartes solution was to find one thought among these illusions and deceptions that is indubitable: *"I am, I exist,"* and that this *"is necessarily true every time I express it or conceive of it in my mind."*[7] In *The Discourse on Method*, it is expressed in the form of a proof: *"I think, therefore I am."*[8]

Then, in his Second Meditation, Descartes meditates on a piece of wax beside the fire, and demonstrably concludes the existence of, not the wax or the fire, but his own mind. Next, in the Third Meditation, the concept of God 'who is infinitely perfect' presents itself to his mind. Can he doubt the existence of an infinitely perfect God? *"I cannot conceive a God without existence, any more than I can conceive a mountain without a valley,"*[9] he concludes. Like the triangle whose angles must equal 180°, an infinitely perfect God, to be perfect, must also exist. Its truth is self-evident.

In the remaining Meditations, the creation itself unfolds, in accord with *"the order and disposition that God has established in created things."*[10] And because of God's unwillingness to deceive him, Descartes was able to accept and demonstrate that the entire cosmos – 'the heavens, the air and the earth; colours, shapes and sounds; eyes, flesh and blood' – truly existed.

III. Announcing Thresholds
From Within

Having reviewed the substance of the Method discovered that day, we may now review Descartes' dream of that night. As Descartes' first dream begins, he is *walking through the streets*, but his progress is hindered in a variety of mysterious ways. Although the question of 'what road to follow in life' will only appear in the third dream, the *street* that Descartes is walking along here seems to be none other than 'the road to follow in life.'

And, as his troubled movements indicate, his life has suddenly become open and exposed to malevolent influences. Descartes experiences *terrifying phantoms* and *a great gust of wind* which force him *to the left* and then spin him round *on his left foot.* Indeed, with each step, he fears *he will fall.* He had made an important discovery that day – his Method – which marked a most important threshold crossing. And now, at night, he was experiencing *the fearful, uncertain, and even malevolent* consequences of that discovery.

As a result of these troubled movements, a task is gradually imposed on the dream-I: *to find a college chapel where he may pray.* But why would a college and its chapel offer the way out of his troubled situation?

Remembering that the dream-I extends along the full course of the dreamer's life, then Descartes' response is to seek those places which offered him shelter and security as a child. The first is *a college* – for eight years, Descartes studied under the Jesuits at the *Collège de la Flèche,* beginning at the age of eight. The second is *a chapel.* When asked directly about his religion, Descartes replied *"My religion is that of my nurse,"*[11] meaning that the simple prayers which the motherless child said at chapel remained his religion for the rest of his life.

But Descartes is not able to return to the schooling and beliefs of his childhood. As the subsequent movements of the dream-I show, he is not able to go back because of all the thresholds he has crossed since that time: he has become a gentleman (*greeting an acquaintance he unwittingly ignored*) and has travelled widely, reaping all the fruits of those experiences (*Mr. N's gift of a melon brought from a foreign land*). And as a scholar, he now carries on knowledgeable discussions with his colleagues – *though he is still hunched and wobbling about from the wind.* The evil influence of the *mauvais génie* remains with him to the end of the dream.

By the end of the dream, Descartes does *not* complete the dream-task. Only after waking will he be able to say his prayers – asking that he be protected from '*the mauvais génie leading him astray*'.

It is worth noting that, just as Descartes prays after waking from the first dream, so does he seek out Philosophy after waking from the second dream. Although *a tremendous thunderclap frightens him into wakefulness,* he resorts to various 'methods' to solve its mystery, deciding in the end that '*the thunder I heard signaled the descent of the Spirit of Truth*'. As we shall see, Descartes will answer many of the disturbing questions raised by this dream through his *Meditations on the First Philosophy.*

In the third dream, feelings of *fear* are noticeably absent. Instead, there is the *delight* of *discovering* something – in this case, the dictionary – *which may have some future use.* It is not so much *what* he discovers, but *that* he discovers something, causing him to feel tremendous joy and hope. The third dream is 'announcing from within' his recent threshold-crossing: that day's discovering of his philosophical Method.

But that is not all. A *second book* appears, a poetry anthology, and like the first, he *has no idea where it came from* – just as his Method came to him unexpectedly, and by *'a revelation and inspiration favouring him'*. Curious about the second book, he opens it at random to find the line *Quod vitae sectabor iter?* – "What road shall I follow in life?"*

The all-important question has been phrased. Does the dream now provide an answer? A man whom Descartes *does not know* hands him a piece of verse beginning *Est & Non* – *"Yes & No"*. The man is an aspect of Descartes himself – the aspect of himself he does not know, or perhaps, does not *yet* know. This man tells him, basically, that 'you have the choice; all things are possible (Yes *and* No)'.

Descartes himself responds to this by *claiming to know the poem*, and *searches for it* in the Anthology. Where the mysterious man responded to the life-question in an enigmatic way full of possibilities, Descartes can only respond to it by demonstrating his knowledge of sources and authorities, like a pupil being examined by his Jesuit masters. The dream-I is returning to the academic methods of his youth.

It is no wonder the mysterious man then asks him 'where he had come upon the book.' He is reminding Descartes of the discovery he had made that day: the Method preferring 'self-evidence', which came to him *'as a revelation'*. But Descartes persists in his schoolish mode of behaviour, looking more and more like a fool: the book *disappears* and then suddenly *re-appears*, but now *less complete*. Since Descartes fails to locate the source of *'Yes & No',* the man asks him to find instead the source of *'what road shall I follow in life'* – again reminding him of his discovery, and of the important threshold he has crossed.

But who is the man? One of his Jesuit masters? Or is it an older and wiser aspect of Descartes himself, who is now testing his younger self? The dream presents – simultaneously – the younger Descartes of his Jesuit days, and the older Descartes who acknowledges the discovery he had made that day: the Method that uses 'self-evidence' as the foundation of his philosophy.

Like the first dream, the third dream is structured through task acquisition and accomplishment. His task, at first, is to find the poem with the words *'Est & Non'*. And though he tries desperately to accomplish this task, various digressions and distractions intervene (the book *disappearing* and *re-appearing*). Then, a new task is given: the mysterious man asks him to locate the source of the words *'Quod vitae sectabor iter.'* And again, the

*The first part of the poem in question runs: *"Quod vitae sectabor iter? Si plena tumultu / Sunt fara; Si curus domus anxia: si peregrinos / Cura domos..."* "What road shall I follow in life? When the streets are full of turmoil, and home beset by worry?"[12]

accomplishment of this task is deflected along various courses (the *copper engravings*).

However, in the final part of the dream, Descartes realizes that the book in which he sought the source of these two lines is nothing other than *'Philosophy and Wisdom combined'*. Hence, as the final moments of the dream show, the road to follow in life, offering it as many choices as possible, is the pursuit of Philosophy. And so, the accomplishment of the dream-task lies ultimately, in his day-time pursuit of Philosophy.

When we compare all three of these dreams to myths, it becomes clear that the first and third are structured through the tasks imposed upon the dream-I, and its attempts to accomplish them by the dream's end. Like myths, the images of these dreams are held together by *the iconologue of task completion*.

As well, the imagery in the dreams relate to specific life-threshold crossings. Some of these reveal earlier modes of behaviour, others manifest future ones. At the final, nadir moment of the last dream, the enigmatic phrase recurs: *'What road shall I follow in life'* This indicates that all the dreams are ultimately concerned with his present life-threshold crossing. In particular, they are concerned with the life-threshold *of profession*, or rather, *vocation*: 'what is my calling in life?' *Quod vitae sectabor iter?* 'What road shall I follow?'

At the point in the dream when Descartes attempts to interpret the enigmatic phrase, he wakes up. This phrase, like a Threshold Image, is capable of transforming his life entirely, if only he can *enter through* it. The way through these words, he realizes by the end of the dream, is Philosophy. *That* is his vocation; *that* is the task which the dream has given him, and which he must pursue in his waking life. For, in Philosophy lay the answers to those disturbing questions which arose during the dream's more disquieting experiences.

IV. The Philosophy of a Nightmare

He had crossed an important life-threshold the day before, and the dreams were not only announcing this from within, but causing him to experience the full implications of that discovery. Descartes himself felt that the dreams of that night were a result of the same revelation and inspiration that attended him that day during the discovery of his Method. Hence, it may very well be that the Philosophy he subsequently developed in his *Meditations* was in response to, not only the new Method he arrived at consciously that day, but the dreams he experienced unconsciously that night.

And so he would only realize the philosophical implications of, not only his Method, but also his dream, in his Philosophy – which he subsequently published in his *Meditations on the First Philosophy*. Were there certain experiences within the dream that caused him to develop particular aspects of his Philosophy?

In order for the truth to reveal itself through his Method, Descartes had to do something which no Doctor of Theology had done till then – *doubt*, and doubt not only the existence of sublunary things, but *even the existence of God*.

It is this doubt, which is such an integral part of his Method, that suddenly threw him open to fearful, uncertain, and even malevolent influences. In the day-lit world of his rationality, this was a simple and necessary stage in his thinking. But in the night-time world of his dreams, where age-old beliefs and their infantile fears still persisted, this exposed him to the wiles and deceptions of evil spirits, and even the threat of eternal damnation.

Certainly, in the dreams of that night, Descartes felt threatened by a *mauvais génie*. We can now see that the terrifying phantoms causing him to lean *leftward*, and the *tourbillon* that spun him around on his *left* foot, were indeed those *sinister* forces to which he had exposed himself that day (our English translation obscures this connection, whereas, in Latin, the word *sinister* means both *left* and *malevolent*). But more than that, the abyss into which *he feared he would fall with every step* was indeed the torments of Hell attending each step of his inquiry.

Descartes had crossed a most significant threshold that day, but to do so he had put his soul at tremendous risk. The dream-I as encountered at the beginning of the dream is Descartes on the other side of the threshold, but only gradually becoming aware of the malevolent forces to which he had exposed himself.

We now see more clearly why his response was to seek out the college chapel and to pray: he sought to *cross back* over the threshold of that day, returning to the security of his childhood. But he could not go back. Due to the other thresholds he had crossed – becoming a well-travelled gentleman and scholar – he could not return to his childhood. Nor could he go back to being a Jesuit scholar. While his learnèd colleagues, enclosed in the courtyard, had stayed within the disputory methods of the Jesuits, and so *were unaffected by the malevolent wind*, he had passed beyond them, and was still being menaced by the wind at the dream's end.

It is for good reason that Descartes, after waking, spent two hours in thought about *the good and evil that attend us in this world;* that he prayed to God for *protection from evil;* and that he asked God to preserve him from *the woe that might befall him*. Nevertheless, the second dream redounded with a thunderclap that was indeed a revelation of God's just retribution: *'the bolts of heaven's vengeance crashing on his head.'* He was damned. The first dream, in all its horror, had revealed the fearful, uncertain, and even malevolent consequences of doubting God's existence. The second dream, in its all-too-brief but apocalyptic moment, revealed God's own wrathful judgement upon his soul.

For Descartes then, the second dream was nothing less than a momentary epiphany – a kind of vengeance upon him for doubting God's existence. As the philosopher himself noted later, God was capable of inspiring in people a *"...Divine revelation* [that] *raises us at a stroke to infallible belief"*[13] Indeed, from this momentary 'stroke' – 'the bolts of heaven's vengeance crashing on his head' – Descartes certainly learned that God *revealed his own existence.*

While earlier philosophers, such as Anselm, had attempted to prove God's existence using the concept of perfection, Descartes was the first to use perfection so as to demonstrate that God's existence was 'self-evident'. From the dream, then, Descartes acquired an aspect of his philosophy which later showed up in *The Meditations:* that God's existence was 'self-evident' because *it revealed itself.*

Descartes also encountered that night, what eventually became, the *'mauvais génie'* of *The Meditations*, who was *"no less cunning and deceiving than powerful,* [and] *has used all his artifice to deceive me."*[14] After the dream, Descartes himself interpreted the *tourbillon* that spun him round and knocked him back violently, as *'a mauvais génie leading me astray'.* This was his greatest reason for doubting – so essential to the Method used in *The Meditations* – with one, final exception.

V. I Dream, therefore, I am

What he also discovered and experienced so intensely that night was the potency of *a dream* to deceive him. Throughout *The Meditations*, Descartes refers to the imagination and dreams time and again, describing their extraordinary power to deceive, so that he cannot distinguish clearly and distinctly whether he is dreaming or awake. *"How many times have I dreamt at night that I was in this place, dressed, by the fire, although I was quite naked in my bed?"*[15] he asks, and concludes: *"There are no conclusive signs by means of which one can distinguish clearly between being awake and being asleep... I am quite astonished by it; and my astonishment is such that it is almost capable of persuading me that I am asleep now."*[16]

As a matter of fact, for the remainder of *The Meditations*, Descartes does not demonstrate that he is awake. Only at the end of *The Meditations* is he able to establish that he was *not dreaming* because dreams, unlike wakingness, are too disconnected, and lack continuity with 'the general course of our lives':

> *I must reject all the doubts of the last few days... particularly the general uncertainty about sleep, which I could not distinguish from the wakeful state: for I now see a very notable difference between the two states in that our memory can never connect our dreams with one another, and with the general course of our lives, as it is in the habit of connecting the things which happen to us when we are awake.*[17]

Our review of Descartes' dream has suggested that he did indeed experience certain things in his dreams which then contributed to his Philosophy as expressed in *The Meditations*. In particular, that he experienced God, the devil, and even of the ability of dreams to deceive him, and that all of these eventually arrived in his Philosophy as well.

Particularly the third dream offered him new possibilities regarding 'the path to follow in life'. And, by accomplishing in deed what was left unaccomplished in dreams, Descartes was able to pursue new pathways in his thinking – which subsequently became his *Meditations of the First Philosophy*. But, it was the dream which posed the life questions to which his Philosophy eventually offered this answer.

VI. To Transfer the Hero's task

"Myths which day has forgotten continue to be told by night"[18] Jung has said. It is entirely possible that the narrative structures which we have encountered in myths had their earliest source in dreams. In dreams, narrative structures emerge freely and spontaneously. After a few random arrangements in the earlier part of the dream, the dream-I acquires a certain task. Then, subsequent images involving the dream-I become linked into a descending series. The images surrounding the dream-I reveal their contexts to be earlier or later life-threshold crossings, and the dream-I's behaviour reflects a free movement back and forth over these earlier or later life-thresholds, so as to present the present task within the greater context of the dreamer's life *as a whole*. Though the dream-I may digress in its given task, the series of more minor threshold crossings culminates finally in a nadir Threshold Image where the dream-I comes face to face with a major and more recent life-threshold crossing.

In some dreams, the dream-I may indeed *accomplish* its task at this threshold – offering the waking-I new paths to pursue through life. Or, it may leave that task uncompleted, which now falls onto the waking-I to not only accomplish but *integrate* into its own life. Either way, at the nadir of the dream, an oneiric Threshold Image arises, which presents its image of a certain life-threshold to the waking-I. And so, in dreams, the life-threshold is 'announced from within'. And, in meditation or in life itself, the waking-I must now *enter through* this oneiric Threshold Image.

If we redraw our iconologue of task completion, but now as it appears in dreams, we may see how the *accomplishment* of the dream-task and its *integration* into life transfers from the dream-I to the waking-I. This variation is, what we shall call, *the Iconologue of Dream-Task Completion*:

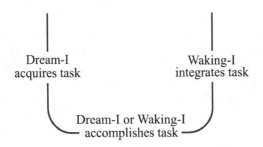

By comparing oneiric Threshold Images with their more sacred equivalents, we may see how our life-threshold crossings reveal life's more sacred aspects. In myth, the hero acquires a certain task, then descends to the dark underworld to accomplish it. At the nadir, he experiences a moment of epiphany, as the Sacred reveals itself through a 'meeting with the Goddess', an 'atonement with the Father' or his own 'apotheosis'. Because these Threshold Images offer us a momentary revelation of the Sacred, they become symbols, and are preserved for all time in sacred and Visionary art.

Just as the figures of ancient myth beseech us across their silent thresholds, so do the figures of dreams. And, if our oneiric Threshold Images are elucidated through sacred symbols, then each life-threshold crossing may also be experienced as a momentary epiphany. ...Through dreams, life itself becomes a gradual awakening to the Sacred.

VII. The Oneiric Path

Through the dreams of Baudelaire and Descartes, we have come to a clearer understanding of the Oneiric Path. This path differs from the Mythic and Symbolic Paths because the dream's images are related to specific life-threshold crossings.

When a dream is laid out on the Ancient Template, its narrative unfolding and nadir Threshold Image reveal a source of unity at the centre of the template – that which we have called 'the innermost Self'. This Self has lived through each past stage of our growth, and will continue to live through the following ones. It transcends each life-threshold crossing, uniting all the stages of our existence into a greater whole. Hence the Self lies behind the dream-I's illusory movements back and forth over our life-thresholds, because it stands at the very source of the dream, as 'the Dreamsource'.

Like the Sacred at the source of the cosmos, the Self lies at the source of the oneiric cosmos. When seen in this manner, the Self creates the dream as a series of images through which *it may reflect upon itself*. It does this, not only through *singular* images, such as the oneiric Threshold Image at the dream's nadir, but through *a whole series* of images, as the dream-I mythically descends through the dream's depths. As such, a dream is much like a myth, offering a grand *temporal* reflection of the innermost Self.

By laying out a dream on the Ancient Template, we may come to see how all its images reflect the Self at the source of the dream. In order to read these images, we follow their Oneiric path through the spiralling mists. That path must be followed *twice*: first in the dream's initial unfolding, and a second time during its elucidation.

During the dream's initial unfolding, the images are arranged according to certain recognizable iconologues: time, narrative and the hero's task (although this latter becomes the dream task). The Self reflects upon itself through this 'mythic' arrangement of descent, nadir-deed, and (perhaps) re-ascent. Everything unfolds in a forward linear progression, until the nadir moment when an oneiric Threshold Image appears.

Like the hero of a myth, the dream-I is nothing less than an image of the Self as it *acts* within its own created cosmos. At the nadir, the dream-I performs a specific deed which renders a clear symbol and mythologem of the innermost Self. That deed involves an important life-threshold crossing, a momentary epiphany of life's unfolding in the context of its greater wholeness. Through that image, the Self *reflects upon itself* – as the *totality* underlying life's linear unfolding.

During the dream's elucidation, the dream is laid out on the Ancient Template, and the Oneiric Path is followed a second time. However, the waking-I is now aware of the dream-I's movements through the dream. The waking-I takes conscious note of the mythic iconologues: how time, narrative and the hero's task have created a seemingly linear movement of descent, nadir-deed and (perhaps) re-ascent. It even takes note of symbolic iconologues: how opposites, combinations and opposites-in-union have created the dream-I's movement from the world above to the world below.

Most of all, the waking-I takes note of how the dream-I has passed back and forth over numerous life-thresholds, creating a jumbled and disordered view unto life. To elucidate the dream, the waking-I must uncover numerous other iconologues: how time has actually *regressed* in dreams, how moments from life have been variously *displaced* and *condensed*, how the dream-task has *digressed* or been *transformed*. In Part IV. we will analyze all these iconologues in depth.

To successfully elucidate the dream, the waking-I must associate its random images with specific life-thresholds, and re-reconstruct the whole so that it finally reflects *life's* greater unfolding. That is to say, he must become aware of the innermost Self, which encompasses each stage of life and unites them all into a greater whole. That Self, as the Dreamsource, was responsible for the dream's strange and enigmatic creation.

The moment the waking-I successfully elucidates the dream, he has a clear view onto the Self. And the Self, in turn, has a clear view onto him. The distorted mirror is destroyed, and each becomes a clear reflection of the other. That is the moment of epiphany: the dreamer has knowingly and successfully followed the Oneiric Path through the spiralling mists to behold the circle of light at the centre.

He has done this because he has achieved a broader view onto his life *as a whole*. And the moment he sees the Self, the Self *sees him*: the Self finds its true reflection in the awakened dreamer. In this way, the Oneiric Path has been pursued to its very end, and all the dream's images have been successfully *entered through*.

PART IV

ICONOLOGUES

The toadstools... there – that's where it is.
Have you seen how they grow in patterns?
If only one could read them...
– Woyzeck, in Büchner's
drama of the same name[1]

From the configuration of pebbles...
from the indentations of leaves...
I saw emerge hitherto-unrecognized
harmonious patterns.
– Gérard de Nerval
Aurélia[2]

CHAPTER XVI

Oneiro–Mythic Iconologues

Arouse the secret
From obscurity.
– Leonard Cohen[3]

I. The Anatomy of Iconologic

In 1907, August Strindberg wrote a pioneering piece of theatre in which the characters variously split, condense, dissolve and merge. As the playwright explains in his introduction: *"In this Dream Play... the author has sought to reproduce the disconnected but apparently logical form of a dream."*[4] Strindberg suggests here that dreams, despite their 'disconnected form', still betray an underlying logic. This elusive logic, which also appears in art and myth, is what we have intended by the term *iconologic*.

And, the greater part of our study has been dedicated to uncovering those symbols and mythologems which constitute our most basic iconologues. We have established that sacred symbols, independently of their associated myths, reveal themselves to be specific *cyphers* of the Divine. Each symbol reflects a unique aspect of the Sacred as it appears on our visual horizon. As such, they may be thought of as the *nomen* or *nouns* of our iconologic.

Mythologems accomplish a similar purpose, but through sacred *actions:* now a particular deed participates in a momentary evocation of the Sacred. As such, mythologems are more like *the verbs* of our iconologic. Both symbols and mythologems constitute our most rudimentary iconologues.

Meanwhile, myth, art and dreams create much larger configurations of images. Myths arrange images through the iconologues of time, narrative and the hero-task while works of art variously combine or displace their symbols and mythologems. Dreams, we could say, make free use of all these iconologues. As such, myth, art and dreams resemble *sentences* rather than verbs and nouns: they make a more complete statement on the mysterious nature of the Sacred.

"Myth," Joseph Campbell writes, *"is a picture language. But the language has to be studied to be read. In the first place, this language is the native speech of the dream."*[5] Campbell speaks here of a 'picture language' or *Bildsprache*, which we have called iconologic (from *icon* - 'image', and *logic* - 'language'). It is a language which, once its elusive rules have been learned, may be understood and even spoken.

Having pursued the mythic, symbolic and oneiric paths through the spiralling labyrinth, we are now prepared to analyze this *Bildsprache* or 'ancient image-language' in detail. In each case, we shall search out a specific iconologue – that is, 'an image-cluster which betrays some kind of recognizable meaning and arrangement' – and analyze it in detail.

But iconologues, in their vast mystery and variety, are not at all easy to detect. We are reminded of Woyzeck in Büchner's drama. On the brink of madness, this Prussian soldier began to notice how toadstools 'grow in patterns' and remarked: *"If only one could read them!"* In a similar manner, Gérard de Nerval remarked, while in the depths of delirium, that the 'indentations of leaves and configurations of pebbles' revealed *"hitherto-unrecognized harmonious patterns."* Iconologues possess this same, elusive quality. In each case we must – as Leonard Cohen says – *"arouse the secret from obscurity."*

Some iconologues, such as *combined symbols* or *shared mythologems*, have appeared before. Others will be entirely new. All these iconologues constitute the basic grammar or syntax of our image-language; they provide our *Bildsprache* with its logical rules and constructs. Just as 'and', 'or', 'not', and 'if...then' describe the different ways in which traditional logic has meaningfully arranged subjects and predicates into propositions, so do these iconologues organize symbols and mythologems into myths, works of art, and the dreams at their source.

In each case, we shall begin with examples drawn from dreams. Since our culture has made use of these iconologues from time immemorial, we shall seek out parallel examples in art and myth – which not only amplify the iconologue's meaning but elucidate its sacred intention.

Iconologues show how we may take a series of symbols or mythologems and, by placing them spatially next each other, or temporally one after another, create a series of steps in our iconological thinking. In myths, iconologues organize images into *temporal* arrangements while, in works of art, those same images may be arranged *spatially*. Dreams, meanwhile, arrange their images *in both*. But the iconologues themselves are independent of the space and time they operate within. The process of *thinking through* spatial or temporal arrangements remains free of those limitations.

We shall concern ourselves, in this chapter, with *oneiro-mythic iconologues*. Since they tend to measure *time*, they appear in dreams and myths alike. In the chapter after that, we shall concentrate on *oneiro-artistic iconologues* which, because they arrange images *in space*, are shared by dreams and art. This will be followed, logically, by two final chapters on *condensation* and *displacement*, since these dream iconologues arrange their images in art and myth *equally*.

Iconologues show us the numerous *possible* ways in which images may be ordered and arranged. And they guarantee, thereby, that the cluster or configuration possesses some underlying sense. But they do not make any statement regarding the truth or falsity of these arrangements. It is the culture in question that renders such a judgement. Nevertheless, whether we *enter through* the images of one cultural myth or another, it is the same sacred unity that is revealed behind all of them.

This anatomy of iconologues is by no means complete, nor should it be. Dreams are a continuously creative expression, a manifestation of the inner Dreamsource, which is as infinite in its varieties of expression as God's creative cosmos. And just as that cosmos may move in accord with certain laws, so may the interior world of the dream.

Granted, this apparent order may be one which we ourselves impose upon it, causing us to ignore a more magnificent chaos. And it may indeed be true that the imposition of order only reflects our own inner sense of symmetry. But, in this particular case, that is precisely what we are seeking: the mind's own creation of an image-logic for its interior world.

II. Our Dream Sources

Our exposition of dream-iconologica arises from a careful observation of dreams, aided by the insights of Saint-Denys, Freud, Stekel, and Jung.[6]

Jean-Marie Léon Marquis d'Hervey de Saint-Denys (1823 – 1892) taught Chinese Sinology, Language and Literature at the *Collège de France* in the mid–1800's. From the age of thirteen, he began keeping a dream journal, where he recorded and even drew his dreams. After thirty years of observing dreams, he wrote his pioneering study, *Dreams and the Means to Direct Them* (*Les Rêves et les Moyens de les Diriger - 1867*).[7] Although the work was published anonymously, in an edition of only fifty exemplars, it became a pioneering work in dream analysis, and remains relevant even to this day.

Léon d'Hervey de Saint-Denys

One reason is that it is the first detailed study of 'lucid dreaming'. Saint-Denys discovered he could become conscious while dreaming, and so conducted a number of experiments on himself in this state. But, more relevant to our theme, his book also pioneered much of the research into those structures of our dream-thinking which Freud later identified in his work. Saint-Denys described various forms of displacement and condensation in detail, as well as recognizing other forms of dream-thinking which Freud had neglected: transformation, superimposition, etc.

Unfortunately for the history of dream theory, Freud never read Saint-Denys – admitting in *The Interpretation of Dreams* that Saint-Denys' *"...book, in spite of all my efforts,* [is one] *I have not succeeded in procuring."*[8] Nevertheless, in our quest for dream iconologues, Saint-Denys' work remains of inestimable value, and so we may offer him belated recognition as one of the great dream pioneers. Also of historical importance are the dreams he furnishes, since the selection is generous, honest, and not biased by the concern of illustrating the theories of depth psychology (as is the case in almost all later dream studies). Instead, his many dreams offer us a view into the oneiric universe of a single man.

Freud's *Interpretation of Dreams*, (*Traumdeutung, 1900*) is undoubtedly a revolutionary piece of work. And like all great works, the personality of its author may be felt through and through. Curiously, the text may be deconstructed to reveal Freud's autobiography, as it gives accounts of his birth, early childhood, later education and psychiatric practice. It also renders many dreams from Freud's patients, and their cultural *milieu* of Hapsburg Vienna in decline. Hence, his book also has value as a historical document. It furnishes many examples, not only from Freud himself, but the citizens of *fin-de-siècle* Vienna. Of particular interest to our study is the chapter on 'the Means of Representation in Dreams' since, here, he identifies many important iconologues.

Wilhelm Stekel was a member of Freud's inner circle (who met every Wednesday evening at Stekel's home), and wrote two important books on dreams: *The Language of Dreams* (*Die Sprache des Traumes, 1911*)[9] and *Poets' Dreams* (*Traüme der Dichter, 1912*).[10] In the *Interpretation of Dreams*, Freud acknowledged Stekel's contribution to the study of dreams,[11] and his books render us the service of gathering together more sample dream-material from the *kaiserlich und königlich* epoch of Vienna's decline. For, it is important that we select dreams which not only have personal symbols and references for the dreamer, but also more cultural

Psycho-analyst
Wilhelm Stekel
(1868 - 1940)

symbols and references recognizable to us through epoch and locale. We shall find this in the *Zeitgeist* of Hapsburg Vienna during its 'last days'.*

Finally, Freud's most gifted apprentice, C.G. Jung, brought the study of dreams into a proper relationship with myths through his 'analytic' approach, based on the Archetypes. The study of dreams is spread throughout Jung's *Nachlass* and, unfortunately, he never dedicated an extended volume to dreams like Freud's breakthrough work.† However, just before his death, he wrote (and partially dictated) his autobiography, *Memories, Dreams, Reflections*, which is a valuable document because of the many personal dreams it offers. As well, in this document, Jung comes closest to explaining dreams as none other than *somnia* – those dreams that expand from personal significance to sacred revelations.

The works of these four dream explorers shall aid us as we investigate the iconologues of dreams. Oneiric iconologues announce themselves in those arrangements of images which strike us, after waking, as peculiar. They are peculiar precisely because we have no way of thinking through them with our waking logic. And yet, the events of a dream, no matter how peculiar to the waking-I, are accepted as normal to the dream-I and, indeed, as capable of leading it even further into the dream. And so, to uncover the iconologues of dreams, our starting point are those arrangements of images which strike the waking-I as strange...

III. Oneiro-Mythic Iconologues: Task Completion

When we awaken from dreams, we may only be able to remember a series of fragments or impressions. But if we are fortunate enough to recover a longer series of images, we often find that these are related to one another through the *iconologue of task completion*. It is the *acquisition* of this task and the attempt to *accomplish* it that actually holds the images together and combines them into a dream. It is not necessary for the acquired task to be completed. The expectation is enough to be bind these images together into one dream.

---

*The expression 'last days' comes from the Viennese satirist Karl Kraus and his unstageable epic play of Vienna's decline, *The Last Days of Mankind*.

†But Jung's *Transformations and Symbols of the Libido* (*Wandlungen und Symbole der Libido*, 1911) later re-worked into *Symbols of Transformation* (*Symbole der Wandlung*, 1946) became a breakthrough work for him, as it was his first attempt to expand the meaning of unconscious imagery with the aid of mythology. His extended essay *'Individual Dream Symbolism in Relation to Alchemy'* (collected in the volume *Psychology and Alchemy*) extended this amplification of hypnagogic and dream imagery with the aid of alchemy. The transcripts of his 1928 – 1930 Seminars on *Dream Analysis* (delivered in English) should also not be neglected, as they provide clear examples of the extent to which he amplified dream material with the aid of ancient myth so as to reveal the Archetypes at their source.

Task acquisition does not immediately appear in dreams, nor is its relevance to one's *life*-task a simple *fait accompli*. Rather, the dream-task may undergo a number of digressions, displacements and transformations before its deeper significance becomes evident. Typically, it first manifests itself in a momentary realization such as Baudelaire's *'I felt it a duty of sorts to present the madam of a large whorehouse with a book of mine which had just come out.'* This momentary realization sets in motion a whole series of actions, in which the dream-I either succeeds or fails in realizing its acquired task.

Baudelaire's dream-task, as we have seen, was transformed, displaced, and digressed into a whole series of strange sub-tasks: to 'screw one of the tarts in passing' (transformation), to not present himself at the whorehouse in such a childish manner (regression), to admire the displays in the medical museum (digression), and finally, to question the serpentine gnome squatting on a pedestal (nadir-moment). And yet, the result of this obfuscation was to eventually reveal the greater *life*-task concealed in the lesser dream-task.

The task presented to the dream-I was *not* accomplished over the course of Baudelaire's dream. Nevertheless, despite its incompletion, despite is transformations, displacements and digressions, it did reveal the life-task immanent in it. The accomplishment and eventual integration of that life-task then fell upon the waking-I. In a backward movement through the dream, and in a forward movement through life, the final image of the dream could be *entered through*.

Hence, due to the *iconologue of task completion*, a sequence of images were arranged over time, and held together as *one dream*. And because dreams and myths share this same iconologue, that dream could become his more personal life-myth.

Meanwhile, the series of transformations, displacements and digressions offer us important variations on the task-completion iconologue. In the case of *task transformation* and *task digression*, the change is more or less absolute. With *task displacement*, the task remains the same, but is displaced onto another situation.

In one of Freud's more famous dreams – the dream of Count Thun – we find examples of all three. The dream begins with a preliminary passage where Count Thun, an Austrian politician of Freud's day, makes a speech against the Germans. This causes Freud to become enraged. Then there is a shift in the dream.

> *It was as though we were in the* Aula [or Great Hall of the university]*; the entrances were cordoned off and we had to escape. I made my way through a series of beautifully furnished rooms... At last I came to a corridor, in which a housekeeper was sitting, an elderly stout woman. I avoided speaking to her, but she evidently thought I had*

the right to pass, for she asked whether she should accompany me with
the lamp. I indicated to her, by word or gesture, that she was to stop on
the staircase... I got downstairs and found a narrow descending path,
along which I went.

(Becoming indistinct again) It was as though the second problem
was to get out of the town, just as the first one had been to get out of
the house. I was driving in a cab and ordered the driver to drive me
to a station... He raised some objection, as if I had overtired him...
The stations were cordoned off. I wondered whether to go to Krems or
Znaim, but ...decided in favour of Graz or some such place.

I was now sitting in the compartment, which was like a carriage
on the Stadtbahn; *and in my buttonhole I had a peculiar plaited, long-*
shaped object, and beside it some violet-brown violets made of stiff ma-
terial. This greatly struck people. (At this point, the scene broke off.)

...I was in front of the station, but this time in the company of an
elderly gentleman. I thought of a plan for remaining unrecognized; and
then saw that this plan had already been put into effect... He appeared
to be blind, at all events, in one eye, and I handed him a male glass
urinal... So I was a sick-nurse, and had to give him the urinal...[12]

The dream-task, clearly, is to escape. But, over the course of the
dream, that task undergoes a series of alterations. First, *task displacement*
occurs: Freud successfully escapes from the house, but finds he must now
escape from the town. A new series of images were regrouped around the
same dream-task. Then, there is *task digression*: while sitting in the train
compartment (again he has succeeded in escaping, but does not notice it),
Freud's attention wanders onto the object in his lapel, what it is made of,
how it impresses people, etc. The dream-I digresses so far from its task that
the dream eventually breaks off. Finally, a *task transformation* occurs: the
original task returns, but now Freud wishes to escape, not by fleeing, but by
disguising himself. He and the old man will act like sick-nurse and patient.

Although these changes in the dream-task appear to be without purpose,
they actually aid us in revealing the more immanent life-task. In the case
of this dream, Freud is clearly trying to escape, though why or from what
remains unknown. First he is aided by an elderly woman, then a cab driver,
and finally by the old man. With the old man, his strategy changes from
fleeing to disguising himself. In the final image of the dream, Freud must
render aid to the old man's urinary needs.

By freely associating on this final image, Freud identified the old man
as his father. As well, this image was the *reversal* of a childhood memory. As
a child of seven or eight, he had 'obeyed the calls of nature in his parents'
bedroom', causing his father to exclaim that 'the boy will come to nothing.'

Now, the roles were reversed: his father was the one with urinary needs, and Freud was rendering medical aid. The greater life-task immanent in the dream-task concerned Freud, his ambitions of becoming a doctor, and his father's claims that he would come to nothing. The life-threshold of profession, as the inheritance of the father world, was thus revealed through this final image of the dream.

The dream-task may then be explained in light of the final image. We know that the dream-I's task was *to escape* – though *the threat* causing him to flee remained hidden. In order to escape, the dream-I had to cross two thresholds, one posed by the university and the other by the town (each of which was *cordoned off*). Aided by the elderly woman and the cab-driver, the dream-I actually succeeded in crossing both thresholds, without even realizing it. If, as the final image reveals, the hidden threat was nothing less than *his father's threat* that 'the boy will come to nothing', then the two crossed thresholds refer to his successful completion of his studies and his travels abroad.

But that was obviously not enough. Freud's father stood at the last threshold, as the final embodiment of all to be expected from the Father: profession, character, and 'coming to be something' in this world. This time, he could not cross the threshold 'by fleeing' but only 'by disguising himself'. That is to say, he had to transform himself in some way. In the image of Freud rendering medical aid to the old man's urinary needs, the *reversal* became complete: Freud was now the learnèd and well-travelled doctor, while his father had become half-blind and helpless. The life-threshold had been crossed, but at a certain price.

IV. The Iconologue of Time's Measure

In dreams, as in myths, images are arranged *over time*. How that time is to be measured – as a segment or cycle, as a movement forward or backward – is determined, ultimately, by what we have called the *Iconologue of Time's Measure*. In dreams, time usually moves forward along linear segments. But, sudden jumps may occur, or disparate segments of time may be enjambed. As well, a dream may regress to earlier, more infantile memories and means of behaviour. Or, through the repetition of the dream-task over many dreams, time may even appear to cycle round.

Ultimately dreams transpire in that timeless *tep zepi, apeiron,* and *aeternitas* familiar to us from myths – a time which passes *without measure*. Our more mythic dreams are ageless and archetypal, yet also ever-present. For, with each retelling of a myth or recollection of a dream, their timeless moments are brought into our more mundane present. As we re-enter the dream-time, we witness how the hero acquires a certain task, then passes over a series of thresholds to complete it.

Through the lesser deeds committed at each threshold, the hero creates a particular sense of time – be it linear-historic or ever-cyclic – which comes to encompass us in the present moment. But then, at the nadir threshold, he commits that life-altering deed which opens a doorway out of those bounding linear segments or repeating cycles. For one brief but epiphanous moment, he reveals time as a more measureless eternity.

Each time the eternal myths are retold, we impose our mortal measure upon them, situating their sacred actions in a more mundane passage of time. The measures of time we impose upon our myths are given to us by their sacred heroes. Adam, Moses, the Prophets and Christ all created a linear-historical sense of time essential to Judæo-Christianity, while the Hindu *Trimurti* of Brahma, Vishnu and Shiva, as well as the Bodhisattvas prior to the Buddha, created a similar sense of ever-recurring cyclic time in Hindu-Buddhism. As we imagine the myth, these different measures of time become manifest, revealing thereby the *iconologue of time's measure*.

Like the hero of a myth, it is the dream-I who creates the dream's particular measure of time. Through the deeds he commits in a variety of situations, the dream transpires along linear segments of time determined by the dream-task and its completion. In the case of recurring dreams, time may even take on the appearance of ever-recurring cycles. However, linear segments and repeating cycles are not the only two temporal arrangements which manifest themselves in dreams.

With each of his actions, the dream-I may also manifest attitudes and actions that remind the waking-I of earlier times. Certain distinct moments from the day before (day-residue) or from the distant past (infantile elements) may arise over the course of the dream. Meanwhile, the dream-I may also act in certain ways or assume attitudes that seem quite forward-looking and advanced. And, in the case of *rêves prophetiques*, *déjà vu*, or premonition dreams, future events seem to have arisen in dreams.

Naturally, the waking-I finds all of this to be rather disturbing, as it cannot divine why the linear unfolding of the dream has rendered such a jumbled image of life. Why have moments from the distant past and unforeseeable future arisen in the dream's present, which transpired as a seemingly continuous narrative? Should not the dream's linear progression reflect the linear progression of life itself? What new measures of time have appeared? It is only when the waking-I begins to *enter through* the images of the dream, distinguishing the various life-thresholds to which they refer, that the actions of the dream-I come to make more sense.

As we *enter through* the dream, we slowly realize that our temporal view on life is somewhat limited. For we tend to see life as a linear progression of moments leading up to the present. The past and the future meet in the present, where they are forever altered through the exercise of the will. Even though our ego is, at present, the latest and best incarnation of the innermost Self, its will does not extend very far beyond the immediate past and future. The ego is bounded, more or less, by its own incarnation. Forced to act in the present, its temporal concerns become more immediate. Through the exercise of the will, it seeks to cross over life's next threshold, while its interest does not extend much further back than the last threshold just crossed. In the end, the waking-I, like our present ego-incarnation, is extremely *limited* in its understanding of time, seeing the forward movement through linear time as the only interesting one.

Meanwhile, the dream-I extends across *all* of life's thresholds. It manifests a much *broader* sense of time, freely moving through disparate moments from the present, future, and long-forgotten past. All these disparate moments may thus be enjambed and combined to render an image of life as a greater whole. In order to *enter through* the greater image of life presented by the dream-I, *the waking-I must regain this broader sense of its own temporal existence.* As well, it must forego the forward-moving linear measure it imposes upon life, and see it instead as a vast number of moments, any one of which could liberate it from time's measure. Such is the greater image of life reflected in dreams.

But the value of the iconologue of time's measure, with its linear (and sometimes cyclic) measures of time, must not be underestimated. Without this iconologue, the sense of continuity between task acquisition and accomplishment would be lost, and the dream itself would deteriorate into a mere collage of jumbled moments. Hence, our task, at the moment, is to determine the ways in which disparate moments may be combined in dreams – while still appearing as a continuous flow imposed by the iconologue of time's measure.

V. The Simultaneity Iconologue

Consider the following dream fragments from Stekel's work:

> ...*I was walking through one of the rooms and saw Mama, but she appeared much younger and thinner...*[13]

> *I saw myself as a child – with the traits of an adult...*[14]

> ...*And then suddenly (without any connection), I saw myself in the house of my childhood, and discovered, to my great fear, that the ceiling above me was bending downward under great stress...* (Scherner)[15]

> *During the night, I dreamt that I was a child on Christmas morning in the servants' quarters of P.'s farmhouse, where I had spent many hours in my childhood.* (Hebbel)[16]

In all of these dream fragments, disparate moments in time are combined. In the first dream, the dreamer's mother appears in the present but with features from the past. In the remaining dreams, it is the dreamer himself who bears features from the past while being in the present. In all of these dreams, disparate life moments are combined and felt *'at once'*. This temporal oneness is best described by the word 'simultaneity'.

In dreams, the *Simultaneity Iconologue* is silently at work when two disparate historical moments (recognizable to the waking-I) transpire within a single dream moment. While *both* of these historical moments may be taken from the dreamer's past, the dream is more relevant to the waking-I when one of those moments exists in the present. And indeed, when the waking-I attempts to *enter through* the images of last night's dream, it must, *per force*, identify the *present* moment with moments from the dream's past. Every time the waking-I identifies itself with the dream-I, it does so through the simultaneity iconologue.

Naturally, whenever we *enter through* the images of myths and works of art, this iconologue is again at work. However, the historical moments which become simultaneous with our own present are not merely from our own life's more immediate past, but from our culture's more epic past. And, through simultaneity with the more timeless moments of myths and art, we may return to that moment before the Beginning, when time transpired as a measureless eternity.

In all, the simultaneity iconologue creates a momentary union between two moments in the past, or between a past moment and the present. If premonitory and *déjà vu* dreams do indeed transpire, then this iconologue may also create a momentary union between the present and the future.

Recurring dreams, though frustrating to the extreme, remind us that time may be constructed as an ever-repeating cycle. Because of this iconologue, our recent failings momentarily repeat themselves in the dream's present. Usually, the images of such dreams evoke a certain life-threshold that has been repeatedly come up against and cannot be crossed. And through these repeated failures – breaks in relationships, exams not passed – we at least become aware of our shortcomings. As Hesse phrased it in *Siddhartha*, *"Everything that was not suffered to the end and finally concluded, recurred, and the same sorrows were undergone."*[17] And so, the Hindu-Buddhist iconologue of time's measure also appears here in the West, in our dreams. By virtue of the life-thresholds we repeatedly run up against unsuccessfully, time acquires an ever-recurring aspect in the very midsts of its linear extension.

Finally, if we succeed in making the present moment simultaneous with the more sacred and eternal moment that exists in myth, art, and even dream, then mundane time's more linear or cyclic bounds may be transcended so as to reveal the timeless *oneiro-mythic time*. This usually occurs at the moment of epiphany experienced during the crossing of a life-threshold. Then, for a few brief moments, the simultaneity iconologue makes eternity one with the present. Time reveals its underlying unity.

VI. The Transformation Iconologue

Saint-Denys was perhaps the first to remark upon the phenomenon of *Transformation* in dreams:

> The [dream] *image of a flower, of a leaf, of a pebble can sometimes remain before the mind's eye for quite a long time without any change. On the other hand... a capricious series of transformations often occur. Sometimes these are rapid substitutions by way of resemblance, other times they are frightening metamorphoses or hideous transformations...*[18]

Saint-Denys dedicated the latter part of his study of dreams to *"the ways in which ideas are linked and their associated images dissolve, transform, or substitute one for the other."*[19] He identified three basic types of transformation.

In the first case, *'transition via substitution'*, a connection between two ideas causes an *immediate* replacement of one image with another. We shall, like Saint-Denys, call this a *substitution*.

In the second case, *'transition via superimposition'*, the connection between two ideas causes their associated images to be slowly superimposed over time. The result is a figure whose different qualities gradually change over time. This may happen to such an extent that one figure slowly dissolves into another. We shall call this a *dissolve*.

In the third case, a visual resemblance between two images may create a *'transition via resemblance'*, where one image gradually metamorphoses into another due to their similar shapes. This is a specific type of dissolve, which we shall call *metamorphosis* (lit. 'a change in shape').*

Saint-Denys furnishes us with many examples of transformation. The following dream contains both *metamorphosis* and *substitution*:

*Saint-Denys describes the first two, substitution and superimposition, as follows:

"While recalling a series of memory-images [enchaînement de souvenirs], *an image presented itself, of a commissioner who once gave me a letter... I had only seen this commissioner once, and even then I had seen him indistinctly. Given this cloudy tableau, my memory seized another ensemble, of a man with more recognizable features: a famous professor whose lectures I had attended. The commissioner vanished from my thoughts, and I found myself following my professor's lesson.*

"But this transition could have transpired in another manner. The face of the professor could have been framed purely and simply by the silhouette of the commissioner, and I would have seen this professor standing at the corner of a street [but, like the commissioner] *he would have a medal on his chest. Or I would have imagined the professor climbing into a carriage,* [but, like the commissioner, he would have] *a velvet blazer over his shoulder and the traditional lanyard hook under his arm.*

"In the first case, there would have been, what I call, 'transition via substitution'. In the second case, 'transition via superimposition of images'. These two kinds of association will always cause a lot of confusion in the course of the dream."[20]

I was lunching in a café. I took the little spoon I was holding in my hand, and laid it on the table. It bore some resemblance to the silver key to my home. All at once, the spoon transformed into that very key. [metamorphosis].

As I took the key and put it in my pocket, I had the idea of returning home. The thought of myself before my door transported me instantaneously from the café to my home. Now my key was turning in the lock. [substitution].[21]

Meanwhile, *dissolves* occur particularly during those moments when we are just falling asleep.

I closed my eyes to fall asleep and thought about some objects that I had noticed the same night in a boutique on Rue de Rivoli. The arcade of the street reappeared in my memory, and I saw it as luminous, with its arches extending repeatedly into the distance.

Then, before my mind's eye, I saw it as an uncoiling serpent covered with phosphorescent scales. It was enframed by an infinity of imprecise images. I remained in a period of confusion as the tableaus altered and disappeared extremely quickly. Then, the long fiery serpent took on the aspect of a long dirt road, burning in the summer sun.[22]

Mythology makes constant use of oneiric iconologues, especially transformations of various types. Consider the following dream by Saint-Denys and by a patient of Stekel's called 'Herr Epsilon'*.

I was telling myself that the features of Mlle V. reminded me of an antique statue: that her neck was whiter than ivory; her eyes, like sapphires, and her lips, the colour of pink coral. From this movement of ideas... I found myself contemplating a beautiful statue formed of precious materials, like the Minerva of the Parthenon.[23]

I was walking in a red-light district, and went inside to one of the women. As I entered, she transformed into a man, who was lying half-undressed on the sofa.[24]

In Ovid's *Metamorphoses*, countless mythic examples of transformation are offered up for our pleasure, amusement, and contemplation. Most worthy of our attention, at present, are the myths of Pygmalion and Tiresias.

In the well-known tale of Pygmalion, this sculptor from Cyprus *"skillfully carved a snowy-white statue. He made it lovelier than any woman born, and soon fell in love with his own creation."*[25] At the next festival of Venus, Pygmalion prayed to the goddess of love for a wife as beautiful as his ivory statue. *"When Pygmalion returned home, he made straight for the statue of the girl he loved... and kissed her. She seemed warm; he laid his lips on hers again, and touched her breast with his hands – at his touch, the ivory lost its hardness, and grew soft."*[26]

*Following a custom initiated by Freud, Stekel conceals the identity of his dreamers by replacing their surname with a letter from the Greek alphabet. Hence, any dream attributed to Herr Alpha, Frau Beta, or Fräulein Gamma was dreamt by one of his Viennese patients.

In Ovid's tale, what happens to the ivory statue is an exact reversal of what happened to Mlle V. in Saint-Denys' dream: where Mlle V. became an ivory statue, Pygmalion's venus transformed, instead, into a woman of flesh and blood.

In the myth of Tiresias, the man who would later become the famed blind prophet was once walking along a path on Mount Cyllene. He came across two snakes in the act of coupling and struck at them with his staff. The moment he killed the female, he was transformed into a woman. Finding himself thus in a female body, he enjoyed its gifts and eventually became a celebrated harlot. Seven years later, as he was walking along the same path on Mount Cyllene, he came across the same scene of two snakes coupling. This time he killed the male serpent, and was transformed again into a man.*

In Ovid's myth, as in Herr Epsilon's dream, a prostitute transforms from one gender to another. Like *simultaneity*, the *transformation* iconologue arranges a series of moments *in time*. Encompassing these momentary arrangements is the *iconologue of time's measure*, which imposes a much larger arrangement, such as time's linear progression. However, in the particular case of *Regression*, time undergoes, instead, a seeming backward movement.

VII. The Regression Iconologue

In dream regression, memories from the past are arranged in reverse order. As the dream-I moves forward through the dream, it finds itself in situations that harken back to ever earlier modes of behaviour or manners of thought. The dream-I may be seemingly unaware of this regression, though the waking-I notices it immediately upon waking.

Such a regression, or *'chronological reversal'* as Freud called it, appears constantly in dreams. We may take, as our first example of regression, this rather amusing dream of Saint-Denys:

> *I dreamt that I was arranging my hair before a mirror, as I had been invited out to a ball (the scene took place in my current house, where I have been installed for the last six years). My hair was in such disorder that I deemed it indispensable to call my neighbour, who was a coiffeur.*
>
> *While waiting for him, not exactly knowing whether he would come or not, I still tried to achieve something with comb and brush. I managed to achieve a clear parting of my hair on one side. But this hairstyle was something which I had abandoned ten years before. Its reflection brought me back to the time when I was living in another house. With this movement of thought, the dream also changed.*

*Later, when Zeus and Hera were arguing over who enjoyed the sexual act more, they consulted Tiresias. He responded 'If the parts of love's pleasure be counted as ten, then thrice three goes to the woman, and only one to the man.' In a rage, Hera blinded Tiresias, but Zeus compensated by giving him the gift of prophecy.[27]

> *Now I was in my old apartment, and the* coiffeur *had meanwhile come in. But it was not, as I thought at first, my neighbour. Instead, it was another* coiffeur *who used to come to my house in the past, and who had long since passed away. – This modification did not prevent me, in the end, from going to the ball.*[28]

It is worth noting in this example that the completion of the dream task was not disrupted by the regression. Nor was the iconologue of time's measure lost or destroyed. Though there was a regression in locale and in the dream figure of the *coiffure*, the dream itself maintained a forward linear flow.

The same is true of the following dream which Jung had during his 'confrontation with the unconscious'. But, whereas Saint-Denys' dream evoked personal memory-images, Jung's dream evoked collective memory-images, which he called 'archaic vestiges' of the collective unconscious. After waking, Jung realized that such archaic vestiges *"are not dead, outmoded forms, but belong to our living being."*[29] Later, he recognized them as the Archetypes.

> *I was in a region like the Alyscamps near Arles. There they have a lane of sarcophagi which go back to Merovingian times. In the dream, I was coming from the city, and saw before me a similar lane with a long row of tombs. They were pedestals on stone slabs on which I saw the dead lay... They were not hewn out of stone, but mummified in a curious fashion.*
>
> *I stood still in front of the first grave and looked at the dead man, who was a person of the eighteen thirties. I looked at his clothes with interest, whereupon he suddenly moved and came to life. He unclasped his hands; but that was only because I was looking at him. I had an extremely unpleasant feeling, but walked on and came to another body.*
>
> *He belonged to the eighteenth century. There, exactly the same thing happened... So I went down the whole row, until I came to the twelfth century – that is, to a crusader in chain mail who lay there with clasped hands. His figure seemed carved out of wood. For a long time I looked at him and thought he was really dead. Suddenly, I saw that a finger of his left hand was starting to move gently...*[30]

VIII. The Solitary yet Eternal Moment

The following dream of Saint-Denys manages to reveal, over the brief and terrifying course of its unfoldment, the essential nature of time in dreams:

> *I was staring at myself in a magic mirror where I saw myself changing degree by degree from one aspect to another: fully combed and shaved, first younger, rejuvenated, and made more beautiful, then puffed up, jaundiced, toothless, twenty years older. My face gradually passed through a succession of modifications, and finally took on such a frightening aspect that I awoke in shock.*[31]

Compare this to the image of Christ from *The Apocryphon of John:*

> *Straightaway, while I was contemplating these things, behold the heavens opened and the whole creation which is under heaven shone and the world was shaken. And I was afraid, and behold I saw in the light a child who stood by me. While I looked at him he became like an old man. And he changed his form again, becoming like a young person. There was not a plurality before me, but there was one image with multiple forms in the light, and the forms appeared through each other, and the image had three forms.*
>
> *He said to me, 'John, John, why do you doubt and why are you afraid? You are not familiar with this likeness, are you? That is to say, be not afraid! I am the one who is with you forever.*[32]

In Saint-Denys' dream, disparate moments from his youth, middle, and old age were combined to render an image of himself across time. During the dream's linear unfolding (*iconologue of time's measure*), the dream-I continually moved forward (*progression*) and backward (*regression*) over life-thresholds to render this temporally-expanded image of himself. As well, a series of *transformations* were used to combine past and future images of himself which, through the *simultaneity iconologue*, became one with the present. Hence, through these numerous iconologues, moments from the dreamer's past, present, and future fell into union so as to create a frightening image of life as a greater whole.

It is no wonder that Saint-Denys awoke in shock. Nor is it surprising that John 'was so afraid'. For they were beholding an image of themselves encompassing all the thresholds of life. That is to say, they gazed for a solitary yet eternal moment at their own innermost Self. Where Saint-Denys saw himself reflected in the more timeless image of the dream-I (*'I was staring at myself in a magic mirror'*), John saw himself in the image of Christ (*'Be not afraid! I am the one who is with you forever'*) .

Although the dream-I creates a linear sense of time in dreams, it may also, like Christ, *show us the way out of that linear bound.* For time's linear unfolding, be it in a myth or in a dream, *is merely one measure* created by the dream. Like Christ, the dream-I may also *transcend* that measure to reveal the underlying, more timeless 'dream-time'.

Finally, at the dream's source, we encounter the innermost Self, which has persisted through *all* the thresholds of life. That Self manifests a broader, indeed timeless and unified vision of life. It gathers all of life's moments into one, so that life as a whole may be experienced, in one moment, as a greater interior oneness.

CHAPTER XVII

Oneiro-Artistic Iconologues

And what of our human art?
Must we not say that... it produces
...a man-made dream for waking eyes?
– Plato, Sophist (266c)[1]

While dreams are the individual man's play with reality,
the sculptor's art is the play with dreams.
– Nietzsche[2]

I. The Elaboration of a Dream

Before falling asleep, an intermediary period of half-sleep and half-wakefulness occurs. From a variety of coloured shapes, hypnagogic images gradually materialize. Though isolated at first, these may transform into more elaborate narratives.

Saint-Denys furnishes us with a fine example of the dream's first few moments:

> *Hardly have some people closed their eyes for sleep when they see a swarm of odd shapes... luminous spinning wheels, small suns turning round, multi-hued bubbles going up and down. Or they see luminous threads of silver and gold, purple and emerald green, interlacing in a thousand different symmetrical patterns. All of them glow and vibrate, forming a vast array of interlocking diamonds, circles, and other constant shapes, resembling the fine mosaic-work of Byzantine images.*
> *...These are embryonic visions. But they contain within them the transitions to more fully-formed dreams.*[3]

Bit by bit, these initial abstractions give way to hypnagogic images. This dream material, though distinct as images, quickly transforms from one fleeting image to another. Saint-Denys reports:

> *At first I see a hedge, brightly lit by the sun. Through this hedge, a young woman emerges, all dressed in white linen. Then, the branches of the hedge interlace, forming a symmetrical pattern. At once, the foliage disappears and the young girl also vanishes. Instead, I see a woven basket, and it is filled with white linen.*[4]

Like the interlocking patterns of the earliest dream phase, the first hypnagogic images undergo a series of transformations, based on the most superficial of resemblances.

But, these transitions also betray the first confused steps in our image-thinking. Primitive iconologues have emerged, arranging images into brief sequential patterns. With a little more time, the dream will evolve into a more elaborate narrative. Saint-Denys furnishes us with an example of the third stage:

> *I dream that I'm staying at an auberge in a strange town. Since I want to go out riding after dinner, I ask what time the meal will be served. It turns out that dinner will be served here at the exact same time as it usually is in my country residence. This thought transports me to the kitchen of my country residence.*
>
> *From that kitchen, I cross the hallway, go out onto the terrace, and take a stroll through the alleys of the park nearby. There is no hint of the streets around the auberge, but my original intentions have not been forgotten. At the iron gates of the park, a horse is waiting for me, and the dream continues as intended.*[5]

Despite the abrupt transition in locales, a narrative has developed and the dream-task has persisted from beginning to end. The first dream of the night has occurred.

II. The Iconologue of Space's Measure

Dreams transpire in a time and space removed from our waking world. In the last chapter, we examined the ways in which oneiro-mythic iconologues arrange their images *over time*. Now, we are more concerned with *oneiro-artistic iconologues*, and the manner in which they manifest their arrangements *in space* – whether that be in a dream's imagined locale or a painting's embroidered expanse of canvas. What, then, are the oneiro-artistic iconologues used from time immemorial to frame images in space?

To answer this question, we turn to a dream which Jung dreamt in 1909:

> *I was in a house I did not know, which had two storeys. It was 'my house'. I found myself in the upper storey, where there was a kind of salon furnished with fine old pieces in rococo style... Descending the stairs, I reached the ground floor. There I realized that everything was much older, and I realized that this part of the house must date from around the fifteenth or sixteenth century...*
>
> *I went from one room to another, thinking, 'Now I really must explore the whole house'. I came upon a heavy door and opened it. Beyond it I discovered a stone stairway that led down into the cellar.*
>
> *Descending again, I found myself in a beautifully vaulted room which looked exceedingly ancient. Examining the walls, I discovered layers of brick that... dated from Roman times. My interest by now was intense. I looked more closely at the floor and... saw a stairway of narrow stone steps leading down into the depths.*
>
> *These, too, I descended, and entered a low cave cut into the rock. Thick dust lay on the floor, and in the dust were scattered bones and broken pottery, like the remains of a primitive culture. I discovered two human skulls, obviously very old and half disintegrated. Then I awoke.*[6]

In this dream, there is a clear case of *temporal regression*. But what interests us is the manner in which the dream-I moved further *through space*. Here, the architectural constructions continually beckoned the dreamer onward through the new spaces they created.

But we must be careful in our use of this word 'space'. Just as the ancients had a much different outlook onto time and its measure, so did they onto space. The modern understanding of space and time as a pre-existent 'field' in which events transpire was unknown to the ancients. When we read their creation myths, we gain a clearer understanding of their outlook.

In, for example, the *Apocryphon of John*, each image appearing in the watery light surrounding the One extended time and space one step further into, what the Gnostics called, 'the aeons'. These aeons or 'extensions of the One' did not proceed into a pre-existent field of time and space. Rather, each image *created a new moment* 'in time', as well as *a new place* 'in space'. Each *moment*, each *place*, was a unique extension of the One as it imposed its *measure* upon the eternal time and boundless space of 'the aeons'.

And the same can be said of the innermost Self as the Dreamsource: through images and through the movements of the dream-I, it creates *new measures* in oneiric space and time. Fundamentally, the dream-time is like Eliade's *mythic time* – eternal and *without measure*. And by that same token, dream-*space* is like the mythic *space* of our imagination – unlimited and boundless.

Returning to Jung's dream, we may see how 'space' is created through the extension of one architectural *place* onto the next. The architecture – its bounding walls and floors; its doors and stairs leading from one room to the next – create these extensions. The dream-I's movements, and the image of each room, thus becomes *a new measure* of the dream-space.

However, dream-space is not bound by the same laws as the space of wakingness. One room recognizable to the dreamer may open out to another room equally recognizable, but in a far different locale in the waking world. The spatial confusion exists only for the waking-I. The dream-I accepts this new extension in the dream-space, and willingly *enters through* the image creating its measure.

One example already occurred in the dream just recounted by Saint-Denys, which we may call *replacement* as a variation in the *iconologues of space's measure*. Though Saint-Denys was in the kitchen of the Auberge, he suddenly found himself in the kitchen of his country residence. Thus, one spatial measure was exchanged for another. The dream-I accepted this replacement, and even pursued the dream-task in the new spatial measure: Saint-Denys found his riding horse at the gates of the park.

III. Sacred Geometry & Perspective

When we turn our gaze onto works of art, we see that they also impose different measures on space. Before the Renaissance, sacred art did this through geometry, while after that, painting accomplished this through perspective. The former may be referred to as 'hieratic art' – depicting images of the Holy, such as gods and sacred heroes. The latter is a more 'humanist art' depicting Christ or the Virgin Mary in such a way as to evoke our more human emotions of suffering and pity. Each imposes its own *iconologue of space's measure*.

In hieratic works of art, space is constructed through sacred geometry. Using 'perfect shapes' such as circles or squares, the proportions of a figure and of the composition as a whole are built up like a grid. Countless studies have revealed the sacred geometry underlying Egyptian, Gothic, Buddhist, even Olmec works in the hieratic style.

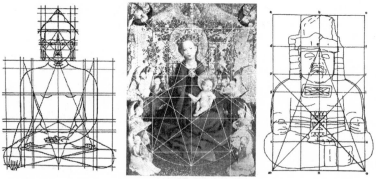

The sacred proportions underlying Buddhist, Christian and Olmec art

There is a marked preference in sacred art for symmetry, which betrays a deeper interest in centeredness. Whether in the *tympanum* of a Gothic cathedral or the *thangka* of a Buddhist temple, the same symmetry and centeredness inhere: Christ appears in the middle of the four evangelists or the Buddha appears at the centre of his many Bodhisattva incarnations. Like the arabesques of a Persian rug, all these figures and their geometric shapes point to the same, sacred centre.

But perspectival space is different. Granted, the lines in a Renaissance painting all meet at one point on the horizon. But that point is defined *by the viewer*, who stands outside the painting and looks *into* its narrowing perspectival space. Renaissance perspective is *humanist*, because all the objects in space are arranged according to the central point in the perspectival vision of the 'human all-too-human' viewer.

And, once we have become accustomed to it, perspectival vision is not easily abandoned. No matter where we turn our gaze, we notice that all lines converge unto a point at their centre. While looking at a work of art, we expect the same: that the measure of its space resemble *our* perspectival measure. This is, essentially, a *narcissistic* point of view, manifesting our more finite, ego-centered view onto the world.

Blake was conscious of this when he wrote, *"If the doors of perception were cleansed, everything would appear to Man as it is – infinite."* But he added lamentingly, *"Man has closed himself up, till he sees all things through the narrow chinks of his cavern."*[7]

Hieratic works lack the ego-centric perspective of humanist art: they are centered in the Sacred. By fixing our gaze onto them, we may free ourselves of our limited ego-centric perspective. We may free ourselves from that humanist *iconologue of space's measure* which has narrowed down our vision, so that we only see 'through the narrow chinks of our cavern'.

After a prolonged meditation on a hieratic work of art, we may use its symmetry and sacred geometry to center ourselves, instead, in the Sacred. And in one final step, we may move beyond even these hieratic *iconologues of space's measure*, to *enter through* the image. With our vision cleansed, we see space *'as it is – infinite'* ...as Blake said. We enter the *boundless* space revealed to us by our mythic imagination ...and by dreams.

The word *perspective*, based on the Latin *perspicere*, means literally 'to see clearly'. But, as Dürer defined it, it also means 'to see through' (*durchsehen*). One aid to 'seeing clearly' would be to combine *both* humanist and hieratic iconologues of space's measure in a *single* work of art. In this case, perspective and sacred geometry would *combine*, such that the point of perspective falls onto the central point determined by sacred geometry. Then, our more mundane, ego-centered point of view would find its true centre in the Sacred. But moving beyond this, we must learn 'to see through' (*durchsehen*) the painting's surface imagery to the Sacred that ultimately transcends it.

Numerous points of perspective, Shifting objects
Salvador Dalí: The Lugubrious Game (1929)

IV. The Lugubrious Game

Instead, 20th century artists made a more desperate attempt to deconstruct, distort or destroy our ego-centric perspective. In their Cubist paintings, Picasso and Braque centered several points of perspective onto the *object* rather than the subject. De Chirico and Dalí de-constructed perspective by painting landscapes with *numerous, conflicting* vanishing points. All of these systems must be seen as interesting, oneiric variations on perspective as an iconologue of space's measure.

In a painting such as Dalí's *Lugubrious Game*, the numerous points of perspective and the shifting size of the objects continually alters our ego-centric view onto the canvas. Our waking-I becomes disoriented, unable to maintain a proper distance from the objects and their horizon. An invitation is rendered unto us: forego all conscious expectations, and surrender yourself to the dream.

We *enter through* the image, much like the dream-I enters ever further through the space of a dream. Each object becomes a unique measure of the dream-space: this face, this arm, this hand – each extends us one step further into the dream-canvas, creating a new measure for its measureless expanse. Each object creates a unique sense of place, which moves from one image to the next. Each object is encountered, first in isolation, then in combination with the next. We forego all ideas of a spatial field, and enter into the series of associations arising from these combinations of images.

Moving further into the image, we associate memories with the images – more memories than the artist ever intended. The work becomes personal and biographical – a rare gaze into our own memory associations. In this particular painting, the numerous life-thresholds associated with sexual awakening, from infancy to adolescence, are evoked through images. Longing, shame, disgust and desire accumulate and constellate a series of memory-images around them. To re-experience these memories, we cross backward over their life-altering thresholds.

The spatial dimensions of our journey have nothing to do with the painting's lines of perspective or the relative size of its images. Space is now determined by the *place* in our memory where each image brings us. We have moved beyond the painting's *illusory* measures of space. The objects in the painting now reflect our mind's interior space, each evoking its own unique locale in our memory. Stepping back, we may behold the greater expanse of that interior world. Its extent is bounded only by our imagination, and the magnitude of our personal and cultural memories...

In describing his working method for this 'oneiric landscape', Dalí relates:

> *All the phantasies and representations of my childhood period again victoriously took possession of my brain. Again I saw passing before my ecstatic and wandering eyes infinite images which I could not localize precisely in time or space, but which I knew with certainty I had seen when I was little...*
>
> *I finally decided to undertake a picture in which I would limit myself exclusively to reproducing each of these images as scrupulously as it was possible for me to do, according to the order and intensity of their impact, and following as a criterion and norm for their arrangement only the most automatic feelings that their sentimental proximity and linking would dictate.*[8]

V. Similarity of Form

In a passage on dreams from *Human All-too-Human*, Nietzsche writes: "*Arbitrary and confused as it is,* [the dream] *continually mistakes things on the basis of the most* superficial similarities; *but it was the same arbitrarism and confusion with which the tribes composed their mythologies...*"[9]

We have seen how, in the early phases of a dream, hypnagogic images undergo transformations based on 'the most superficial similarities'. Saint-Denys provides us with two more examples from dreams:

> *I'm trying to remember something that has just slipped my memory. Recalling that it was square in shape, a whole series of square objects pass before me in quick succession: journals, glazed tiles, playing cards, match-boxes, etc.*[10]

> *I dream that I'm in a carriage with an actress from my favourite theatre. This actress reminds me of another. I watch as, beside me, a succession of actresses pass in review, without the idea of the carriage ride being interrupted by this continuous series of substitutions.*[11]

In these examples, a fascinating series of metamorphoses and transformations occurs. In the last chapter, we examined how these transformations occur over time. But what interests us now is how these transformations take place *in space*, through the *Similarity of Form Iconologue*.

In the first example, a rectangular shape persisted in space – the square tiles, playing cards and match boxes – even though the objects themselves transformed from one to another. The same could be said of the actress and her colleagues – her face transformed while her singular form remained beside him (and the coach journey continued uninterrupted). All of these images share a certain *similarity of form* which the dream delineates *spatially*.

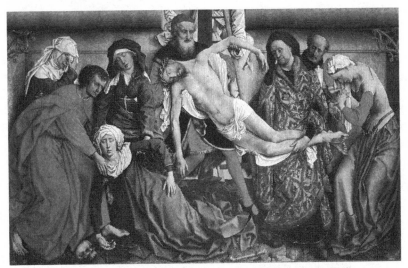

Morphological Echoes
Rogier Van der Weyden: Deposition from the Cross (c. 1440)

In dreams, the similarity of form iconologue is used time and again while also manifesting some fascinating variations. In the first variation, two images share a similarity of form, but these images exist *side-by-side* in space. We may identify this as a *morphological echo*.[12] In the second variation, two images share a similarity of form, but they exist *in one place only*, as super-imposed. We may identify this, instead, as a *double image*. Both find admirable examples in painting...

VI. Morphological Echoes in the Gothic Period

Rogier Van der Weyden was born in Tournai around 1400 and died some sixty-four years later. Not much else is known about his life, and it was only in the last century that his works were gathered together and considered the *œuvre* of one man. Nevertheless, his vision is undoubtedly unique, and reveals a life-long fascination with the Christian myth – as well as one of its 'untold' narratives...

When we concentrate our gaze on his *Deposition from the Cross*, a most striking feature appears: the figures of Christ and the Madonna *echo* one another in their falleness. Indeed, contrary to all the vertical figures standing behind them, Christ and the Madonna manifest a disturbing *similarity of form*. But what mysterious relationship is Van der Weyden trying to evoke through these figures?

We know, in accord with the Passion narrative, that *death* is the abyss into which Christ has fallen. The Madonna, on the other hand, has swooned at the foot of the cross, undergoing her own interior collapse.

The myth of Christ's death and resurrection is indeed profound, but the Madonna's unspoken myth, manifest here, is that during the crucifixion there transpired, not only Christ's *Passion*, but the Madonna's *Compassion* (literally, *'shared suffering'*).

The Madonna has swooned at the base of the cross because, *through compassion*, she has participated fully and absolutely in her son's death. But, rather than falling into the abyss of death, she has fallen into the interior abyss of her own suffering, wisdom and awakening *to* compassion.

This hidden myth of the Madonna, though neglected in the gospels, was expanded by Gothic Art to rival even the myth of Christ. During the Gothic period, the image of the Virgin Mary took root and suddenly blossomed – appearing at the very centre of those cathedrals and spiralling rose windows dedicated to *'Notre Dame'*. Soon, images *of her own death and resurrection* spontaneously appeared on the cathedrals' facades – her Dormition* and Assumption. She was also portrayed kneeling beside the throne of Christ-Judge, so that she, together with John, could beseech *mercy* on behalf of our souls.† For it was the Madonna, and not Christ-Judge, who felt a profound compassion for our suffering.

Through the *morphological echoes* in his painting, Van der Weyden has evoked this lost and neglected myth of the Madonna. In his moving representation of the Virgin, he has also recovered a collective memory-image which would otherwise have been lost to our culture forever. But our culture will only regain this forgotten Threshold Image once we, in our meditations, *enter* anew *through* its image...

VII. Morphological Echoes in Surrealism

In his *Metamorphosis of Narcissus* (1937), Dalí refined *morphological echoes* to the point of creating a veritable masterpiece. Although the myth of Narcissus aids us in deciphering its enigmatic images, the echoing forms of Narcissus and the upheld flower betray the silent presence of the *similarity of form iconologue*. Not only the myth, but this iconologue develop a hidden relationship between Narcissus and his flower.

According to the myth as told by Ovid, Narcissus (his name is related to *narké*, meaning the numbness associated with narcotics) was born a most beautiful creature. Tiresias prophesied he would live a long life, provided *"he does not come to know himself."*[13] While he rejected the love proffered by others (particularly the nymph Echo, who *echoed* all that he said), he was cursed to fall in love with his own reflection in a pool.

He lamented: *"I am you! I realize it; my reflection does not deceive me; I burn with love for myself."*[14] But he could not embrace the watery image. Finally, he could stand the separation no longer, proclaiming aloud: *"As it is, we two who are one in life shall die together!"*[15] He disappeared from the banks of the pond, and all that was left was a yellow flower with a circle of white petals in its centre – the narcissus flower.

* For an image of the Virgin's Dormition, see page 278.
† For an image of the Virgin beside the throne of Christ-Judge, see page 265.

Morphological Echoes
Salvador Dalí: The Metamorphosis of Narcissus (1937)

In Dalí's painting, the figure of Narcissus does not find his reflection in the pool; it is echoed instead by the hand upholding a cracked egg with a flower. This, we realize, is the true reflection of himself. Why a cracked egg with a flower?

In a text accompanying his painting, Dali went to great lengths to explain 'the metamorphosis' mentioned in the title:

> *If, with a certain distance and a 'playful regard', we concentrate on the stilled figure of Narcissus, he gradually disappears. At this precise moment, the metamorphosis of the myth takes place: the image of Narcissus transforms into that hand which arises from his own proper reflection. This hand holds an egg, a seed, a bulb from which is born the new Narcissus – the flower.*[16]

Dali even wrote a poem that dramatizes Narcissus' death and rebirth: *"In the cosmic vortex, Narcissus annihilates himself... In the abyss of his reflection, Narcissus loses his form."*[17] *"Then, the mystery draws near, the epic metamorphosis occurs."*[18] In the final moments, *"Nothing remains of Narcissus but the white oval of his delirious head... held deftly in fingers... of a deathly hand, which reflects none other than himself. When this head cracks open, the flower will emerge – of Narcissus made anew."*[19]

Through *the similarity of forms*, Dali has shown us Narcissus' *death and rebirth*. And it is this *mythologem* which underlies the painting's *morphological echoes*. This mythologem is one we have met with before and will meet again. It offers us the Threshold Image of our own life's continuous transformation, as we ourselves metamorphose from one life-threshold to the next.

VIII. Double Images

The similarities of form considered thus far presented two images side by side, in the form of morphological echoes. But Dali excelled in those double-images which superimposed one image over another.

Saint-Denys reveals that these super-impositions occur, first of all, in dreams:

> As I gradually descended into the dream-state, I thought I saw a chateau in the style of Louis XV. It glistened in the bright sunlight. Suddenly another chateau, in a completely different style, descended before the first without obscuring it completely. In fact, it seemed to be painted on a transparent screen, which moved between me and the other chateau. It was raised and lowered several times, offering me the spectacle of two super-imposed images – one fixed and solid, the other fleeting and transparent. This lasted for several seconds and then the whole disappeared.[20]

We shall meet with super-impositions again in the next chapter. For now, we are interested in the way they present two seemingly different images in one and the same place.

Without a doubt, the master of the double-image was Salvador Dali. In many of his works, a woman's head in profile may suddenly become a jug, or a bouquet of flowers may be mistaken for a female nude. In one of his more famous works, two women at the market suddenly transform into a bust of Voltaire. In each case, the double-image arises due to a similarity of form where, uniquely, the two forms occupy the same position in space.

Dali described the double-image as "...the representation of an object that is also, without the slightest figurative or anatomical

Double Image
Salvador Dali: Slave Market with Disappearing Bust of Voltaire (1940)

change, the representation of another entirely different object."[21]

For him, the elaboration of the double image comes about through 'the paranoia-critical method'. In the peculiarly Dalínian prose of *The Conquest of the Irrational* (1935), he described the paranoia-critical method as "...an experimental method based on the unexpected power of those systematic associations peculiar to paranoia."[22]

Expanding on this idea, Dali explained that the paranoiac mistakes one object for another due to an 'obsessive idea'. If one has a fear of spiders, then every black speck or spot will be mistaken for a hairy, creepy-crawling arachnid. All of us have the potential in us to develop this 'paranoiac faculty', which can then be applied in a systematic and 'critical' way:

> *Theoretically, a person sufficiently endowed with the* [paranoiac] *faculty may, at will, see the form of any real object go through successive changes, exactly as in voluntary hallucination, but with the devastatingly important difference that the various forms assumed by the object in question will be controllable and recognizable by all.*[23]

As an artist of notable skill, Dali tried to provide us with those double and even multiple-images which provoke fear, shame or desire. By fixing our gaze upon them, we could exercise and refine our paranoiac faculties: *"The double-image can be prolonged and, following the paranoid progression, the presence of another dominating idea then suffices for the third image to appear...and so on, until the number of images are limited only by the mind's capacity to produce degrees of paranoia."*[24]

The entire aim of this activity, in the end, is to *subvert* reality. In accord with Surrealist doctrine, Dali wanted to use the mechanisms of dreams and madness to *transform* our experience of reality: *"I believe that the moment is near when, by thought processes of a paranoiac and active character, it will be possible... to systemize confusion, and thus contribute to discrediting completely the world of reality."*[25] In its place, the double image *"...will make the very world of delirium pass to the level of reality."*[26]

By recognizing the iconologues of dreams and reproducing them in his art, Dali tried to integrate forms of madness and 'dream-thinking' into our culture. This more mythopoeic logic – or 'iconologic' – would, thus, *elevate our vision* to a 'higher reality' or *sur-réalité...*

IX. Shared Mythologems

In their attempts to uncover divine forebodings of Christ in the Old Testament, the early Church Fathers used 'types' as a hermeneutic device. This began as early as the New Testament, where Matthew wrote: *"Even as Jonah was three days and three nights in the belly of the whale, so shall the Son of Man be three days and three nights in the depths of the earth."* (Mt 12:40). And John created his own intriguing comparison: *"As Moses lifted up the serpent in the wilderness, even so must the Son of Man be lifted up."* (Jn 3:14)

All of these 'types' (Jonah, the brazen serpent) were used to see 'veiled forebodings' of Christ in the Old Testament, which the New Testament revealed when Christ 'rent the veil from top to bottom'.

But the early Church Fathers went a step further, and identified divine forebodings of Christ even in the 'pagan' prophecies of Hellenic culture. That Christ was born of a virgin mother, for example, fulfilled the prophecy uttered in trance by the Sibylline Oracles, and recorded by Virgil in 40 BC:

> *Now the last age is coming*
> *As it was written in the Sibyl's book*
> *The great circle of the centuries begins again*
> *...The Virgin has returned to earth*
> *...For the birth of the boy, the blessed boy*
> *For whom they will beat their swords into ploughshares.*[27]

Through this use of 'types', the Church Fathers were able to see mythic analogues to Christ in both Hebrew and Hellenic culture. A definite iconologue is at work here, which we may detect once all these myths are laid side by side.

In the Old Testament myth, Jonah descended into the belly of a whale, where he remained for three days, and then re-ascended. In the New Testament myth, Christ descended into Hades, where he remained for three days, and then re-ascended ('the Harrowing of Hell'). The two heroic figures *share the same mythologem* of descending three days into a monstral darkness. And, as a result of the *shared mythologem*, the two myths cross at their nadir.

In sacred works of art, these shared mythologems are made explicit by arranging *their images side by side*. Particularly in the carved stone and stained-glass windows of the Gothic period, mediæval craftsmen went to great pains to arrange images from the Old Testament next to the new.

In the cathedral of Le Mans, for example (see right), the crucified Christ is depicted at the centre of one *vitrail* while, just below to the right, Moses is seen uplifting the brazen serpent. By placing such images side by side, their *shared mythologems* are made explicit. Indeed, the entire programme for the stained-glass windows and sculpted facades of Gothic cathedrals was based on the *iconologue of the shared mythologem*.

X. Shared Mythologems in Gothic Christianity

Hence, each time we pause to admire the Christian symbols adorning Gothic facades, image-pairings rise before our eyes. Their shared mythologems appear, not only between Old and New Testament figures, but even between human and animal forms.

In the stained-glass window from Le Mans, there is not only Moses and the Brazen Serpent on the lower right, but a pelican and her young on the upper left. Why a pelican? Because it was believed that the pelican killed her own young, and then, after three days, opened a hole in her breast to revive them by sprinkling her blood upon them. And Christ, as we all know, died

Shared Mythologems
Stained-glass window from the Cathedral of Le Mans
Upper register: Pelican and her young, Lion and her young
Lower: Moses striking a rock that brings forth water, Moses and the brazen serpent
Centre: Christ flanked by Mary and John during the crucifixion

and rose again on the third day. Though these symbols differ in appearance, they both share the same *mythologem of death and rebirth*.

After a lifetime of studying French cathedrals, Emile Mâle discovered Honorius of Autun's 12th century book *Speculum Ecclesiæ* (The Mirror of the Church), which identified in print those forgotten mythologems whose forms could still be found in the cathedrals' sculptures and stained-glass ornaments. Honorius saw Christian types, not only in the Old Testament, but *"endeavoured to discern an image of the life and death of Christ even in the habits of animals,"* Mâle says.[28]

With the aid of contemporary *Bestiaries* (a fascinating compendium of mediæval lore), Honorius saw the image of Christ in, first of all, the unicorn. For the unicorn *"is a beast so savage that it can only be caught by the help of a young maiden. When he sees her, the creature comes and lies down in her lap."*[29] In a similar manner, we find images of Christ cradled, lying in death, and finally enthroned in the lap of the Virgin.

Of equal interest are images of the lion, eagle, and *charadrius* which, in the Cathedral of Lyons' stained-glass, flank the central medallions of Christ's resurrection and ascension. While an image of Jonah in the belly of the whale, as its type, naturally flanks the medallion of Christ's resurrection, so too does the image of a lion (*Leo*) with her cubs.

For, according to Honorius, *"the lioness gives birth to lifeless cubs but, after three days, the roaring of the lion brings them to life."*[30] (The image of the lioness and her young may also be seen on the right side of the central medallion of Christ's crucifixion in the Le Mans window).

Meanwhile, in Lyons, the medallion of Christ's ascension is flanked on one side by the image of an eagle (*Aquila*) and her young flying into the sun, and is flanked on the other side by the image of a bird labelled the *Kladrius* hovering over a deathbed.

The *shared mythologem* of Christ's resurrection and the eagle's flight is identified by Honorius as follows: *"The eagle is of all creatures that which flies the highest, and alone dares to gaze straight into the sun... Even so did Christ ascend into heaven."*[31]

*Stained-glass vignettes
from the Cathedral of Lyons*

Finally, the mystery of the 'Kladrius' is revealed by an obscure passage in Honorius: *"There is a bird named* charadrius *to whom it is given to know whether or not the sick will escape death. Placed near a sick man, if the sickness is unto death, the bird turns away its head; if the man will live it fixes its eyes on him and with an open beak absorbs the illness. Then it flies away into the rays of the sun...* The white charadrius *is Christ* [who] *looked towards us and bare our sickness on the cross... Then, returning to his Father with our flesh, he brought salvation upon us all."*[32]

XI. Shared Mythologems in Hinduism

In the myths and art of Asia, this same *iconologue of the shared mythologem* is at work, particularly in 'the Avatars' of Vishnu. The Hindu god Vishnu is the preserver of this world, which is periodically destroyed by Shiva and created again by Brahma. In the moments between the world's creation and destruction, Vishnu sleeps upon the cosmic waters. He is a *colossus*, lying on his side, partly submerged and partly afloat upon the endless ocean, which symbolizes *Maya*, the fluid appearance of all things. He also reposes upon the coils of his serpent, *Sesha*, who symbolizes time's ever-cycling. In deep, undisturbed sleep, Vishnu dreams this illusory universe with its endless emanations cycling round. He also dreams of himself, entering into and out of these many worlds, as one of its timely saviours or *avatars*.

There are primarily ten avatars of Vishnu, though the number is sometimes twenty-four, and other times, infinite. This is because all the figures of mythology and, indeed, the singular and unique life-myth of every living person, is a creation of Vishnu's great, all-embracing, life-sustaining dream. Each of the ten avatars constitutes one of Vishnu's 'descents' (the literal meaning of *avatar*) into the world-dream, appearing thus to himself, to alter the dream's course.

Vishnu Trivikrama (c. 1200)

In deep, undisturbed sleep, Vishnu dreams of himself
entering into and out of the world as one of its avatars.

For example, before the world was to be cleansed by a massive flood, Vishnu warned the elderly and wise Manu of the ensuing cataclysm, instructing him to build an ark that would hold seeds of every plant, and two of every living creature. When the great deluge arrived, Manu's ark kept afloat above its churning waters, but was tossed and turned about wildly. Then, in the midsts of the mælstrom, Vishnu appeared in the form of *Matsya*, half-man, half-fish, and towed the ark to safety. Mankind, all the plants, and all the animals, thus survived and replenished the world, because of its saviour, Matsya, the first of Vishnu's avatars.

Later, when the world was flooded again, Vishnu appeared in the form of *Varahavatara*, the Wild Boar. At the bottom of the churning waters, the Goddess of the Earth was held captive by the demons who had instigated the flood. *Varahavatara* dashed across heaven and dived into the waters, defeating the demons in battle and then lifting the goddess to the surface, so as to replenish the earth once more. In the form of the wild boar *Varahavatara*, Vishnu again saved the world.

As the Tortoise, the Man-lion and the Dwarf; as *Rama, Krishna* and the Buddha; and finally as the future messiah, *Kalkin*, Vishnu has appeared and shall appear an endless number of times to save the world in the course of its ever-repeating catastrophes and resolutions.

But, earlier extant versions of the above flood myth reveal that the figure of Vishnu was only *interpolated* into the text at a later date. Indeed, it is quite possible that the image of the flood, which is also present in the disturbingly familiar Hebrew myth of the deluge, was derived from a common source: the Mesopotamian *Epic of the Deluge* which is included in the Legend of Gilgamesh. This mythic motif then travelled West, with the Hebrew god aiding Noah in his ark, and East, with Vishnu as the Hindu god offering aid to Manu in his ark.

In this manner, the Hindu god Vishnu was able to *appropriate* the mythologems of countless other figures, which were usually the cult animal of a long forgotten myth. But, rather than placing images of this animal and the saviour *side by side*, as in Christian art, the two were *combined* into a single image. For example, the Matsya avatar was depicted as a human figure with a fish's tail.

Hindu avatarism and Christian typology also differ radically by virtue of their differing conceptions of time. Because Christianity possesses a linear and historical sense of time, the myths of other cultures could only be encountered *historically*, as *pre-dating* Christianity. And so the mythologems they shared with Christianity were read as prophecies and oracles, which foretold and in some sense pre-validated the coming of Christ in one historical moment in time.

Hinduism, on the other hand, possesses an ever-repeating cycle of time, and so the myths of other cultures were encountered as the *repeated tellings* of a contemporary myth in its antiquated and more ancient guise. Though, in this *yuga*, Vishnu assumes the form of *Matsya*, half-man half-fish, to save Manu from the flood, in previous *yugas*, and in the more ancient version of the myth still preserved, a *jhasha* fish alone was responsible for saving Manu from the flood.[33]

But, many of Vishnu's avatars fail to reveal their underlying sources. The earlier figures are wholly subsumed under the manifest figure of Vishnu, and so become 'immanent' in him. In the next chapter, we shall examine these combined figures in depth. For, in this case, a mythologem is shared, but its underlying presence is more difficult to detect – as it was *completely combined or displaced*, with little sign remaining...

CHAPTER XVIII

Condensation

Through dreams, a door is opened to mythology.
– Joseph Campbell[1]

*There is no mythic motive or scenario of initiation
which is not also presented, in one way or the other,
in dreams.*
– Mircea Eliade[2]

I. The Combinations Iconologue

Toward the end of his life, Gérard de Nerval had a dream which he described in his final work *Aurélia*. This unfinished piece of prose, haunted by nightmares and visions, was partly inspired by the poet's own fight against his incipient madness. Its completion was cut short when de Nerval took his own life in January of 1855.

> *I suddenly found myself in a room which formed part of my grandfather's house, only it seemed to have grown larger. The old furniture glowed with a miraculous polish, the carpets and curtains were as if new again, daylight three times more brilliant than natural day came in through the windows and the door, and in the air there was a freshness and perfume like the first warm morning of spring.*
> *Three women were working in the room and, without exactly resembling them, they stood for relatives and friends of my youth. Each seemed to have the features of several of them. Their facial contours changed like the flames of a lamp, and all the time something of one was passing to the other. Their smiles, the colour of their eyes and hair, their figures and familiar gestures, all these were exchanged...*[3]

In one short sequence, this dream manifests the unlimited resources and ever-creative power of the oneiric imagination. How many iconologues are here at work? As seen before, there are transformations and temporal regressions. But, what is more, figures appear which 'seem to have the features of the others'. This unique combination of figures in de Nerval's dream can best be characterized as *'condensation'*.

As Freud discovered in his analysis of dreams, *symbolization* is not the only way the dreamwork may arrange its images. For him, *condensation* and *displacement* also play major roles. These iconologues are used to create, not only our individual dreams, but the collective dreams of an entire culture. For, as Campbell reminds us, *"Dream is the personalized myth, myth is the depersonalized dream."*[4]

In this chapter we shall concentrate on *condensations* of images while, in the next, *displacements* will come more to the fore. Although these iconologues occur, first of all, in dreams, they may manifest themselves *equally* in art or in myths.

In 'the Means of Representation in Dreams', Freud analyzes *condensation* in depth and gives us three different varieties. In the first two types – 'collective' and 'composite' figures – the combination of figures remains *manifest* in the dream image. Meanwhile, in the last type – what Freud called 'identification' – at least one of the figures combined in the dream-image remains *latent* or hidden. We shall identify the latter type as the *Immanence iconologue*, and deal with it afterwards.

For now, we must distinguish between Freud's 'collective' and 'composite' forms of *condensation*. According to him, *"a 'collective figure' can be produced for purposes of dream-condensation, namely, by uniting the actual features of two or more people into a single dream-image."*[5] In this case, different aspects are combined in one figure. This was certainly the case with de Nerval's dream, where 'each women seemed to have the features of the others'.

Meanwhile, with 'composite figures', it is the *similarities* that come to the fore. Freud reports that in one of his dreams,

> *...the dream-image was constructed in yet another way. I did not combine the features of one person with those of another and in the process omit from the memory-picture certain features of each of them. What I did was to adopt the procedure by means of which Galton produced family portraits: namely, by projecting two images onto a single plate, so that certain features common to both are emphasized, while those which fail to fit in with one another cancel one another out and are indistinct in the picture.*[6]

Here, the *similarities* become manifest, and these are combined in one figure.*

If we now examine several dreams dreamt by Freud himself, we will find examples of these two types of condensation. In the first dream, the images were so arranged as to create a 'collective figure' who *"...bore the name of Dr M., spoke and acted like him, but his physical characteristics and his malady belonged to someone else, namely my eldest brother."*[8]

In the second dream, the images were arranged in a different way, so as to create a 'composite figure': *"My friend R. was my uncle. – I had a great feeling of affection for him. I saw before me his face, somewhat changed. It was as though it had been drawn out lengthwise. A yellow beard that surrounded it stood out especially clearly."*[9] Both R. and Freud's uncle possessed beards, and so the similarities between the two were combined and emphasized (*'the yellow beard stood out especially clearly'*). Meanwhile, due to a combination of the differences in their faces, the composite face was distorted and *'drawn out lengthwise'*.

All of Freud's condensations may be characterized as *iconologues of combination*. Simply put, the 'collective figures' are combinations *of differences*, while the 'composite figures' are combinations *of similarities*.

Examples of these two types may be clearly drawn from mythology. From time immemorial, mythic figures have emerged which combine the male and female genders into one person. Such figures have been described variously as 'hermaphrodites' or 'androgynes'. But there is more than one way to create such a figure...

As Ovid tells in his myth of *Hermaphroditus*, this son of Hermes and Aphrodite once wandered far from his home, and became entranced by his own reflection in a pool (much like Narcissus). The *naiad* of that pond, a comely young maiden, also became entranced by his beautiful reflection.

---

*The discovery of dream condensation must be accredited to Saint-Denys, who first mentions this phenomenon in 1867. While describing 'the connections between memory images' (*l'enchaînement des clichés souvenirs*), he uses an extended metaphor:

If you attempt to pass a second glass slide into a magic lantern before removing the first, two things will happen: either the painted figures on both slides, appearing one beside the other, will form a heterogeneous composition in which Bluebeard finds himself face to face with Tom Thumb; or they will appear superimposed, in which case Bluebeard will have two different heads, four legs, and a menacing arm jutting out of his ear.[7]

Although Saint-Denys offers us two examples, both of them describe 'composite figures': the first is a composite 'scene' and the second is a composite 'figure' (which Saint-Denys calls 'superimposition'). Saint-Denys uses 'superimposition' to demonstrate changes in dream imagery *over time*, as 'transitions via resemblance, substitution, and superimposition'. We have already investigated these under the *transformation iconologue*. Meanwhile, in the dream of the two chateaux – one real, one on a screen – these two existed together *in one place*. We examined this type of 'superimposition' as a *double image*. Nevertheless, all these examples show Saint-Denys' prior awareness of combined images, which Freud called 'condensation'.

Hence, when the young man removed his clothes and dived into the pool, the lovestruck *naiad* seized him and clutched him to her in a loving embrace. The youth tried to escape, but the more he struggled against her, the more she clung to him. In fear of losing him forever, the *naiad* called aloud 'May the gods so ordain that we never be separated in future time, neither you from me nor me from you.' And, as Ovid tells, 'the Gods accepted her prayer. For their two bodies were joined together as they entwined.' Henceforth, he was called Hermaphroditus, for he bore the features of both his mother and his father.

Meanwhile, an androgyne is created differently. As we have seen in Gnostic myth, the Mother and Father both emerged from an androgynous unity called 'the One'. In a similar way, Christ and Sophia became the male and female aspects of one androgynous figure called 'the Child'. A child (like the androgynous One) does not possess two genders, but is considered gender*less*. It only manifests its gender difference later on.

In the case of *Hermaphroditus*, this mythic figure clearly manifests both its masculine and feminine genders – combining these *differences* into one 'collective figure'. But, in the case of 'the Child', this androgynous figure eludes gender distinction – eliminating the masculine and feminine differences, while combining their remaining *similarities* into one 'composite figure'.

II. Combinations
of Human and Animal Mythologems

Many of mythology's more fantastic creatures were first conjured forth in dreams. While Freud remained an avid collector of Egyptian statuary all his life, his first encounter with their combinatory figures occurred in a nightmare from his seventh or eighth year:

> *I saw my beloved mother, with a peculiarly peaceful, sleeping expression on her features, being carried into the room by two (or three) people with bird's beaks, and laid upon the bed. I awoke in tears and screaming...*[10]

Not only does this dream combine human and animal features into collective figures, but in its analysis, Freud recognized that *"the expression on my mother's features in the dream was copied from the view I had had of my grandfather a few days before his death as he lay sleeping in a coma."*[11] Through this expression, his mother became, instead, a composite figure.

The gods of ancient Egypt are a rich compendium of possible ways in which the human figure may be combined with an animal's form. In the process, an image is rendered unto us through which we may behold the Sacred. Although these figures combine human and animal forms, it is their *combined mythologems* which fascinate us, and allow us to think further through their combined image.

Combined mythologems differ from the *shared mythologems* we examined in the last chapter. There, a certain *similarity* between, say, the risen Christ and a flying eagle, allowed us to identify one with the other (through the mythologems they shared). Rather, it is now the *differences* in mythologems that interests us, and the way in which these differences may be combined.

As we saw with the example of *an angel* in 'symbolic thinking', man's unique ability 'to think' may be combined with the bird's unique ability 'to fly' to render a higher, indeed 'more elevated vision' of the world. In Egyptian mythology, Horus combines man's thinking with a falcon's flight. This falcon hunts by day and was considered a sun-bird. Thoth also combines man's thinking with bird-flight, except that bird was an ibis which, on the contrary, hunts by night, and was considered a lunar-bird. Both manifest a view of the world 'as seen from above'.

The jackal-headed God Anubis is he who, like the jackal, walks among the dead knowingly and without fear. Sakhmet is a lion-headed goddess who, with feline ferocity, engages knowingly and without pity in human destruction – for which reason she became 'the great beast' in the Egyptian Apocalypse. According to this cataclismic myth, Re sent Sakhmet out into the desert to destroy the first race of men due to their lack of faith. In the ecstasy of slaughter, the raging lioness waded through rivers of blood, but finally spared mankind from complete destruction.

Hence, whenever we gaze upon the image of an Egyptian god, an invitation is offered us: to combine our more human thinking with this animal's unique manner of moving through the world.* When these two mythologems *are combined*, we *think through* this composite image. And the moment the image is *entered through*, we gain a frightening awareness of the Sacred at the source of *all* life.

III. Combinations of Animal Mythologems

In *The Language of Dreams*, Wilhelm Stekel rendered an account of one of his own oneiric creations:

> *I am in a large hall. A combined being appears on a podium, similar to a centaur: half-horse and half-wolf or tiger. I am standing at the entrance to the hall, because I am afraid it could escape. Suddenly the tiger separates itself from the horse and springs with large strides toward the door. Quickly, I get behind the door and bolt it shut.[14]*

*In his classic study, *Shamanism: Archaic Techniques of Ecstasy*, Eliade notes that the shaman, through ecstatic trance, is able to knowingly enter animal states of being, and so, return to the time 'at the beginning': "*Each time a shaman succeeds in sharing in the animal mode of being, he in a manner re-establishes the situation that existed* in illo tempore, *in mythical times, when the divorce between man and animal had not yet occurred.*"[12]

Under the influence of LSD, many of Grof's subjects claimed a similar ability to "*...transcend the limits of specifically human experience and tune in to what appears to be the consciousness of animals, plants, or even inanimate objects.*"[13]

Egyptian Book of the Dead; Judgement scene:
Horus, the falcon-headed god, presents the defunct before the scales of judgement.
Anubis, the Jackal-headed god, tends to the scales
while Thoth, the Ibis-headed god, records the outcome.
If the defunct's heart does not balance against the feather of truth,
it will be eaten by Ammit, 'the devourer of hearts'.

It is no co-incidence that Stekel dreamt of this horse-tiger as something menacing and fearful. Since the image combines two animal mythologems, it moves in ways that are utterly unknown to mankind. Unlike the examples above, we cannot easily combine our thinking with this creature's swift and ferocious ways.

Granted, two animal mythologems may be combined to form a fantastic creature that strikes us as wondrous and heavenly, such as the winged horse Pegasus, the chimera, the gryphon and the gentle unicorn. But most combinatory animals, since they manifest instincts, appetites and actions unknown to consciousness, have a much darker purpose...

Witness, for example, the Egyptian *Am-mit*, a tripartite creature with the jaws of a crocodile, the claws of a lion, and the body of a small hippo. As the 'devourer of hearts', he perched beneath the scales in the judgement hall of Osiris and awaited the moment that one's heart, when weighed against the feather of truth, was found to be lacking – for then it was thrown into *Ammit's* open mouth. With the swiftness of a lion, the lancet teeth of a crocodile, and the appetite of a hippo, the 'great beast' mercilessly devoured the heart of the damned.

The 12th Book of Revelation
The woman "clothed with the sun and with the moon under her feet"
gives birth to a child, which the "great red dragon with seven heads"
hopes to devour, but "the child was snatched away and taken to his throne."

In a similar image, Satan appears during the Last Judgement as *"a great red dragon, with seven heads, ten horns, and seven diadems on his heads."* (Rev 12:3) This combined image emphasizes the beasts' primæval (dragon), multiple (seven heads) and vicious (horns) nature. Since *"this ancient serpent was seized and thrown into the pit of the underworld"* (Rev 20:1) mediæval Christianity transformed this dragon into the fearful image of 'the Hell mouth'* where the damned descended after judgement. Hence, in Christianity as in Egypt, the same image recurs: those souls whom the scales of judgement find to be lacking are thrown into the open mouth of 'the great beast'.

IV. Combinations
of Objects and Attributes

But it is not only human or animal figures that may be variously combined. The Combination iconologue may also compound several objects, creating new inventions and even composing hybrid forms of architecture. Over a three-year period Friedrich Huch recorded his dreams and gathered them together in his 1904 book *Träume ('Dreams')*. From that collection comes the following:

*See the image of *The Harrowing of Hell* on pg. 56, where the Hell mouth appears on the far right.

I thought of my pocket-watch, and pulled it out. It had stopped. I tried to wind it, and while winding it, realized that something was wrong. The watch began to hum, and the hands suddenly began to spin wildly round. I looked at it in fear: a red drop of blood slowly emerged from the centre of the watch face. The blood began forcing its way over the watch face, its rounded glass expanding further and further...[15]

This dream's nightmarish quality is accomplished through a combination of the mechanic and organic. Though his pocket-watch has stopped, it is not 'dead'. Indeed, it has come to life in a most shocking manner.

And yet, not all objects conjured forth in dreams need inspire our fears. Sometimes they may acquire a more visionary and mystical quality. Take for example this dream of Saint-Denys:

A glass apparatus of unusual design was placed before me on a low table. It appeared to be full of water and someone, I don't know who, told me that the liquid had the power to render things transparent for a few instants. I was amazed and also doubtful. At that moment, I heard a cat meowing in the corner. I took the cat and threw it in the water to see what would happen. I watched as, bit by bit, the animal lost its first appearances and became luminous, translucid, diaphanous, and finally, like crystal.[16]

In the world of myth, the hero may also possess such a marvelous invention – a special charm, talisman, weapon or vestment blessed with benevolent power. The most familiar are the winged sandals and cap of darkness which Athena gave to Perseus to slay the Medusa. The sandals allowed him to fly, and the cap – like the dream-apparatus of Saint-Denys – rendered him invisible...

Later, Hermes acquired these instruments for himself, and they became emblems of his power. The gods of the ancient world were always depicted with such emblems. Athena held a spear – and a shield emblazoned with the head of the Medusa. Osiris held the shepherd's crook and flail. Baal held his thunderbolts overhead. The angels behind Christ bore the instruments of his passion, and the Saints, the implements of their martyrdom. The gods of India held many emblems in their four hands: thunderbolts, tridents, drums, begging bowls and bells.

As a result, many gods manifest themselves sheerly through their emblems, which thus became *symbols* of their power. In Egypt, we find the symbols of the *ankh*, *djed* column and *was* sceptre combined

Ptah's sceptre combining the ankh djed column and was sceptre

into one object manifesting Ptah's life-giving, life-restoring and eternally-prospering power. In Russia, the Byzantine crucifix is an abstract rendering of the cross, spear and crown of thorns: all are combined into one symbol of Christ's suffering, humiliation and sacrifice.

As is clear from India's sculptures, such symbols may be combined variously to demonstrate each god's particular blend or mixture of power. In his four hands, Brahma holds a water jug, lotus, prayer beads and book – each a mythic object manifesting his all-creative power. Vishnu holds a conch shell, chakra, club and lotus flower – similar such emblems of his all-preserving power. And as the destroyer-of-all, Shiva holds the drum, trident, begging bowl and mirror. Meanwhile, as the great *Trimurti*, these three gods merely reflect different aspects of one unity. Thus, each of their emblems becomes a particular inflection of the *one* sacred power which, variously refracted and combined, emanates from the same source.

Byzantine cross

V. The Immanence Iconologue

The third type of condensation, as described by Freud, is 'identification'. With 'composite' and 'collective' figures, the combination of two or more figures becomes *manifest* in the dream image. Meanwhile, in 'identification' at least one of the figures combined in the dream-image remains *latent* or hidden.

Freud writes:

> *In identification, only one of the persons who are linked by a common element* [in the latent dream-thoughts] *succeeds in being represented in the manifest content of the dream, while the second or remaining persons seem to be suppressed in it. But this single covering figure appears in the dream in all the relations and situations which apply either to him or to the figures which he covers.*[17]

As an example, Freud cites his own dream of Irma's Injection.[18] In this oft-cited dream, Freud meets his patient Irma at a large gathering, and is struck by her pale appearance. He takes her to the window and, with a number of other doctors, begins examining her. They conclude that she must have become infected when given an injection from a dirty syringe.

In the interpretation of this 'specimen dream', Freud recovers a number of latent dream-thoughts through free-association. He concludes that, in creating this dream, the dreamwork *identified* all of the figures from his latent dream-thoughts with this one manifest figure of Irma, due to their shared 'common elements':

The principal figure in the dream-content was my patient Irma. She appeared with the features which were hers in real life, and thus, in the first instance, represented herself. But the position in which I examined her by the window was derived from someone else, the lady for whom, as the dream-thoughts showed, I wanted to exchange my patient. In so far as Irma appeared to have a diphtheritic membrane, which recalled my anxiety about my eldest daughter, she stood for that child and, behind her, through her possession of the same name as my daughter, was hidden the figure of my patient who succumbed to poisoning. In the further course of the dream the figure of Irma acquired still other meanings, without any alteration occurring in the visual representation of her in the dream.[19]

Perhaps the easiest way of explaining this phenomenon is to say that the other figures were not visibly present in the figure of Irma, but were nevertheless *immanent* in her. As such, identification may be characterized by the *Immanence Iconologue*. Detecting immanence is no easy task, since there is very little in the manifest content to indicate the latent figures. Apparently, it is only 'their relationship to the dreamer' and 'the situations in which he remembers them' that indicate their presence.

And yet, the shared 'common elements' demonstrated by Freud in the above example included the act of examining the patient by the window, and the transfer of his daughter's malady onto Irma. That is to say, certain features, gestures and even actions (hence, mythologems) had been 'displaced' from the latent figures onto Irma.

In our next chapter, on Displacement, we shall see how the figure of one myth may appropriate the features, gestures and especially the mythologems of another figure from an earlier myth *–with little signs remaining*, since the latter is hidden, undepicted or even *repressed*. In fact, the presence of this hidden figure can only be detected through the shared mythologem, which has undergone an important *shift* in meaning during its displacement. In this way, the hidden figure of an earlier myth survives, but as *immanent* in the manifest figure of a later myth. Detecting the presence of these hidden figures is difficult, but necessary, insofar as the ancient and repressed deities of earlier cultures may thereby be recovered and remembered.

In the dream of Irma's Injection, Freud's daughter and the patient shared certain features, gestures and actions with Irma, but these figures were not successfully depicted in the dream. Due to displacement, the figures were not *combined* with Irma in a manifest way, but are *identified* with her in a more latent manner. They become *immanent* in her.

Every time we recollect a dream, read a myth, or look at a sacred work of art, we *identify ourselves* with the main figure. Although our presence remains hidden, we too become immanent in the main figure. Seeing ourselves as

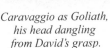

Caravaggio as Goliath, *Dürer as Christ* *Michelangelo as*
his head dangling *"I live, yet not I, but* *St. Bartholomew holding*
from David's grasp. *Christ liveth in me."* *his own skinned husk.*

immanent in the mythic hero requires a more ancient way of thinking, which we first learned in dreams long ago, and have since transferred onto myths and works of art. According, once more, to Freud:

> *Dreams are completely egoistic. Whenever my own ego does not appear in the content of the dream, but only some extraneous person, I may safely assume that my own ego lies concealed, by identification, behind this other person; I can insert my own ego into the context.*[20]

Through the *immanence iconologue*, we have learned to see ourselves in all the great figures of myth. And many of the world's greatest artists have not hesitated to depict *themselves* in their works, so strong was their identification with their mythic subject. In doing so, they made this hidden identification explicit.

For example, in his stunningly graphic image of *David and Goliath*, it is Caravaggio's own severed head which dangles from David's grasp. In the Sistine Chapel *Last Judgement*, it is Michelangelo's own skin which has been torn off and now hangs from St. Bartholomew's hand. In this way, both of these *peintres maudits* saw a mirror-image of themselves in their martyred victims.

Meanwhile, in his strangely moving *Self-portrait* of 1500, Dürer uses the *immanence iconologue* to display, not only himself, but the Christ-in-him, following Galatians 2:20: *"I live, yet not I, but Christ liveth in me."* Through his artistry, Dürer saw his own image reflected in Christ. And Christ, we should recall, is the mirror-image of our own soul in eternity: we die and rise *in him* to become one with the Sacred. Through this hieratic self-portrait, Dürer has offered us a 'sacred mirror' of the invisible Christ-within.

VI. The Iconologue of Opposites

When we awaken from dreams, we may often detect the presence of opposites. Stekel provides us with an interesting dream fragment, complements of a certain 'Fräulein Etha':

> *I saw a wide river divided in the middle: one half was flowing in one direction; the other, in the opposite.*[21]

In the course of a lucid dream, Saint-Denys noted that certain options were offered him:

> *Now two paths open before me. The one on the right seems to disappear in a dense forest; the other, on the left, leads to a sort of manor in ruins. I can well sense that I have the freedom to turn right or left.*[22]

Opposites are a specific type of condensation where two images are combined to manifest a *contrary* relationship. In the above examples, a curious *difference* at first becomes manifest: the river flows *this way and the other*; the path divides *left and right*. But a hidden *similarity* also inheres, since *one river* flows this way and the other; *one path* divides left and right.

As such, opposites possess an important similarity which remains hidden or de-emphasized. If, however, this similarity were entirely absent, then we would simply have two different images in combination, with no common ground to create the opposition.

We are reminded of the fragment from Heraclitus: *"The way up and the way down are one and the same."* The logic of 'similarity and difference' underlies this iconologue, which uses both similarities and differences to construct the resulting image.

Opposites exists in a fascinating variety of examples. In each case, we cannot say that they are simply the result of a random arrangement of images. Rather, it is our iconological manner of thinking that creates these oppositions, in order to *think further through them*.

Let us take another example from a dream which the 19th century German dramatist and diarist Friedrich Hebbel recorded in his Dream Journal:

> *Dec 16, 1846. During the night a dream: a small friendly street, brightly lit by the sun into which I turned. Then, a long bridge, then a gloomy passage between houses with windows one could not see. Shadowy forms of beggars at the entrance and inside of the passage. It was not quite dark and trees gleamed at the far end. The forms became more menacing. "Where does this passage lead?" I asked. "To the churchyard!" was the answer. They hoarded round me, without harming me. I turned around.*[23]

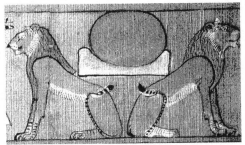

Threshold Guardians:
Top: the Egyptian Aker
Left: Vishnu's Nrisimha avatar

The images of this dream are arranged through a series of oppositions: a friendly, bright, sun-lit street becomes a shadowy, gloomy, menacing passage. Hebbel willingly *turns into* the bright street, but later *turns round* from the gloomy passage. A bridge connects the two. The oppositions in Hebbel's dream are not only spatial or directional, as they were in the previous two examples, but qualitative, emotional, and even temporal (how the dream begins is the opposite of how it ends).

If we now turn to art and myth for elucidations of this dream-phenomenon, we find that the *iconologue of opposites* appears time and again. As we have seen in Campbell's Monomyth, almost all myths move from the light overworld into a dark underworld, just as in Hebbel's dream. The journey begins in a world of clear sunlight and friendly forces, but then crosses the threshold of adventure into a dark underworld full of menacing forms. The underworld and overworld may thus be distinguished through the contraries of upper and lower, dark and light, clear and smokey, friendly and menacing.

At the threshold between these two worlds stands, what Campbell has called, *the Threshold Guardian.* The Egyptian image of the *Aker* is one such threshold guardian: with one visage it faces the Manu gate, where the sun descends into the underworld at dusk; with the other visage it faces the Bakhu gate, where the sun rises into the heavens at dawn. The sacred Roman figure of *Janus bifrons* is a similar such 'god of doorways': his two-faced figure was so stationed as to face both sides of all public gates (*jani*). And, he was honoured on the first day of the first month (*Janarius*). This means, he stood on the threshold between the year past and the year coming, facing both the past and the future.

Even more fascinating is the *Nrisimha* avatar of Vishnu. During one of this world's many permutations, a demon acquired great power and, indeed, became king of all the earth, since he could not be slain either by man or beast, neither inside nor outside his palace, and neither by day nor night. To

The Scales of Judgement:
In the Egyptian scheme (above), Osiris presides over the judgement
while, in the Christian scheme (right), it is Christ. St. Micheal holds the scales

save the world of this tyranny, Vishnu assumed the form of *Nrisimha*. Then, at dusk, he hid himself in a pillar at the doorway to the palace. When the demon passed into his abode, *Nrisimha* broke out of the pillar, seized the demon in his claws, and tore out his entrails. Vishnu was able to slaughter the demon because, as *Nrisimha* he was a 'lion-man' (neither man nor beast). He attacked at dusk (neither day nor night), and from a pillar at the threshold of the palace (neither inside nor outside).

In the movement from mundane time to the eternal *mythic time*, the threshold guardian appears once more in images of the Last Judgement. The Apocalypse occurs during *the twilight* – at the threshold between endless day and endless night. Whether the threshold guardian be Christ in *The Book of Revelation*, Osiris in *The Book of Am Duat*, or Yama Raja in *The Bardo Thödol*, an opposition within the soul of the deceased is weighed, reflected upon, and judged.

In the Christian scenario of Doomsday, scales held aloft by the archangel Michael manifest the soul's internal opposition of good and evil. In Osiris' hall of judgement, the scales manifest the opposition (or hopeful accord) between one's heart and Maat's feather of truth. And in the court of Yama Raja, the scales reflect the soul's karmic opposition through the black and white pebbles placed on the pan by the genii of good and evil. Yama Raja stands above these scales, holding a sword in his right hand and the mirror of

Rogier Van der Weyden:
Altar of Beaune Last Judgement (1451)

karma in his left – a mirror which reflects the good and evil deeds performed over several lifetimes.[24] Hence, the *iconologue of opposites* is used repeatedly in images of the Last Judgement to reflect the soul's internal opposites.

In the image of the Divine Twins, the iconologue of opposites again becomes manifest. For example, around the ancient astrological image of the Gemini, a series of myths have been woven throughout time. The ancient Greeks called them the *dioscuri* – the twins Castor and Polydeuces (Roman: Pollux) who appear side by side in the heavens. As one legend tells, Zeus was so moved by Polydeuces' pleas for his dead brother, that he placed the image of the two in the heavens. But only one of the twins was allowed into upper Olympus while the other had to suffer under the earth in Therapne. As a result, each day the twins alternated with each other: one below, one above.

In Mithraic mythology, the *dadophores* appear beside the central image of Mithra slaying the primæval bull (*Mithra Tauroctonus*). *Cautes* and *Cautopates* by name, these twins appear bearing torches: one holds his torch upward and the other, down. They are thought to symbolize the sunrise and sunset, as well as the autumnal and vernal equinox. For, in an earlier epoch, the bull (Taurus) and the scorpion beneath him (Scorpio) appeared in the heavens during the autumnal and vernal equinox. The two thieves crucified

Mithra Tauroctonus
The twins Cautes and Cautopates appear on either side of Mithra,
who is slaying the primæval bull. One of the dadophores
holds his torch upward, the other, down.

on either side of Christ are a similar image: one ascends to Heaven while the other descends to Hell. Hence, we have not only the contrary symbols of the good and bad thieves, but the *opposite mythologems* of one ascending while the other descends.

Finally, there are the Gemini themselves – the original 'Twin Giants' *Lugal-irra* and *Meslamta-ea* of Sumer – whose astrological image harkens back to a time before recorded myth. Their twin effigies have always been found at doorways, in classical Sumerian stance, with an axe upheld. They may have been guardians to the gates of the underworld or, in a lost myth, they may have been condemned like Castor and Polydeuces to a shared eternity on either side of its dark threshold. In all of these images, *the iconologue of opposites* silently appears, arranging two similar figures into contrary forces.

The eagle and the serpent, the sun and the moon, the sky and the earth, the masculine and feminine, the king and the queen – the iconologue of opposites is inherent in all of these pairs. The ascent and descent, to enter into and to flee from, to be born and to die – all of these contrary movements constitute opposing mythologems, which become the substance of a mythic journey through the two worlds. The two worlds, the threshold guardians that stand between them, and Twins who exist on either side of that threshold – all of these embody, through their very form, an inherent opposition.

VII. The Iconologue of Opposites-in-Union

In *The Language of Dreams*, Stekel describes a *Phantasietraum* of a certain Herr Beta. The man imagined he was accused of a crime, tried in court, and finally found guilty – even though quite innocent. He made no defense, and so was sentenced to life imprisonment. While in prison, he came to be revered by all, even the guards, as a kind of miracle worker. Then:

> *...It is completely revealed that he is Christ himself. His great triumph is that, through his holiness, he has lost his genitals. He is sexless, and ascends as an infinite beam of light to Heaven.*[25]

The arrangement of images in this dream-fantasy may appear, at first glance, to be nothing but the delusions of a severe neurotic. And yet, when the *Nag Hammadi* corpus was published sixty years later, the same arrangements of images could be found in its aged pages.

For the Gnostics, this world is a prison, one into which Christ descends so as to reveal to us 'the hidden spark'. That spark, let us not forget, is the remembrance of the One *'who ...being both male and female, exists in unity.'* And Christ himself, through his consort Sophia, is also an androgynous being, which first appeared in the light as 'the Child'. We recall: *"the Child... produced a bright androgynous light. The masculine name of that light is Saviour... and the feminine name is Sophia... Then the Saviour consented with his consort Sophia. "*[26] The dyad of Christ and Sophia, as masculine and feminine opposites, re-unite in the Child.

That is why the Gnostic *Gospel of Philip* says: *"Christ came to repair the separation which was from the beginning, and again unite the two."*[27] Gnosticism reveals a hidden, indeed heretical teaching: if we, like Christ and Sophia, unite the masculine and feminine aspects in ourselves, then we may return to the One, who is 'both male and female existing in unity'.

The image of Christ in the *Phantasietraum of Herr Beta* and the Gnostic *Gospel of Philip* manifests *the union of opposites.* Such an image, though heretical, persisted throughout history, and became particularly evident in the Hermetic traditions of alchemy and the Tarot. In the last card of the *Major Arcana* from the *Tarot de Marseilles*, an androgynous figure with breasts (and sex veiled) appears between the traditional Christian *tetramorph* of the four evangelists: the angel (Matthew), bull (Luke), lion (Mark) and eagle (John). Given that this is the final card in a series which includes the Emperor and Empress, Pope and Papess, Sun and Moon, it becomes a mysterious image of unity: the androgynous saviour – who we may now recognize as Christ and Sophia *re-united.*

The latter part of Jung's life was dedicated to identifying oneiric and mythic imagery where opposites-in-union occurred. He found an ancient exemplar of this principle in Heraclitus, who *"...called it* enantiodromia, *a running contrariwise, by which he meant that sooner or later everything runs into its opposite."*[28] He also found the union-of-opposites in the *mythologem of the coniunctio*, particularly the alchemical images of the *Mysterium Coniunctionis* and the *hermaphroditus.*

But more generally, the iconologue of the opposites-in-union could be found in almost *all* traditional symbols of the Sacred, uniting their parts into a unified whole. Jung writes:

> *The God-image is not something invented, it is an experience that comes upon man spontaneously... As a rule* [it appears in] *uniting symbols, representing the conjunction of a single or double pair of opposites, the result being either a dyad or quaternion... The circle is a well-known symbol for God; and so (in a certain sense) is the cross, the quaternity in all its forms, e.g., Ezkiel's vision, the* rex gloriæ *with the four evangelists, the Gnostic Barbelo ('God in four') and Kolorbas ('all four'); the duality (tao, hermaphrodite, mother/father); and finally, the human form (child, son, anthropos) and the individual personality (Christ and Buddha), to name only the most important of the motifs.*[29]

In works of art, the opposites-in-union may be found time and again in mandala imagery. *"In the products of the unconscious,"* Jung remarked, *"we discover mandala symbols, that is, circular and quaternary figures which express wholeness."*[30] In a more personal remark regarding his encounters with mandalas, Jung wrote: *"Only gradually did I discover what a mandala really is:* 'Formation, Transformation, Eternal Mind's eternal recreation." [Goethe, Faust Part II] *...When I began drawing mandalas, I saw that everything, all the paths I had been following, all the steps I had taken, were leading back to a single point – namely, to the mid-point. It became increasingly plain to me that the mandala is the centre. It is the exponent of all paths. It is the path to the centre..."*[31] Mandalas arrange images so as to display the opposites-in-union as 'the way' and 'the path' to the centre. Such imagery occurs all over the world – as the spontaneous product of dreams, and the perennial constituents of art and myth.

The union of opposites constitutes one of the most important steps in our iconological thinking. All of the opposites we encountered previously, stressing the contrary nature of their forms, are now transcended in favour of a greater unity. When the opposites merge, the result is an *epiphany* of the rarest sort: a direct view into the Sacred as the *Unio oppositorum.*

CHAPTER XIX

*I had resolved to fix my dreams clearly in my memory,
and to discover their hidden meaning. I asked myself,
'...Is it not possible to tame this fascinating awesome chimera?'*
– Gérard de Nerval[1]

I. Displaced Mythologems

In *The Interpretation of Dreams*, Freud gives us the dream of a patient when she was four year's old:

> *A whole crowd of children – all her brothers, sisters, and cousins of both sexes – were romping in a field. Suddenly, they all grew wings, flew away, and disappeared.*[2]

And Jung, in *Memories, Dreams, Reflections*, recalls how he dreamt one night of his deceased wife:

> *I dreamt that my wife's bed was a deep pit with stone walls. It was a grave, and somehow had a suggestion of classical antiquity about it. Then I heard a deep sigh, as if someone were giving up the ghost. A figure that resembled my wife sat up in the pit and floated upward. It wore a white gown into which curious black symbols were woven. I awoke...*[3]

In dreams, *Displacement* occurs so often that it is often difficult to detect. It becomes most obvious in those cases when the dreamer performs an almost *impossible act*, such as leaping tremendous distances, floating slowly upward, or suddenly growing wings and taking flight. In these cases, the actions of another creature have been strangely *displaced* onto us. And, our perception of the world is altered thereby, as we now experience it from this new perspective.

But, rather than gliding or floating through the air (like a bird), we may instead move underwater (like a fish), run extremely fast, (like a swift animal) or glide over ice, etc. Even the qualities of other objects may be displaced onto us, so that we glow, burst aflame, turn to stone, become invisible, walk through walls, etc.

This dream phenomenon of displacement was described by Saint-Denys many years before Freud, as a 'transition via abstraction' or a 'double abstraction':

> *'Abstraction' occurs when the mind detaches certain details from the complex whole to which they belong... In wakingness as in sleep, 'abstractions' form ordinary associations of ideas. The difference is, in wakingness, a simple association of ideas occurs without the mind mixing or confounding things as* [details] *pass from one subject to another. Meanwhile, in the realm of sleep, a single thought may bring about the immediate appearance of numerous related images. 'Abstraction' brings together two ideas in such a way that a real fusion or confusion occurs between them. From whence, many incoherences and monstrosities may follow. We may now pass over several examples in review...*
>
> *Through a play upon our memory, we may dream that a statue becomes a living person; or, a man who we are speaking to may transform into a statue.*[4]

In the child's dream, because her siblings grow wings, the collective image makes the *shared mythologem* explicit, thus revealing its displacement. But in Jung's dream, many displacements occur, and these have a less obvious character. His wife's bed is a grave that 'has a suggestion of classical antiquity about it'; an indistinct figure 'resembles his wife'; this figure then 'floats upward'. To what may we compare this floating upward? A mythologem has undoubtedly been displaced onto this figure, but its source remains quite hidden...

II. 'Displacement of Importance'

In *The Interpretation of Dreams* Freud defines displacement through an allusion to Nietzsche's 'transvaluation of all values'. This particular psychologem was used by Nietzsche in his *Genealogy of Morals* to describe the *Umwertung aller Werte* which transpired in the movement from ancient Antiquity to early Christianity: due to Christian *ressentiment*, the virtues of Antiquity – to be brave, valorous, wise and just – were *devalued* as 'evil'; while their opposites – to be meek, mournful and poor in spirit – were *elevated* into the Christian 'good'. For Freud, a similar such 'transvaluation of all *psychical* values' occurs in dreams. Certain thoughts of high psychical value may be *devalued* in dreams, while corresponding thoughts of low psychical value can actually be *inflated*.

This becomes apparent through the relative emphasis or de-emphasis placed upon the images themselves. We know a devaluation has occurred because *"what occupies a dominating position in the dream-thoughts can often only be discovered precisely in some transitory element of the dream, which is quite overshadowed by more powerful images."*[5] Meanwhile, psychical *inflation* is evident in cases where something of little importance *"was expanded to a disproportionate extent."*[6] Essentially, a shift of emphasis occurs, so *"the dream appears differently centered and strange."*[7] Such shifts of emphasis in dreams betray the presence of, what we shall call, the *Displacement of Importance Iconologue*.

However, it is not only 'psychical values' which are displaced in dreams. In another case mentioned by Freud, a displacement occurs in the 'common elements' shared by two figures. These 'common elements', as we have seen, may be shared features, gestures, or even actions (and hence, *shared mythologems*):

> *When a common element between two persons is represented in a dream, it is usually a hint for us to look for another, concealed common element whose representation has been made impossible by censorship. A displacement in regard to the common element has been made...*
>
> *Accordingly, identification... serves various purposes in dreams: firstly to represent an element common to two persons, secondly to represent a* displaced *common element.*[8]

Whenever a displacement of importance occurs, there are often hints that *a mythologem has been displaced* as well. But, as in cases of *immanence* (identification), there is very little in the manifest image to indicate this. The displaced mythologems only become evident when we compare earlier and later versions of the same myth. Then, we can see that the shared mythologem has acquired a *different* meaning, betraying its displacement. The earlier mythologem lives on *in form only*, while its *meaning* has been changed dramatically. Indeed its meaning may have been *inverted* entirely, with a complete change of emphasis and importance. All of these peculiarities hint at its earlier existence in other myths, though now, through displacement, it has been partially hidden or entirely repressed.

In Gnosticism, particularly in its later development as Christian Gnosticism, evidence of displacement may be detected time and again, as this iconologue underlies many of its more peculiar symbols. For example, the figure of Sophia was regarded as 'fallen' and a 'whore', though the epithet of 'Mother of All' remained – identifying her with the Goddesses of Fertility of more ancient times.

Throughout the Nag Hammadi corpus, a variety of names and epithets were attributed to this goddess figure, branding her as either all-generating mother or all-accommodating whore. Positively, she was identified as 'the upper Wisdom' (Barbelo), the source of life and 'the womb of everything'; negatively, she was 'the lower Wisdom' (Sophia), the fallen *Prunikos* and 'corrupted whore' who caused this world of suffering. In one particular codex, this duality came out explicitly:

> *I am the honoured and the scorned one,*
> *I am the whore and the holy one,*
> *I am the wife and the virgin*
> *...I, I am sinless, and the root of sin derives from me*
> *...I am senseless and I am wise*
> *...I, I am compassionate and I am cruel.*[9]
> ('Thunder Perfect Mind')

What we witness in Gnosticism is the moment of 'the great inversion' when the values placed upon the all-giving Mother Goddess were *inverted* during the course of Western history: once valued as wise, compassionate and virginal, she was debased as corrupted, sinful and a harlot – due to those very fertile powers for which she was once worshipped and praised.

The body, though vigorous, erotic, powerful and playful (especially as conceived by the ancient Greeks in their sculpture), was also devalued to a corpse, a tomb (*sema soma*, the body is a tomb) and a prison, because of the newly-discovered *pneuma* or 'divine spark' residing within it.

In order for the Great Goddess of ancient Near Eastern culture to survive into Christian times, she had to become 'the Virgin'. Meanwhile, the darker, shadow-side of her personality also persisted, but in the guise of a 'reformed prostitute' who we all now know as Mary Magdalene...

But orthodox Christianity went to great lengths to suppress this shadow-side of the Goddess. As Gnosticism and Christianity merged into Christian Gnosticism, the early church condemned the Gnostic gospels as sheer heresy – to be buried in the Nag Hammadi cliffs and forgotten (they hoped) for all time...

But, once those texts were rediscovered, we were also able to discover how the image of the ancient Goddess had persisted in Christian Gnosticism – not in the form of the Madonna, but the Magdalene.

In Christian Gnosticism, the heavenly Christ descended into Jesus, while the heavenly Sophia came to exist *in Magdalene*. And it was *she*, as the fallen Wisdom, who became the last clear vestige of the ancient Goddess of Fertility. For *her*, the Gnostic Christ descended, in order to redeem Sophia, reveal the *'gnosis'* and return with her to the upper heavens.

This Gnostic inversion of the Great Goddess, from fertile mother to corrupted whore, leads to a major displacement in the myths' mythologems. *A shift of emphasis* has occurred, so that the Great Goddess – once the dominant divinity in all of Near Eastern mythology – is relegated to a more minor position. And now her consort 'the dying and rising Son of the Abyss' is elevated to a superior status.

These figures have been *regrouped around a different theme*, because all of creation, rather than being something bountiful and beneficial – to be propitiated by fertile rituals which extend the on-going process of creation – is now viewed as something evil and corrupt – to be terminated apocalyptically as soon as possible, and so transcended.

The ever-dying/rising god, now appearing in the guise of the Gnostic Christ, must descend from above to rescue the fallen goddess Sophia, and it is this heroic deed that shall restore creation to its original, untainted state. When he ascends once more, he shall raise her up with him. This means that the ever-dying/rising god, who was once the consort of the Great Goddess, has instead become 'the Saviour', and the Great Goddess now plays a passive role – 'the Lost Sheep' and fallen Magdalene, waiting to be saved or, worse, 'redeemed'.

Essentially, this shift in the Goddess' fertile value caused the mythologems of her myth to be displaced – including one particular mythologem which, in this case, is recognizable as the mythologem of death and rebirth. The ever-dying/rising god of fertility no longer *dies and rises again* to perpetuate the Goddess' abundance. Instead, as 'the Saviour', he *dies and rises again* to redeem her from the corrupted world which *she* created...

As the mythologem moves from one myth to another, the elements around it are regrouped, but the new myth appears *differently centered and strange*. The ever-dying/rising god of fertility, as the Saviour, now becomes *the hero*, the main focus of the myth, while the Great Goddess is relegated to a minor, secondary role.

In orthodox Christianity, Mary Magdalene (barely recognizable as the last vestige of the Great Goddess) plays such a small and pitiful role that this displacement is barely recognizable. Christian Gnosticism, by expanding Magdalene's role in the gospels, brought out this displacement and at least made it more explicit.* Which is perhaps one reason why the early church banned Gnosticism: they preferred to eliminate *all traces* of the Great Goddess. Still, in at least one of the canonical gospels, it is Magdalene who discovers Christ risen from the tomb (Jn 20:11). That is to say, like the Goddess of ancient times, she mourns for the return of her lost lover and consort.

---

*Although traditional Christianity either ignores the Goddess of Fertility or represses her entirely, her devaluation does emerge explicitly in a few places. For example, when a woman praises the Virgin Mary for her fertile aspect, Jesus contradicts her, praising the *logos* over *eros*: "A woman in the crowd raised her voice, and said to him, 'Blessed is the womb that bore you, and the breasts that you sucked!' But he [Jesus] said, 'Blessed rather are those who hear the word of God and keep it!'"(Lk 11:27)

III. Displaced Themes and
Regrouping around a Different Centre

In his description of displacement, Freud mentions that the resulting dream may appear *'differently centered and strange'*. This 'Regrouping around a Different Centre' is more difficult to discern, for it is not only the importance that is shifted, or a particular mythologem that is displaced, but the entire theme or centre around which the elements are re-grouped.

For example, *"two dreams may have sprung from different centres in the dream material, and their content may overlap, so that what is the centre in one dream is present as a mere hint in the other, and vice versa,"*[10] Freud says. In the realms of myth and art, such regroupings become more patently manifest.

The re-arrangement of the myth of 'the Goddess and ever-dying/ rising Son of the Abyss' into the myth of 'the Saviour and the Lost Sheep' is only one small example of a much larger trend that occurred throughout the Near East during the Bronze Age. As Campbell describes eloquently in his *Occidental Mythology*, the emergence of the 'thunder-hurling god' in the Tigris-Euphrates valley caused the gradual displacement and eventual extinction of the Great Goddess. Rather than the Goddess engendering the world through her fertile womb, it is now the Bronze Age God who creates the cosmos through his heroic act.

In many of the myths mentioned thus far – Marduk's victory over Tiamat, or Zeus over Typhon – the hero triumphs over the Great Goddess by symbolically defeating her emblem, the serpent. Though Tiamat is regarded as a force of chaos and evil, giving birth to the seven-headed snake monster *Musmahhu,* the myth cannot hide the fact that she is still the feminine source of all creation. As Marduk defeats her beasts in battle and then separates her body into the sweet waters above and the salty seas below, the traces of a more ancient creation myth can still be detected – where the Goddess herself is the cause and substance of all creation.

But the emblems and motifs from these earlier myths have been shifted, revalued, and then *regrouped around a new theme.* Despite their mythic re-arrangement, the vestiges of the Goddess's power remain, and may be heard if we allow the images to speak for themselves.

We now see the relevance of Freud's remarks that *"by the displacement of the accent and regrouping of the elements, the manifest content is made so unlike the latent thoughts that nobody would suspect the presence of the latter behind the former."*[11] In the history of mythology, similar such displacements have occurred where, according to Campbell, *"...a distracting secondary theme is introduced, around which the elements of a situation are regrouped; revelatory scenes, acts, or remarks are omitted, reinterpreted or only remotely suggested; and 'a sense of something far more deeply interfused' consequently permeates the whole."*[12]

Citing the above passage from Freud, Campbell goes on to remark in his exposition on the Goddess's decline:

> *And so it has been throughout all patriarchal mythologies. The function of the female has been systematically devalued... Just as her role is cut down, or even out, in myths of the origin of the universe, so also in hero legends. It is, in fact, amazing to what extent the female figures...have been depicted as incarnate demons, or as mere allies of the masculine will.*[13]

In more modern works of literature and art, similar such *Displacements of Theme* occur. Such is the case, for example, in Nikos Kazantzakis' *Last Temptation*. Although Jesus, Judas and Mary Magdalene form the three main characters of this work, and even though it closely follows the narrative thread of the gospels – ancient Greek and even Buddhist themes are woven into the resulting tapestry. As a modern interpreter of *The Odyssey*, who was also steeped in Buddhist lore, Kazantzakis naturally absorbed mythic motifs from all these traditions. In his novel, the Nazarene displays unmistakeable traits from both Odysseus and the Buddha. The saviour's path to Golgotha is very much like Odysseus' episodic wanderings from one island of encounters to the next, and his final crucifixion bears many similarities to the Buddha's visionary battle with Kama-Mara beneath the Bodhi tree. The result – contrary to the much narrower vision of the church – is a successful *expansion* of the figure of Christ: *through his image*, we may *enter into* these other mythologies...

In the Visionary works of Ernst Fuchs, we discover a similar tendency to *enter*, through the image of Christ, *into* other myths. His *Triumph of Christ* displaces the Buddha's lotus position and *vitarka mudra* onto Christ's hands and feet (while also transferring his own features onto Christ's visage, and his wife's onto the angel behind him). Themes from other myths are thus *displaced* onto this work.

In another amazing image, *The Marriage of the Unicorn*, we behold a unicorn and his naked bride in postures very reminiscent of Van Eyck's *Arnolfini Marriage Portait*. At their feet, a most amazing spectacle transpires: six mocking babies bend branches over the

Ernst Fuchs:
The Triumph of Christ (1965)
(detail)

Ernst Fuchs: The Marriage of the Unicorn (1960)

head of a swan-like being crowned with thorns. Due to a *displacement of centre*, this image acquires a bizarre, dream-like quality. Yet, the displacement is so complete, that we are thrown into several directions to seek out its origins.

The curious motif of 'the crossed branches over a crown of thorns' is taken from a theme common to Gothic painting, called the *'Dornenkrönung'*. See for example Dürer's engraving or Holbein the Elder's *Crowning with Thorns*, where several malicious assistants press the crown of thorns so force-

Hans Holbein the Elder:
Crowning with Thorns

fully upon Christ's brow that one of the two branches actually breaks.

But what of the six children? In his autobiography, Fuchs describes this painting as 'a wedding portrait' of himself (as the unicorn) and the woman who became the mother of his third child. *"In The Marriage of the Unicorn,"* he writes, *"I accurately portrayed our son in a repeating series..."*[14]

This adds a very different dimension to the picture, as the couple's singular child is multiplied six times into the infants mocking the swan-like being. Interpretations aside, the malicious children have clearly been *re-grouped around a different centre*, mainly, that of the 'crowning with thorns'. Meanwhile, the interpretation of this image remains an endless enigma, since the displacement hides the artist's original aims and intention.

IV. The Reversal Iconologue

One particular variation of the above iconologue occurs in cases of *Reversal*. Here, it is not a random re-grouping of elements around a different centre, but a very clear case of a reversal of the elements involved. This reversal may manifest itself in one of two ways. In the first case, all the elements involved remain manifest, and so the reversal of their relationship also remains clearly evident. In the second case, an earlier and now forgotten relationship remains hidden, and only its reversal appears in the manifest dream, myth, or work of art.

A patient of Freud's provides us with an example of the first case:

> He arrived at a railway station just as a train was coming in. What then happened was that the platform moved towards the train, while the train stopped still.[15]

Dormition of the Virgin
Tympanum of Strasbourg Cathedral, South facade (c.1230)
Christ cradles the soul of the Virgin

Mediæval art furnishes us with an even clearer example. In the South facade of Strasbourg cathedral, we find a free-standing statue of the Virgin cradling the Christ-child in her arms. Meanwhile on the tympanum just below apears the apocryphal relief of the Virgin's Dormition (see above). Here, we find the exact *reversal* of the first image. Just above the supine Virgin, we can see Christ cradling her risen soul in his arms, as if her soul were a little child. One composite figure is an exact reversal of the other.

In *The Interpretation of Dreams*, Freud was more concerned with the second type of reversal, in which a certain relationship remains latent, while its reversal *"reveals its presence through the fact that some piece of the dream content... is turned round the other way."*[16] Freud cites as an example his own dream, already mentioned, of his bearded friend R. resembling his bearded uncle Josef (creating a composite figure of them both).

In the manifest content of the dream, Freud *"felt a great feeling of affection for him."*[17] Meanwhile, the interpretation revealed the contrary: *"My dream-thoughts had contained a slander against R.; and, in order that I might not notice this, what appeared in the dream was the opposite, a feeling of affection for him."*[18]

Hence, the relationship between Freud and R. manifest in the dream was exactly the opposite of that suppressed in his unconscious. The many examples found by Freud caused him to conclude that *"reversal or the turning of a thing into its opposite is one of the means of representation most favoured by the dreamwork, and one which is capable of employment in the most diverse directions."*[19]

Jung came to recognize such reversals as an essential component for the interpretation of dreams. According to his theory of 'dream compensation', dreams respond to the narrower and more extreme positions taken by our consciousness, and try to compensate for them by depicting 'just the reverse'. One example he gives is a dream involving one of his patients:

> *I was walking down a highway through a valley in the late afternoon sunlight. To my right was a steep hill. At its top stood a castle, and on the highest tower there was a woman sitting on a kind of balustrade. In order to see her properly, I had to bend my neck far back. I awoke with a crick in the back of my neck.*
>
> *Even in the dream I had recognized the woman as my patient. The interpretation was immediately apparent to me. If in the dream I had to look up at the patient in this fashion, in reality I had probably been looking down on her. Dreams are, after all, compensations for the conscious attitude.*[20]

In the area of mythology, we have already found an example of reversal in the relationship between the Great Goddess and the Saviour. In *The Masks of God*, Campbell finds several historical examples where an attempt was made to remedy – or rather, *to compensate for* – this reversal: the cult of Kali, the Grail Legend, and Alchemy to name a few.

In his reading of *The Iliad* and *The Odyssey*, Campbell also sees the latter as a compensation for the former's heroic and patriarchal attitude towards women. In *The Iliad*, women are nothing more than bounty (Helen), or else, 'mere allies of the masculine will' (Athene). But in *The Odyssey*, during his seven-year journey home from Troy, Odysseus meets with Circe, Calypso and Nausicaa – three nymphs who reveal to him various aspects of the feminine that formerly lay beyond his ken. Through them, his vision of the feminine expands into a much greater image of the Goddess. Only then is Odysseus sufficiently prepared to return home and be re-united with his wife.[21]

The entire cult of the Virgin Mary – the growth and sudden blossoming of so many ligneous, rose-windowed cathedrals dedicated to 'Our Lady' during the Middle Ages – can be seen as a similar such compensation in art for the Goddess' devaluation during the history of Christianity. Through the numerous statues of her placed variously on mountain peaks, overlooking fields, and deep in the caverns of the earth, the image of the Christian goddess spread across all of Europe. Though veiled in robes of virgin purity, the Great Goddess of antiquity was born again...

V. The Iconologue of Division and Re-union

In *Poets' Dreams*, Stekel cites a dream by Gottfried Keller. Through this dream, the 19th century Swiss novelist gives us a fascinating glimpse into his nocturnal world:

I was standing in the midst of a large crowd which had gathered at twilight in the Rathausplatz*... A soft, tender hand wrapped itself in mine. It was a girl entirely unknown to me, perhaps fifteen years of age. With eyes glistening in the darkness, she whispered in my ear, 'Gottfried Keller, come home with me.' Deftly, gingerly, she led me through the crowd. We traversed dark alleys, which were quite unknown to me and certainly do not exist in Zürich. The girl kept herself close to me. She was unspeakably dear, and made me feel completely at ease. I was not surprised therefore, when she suddenly became two, each of which pressed to either side of me. They were entirely identical, with only the slight difference of a younger and older sister.*[22]

In this strange and extraordinary dream, we witness the division of one figure into two. It is a movement which defies all rational expectation, and yet, makes sense in our mythopoeic world. Since dreams and myths continually move in their imagery towards unity, it should not surprise us if, on occasion, they also move from unity towards a greater multiplicity. Certainly, this is the case in creation myths, which begin with an original unity that first divides into a primal dyad, and then gradually emanates outward further into a many-layered cosmos.

This division requires a certain movement in both space and time. In Keller's dream, the division occured temporally, since the girl who was singular one moment became two the next. But it also occured spatially, insofar as the two girls were constellated on either side of the dreamer.

Since dreams are essentially egotistical, we should not be surprised if, in other dreams, the figure who divides into two is the dreamer himself. In the first case, this may occur spatially, where the dream-I appears simultaneously in several places, and under several guises. But, in the second case, it may also occur temporally, where the dream-I appears as itself one moment, and as another figure the next.

Regarding the first case, Freud noted the importance of *"the fact that the dreamer's own ego appears several times, and in several forms, in a dream..."*[23] Usually, the dreamer's ego remains *latent*, and hence *immanent* in other figures, as is the case with *"dreams in which my ego appears along with other people who, when the identification is resolved, are revealed once again as my ego."*[24]

But thirty years before *The Interpretation of Dreams*, Saint-Denys noted a case where the dreamer's ego actually became *manifest* in another figure. This division occured, as in the second case, over time. And the result was not only a division, but a subsequent *re-union*, involving identification or 'immanence'.

Due to extreme pity or compassion, Saint-Denys realized that *"...dreams occur in which we are suddenly immersed into a situation which we imagined, at first, to be outside of ourselves."*[25] He cites, as an example, the following dream-fragment:

> *I am rendering aid at a terrible accident; the sight of the wounded man fills me with deep pity. I imagine what he must be suffering; and then, it is I who am the wounded man.*[26]

In this case, there was a brief moment of pity when the dream-I felt, as it were, *torn in two*: 'I imagine what he must be suffering'. Then, due to his strong *identification* with the victim, Saint-Denys ceased to exist *outside* the event, and became wholly *immanent* in it. From overwhelming compassion, he himself became the victim.

C.G. Jung perceived a more metaphysical significance to this ego-division and re-union. In one dream, he came to understand how his ego was nothing more than a projection of the Self into the world:

> *I had dreamed once before of the problem of the Self and the ego. In that earlier dream, I was on a hiking trip. I was walking along a little road through a hilly landscape; the sun was shining and I had a wide view in all directions. Then I came to a small wayside chapel. The door was ajar, and I went in. To my surprise, there was no image of the Virgin on the altar, and no crucifix either, but only a wonderful flower arrangement.*
>
> *But then I saw that on the floor in front of the altar, facing me, sat a yogi – in lotus posture, in deep meditation. When I looked at him more closely, I realized that he had my face. I started in profound fright, and awoke with the thought: aha, so he is the one meditating me. He has a dream, and I am it.*[27]

While the dream-ego appeared in this dream in two roles simultaneously, as the wanderer and the yogi, there was also a strong *identification* between the two. Not only had *the iconologue of division* silently separated them; *the immanence iconologue* joined them together once more. But this form of union was new and different: the yogi revealed to the wanderer a higher, indeed transcendent dimension within himself. The dream-I, we could say, had come face to face with the Dreamsource.

But, it was only *after* he awoke that Jung recognized the true nature of the Dreamsource: 'He has a dream, and I am it'. At that moment, the *waking-I*, we could say, had *also* come face to face with the Dreamsource. Then, *who*, we may ask, is the dreamer? And *who* is the one dreaming the dream..?

CONCLUSION

Labyrinth from the floor of Chartres cathedral (c1200)

CHAPTER XX

The Eternal Labyrinth

Where the source of things is,
to that place they must also pass away,
– according to necessity –
for they must pay penance
and be judged for their injustices
in accordance with
the ordinance
of time.
– Fragment from
Anaximander[1]
c. 560 B.C.

I. A Backward Glance

At the outset of our exposition, we had only a dim foreboding of the encounters that awaited. Three paths appeared through the mists, and each became a new voyage of discovery. Fortunately, various mythographers, dream-explorers, artists and writers were invoked as our guides. For, what we sought at the outset was a more ancient manner of thinking, and they too had traced its dim outlines in their works.

With the hope of exposing the lost and forgotten language of images we set out, seeking examples first of all in the art and myth-making of the last century. Here, we had the first intimations of iconologic's higher, more sacred purpose. And through an intensive study of ancient myths and symbols, we eventually discovered its eternal purpose: to awaken in us a view onto life as a more sacred unfolding.

This came about gradually. First of all, we had to learn how to 'enter through the image'. We began with an image of the Madonna and Child, and then moved on to an archaic image which served us as a template for 'thinking through images'.

What was required of us, first of all, was to approach images with a mixture of feeling and imagination. We allowed the images to conjure up certain feelings in us, so as to call forth the series of personal memory-images constellated around them. We then tried to follow these feelings backward, regressing through the personal memory-images they constellated – *entering through* each image in succession.

But, as that regression came to a frustrating end, collective memory-images inevitably uprose, to replace the personal memory-images we lacked. Our myths and our art offered us those key-images which extended our journey through memory ever further. And now, *entering through* these more ancient memory-images, we finally arrived at a momentary *epiphany*. We followed the sacred Hero myth to its nadir, and *entered through* its Threshold Image to a momentary suffering and awakening. And, we followed Cosmogonic myths to their beginning and end, then *entered through* their Threshold Images to 'the One' at the source.

We did this by following the Mythic Path through the Ancient Template, whose swirling mists became a kind of 'eternal labyrinth'. On this path, we read the images in remembrance of their mythic arrangement.

Along the Mythic Path, we encountered the two basic types of myth, and discovered how Cosmogonic myths offer us images of the ancient *Sacramentum* at the beginning of the creation or at the end of the apocalypse, while Hero myths offer us an equally timeless image at the mythic nadir – when the hero himself, through his death, rebirth and awakening, becomes a symbol of the Sacred. Since this image offered us a momentary epiphany, we recognized it as a Threshold Image. It's timeless threshold could be crossed if we could but learn how to think in a more ancient manner, and so *enter through* its image.

Along the Mythic Path, we also discovered that three basic iconologues underlie all our mythic creations. Since myths are an arrangement of images *in time*, we recognized that, underlying each such arrangement lies a particular iconologue of time's measure. In the Hero myths of Judæo-Christianity and Hindu-Buddhism, time acquired linear-historical and ever-cycling aspects as, indeed, Christ and the Buddha became those iconologues which *measured time* in these different ways.

We also recognized how the images of their myths were strung together by the iconologue of the *hero task*, which caused them to fall into U- and O-shaped *narrative patterns*. In Ch. VII, *The Sacred Moment in Art*, we identified the hero tasks of Christ and the Buddha. Christ journeyed *forward* through time, bending his will ever higher, to finally transcend time's linear-historical measure through a momentary epiphany. Meanwhile, the Buddha journeyed *backward* through time's illusory cycle, denying his will, until he too transcended its measure in a momentary awakening. As such, at their nadir, each of them became a timeless Threshold Image which we have sought, ever after, to *enter through*.

During that momentary epiphany, time is revealed in its eternal aspect. As well, the eternal Sacred underlying time's linear or cyclic measure assumes symbolic form. Symbols of the Sacred arise, not only at the nadir of a sacred Hero myth, but also at the beginning or end of a Cosmogonic myth. During our exploration of Cosmogonic myths, specifically the *Apocryphon of John*, we learned how to re-enter myths of the creation, reading their succession of images *backward*, until we arrived at a vision of that 'Ancient of Days' which lies at *the source* of creation.

More than that, we realized how the images over the course of this 'journey back' referred, not only to the external cosmos, but the interior of the mind. Cosmogonic myths offered us a more ancient model of the mind which, uniquely, allowed us to think our way through images to the innermost Self. We learned that to return, in myth, to the Sacred at the source of creation was to also return, in mind, to the Self at the centre of all thought. Following ancient writers, we called this timeless source of unity 'the One'.

After exploring ancient Egyptian and Mesopotamian myths, we discovered *a more ancient, mythopoeic understanding of time*. In essence, we discovered that some iconologues measure time in such a way as to create a momentary epiphany each year, each month, indeed, each day. Such was the case with the yearly death and rebirth of Damuzi, the monthly descent and re-ascent of Inanna, and even the daily setting and rising of Atum-Re.

Although images of Christ and the Buddha also measured time, they delayed, over the ensuing æons of linear and cyclic time, their attendant epiphanies. If we could remove the measures of time that their images imposed, and regain the more ancient, mythopoeic understanding of time, then their momentary epiphanies would be experienced *here and now*. They would cease to be iconologues of time's measure, and become instead Threshold Images we could *enter through*.

Each time we successfully *entered through* an image, the measures of linear or cyclic time were removed, and we experienced instead an 'eternal moment'. However, such an experience could not be sustained. Only at the end of an apocalyptic myth are time's measures *permanently removed*. And so, after our *momentary* epiphany – briefly regarding the eternally Sacred – we fell back once more to a mundane passage of time.

Since Cosmogonic myths offer us a more ancient model of the mind, we realized that the Threshold Images of creation myths actually refer to our own life-thresholds. In particular, they refer to those *infantile* life-thresholds which were crossed over before the appearance of the ego on the horizon of our consciousness. Indeed, the Egyptian myth of the sun's *first* rising models that particular moment in life when the ego *first* emerged at the centre of consciousness. And the world-parent myth models the even earlier moment when the mother and father first became distinct in our mind. Each of these cosmogonic Threshold Images models an earlier 'infantile' life-threshold crossing.

With this thought in mind, we came to see how Hero myths model life's *later* threshold crossings. In particular, the hero's 'meeting with the Goddess' or his 'atonement with the Father', modelled the attempt to cross over life's later thresholds of marriage and profession.

This was brought out, not only in our exploration of sacred symbols, involving images of the *Magna Mater* and *Pater Omnipotens*, but also in our exploration of sacred mythologems, involving images of the *Coniunctio* and Conquest. All such arrangements of images model those moments in later life when we come up against a particular threshold involving a life-transformation. But, more than that, they render those moments sacred.

During our explorations into *the mythologem of death and rebirth*, we came to see how the image at the nadir of a sacred Hero myth models *all* our life-threshold crossings. For each life-threshold crossing requires a momentary death, rebirth and awakening. This is brought out explicitly in rituals of initiation, in which the neophyte undergoes a symbolic death and rebirth to pass from child to adolescent, adolescent to adult. Such initiations become, for each of us, those life-threshold crossings which we encounter *over the course of life* – revealing that marriage or skill-acquisition are also momentary epiphanies involving a brief awakening to life's inherent splendor. In this way, *all of life*, with the crossing of each threshold, becomes a gradual unfolding of the Sacred.

By looking at symbols and mythologems in works of art, we discovered a different route through the Ancient Template: the Symbolic Path. This time, the images were read in the absence of their mythic arrangement. We realized that a series of ever more ancient images could be *entered through* in succession, or else *combined* to create more creative paths.

By looking at our more modern works of Visionary art, that creative path to the centre became crystal clear. Symbolic thinking requires that we see images in light of their higher unity. Then, symbols become openings unto the Sacred. And the symbols of different cultures, when combined in modern works of Visionary art, become openings onto the sacred unity that all cultures share at their core.

During our third journey, exploring the Oneiric Path, we discovered how dreams use those same iconologues common to myth and art: the hero-task, narrative patterns and Threshold Images. But first, we had to differentiate between the dream-I, which acts in dreams, and the waking-I, which reflects upon the dream.

By comparing dreams to myths, we saw that images of dreams are also held together by the iconologue of the hero task. At the beginning of the dream, the dream-I acquires a certain task, and then crosses over a series of thresholds to complete it. However, the thresholds revealed in dreams are those particular *life*-thresholds revealed to us over the course of life. And so, we sought out the specific *life*-threshold revealed at the dream's nadir (which is often the end of the dream).

We came to see that the dream-I, over the course of the dream, moved back and forth over many different life-thresholds, reflecting manners of behaviour and modes of thought from different stages of life. We also came to see how dreams, like myths, are models of the mind: their images reflect the historical development of the mind.

Particularly at the nadir-point in the dream, an arrangement of images arises which reflects the life-threshold presently awaiting the dreamer in waking life. We called such an arrangement of images, an oneiric Threshold Image.

After remembering a dream, the task awaiting the dreamer (the waking-I), is to resolve *in life* what was left unresolved *in dreams*. Thus, at the nadir of a dream, the dream-task transfers onto waking life. The dreamer can then accomplish this task by *entering through* the oneiric Threshold Image. This may be accomplished in a backward journey through life, in which the dreamer meditates on the dream's succession of images, and *enters through* its nadir-Threshold Image to a momentary epiphany. Or, it may be accomplished in the forward journey through life, by getting married, acquiring a profession, and so, realizing the sacred nature of our existence.

By meditating on an oneiric Threshold Image, we learned that an Oneiric Path through the Ancient Template also exists. First we constellated personal memory-images around it, and then collective memory-images, so as to *enter through* the image. While artistic and mythic Threshold Images reveal the Sacred at the source of the cosmos, oneiric Threshold Images reveal, at their source, the innermost Self – which is our own internal image of unity.

This Self encompasses all the moments of life, and reflects them to us as one 'wholeness'. It has lived through each past stage of our growth, and will continue to live through the following ones. The I of our dreams, meanwhile, is like the hero of myths: a timeless figure engaged in an endless quest for life's greater wholeness. Thus, the more thresholds the dream-I crosses, the more it reveals the innermost Self. As it crosses back and forth over previous life-thresholds, or approaches our next life-threshold, it reveals our life in the context of the greater whole: it intimates to us its deeper unity. Hence, all these life-threshold crossings, once they are elucidated through art and myth, may thus be elevated into heroic, indeed, sacred events. In this way, life itself is revealed as a series of veils enshrouding the eternally Sacred.

Finally, in the fourth part, we concentrated on Iconologues. We learned that many variations exist in the iconologue of time's measure, since dreams may regress, recur or recombine life's moments into different orders and arrangements. The dream task also underwent numerous changes, such as digression, transformation and displacement. All of these manifest the hidden accord between myths and dreams.

Meanwhile, like works of art, dreams also measured space, and played with its measures in a number of ways: images could echo one another, become double images, or manifest shared mythologems. Ultimately, a boundless dream-space appeared behind the dream's embroidered expanse.

With condensation and displacement, we learned how dreams disguised their true intentions. Sometimes their figures divided into opposites, other times they re-united, or combined to form collective and composite figures. Despite the displacement of theme or importance, and the many reversals and transformations that transpired, the disguised sources of our dream imagery were ultimately revealed. Dreams revealed themselves to be an endless play of the imagination, as the mind continually composed and recomposed imagery in its ongoing attempts to reflect upon itself.

II. The Sacred at the Source

In the innermost depths of the Ancient Template, we beheld a circle of light at the centre of a spiralling abyss. Fragments from ancient myth enabled us to name this circle of light 'the One' (*to Hen*). This, the unified source of all creation, has existed since time immemorial. Yet its presence can only be evoked through art, myths and dreams – which arrange their images in such a way as to reveal its timeless oneness.

Through our reading of the *Apocryphon of John*, we discovered that all of creation is a spacio-temporal mirror in which the One sees itself reflected. Each emanation of the One constitutes a movement in its grand reflection – either being an unfoldment (creation) or infoldment (return) to the One. Over time, a variety of images have appeared in those luminous waters.

Some were arranged into myths of the creation, others into the apocalypse. And finally, sacred Hero myth arranged its images in the cycles or segments of time that seemed to transpire in the time in-between. At the nadir of the Hero myth, a Threshold Image appeared, which also constituted a moment of reflection: the sacred hero, whether through his symbol or mythologem, momentary revealed the One to itself, but now as acting here in the world. What is more, the hero made the One present by discovering its unity in the innermost depths *of himself*. Through him, the One appears and, *in him,* it finds its momentary reflection.

Each of us, in his own life, is engaged on that eternal quest, whether he knows it or not. And, by thinking through images, the hero-path to the Sacred may be made complete. We have found three such paths that return us to the One, and named them respectively the Mythic, Symbolic and Oneiric Paths. Each time one of those paths is successfully followed, we become, in our eternal soul, the sacred hero. At each life-threshold crossing, we become the sacred symbol or mythologem. That moment, we manifest the Sacred. And so, whenever we discover its unity in the innermost depths of ourselves – for that moment – we become an image reflecting the One.

The *Coniunctio* offers us one example of a life-threshold crossing that becomes a sacred symbol or mythologem. Through this mythic image, we may return to an experience of the ancient *Sacramentum*. In Sumer, the Sacred manifest itself as both God and Goddess. In their union transpiring at the moment of creation, the God and Goddess reflected the One to itself as the two-in-one, united at the source. And so, we too may *enter through* this image, so as to participate in the original moment of creation. Through the experience of sexual union here and now, the two may again become one, and so may we return, as two-in-one, to the source. The two become those parts of the creation that reflects the One to itself as God and Goddess, male and female, in union.

In Egypt, a more primordial image of the One arose. The sun's rising from the primæval depths reflected the One's own emergent awareness of itself. Through this image, the One achieves its own self-awareness. Although the sun returns to the primæval depths each evening, the One continues to reflect upon itself through images of the sun's underworld boat journey. Although besieged by dark and demonic images, the sun continues to shine; the One remains conscious over the course of its descent. And, as long as the sun succeeds in rising again, the One's self-consciousness will be fully restored. Hence, though it undergoes periodic immersions into the depths, the One's awareness is sustained and, indeed, realized anew. This image of the sun's eternal sinking and rising on the horizon constitutes the One's grand reflection: the eternal renewal of its own self-awareness.

Each time we see the sun rise on the horizon, illuminating all of creation with its light, we are reminded of our own consciousness: sheerly through awareness, we illuminate all of creation. And each time the sun descends beneath the horizon, we surrender our own consciousness to the dark underworld of dreams. Like the sun, we journey through our own underworld, illuminating its darker images with the light of our awareness. And so too, like the sun, do we emerge to greater consciousness with our awakening. In this way, our continuous dream and awakening reflect the One to itself, as an eternal renewal of self-awareness.

In Hindu-Buddhism, a new series of images revealed this ancient philosophy of unity. Now, it is 'the illuminated one', rather than the rising sun, who symbolizes the One's awareness of itself. But the One does not *think* itself into being; it does not, as in classical Greek and Gnostic thought, reflect upon itself as 'thinking a thought of itself thinking'. Nor does it, as in the Memphite and Hebrew creation, utter those words that speak itself into being – the Ptah who 'commanded thought by the heart and issued from the tongue' or Yahweh that uttered 'I am that I am.' Instead, the One is an *infinite* self-awakening.

In the first unfolding of itself, it awakens to the marvelous beauty it has willed into creation: the wisdom, pleasure, poetry and joy of this world. It becomes Brahma. Then, despite the attempts of each world-saving avatar, it becomes aware of creation's continual decline. It awakens to the sorrow, pain, suffering, sickness and death that sustain it. That is to say, it becomes Vishnu. And finally, it awakens to the utter futility of escape, despite unending attempts to will its destruction. It becomes Shiva. In a final movement, it awakens to the inherent opposition and eventual union of these three – the *Trimurti* of Brahma, Vishnu and Shiva – who continually will the creation, preservation and destruction of the world into its ever-cycling æons. The One sees itself reflected in this tripartite image. And we, by the illusory world we continually create, preserve and destroy, also reflect the One to itself in this manner.

Finally, in the form of the Buddha, the One ceases to will this world's illusion into being. Like the lotus rising from the watery depths and blossoming; like a child emerging from the bloom of that flower (both these Buddhist images are Egyptian in origin), the One sees itself reflected in the image of the Buddha: the illuminated one's own blossoming and infinite self-awakening. It awakens once more, into a more timeless realization: All is one, but is founded upon one nothingness or 'emptiness'. And so, the task is to return, in unity, to the timeless void from whence it came.

For those who wish to *enter through* this image, the task is to return to nothingness. Not, of course, by willing our own death, which would only lead to a re-incarnation and return to endless suffering. The task is to forego the will, and in this manner, seek release. Such may be achieved in a more solitary meditation, as we pass backward through time to its source in the void.

But the Buddha, though awakened, discovered himself to be still in the midst of the swirling illusion of suffering and joy; of death and rebirth. And so, compassionate yet detached, he 'willessly willed' to awaken others. By meditating and then speaking, by showing awareness of others' suffering and then acting towards them with infinite compassion, the way of return was made clear. For each in this way may participate in the One's *infinite* self-awakening – an awakening to its inherent suffering, transcendence and unity, founded upon one nothingness.

In traditional Christianity, images are also found of the One's unfolding and infolding, through the myths of Genesis, the Apocalypse, and Christ's passion – even though Christianity itself does not acknowledge the ancient philosophy that still persists in its images. Nevertheless, they offer a unique variation on that timeless theme, and may still be *entered through* so as to reveal the ancient One at the source of all creation.

In Christianity, the One reveals itself in deed rather than thought. Christ is that unique figure in the creation who, through his sacrifice on the cross, revealed the One to be a loving self-sacrifice. By surrendering his will to God's, he realized God's will. And so, for one brief but epiphanous moment, Christ came to behold the eternally Sacred *act*, in the form of that loving self-sacrifice.

The One performs an act which acts upon itself, thereby acting itself into being. That act, as Christ realized, is one of loving self-sacrifice. In its first movement, or emanation, the One created Adam, the first man. This was a sacrifice of its oneness to become two – God and man. Christ, as the second Adam, sacrificed humanity in order to re-unite man and God. And so, as free-willing men and women, we, may act in such a way as to acknowledge our sacred unity as based upon loving self-sacrifice. By freely sacrificing ourselves out of love, we may return, in deed, to the One.

Such a loving self-surrender may manifest itself in a thousand lesser deeds, such as the daily surrender of husband and wife to each other in marriage, or of father, mother and child to each other in the family, or even of a group of people to one another in a community. Such was the original intention of the Christian community. Through their loving self-sacrifice, the kingdom would come to be felt and experienced here on earth. And so, until the moment of that great Revelation, when that New Jerusalem would finally appear here on earth, each must, in his own way, act in acknowledgement of Christ's momentary revelation. Through their loving self-sacrifice, each would momentarily reflect the One back to itself; each would participate once more in the grand movement of its eternal self-sacrifice.

Through the archaic images of the *Coniunctio*, of 'thinking a thought of itself thinking' and of the rising/setting sun – through all of these images in the luminous waters, the One may come to reflect upon itself. Through the more contemporary images of the Buddha as an infinite self-awakening or of Christ as a loving self-sacrifice – through each of *these* images in the luminous waters, *we* may come to reflect upon ourselves, and see that eternal oneness that lies in our innermost depths. All these images create a mirror 'various and divine' in which the eternal One sees itself reflected in us. And so may we, if we can but learn to *enter through* these images, see our more eternal selves reflected in its depths – in our innermost Self or soul, which all ancient traditions have recognized, ultimately, as our timeless particle of the Sacred.

III. The Labyrinthine Journey

Myths, art and dreams each create their own path through the eternal labyrinth. The Mythic Path uses the movement of life itself – its temporal unfolding – to unconceal the Sacred. Although myths of the creation or apocalypse offer us Threshold Images from life's earliest infancy which we may *enter through*, the epiphany is most apparent at the nadir of the sacred

Hero myth, when a Threshold Image arises from life's later struggles for death and rebirth. At that moment, the sacred hero, be that Christ, the Buddha, or we ourselves, becomes a sacred symbol or mythologem. Through this image, the veil over the eternal One tears in two. Then, *in our image*, the eternal One finds its momentary reflection. Whether at the beginning, nadir, or end, the eternal One is encountered beneath each of myth's temporal reflections.

Threshold Images create the most potent of our symbols and mythologems. But *all* objects and events, *all* animals and figures possess this potential of metamorphosis: in a fleeting and mundane moment, they transform into the eternally Sacred. The Symbolic Path to the centre is wended whenever we successfully *enter through* these symbols and mythologems of the Sacred – which life itself reveals to us over the course of its unfolding. The depths of the sea, the blossoming of a lily, lotus or rose, the flight of a bird, the two lovers their limbs entwined – all, in their own unique way, reflect the One's movement through creation. To move backward through creation, to *enter through* them, we must transcend ourselves: from the profane to the holy; from the personal to the collective; and from the unique here and now to the Sacred for all eternity.

Dreams teach us the way. They sanctify life. First, they identify our life-thresholds and transform them into Threshold Images. Then, they arrange a series of images into myths which, alas, are left incomplete. They transfer the task of each life-threshold crossing onto wakingness, and then offer us a timeless artistic image which may then be *entered through*. And so, on the Oneiric Path, figures from life appear once more as timeless symbols and mythologems. Aided with the sacred codes of art and myth, we learn to recognize their life-altering purpose. By crossing over the thresholds they present, life itself becomes a series of sacred transformations, each revealing its underlying wholeness and holiness. Our view onto existence is utterly transformed: life becomes a gradual awakening to the Divine within.

The three paths to the source may be followed either forwards or backwards through time. In the backward movement, personal memory-images soon give way to more collective memories which our culture has preserved in the archetypes of art and myth. Each of the gods or goddesses of myth, as sacred symbols in art or as archetypes in our dreams, symbolizes one of our life-threshold crossings. They all exist in potentiality before one's life has even begun. Yet, it is only our more unique encounters with these images, as they appear in life *here and now*, that awaken and enliven the collective memories shared by an entire culture. Hence, each life-threshold crossing involves bringing one more unconscious archetype into consciousness – or rather, one more eternal symbol into the present, as uniquely experienced here and now.

And it is because each of us, uniquely, has had these life experiences, that we are able – conversely – to *enter through* collective images to the One. Our life experiences allow us, not only to read or understand a symbol, but live or re-live the threshold experience to which it refers. And, by re-experiencing all these thresholds, life is felt *as a whole.* The movement backward through our life-time becomes a kind of Platonic remembering: the eternal forms are momentarily recalled through the experience of life itself, thus returning us *in memory* to our eternally sacred aspect.

Such a backward movement also has a more Promethean purpose: to encourage us *forward through life,* across each awaited threshold. Each time we step through that doorway, we become one with our ancestors, experiencing with them those eternal thresholds which all must experience over the course of their lives. We feel the same wholeness of life that everyone has experienced, from time immemorial. And so we share with them, become one with them, in the whole. With each death and rebirth, with each threshold crossed, we move one step further through the eternal labyrinth, to life's wholeness and holiness – to the innermost One at the centre. Through the lives we all share, we fall into greater unity with the eternal One. And this includes life's final threshold, which we all must cross over, to become one once again with the eternal source.

And so, with this arcane and forgotten philosophy, we may knowingly
return, in death, to the sacred source from whence we, in birth,
unknowingly proceeded. Otherwise life, in its various stages,
reflects the One to itself in the unfoldment of time.
To live life in accord with its gestation, ripening,
flowering (and even harvest and decay)
is, with each threshold-crossing,
to behold the eternally Sacred
through the full enactment
and participation
in life.

APPENDIX I

The Life of the Buddha

There arose in me vision,
insight, understanding,
there arose in me wisdom,
there arose in me light.
— The First Sermon of the Buddha[1]

I. The One on the Way

The story of the Buddha's life may here be briefly told.[2]

After swirling through time in countless previous incarnations, and achieving twenty-four recognizable incarnations, the Bodhisattva – 'one on the way to Awakening' – descended from heavenly Tusita. While Queen Mayadevi was peacefully slumbering, he entered her from the right side. The immaculate Queen dreamt of him entering her, and saw him coming as a white elephant.

Ten months later, Queen Mayadevi undertook a journey to her parents accompanied by a great entourage of attendants. But, she stopped the entourage in Lumbini Park. Knowing the moment was at hand, she stood beside a tree and, to steady herself, seized one of its branches, which bent toward her. Painlessly, she gave birth to the Bodhisattva, who emerged from her side.

Later legends recount that the gods Indra and Brahma took the babe up in their arms and bathed him. Then, he was stood upon a large lotus flower that suddenly grew up at the place of his birth. While other lotus flowers sprung up spontaneously under his feet, the infant took seven steps to each of the cardinal points, and proclaimed he would vanquish the earth of sickness and death.

Queen Mayadevi and her entourage returned to the palace in Kapilavastu, where King Suddhodana, the Bodhisattva's earthly father, named the new-born child Prince Siddhartha. This child possessed the 'thirty-two bodily marks of greatness'. To the king's great satisfaction, his seers predicted that the child would become a great monarch. But the prophet Asita, who came from afar to worship the child, proclaimed Siddhartha would instead become the Buddha.

His father was determined that his sole heir become a great monarch, so the child was brought up in the palace with its enclosed pleasure gardens. He was taught 'the sixty-four arts', where he excelled in each, and at age of sixteen, he was married to the beautiful and virtuous Yasodhara. In time, they had one son, Rahula.

One day, as his charioteer was driving him to the enclosed pleasure gardens, Siddhartha saw a man withered and decrepit by age. This so disturbed him that they turned back. The next day, they encountered a man enfeebled and bedridden by illness, so they turned back. On the next, they met with a funeral procession, its corpse blackened by death, so they turned back. The future Buddha was so disturbed by these images of age, illness and death, that he sought the means of release from human suffering. Finally, on the fourth day, they encountered a monk begging for alms, who displayed a most remarkable calm and detachment. Seeing this, Prince Siddhartha resolved to renounce the things of this world, and become a wandering mendicant.

On the night of his twenty-ninth birthday, Siddhartha secretly departed from the palace. Legend tells that the gods lifted the hooves of his horse from the ground, so no sound would wake the slumbering inhabitants. On his journey, Kama-Mara, the powerful god of illusion and temptation, tried to sway him from his path, but Siddhartha was unyielding. Still, Kama-Mara would appear again during the future Buddha's quest.

Siddhartha rid himself of his princely garments, shaved his hair, and sent his horse, Kanthaka, back to the palace. (Instead, the faithful mare died of sorrow, and was taken up to Indra's heaven). Henceforth, Siddhartha would lead the life of the itinerant monk Guatama.

Guatama apprenticed himself to several masters, but their teachings failed to grant him release from sorrow. Finally, he set out on his own path, joined by five companions, as Sakyamuni ('sage of the Sakyas'). He practised a form of Hatha Yoga, combined with extreme asceticism, until his strength completely wasted away.

After six years of the strictest fasting, the god Kama-Mara re-entered Gautama's life, but was unable to sway him from this path, for the supreme ascetic remained resolute. Finally, the god Indra appeared to him, and played three strings on his lute. One was too slack, and produced no sound; one was too tight, and broke; it was only the middle string which could sound a harmonious note. Gautama Sakyamuni acknowledged this 'middle path', and abandoned his extreme asceticism.

Legend tells that a young girl, Sujata, was sent by the gods to offer him a handful of succulent rice in a golden bowl. The future Buddha, sitting beneath the Ajapala tree, accepted the rice from her, but threw away the bowl. His companions, seeing him break his fast, became disillusioned and abandoned him.

II. The One Thus Come

Alone, Guatama bathed in the Nairanjana river, then wandered a ways, before finally sitting beneath the Bodhi tree. He sat in the lotus position, his two hands resting flat, one atop the other (*Dhyani mudra*). It was April, the night of the full moon, exactly the thirty-fifth year after his birth. On this night, Guatama became the Buddha.

The evil god Kama-Mara appeared before him once more, and assaulted his senses with a dazzling array of demons, to frighten, torment and distract him. The frightening demons sought to evoke his fear of death, while the voluptuous ones sought instead to arouse attachment to this life. But with meticulous calm, he raised his right hand and, turning the palm outward (*Abhaya mudra*) to Kama-Mara, silently declared his fearlessness of the illusory god. Then, moving his right hand down, he touched the earth (*Bhumisparsa mudra*), and claimed this spot to be the 'immovable spot' in the midsts of Kama-Mara's flux. The earth bore witness to his claim, and the illusory army was dispelled.

In the remaining three watches of that night, Guatama sank into ever more profound depths of meditation. He beheld the unfolding of all his prior existences, and broke through these to their source; this eternal round was recognized to be delusion, and gradually it dissolved before him. He awakened, and through eyes half-open in wonder, beheld the world transformed. He had achieved enlightenment.

The four stages of meditation leading to his awakening had become for him Four Noble Truths. He had seen *suffering*, and the *origin* of suffering, then the *cessation* of suffering, and the *path* which led there. This path he likened to a tree with eight branches, each reaching to the attainment of one perfection. And so he named it the Eightfold Path. By practising goodness of action and purity of thought in various forms, one may finally attain, through meditation, a state of enlightenment.

For seven weeks, the Tathagata Buddha ('the one just come') remained at the site of his enlightenment, engaged in various states of meditation. When a chilling rain threatened to disrupt his meditations, a seven-headed serpent, the Naga of Lake Mucalinda, coiled itself around him and spread its seven hoods over his head to offer warmth and protection. Meanwhile, he wondered to himself if his awakening could be taught, and the thought of others suffering without hope roused in him such a state of compassion, that he resolved to act.

Crossing the Ganges river, he entered the Mrigadava Deer Park in Benares. He sought out and eventually found his five former companions. In his mind was the image of three lotus plants, whose flowers were either immersed in the water and still closed, or at the water's surface and almost opened, or above the water and opened to the sun. The first, who do not recognize the path, and the last, who do not need the path, he could not teach. But those in the middle, who could recognize the path, and needed it, he could teach.

It was June, the night of the full moon. On this night, the Buddha expounded his thought for the first time. During the first watch, he remained silent. He sat in the lotus position, his right hand upheld, with fore-finger and thumb touching (*Vitarka mudra*), and the fingers of his left hand gently touching the palm of the right (*Dharmachakra pravartana mudra*).

During the second watch, he spoke to his five companions, explaining to them the Middle Way he had found. And during the third watch, he expounded to them the Four Noble Truths that had appeared to him. This was his gospel, called the Dharma or 'Good Law', and by expounding it, he was setting a great wheel in motion: 'the Wheel of the Good Law', which would turn back upon the wheel of suffering, and eradicate its endless cycle of death and rebirth.

The Buddha, and the five who now saw the truth of his teachings, began traveling throughout the Ganges basin, begging food and teaching the Dharma to all castes. On the Gayasirsha hill, the Buddha delivered his great 'Fire Sermon', teaching his followers how to extinguish desire through the Eightfold Path (right view, right resolve, right speech, right action, right livelihood, right effort, right mindfulness and right concentration).

All were transported into a state of 'arhant', visionary wonder just short of 'nirvana'. King Bimisara, converted to the teachings, offered his Bamboo Grove, which became the sight of the first Order. Among the many converts, several became disciples; and among these, Ananda became his most simple and devoted, while Devadatta became his most scheming and treacherous.

The Buddha lived to a great age, preaching the Dharma to all, and converting many. When the time came for him to quit his body, he was with his disciples in a grove of sal trees outside Upavartana. It was April, the night of the full moon, exactly the eightieth year after his birth. He stretched himself out on his right side, and asked the disciples gathered round him to continue preaching the Dharma.

During the night's three watches, some disciples, such as Ananda, expressed great grief, while others, further along the path, joined with him in a state of peaceful contemplation. His final words to them were simple: *"All that is corruptible perishes: work diligently towards your own salvation."*[3]

Then, sinking ever deeper into meditation, he entered the domain where all consciousness ceases, and surrendered unto death. Legends tell that all the gods gathered round him, causing the earth to shake and the trees to erupt in a magnificent garland of blossoms.

Over the course of his life, the Buddha had come to realize, as expressed in one of Buddhism's more poetic expressions, *om mani padma hum* – that he, and we all, are but 'the jewel in the lotus'.

APPENDIX II

Life Thresholds in Dreams

Fleeting dreams have two gates:
one is fashioned of horn and one of ivory.
Those which pass through the one of sawn ivory
are deceptive, bringing tidings which come to nought,
but those which issue from the one of polished horn
bring true results when a mortal sees them.
- Homer, The Odyssey Bk XIX, l. 563

I. Life-Thresholds

Every life-altering dream, when it is laid out on the Ancient Template, is able to model contents of the mind otherwise hidden from consciousness. To better understand how dreams, like myths, may become models of the mind, we must now consider in greater depth those dream images concerned with life's threshold-crossings.

Oneiric Threshold Images bear a striking similarity to the archetypes identified by Jung. This should not surprise us, as the archetypes are precisely what myths and dreams share in common. On the other hand, it *is* surprising how rarely Jung's archetypes have been identified with life's thresholds. This, then, shall be one of our concerns in what follows.

But it should also be kept in mind that the number of life-thresholds is in no way *fixed*. Especially in our modern society, life-threshold crossings may be delayed, repeated, or approached only tentatively. Hence, crossing a life-threshold is more like a gradual transition, involving the accumulation of many deeply-moving experiences.

II. First Life-Thresholds

Oneiric Threshold Images will obviously change over the course of the dreamer's life. In infancy, the thresholds awaiting the infantile dreamer are numerous. Typically, they involve the task of autonomously mastering certain bodily functions: toilet-training, walking, speaking, etc. Using pleasure and pain, parents will have enforced a series of opposites upon the child: dirty and clean, right and wrong. Hence, in dreams the child's task is to master its bodily functions, and many images of 'doing something dirty or wrong' will appear. Parents show up as threatening threshold guardians: promising punishment for a task poorly performed. (On the other hand, a task may be successfully performed, and parents become a source of the most wonderful attention).

Such dreams will also lead to the gradual formation of the dream-I: an oneiric sense of identity that is still quite infantile, and hence, fragile (Jung's *Puer Æternus*). It is here, in this image, that many of the opposite meet for the first time. The child becomes this mixture of dirty and clean, good and evil, light and dark, and must act autonomously infavour of one rather than the other.

While joyful dream-images such as solitary play or fortuitous discovery solidify the infant's new-found sense of identity, traumatic memories may also be constellated round this figure. Recurring fears of abandonment or detachment from the parents also manifest themselves in dreams, and siblings may pose a most dangerous threat to this new identity's very fragile existence. In infant dreams, such threats usually appear under the more imaginary guise of vicious animals, pursuing monsters, and even abducting aliens.

III. Adult Life-thresholds

With adolescence, other life-thresholds loom on the horizon. The youth begins to form important relationships outside the family configuration. Acceptance and recognition by one's peers become more important. In dreams, figures of the opposite sex (*Anima/Animus*) and same-gender friends (the *Helper*) or rivals (the *Shadow*) begin to acquire greater power. The task is to appear attractive to the opposite sex, and be judged worthy by one's equals. Now, the life-thresholds of 'a first sexual experience' and of 'demonstrating a worthy skill' appear (as lesser forms of the marriage and profession thresholds).

Usually, the opposite sex appears as an ideal, while the same-gender rivals make worthy opponents. At the end of the dream, images of embrace with the opposite sex or of shared triumph over rivals indicate these underlying life-thresholds. The dream-I need not be successful: even rejection or failure indicate that the threshold is present. The dreamer will have to come up against these thresholds repeatedly before they are successfully crossed. And for this reason, all these images may also acquire darker aspects.

With greater maturity comes an increase in one's powers, and the parents' expectation that these be channelled into certain societal roles. Now the task is to find a partner in marriage and a vocation in life, so as to gain greater autonomy. Hence, in the dream-task, the life-thresholds of 'marriage' and 'profession' can be detected. The presence of the mother may be felt in regard to marriage, while that of the father occurs in regard to profession. (As Jung noted: *"The father... serves his son as a model persona."*[1]) On the other hand, each parent may also play an important role in the other life-domain.

Traditionally, the dream image of the mother embodies our experience of the world itself (*mater = materia*) in all its round of pleasures and pains. She is the *Magna Mater*. To master her powers is to either free one's self of desire and the desireable images of the world she creates (the way of the wandering ascetic) or to surrender one's self, in love, to one or more of her images (the lover and the beloved). Finally, to cross over her threshold is to marry, and so find in the beloved the source of all our hoped-for pleasures and undesired pains (or, given the other option, to abandon this world and enter into a more cloistered existence).

The dream image of the father embodies all those life-skills necessary for survival in this world. Traditionally, he is the *Pater Omnipotens* (though, in our modern society, these traditional roles are changing, and expanding into each other's domain). To acquire the father's powers for one's self is to cross a threshold away from him, and towards independence. That threshold is crossed when one acquires a profession, becomes self-sustaining, and so on.

Dream images of the same and of the opposite sex expand at this time and become more various. The beautiful veil of the ideal is shredded, revealing many darker figures beneath. Same-sex friends and siblings may reveal possible societal roles (the *Persona*) while also becoming rivals, appearing in numerous shadowy guises and gaining access to overwhelming forces (the *Shadow*). Ritualistic elements also appear in dreams, such as the preparation, jewellery, and vestments of a wedding; the teachers, initiations, and tests before graduating; or the required practices, tools and instruments of a profession. The dreamer will repeatedly come up against these thresholds, and seem to never cross them successfully. Recurring dreams, as endless variations on the same theme, tend to occur with frustrating frequency.

Once these thresholds are successfully crossed in life, their implications will be felt. Having acquired and integrated the parental roles, their inner images begin to dwindle in power and influence. The death of the mother or father will be dreamt repeatedly, regardless of the status of the real parents. The 'loss of mother' and 'loss of Father' thresholds are felt through images of the parents' departure, decline, death, or even murder. Our response to these events constitutes the dream-task.

Fortunately, this is compensated by images of new life and the next generation, as the 'birth of the child' constitutes another, contemporaneous life-threshold. The birth of the child means different things to the male and female parent. For the male, this involves 'fathering the child', meaning that (traditionally) the weapons, knowledge and skills for protecting the child become important. Meanwhile, for the female this involves 'mothering the child', and so images of descent into a fertile darkness, vegetation, pregnancy, and birth come to dominate. As well, the image of the child (*Puer Æternus*) will return to both, bearing many similarities to the dreamer as a child. The task is to create some form of relationship with this child.

At this time, the internal image of the parents may re-emerge, but with a new found energy. In response to the new-born child, they become figures of elderly wisdom (Jung's Spirit archetypes of the *Wise Old Man* and *Magna Mater*). They may guide or offer advice. This is accompanied by the dreamer's adjustment into the new life-role of mother or father. The responsibilities associated with these roles are now immanent in the dream-task. Images emerge of the new family configuration: home, shared dinners, yearly celebrations. Over the years, the spouse and children are gradually integrated into the dreamer's own sense of identity.

Building a home, educating the children, cultivating leisure activities - all of these seemingly mundane events recur in dreams, but acquire thereby a greater possible significance. The natural course of life may also be disrupted by unsuspected tragedies: accidents, illness, violence - all of which constitute unexpected life-threshold crossings. Coming to terms with the immense pain and loss is a life-task that now emerges in daily life and in dreams.

IV. Mid-life & the Last Life-thresholds

With middle age comes the dawning awareness that death will eventually remove the dreamer from this family configuration. Despite the powerful emotional ties binding them to one another, death must intervene. This first appearance of the 'death threshold' may cause a sudden and spontaneous backward movement through life (the *mid-life crisis* or *Lebenswende*). And as these past life-thresholds are re-crossed in memory, the dreamer regains a sense of identity independent of the family. This independence may be taken to extremes, and the family configuration abandoned. Then, attempts to crossover old life-thresholds may be made all over again. And indeed, one may actually succeed in crossing – again – over one or more of the old life-thresholds, re-creating once more the husband/wife and family configuration.

In less extreme cases, the first backward movement through life becomes part of a longer and more gradual process (*Individuation*). Past thresholds are repeatedly re-crossed, creating a greater sense of identity extending over the whole course of one's life (*the Self*). Now, images of life's different stages appear in combination. Dreams may depict one's self across time, mixing and superimposing several temporal images. A single dream may relate and combine all of life's major thresholds. Or, a dream may depict all of life's thresholds in a single, all-encompassing image (*mandalas*). Such an image reveals the innermost Self as reaching across all the stages of life.

With old age, more and more people known to the dreamer pass over the 'death threshold'. The 'death of the husband or wife' is one such painful threshold-crossing that may need be encountered. Previously, the 'death of the father or mother' may have prepared the dreamer for this event. All people known to the dreamer who have gone to that Beyond may return in dreams so as to suggest images of what lies beyond. As well, coping with increasing solitude, illness, the loss of bodily powers, and the increasing wisdom or loss of memory that may result from age constitute its many difficult life-thresholds.

All of this is to prepare the dreamer for the final journey *forward*. Death is life's last threshold, and this too must be crossed, in dreams as well as wakingness. As always, dreams will offer us images of that threshold, and even create a way across. Images of departed family and friends may appear as guides. But for the dreamer, a passage, a journey, a crossing awaits, and the task of the dream is to confront it. Successful confrontations may lead to visions of life beyond death's threshold. And whatever passage the dream may leave incomplete, that task will fall then to the dreamer to complete in wakingness. Ultimately, one must make one's own way across the final threshold.

REFERENCES

CH. I. INTRODUCTION

1. 'The Gospel of Philip' 67:9, *The Nag Hammadi Library*, edited by James M.Robinson, Harper & Row, 1978, p. 140.

2. 'The Gospel of Philip' 67:17, *The Nag Hammadi Library*, edited by James M.Robinson, Harper & Row, 1978, p. 140.

3. 'Corpus Hermeticum' IV.11, *Hermetica: The Greek Corpus Hermeticum and the Latin Asclepius*, translated by Brian Copenhave, Cambridge University Press,1992, p. 17.

4. Friedrich Nietzsche, *Human all too Human*, vol I, 13, cited by C. G. Jung *Psychology and Religion* C. W. 11, par 89, translated by R. F. C. Hull, Bollingen XX, Princeton University Press.

5. Friedrich Nietzsche, cited by Heinrich Zimmer, *The King and the Corpse*, edited by Joseph Campbell, Bollingen XI, Princeton University Press, 1948, p. 310

6. For Goethe, see his short essay, 'Epochs of the Spirit' (1817) in 'Geistes-Epochen nach Hermanns neusten Mitteilungen' *Sämtliche Werke nach Epochen seines Schaffens,* Band 11, Karl Richter Verlag, München. For Hegel, see *Aesthetics: Lectures on Fine Art*, trans. T. M. Knox, Oxford University Press, 1975.

7. *"Everyday language is a forgotten and therefore used-up poem, from which there hardly resounds 'a call' anymore."* Martin Heidegger, *Poetry, Language, Thought*, translated by A. Hofstadter, Harper Colophon, Harper & Row, 1971, p. 208.

8. Sigmund Freud, *The Interpretation of Dreams*, Translated by J. Strachey, Penguin, 1976, p. 700.

9. For example, this excerpt from one of Freud's letters to Jung: *"Dear Friend, ...It is remarkable that on the same evening that I formally adopted you as an eldest son, annointing you as my successor and crown prince –* in partibus infidelium *– that then and there you should have divested me of my paternal dignity... I therefore don once more my horn-rimmed paternal spectacles and warn my dear son to keep a cool head... I also shake my wise gray locks..."* C. G. Jung, *Memories, Dreams, Reflections*, recorded and edited by Aniela Jaffé, translated by Richard and Clara Winston, Vintage Random House, 1989, p. 362.

10. Ibid., p. 188.

11. C. G. Jung, *(*C. W. 8), *Structure and Dynamics of the Psyche,* translated by R. F. C. Hull, Bollingen XX, Princeton University Press, p. 247.

12. C. G. Jung, (C. W. 11, par. 88), *Psychology and Religion*, translated by R. F. C. Hull, Bollingen XX, Princeton University Press.

13. Joseph Campbell, *The Masks of God: Creative Mythology*, Penguin, 1968, p. 671.

14. Joseph Campbell, *The Mythic Image,* Bollongen Series C, Princeton University Press, 1974, back cover.

15. Mircea Eliade, *Myths, Dreams, and Mysteries: The Encounter Between Contemporary Faiths and Archaic Realities*, translated by Philip Mairet, Harper Torchbooks, 1960, p. 14.

16. André Breton, *Manifestoes of Surrealism*, translated by R. Seaver and H. Lane, Ann Arbor, University of Michigan Press, 1969, p. 20.

17. Lautréamont, *Les Chants de Maldoror*, cited in Jean-Luc Rispail, *Les surréalists: Une génération entre rêve et l'action*, Gallimard, 1991, pg. 34, 85.

18. Sigmund Freud, *The Interpretation of Dreams*, p. 470.

19. Ibid., p. 473.

20. Ibid., p. 473.
21. See for example, *Ernst Fuchs de Draeger*, Draeger, 1977; *The Fantastic Art of Vienna*, Alessandra Comini, Alfred A. Knopf, 1978; *Inner Visions*, Nevill Drury, Penguin Arkana, 1979; *Die Phantasten*, Gesellschaft bildender Künstler Österreichs, Künstlerhaus,1990.
22. For a resumé of Visionary art, see L. Caruana, *First Draft of A Manifesto of Visionary Art*, Recluse Pub., Paris 2001.
23. Joseph Campbell, *The Hero with a Thousand Faces*, Bollingen XVII, Princeton University Press, 1949, p. 35.
24. Nikos Kazantzakis, *Report to Greco*, Faber and Faber, 1965, p. 150.
25. Hermann Hesse, *The Glass Bead Game*, translated by Richard and Clara Winston, Picador Classics, 1969, p. 40.
26. Ibid., p. 119.

CH. II. THE SACRED EXPERIENCED AS UNITY

1. Dante Alighieri, 'Paradiso' Canto XXXIII, *The Divine Comedy* translated by Dorothy L. Sayers and Barbara Reynolds, Penguin, 1962, p. 346.
2. Plato, *Great Dialogues of Plato*, translated by W. H. D. Rouse, New American Library, 1956, p. 407
3. Aristotle, cited by Lawrence Hatab, *Myth and Philosophy: A Contest of Truths*, Open Court, 1990, p. 259.
4. Plotinus (XI, 9) Dodds translation, cited in Edgar Wind, *Pagan Mysteries in the Renaissance*, W. W. Norton and Company, 1958, p. 5
5. Euripides, 'The Bacchae' l. 201 in M. Morford and R. Lenardon, *Classical Mythology*, Longman, 1977, p. 191.
6. R. T. Rundle Clark, *Myth and Symbol in Ancient Egypt*, Thames and Hudson, 1959, pp. 35 - 36.
7. 'Corpus Hermeticum' I.1, *Hermetica*, p. 1.
8. Ibid., (C. H. V.2), p. 18.
9. Ibid., (C. H. XIII.17), p. 53.
10. Ibid., (Ascl. I.1), p. 17.
11. Hesiod, 'Theogony' l. 115 in John Mansley Robinson, *An Introduction to Early Greek Philosophy: The Chief Fragments and Ancient Testimony*, Houghton, Mifflin Company, 1968, p. 4.
12. Attributed to Orpheus' pupil Musaios by Diogenes Laertios (prooem. 3) in W. K. C. Guthrie, *Orpheus and the Greek Religion: A Study of the Orphic Movement*, Princeton University Press, 1952, pp. 74 - 75.
13. Ibid. (*Orphicum Fragmenta* 71b), p. 137.
14. Ibid. (*Orphicum Fragmenta* 165), p. 139.
15. Anixamander (Diels' fragments 2, A9, A9) in J. M. Robinson, *An Introduction to Early Greek Philosophy*, p. 24.
16. Heraclitus, (Diels' fragments 41, 54, 51, 8, 60, 67, 50, 32) in *Ancilla to the Pre-Socratic Philosophers: A Complete Translation of the Fragments in Diels' Fragmente der Vorsokratiker*, translated by K. Freeman, Harvard University Press, 1948, p. 24 - 34.
17. Parmenides, (Diels' fragments 7, 8), in Ibid., p. 43.
18. Empedocles (Diels' fragments 17, 17, 26, 35, 36) in John Burnet, *Early Greek Philosophy* (4th ed.), Adam & Charles Black, London, 1930, pp. 207 - 211.
19. Empedocles(Diels'fragment115)inJ.M.Robinson,*EarlyGreekPhilosophy*,p.152.
20. Plato, 'Timaeus', *The Collected Dialogues of Plato*, pp. 1151 - 1211.
21. Aristotle, *Aristotle's Metaphysics*, edited by W.D. Ross. Oxford: Clarendon Press, 1924, 1074b - 1075a. Amended.

22. Plotinus 'Enneads' *The Essential Plotinus*, edited and translated by Elmer O'Brian, Hackett, 1981.

CH. III. THE ANCIENT TEMPLATE

1. 'Corpus Hermeticum' I.8, *Hermetica*, p. 2.
2. Ernest Jones, *The Life and Work of Sigmund Freud*, Penguin, 1961, p. 280
3. See Henri Ellenberger's illuminating book *The Discovery of the Unconscious* for a description of this phenomenon. Henri Ellenberger, *The Discovery of the Unconscious: The History and Evolution of Dynamic Psychiatry*, Basic Books, 1970, p. 39.
4. Sigmund Freud, *The Interpretation of Dreams*, p. 47.
5. C. G. Jung, *Memories, Dreams, Reflections*, p. 170.
6. Ibid., p. 177.
7. C. G. Jung, (C.W. 9.i. par 155) 'The Archetypes and the Collective Unconscious' in *The Essential Jung*, edited by Anthony Storr, Princeton University Press, 1983, p. 84.
8. Friedrich Nietzsche, 'On the Genealogy of Morals' II, 3 *On the Genealogy of Morals and Ecce Homo*, translated by Walter Kaufmann and R. J. Hollingdale, Vintage, 1967, p.61.
9. William Blake, 'Songs of Innocence and of Experience' *The Portable Blake*, edited by Alfred Kazin, Penguin, 1946, p. 96.
10. C. G. Jung, *Memories, Dreams, Reflections*, p. 177.
11. Gérard De Nerval, 'Aurelia', *Aurelia followed by Sylvie*, translated by Kendall Lappin, Asylum Arts Publishing, 1993, p. 32.
12. Mircea Eliade, *Myths, Dreams, and Mysteries*, p. 179.

CH. IV. MYTH AS NARRATIVE AND AS A MEASURE OF TIME

1. Joseph Campbell, 'The Art of Reading Myths', cited by Stephen and Robin Larsen, *A Fire in the Mind: The Life of Joseph Campbell*, Doubleday, 1991, p. 338.
2. Mircea Eliade, *Images and Symbols: Studies in Religious Symbolism*, translated by Philip Mairet, Princeton University Press, 1991, p. 72.
3. Mircea Eliade, *The Sacred and the Profane: The Nature of Religion*, translated by Willard R. Trask, Harvest, Harcourt Brace & Company, 1959, p. 157.
4. Northrop Frye, *The Great Code: The Bible and Literature*, Penguin, 1981, p. 92. Ibid., p. 193.
5. Northrop Frye, *The Educated Imagination*, CBC Publications, 1963, pp. 20 - 21.
6. Joseph Campbell, *The Masks of God: Creative Mythology*, p. 216.
7. Joseph Campbell, *The Hero with a Thousand Faces*, pp. 257 - 259 passim.
8. Mircea Eliade, *Patterns in Comparative Religion*, translated by Rosemary Sheed,
9. Meridian Books, 1958, p. 383.
10. Mircea Eliade, *The Myth of the Eternal Return or, Cosmos and History*, translated by Willard R. Trask, Bollingen XLVI, Princeton University Press, 1954. For a more concise explanation, see Mircea Eliade, *The Sacred and the Profane*, pp. 104 - 113.
11. 'Enuma Elish' tablet 1 in *Myths from Mesopotamia: Creation, The Flood, Gilgamesh, and Others*, translated by Stephanie Dalley, Oxford University Press 1991, p. 233.
12. 'Rg Veda' X. 129 in *A Sourcebook in Indian Philosophy*, edited by Savepalli Radhakrishnan and Charles A. Moore, Princeton University Press, 1957, p.23.
13. Northrop Frye, *Fables of Identity: Studies in Poetic Mythology*, Harcourt, Brace, & World, 1963, p. 30.
14. Mircea Eliade, *The Myth of the Eternal Return*, p. 104.

CH. V. MYTHIC NARRATIVE IN
JUDÆO-CHRISTIANITY & HINDU-BUDDHISM

1. Northrop Frye, *The Great Code*, p. 169.
2. Ibid., pp. 170 - 171, which offers a source diagram.
3. C.f. The 'longer' and 'shorter' versions of the Christ myth in Northrop Frye, *The Great Code* pp. 172 - 173.
4. W. B. Yeats, 'The Magi', *Selected Poetry*, edited by Timothy Webb, Penguin 1991, p. 83.
5. 'The Gospel of Nicodemus' (including 'The Acts of Pilate' and 'Christ's descent into Hell') in *New Testament Apocrypha, Vol. I: Gospels and Related Writings*, edited by Wilhelm Schneemelcher, translated by R. McL. Wilson, James Clarke & Co., 1991, p. 521 - 526.
6. Northrop Frye, *Words with Power: Being a Second Study of the Bible and Literature*, Penguin, 1990, p. 103.
7. Cf. 'Phases of Revelation' in Typology II of Northrop Frye, *The Great Code* 1981: *"If we read the Bible sequentially, the Bible becomes a myth... If we 'freeze' the Bible into a a simultaneous unit, it becomes a single, gigantic, complex metaphor... A great mass of additional detail that we missed in the sequential reading then becomes relevant, because all the images are linked with all the other images, not merely with those that follow each other in the narrative."* (p. 63) For us, these 'metaphor clusters' may then be reconstituted into narratives, creating the Bible's 'hidden narratives'.
8. Joseph Campbell, *The Hero with a Thousand Faces*, Bollingen XVII, Princeton University Press, 1949, p. 30.
9. Nikos Kazantzakis, *Report to Greco*, p. 327.

CH. VI. THE MORE ANCIENT
MYTHOPOEIC UNDERSTANDING OF TIME

1. Peter Gabriel, 'The Rhythm of the Heat', *Security,* Geffen Records, 1982.
2. C. G. Jung, *Memories, Dreams, Reflections*, p. 266.
3. Erik Hornung, The Ancient Egyptian Books of the Afterlife, trans. by David Lorton, Cornell U. Press, 1999
4. R. T. Rundle Clark, *Myth and Symbol in Ancient Egypt*, Thames and Hudson, 1959, pp. 36 - 40.
5. Ibid., p. 224.
6. Mircea Eliade, *A History of Religous Ideas, Volume I*, translated by Willard R. Trask, University of Chicago Press, 1978, p. 92.
7. R. T. Rundle Clark, *Myth and Symbol in Ancient Egypt*, p. 264.
8. *"The basic principles of life, nature, and society were determined by the gods long ago, before the establishment of the kingship. This epoch – 'Tep zepi' – 'the First Time' – stretched from the first stirring of the High God in the Primæval Waters to the settling of Horus upon the throne and the redemption of Osiris. All proper myths relate events or manifestations of this epoch."* R. T. Rundle Clark, *Myth and Symbol in Ancient Egypt,* p. 263.
9. Mircea Eliade, *The Sacred and the Profane*, p. 106.
10. Mircea Eliade, *Images and Symbols,* p. 62
11. 'Inanna's Journey to Hell' *Poems of Heaven and Hell from Ancient Mesopotamia*, translated by N. K. Sandars, Penguin, 1971, p. 142.

12. Ibid., p. 147.
13. Ibid., p. 142.
14. Ibid., p. 147.
15. Ibid., p. 156.
16. Ibid., p. 164.
17. Ulla Koch-Westenholz, *Mesopotamian Astrology: An Introduction to Babylonian and Assyrian Celestial Divination*, Museum Tusculanum Press, University of Copenhagen, 1995, p. 132. See also: Micheal Baigent, *From the Omens of Babylon: Astrology and Ancient Mesopotamia*, Penguin Arkana, 1994.
18. Heinrich Zimmer, *Myths and Symbols in Indian Art and Civilization*, edited by Joseph Campbell, Bollingen, Princeton University Press, 1946, p. 11 - 19. Mircea Eliade, *The Myth of the Eternal Return*, pp. 114 - 116.
19. Mircea Eliade, Patterns in Comparative Religion, p. 408.
20. Mircea Eliade, *The Myth of the Eternal Return*, p. 35.

CH. VII. THE SACRED MOMENT IN ART

1. Plato, 'Phaedrus' 275 d, *The Collected Dialogues of Plato*, p. 521.
2. Heinrich Zimmer, *Artistic Form and Yoga in the Sacred Images of India*, translated by Gerald Chapple and James B. Lawson, Princeton University Press, 1984, p. 4.
3. Ibid., p. 33.
4. Ibid., p. 18.
5. Hermann Hesse, Letter 1925, *Hermann Hesse: A Pictorial Biography*, edited by Volker Michels, translated by Theodore and Yetta Aiolkowski, Triad Panther, 1971, p. 145.
6. Hesse, Herman, Preface to Siddhartha, 1958 Persian Edition, *Hermann Hesse: A Pictorial Biography*, p. 145.
7. Hermann Hesse, *Siddhartha*, translated by Hilda Rosner, New Directions, 1951, p. 151.
8. Nikos Kazantzakis, *The Last Temptation*, translated by P. A. Bien, Faber and Faber, 1975, p. 506.
9. It is worth noting that, from the fifth to the eleventh centuries, Christ was portrayed with his head held upward and eyes open. Only after the eleventh century did Christ appear as dead on the cross, his head falling forward and eyes closed. See G. Duchet-Suchaux and M. Pastoureau, *The Bible & Saints, Flammarion Iconographic Guides*, 1994, pg. 106.
10. R. T. Rundle Clark, *Myth and Symbol in Ancient Egypt*, p. 142.
11. See Erik Hornung, The Ancient Egyptian Books of the Afterlife, trans. by David Lorton, Cornell U. Press, 1999.
12. *"Every God has his place in the Boat of Millions of Years."* Ch. 175 of *The Book of the Dead*, cited in R. T. Rundle Clark, *Myth and Symbol in Ancient Egypt*, p. 139
13. Plato, 'Timaeus' 37d, *The Collected Dialogues of Plato*, p. 1167.
14. Coffin Text VII 302e in Erik Hornung, *The Ancient Egyptian Books of the Afterlife*, p 11.
15. Ibid. p. 6.
16. 'Chhandogya Upanishad' VI. xiii, 1 - 3 in *A Sourcebook in Indian Philosophy* p. 70.
17. 'The Tibetan Book of the Golden Precepts' in F. C. Happold, *Mysticism: A Study and an Anthology*, Penguin, 1963, p. 171.

310 ENTER THROUGH THE IMAGE

CH. VIII. COSMOGONIC MYTH AS A MODEL OF THE MIND

1. 'Gospel of Thomas' (18), *The Nag Hammadi Library*, p. 128.
2. 'Corpus Hermeticum' V.10, *Hermetica,* p. 20.
3. Although three versions of the *Apocryphon* were discovered in 1945 in Nag Hammadi, another shorter version had already turned up half a century earlier, in 1896 in Cairo. It was acquired by the Berlin Museum and, due to a series of unfortunate circumstances, the *Papyrus Berolinensis 8502* was not published until 1955. All citations marked 'AJn' are from 'The Apocryphon of John' translated by Frederik Wisse in *The Nag Hammadi Library in English*, edited by James M. Robinson, HarperSanFrancisco, 1988. Comparisons have been made with: 'The Secret Book of John' translated by Marvin Meyer in *The Nag Hammadi Scriptures, International Edition*, edited by Marvin Meyer, HarperOne, 2007.
4. Ibid. AJn 5:5.
5. Ibid., AJn 6:10.
6. Ibid., AJn 9:7.
7. Ibid., AJn 14:3.
8. Ibid., AJn 20:5.
9. 'The Gospel of Thomas' *The Nag Hammadi Library in English*, pp. 118 - 130 passim.
10. Aristotle, *Aristotle's Metaphysics*, edited by W.D. Ross. Oxford: Clarendon Press, 1924, 1074b. Amended.
11. 'Eugnostos the Blessed' 81:21, translated by Douglas M. Parrot in *The Nag Hammadi Library in English*, pp. 232 - 233.
12. 'The Gospel of Philip' 68:23, translated by Wesley W. Isenberg in *The Nag Hammadi Library in English*, p. 150.
13. Ibid. p. 154.

CH. IX. SYMBOLS OF THE SACRED

1. 'The Gospel of Philip' 67:10, *The Nag Hammadi Library*, p. 150.
2. 'The Gospel of Thomas' 47:20, *The Nag Hammadi Library*, p. 135.
3. *An Intermediate Greek-English Lexicon: Founded upon the Seventh Edition of Liddell and Scott's Greek-English Lexicon*, Oxford University Press, 1983 p. 759
4. *"One Almighty is, from whom all things proceed and up to him return... differing but in degree, of kind the same."* This is Milton's poetic phrasing of Macrobius' ancient philosophy, where the One expands into the multiplicity of the cosmos (*'from whom all things proceed'*). And, at the same time, this multiplicity may return to the One's original unity (*'and up to him return'*). To *'differ in degree'*, but be *'of kind the same'* refers to Macrobius' idea of 'similarity and difference'. See John Milton, *Paradise Lost*, Bk V. l. 470 - 490, edited by Northrop Frye, Rinehart & Co., 1951, p. 121.
5. Macrobius, (I. XIV. 15) *Commentary on the Dream of Scipio*, translated by William H Stahl, Columbia University Press, 1990, p. 145.
6. For a more complete description of the Golden Chain of Being, see: E. M. W. Tillyard, *The Elizabethan World Picture*, Vintage Randam House, ch. IV, *passim* and C.S. Lewis, *The Discarded Image: An Introduction to Medieval and Renaissance Literature*, Cambridge University Press, 1964
7. Plotinus 'Enneads' (VI, 9, 7) *The Essential Plotinus*, edited and translated by Elmer O'Brian, Hackett, 1981, pp. 83.
8. Macrobius (II. XV. 25) *Commentary on the Dream of Scipio, p. 237*. See also Steven Kruger, *Dreaming in the Middle Ages*, Cambridge University Press, 1992, p. 34.

REFERENCES

9. The author's circular diagram on p. 121 is based upon an illustration from the 15th century *Clavis Sapientiæ* of Artephius (reproduced p. 120). See: Gareth Roberts, *The Mirror of Alchemy*, The British Library, 1994, p. 48.
10. Macrobius (I. VI. 31) p. 106.
11. Ibid., (I. VI. 33) p. 106.
12. Ibid., (I. VI. 9) p. 101. Verb tense altered.
13. Mircea Eliade, *Myths, Dreams, and Mysteries*, p. 175.
14. Mircea Eliade, *The Myth of the Eternal Return*, p. 4.
15. Aldous Huxley, *The Doors of Perception / Heaven and Hell*, Grafton, HarperCollins, 1974, p. 19.
16. Mircea Eliade, *Myths, Dreams, and Mysteries*, p. 124.
17. Friedrich Nietzsche, *Ecce Homo* ('Zarathustra'¶3) translated by R. J. Hollingdale, Penguin, 1979, p. 103.
18. Mircea Eliade, Images and Symbols, p. 84.
19. Sigmund Freud, *Totem and Taboo: Some Points of Agreement between the Mental Lives of Savages and Neurotics*, translated by James Strachey, W. W. Norton and Company, 1950, p. 154.
20. Hesiod, 'Theogony' l. 824 in M. Morford and R. Lenardon, *Classical Mythology*, Longman, 1977, p. 38.
21. Anne Baring and Jules Cashford, *The Myth of the Goddess: Evolution of an Image*, Viking Arcana, 1991, p. 291.

CH. X. THE MYTHOLOGEM OF 'THE CONIUNCTIO'

1. D. Wolkstein and S. N. Kramer, *Inanna, Queen of Heaven and Earth: Her Stories and Hymns from Sumer*, Rider and co. 1983, p. 36.
2. Joseph Campbell, *The Masks of God: Oriental Mythology*, Penguin, 1962, p. 88.
3. Lucius Apuleius, *The Golden Ass*, translated by Robert Graves, Penguin, 1950, p. 227.
4. Ibid., p. 228.
5. Anne Baring and Jules Cashford, *The Myth of the Goddess: Evolution of an Image*, Viking Arcana, 1991, p. 211.
6. Ibid., p. 211
7. Ibid., p. 213.
8. Ibid., p. 215.
9. Irenaeus, *Contra Hæreses* Bk. I. Ch. XXIII in Philip Schaff, ed. *The Ante-Nicene Fathers, Vol. I. The Apostolic Fathers with Justin Martyr and Irenaeus*, Wm. B. Eerdmans Publishing Company, reprint 2001
10. For an anthology of ancient sources on Simon Magus, see G. R. S. Mead, *Simon Magus: An Essay on the Founder of Simonianism, based on the Ancient Sources*, Ares, 1892.
11. Ibid, p. 54.
12. Simon Magus, cited by Hippolytus in *Refutatio Omnium Hæresium*, Bk VI, Ch. XII, translated by Rev. J. H. MacMahon, in Philip Schaff, ed. *The Ante-Nicene Fathers, Vol V. Fathers of the Third Century*, Wm. B. Eerdmans Publishing Company, reprint 2001
13. Hippolytus, *Refutatio Omnium Hæresium*, Bk VI, Ch. XIII. Amended
14. Irenaeus, *Contra Hæreses* Bk. I. Ch. XXIX.
15. Irenaeus, *Contra Hæreses* Bk. I. Ch. XXXII
16. Ibid.
17. 'The Gospel of Philip' 63:30, translated by Wesley W. Isenberg in *The Nag Hammadi Library in English*, p. 148.
18. Hippolytus, *Refutatio Omnium Hæresium*, Bk VI, Ch. XIII. Amended

312 ENTER THROUGH THE IMAGE

19. Heinrich Zimmer, *Artistic Form and Yoga,* pp. 201 - 202.
20. Heinrich Zimmer, *Myths and Symbols in Indian Art,* p. 137.

CH. XI. COMBINING SYMBOLS AND CROSSING MYTHS

1. Hermann Hesse, *Demian,* p. 105.
2. Hermann Hesse, *Narziss and Goldmund,* translated by Geoffrey Dunlop, Penguin, 1974, p. 146.
3. Ibid., pp. 259 - 260.
4. C. G. Jung, 'The Special Phenomenology of the Child Archetype', in *Psyche and Symbol: A Selection from the Writings of C. G. Jung,* edited by Violet S. de Laszlo, Anchor Doubleday, 1958, p. 145.
5. Mircea Eliade, *Images and Symbols,* p. 174.
6. Martin Heidegger, (SZ ¶44) *Being and Time,* translated by John Macquarrie and Edward Robinson, Harper & Row, 1962 p. 219.
7. Ibid.,(SZ ¶44) p. 222.
8. Heidegger states explicitly in *Being and Time* that, not just individual entities, but the greater Being which underlies and unifies them, is either concealed or unconcealed: *"That which remains hidden...or which relapses and gets covered up again, or which shows itself only 'in disguise', is not just this entity or that, but rather, the Being of entities."* (SZ ¶7c, Being and Time p. 35) What is more: *"Being, as the basic theme of philosophy, is no class or genus of entities; yet it pertains to every entity. Its universality is to be sought higher up... Being is the transcendens pure and simple."* (SZ ¶7c. Being and Time p. 38).
9. Martin Heidegger, *Early Greek Thinking,* p. 73.
10. Friedrich Nietzsche, 'On Truth and Lie in an Extra-Moral Sense', *The Portable Nietzsche,* pp. 46 - 47.
11. Heinrich Zimmer, *Philosophies of India,* edited by Joseph Campbell, Bollingen XXVI, Princeton University Press, p. 1. Cited also in Joseph Campbell, *The Masks of God: Creative Mythology,* p. 625.
12. Joseph Campbell, *The Masks of God: Creative Mythology,* p. 1.
13. Joseph Campbell, *The Masks of God: Creative Mythology,* p. 677.
14. Leonard Cohen, 'Last Year's Man' *Songs of Love and Hate,* Stranger Music, 1971.
15. W. B. Yeats, 'The Second Coming', *Selected Poetry,* edited by Timothy Webb, Penguin 1991, p. 124.
16. Hermann Hesse, *Demian,* translated by W. J. Strachan, Paladin HarperCollins, 1960, p. 117.
17. Heinrich Zimmer, *Philosophies of India,* p. 1.
18. Joseph Campbell, *The Masks of God: Creative Mythology,* p. 678.
19. *Ernst Fuchs: Fantasia,* Artograph Verlag, 1993, p. 58.
20. C. G. Jung, Memories, Dreams, Reflections, p. 331.

CH. XII. SYMBOLS IN MODERN VISIONARY ART

1. Nikos Kazantzakis, *Report to Greco,* Faber and Faber, 1965, p. 173.
2. Ernst Fuchs, *Im Zeichen der Sphinx,* DTF verlag, p. 49. Author's translation.
3. Ernst Fuchs, *Architectura Cælestis: Images of the Hidden Prime of Styles,* Residenz Verlag, 1966, p. 174.
4. Ibid p. 161.
5. Johfra, *Astrologie: Tierkreiszeichen,* Verlag Marco Aldinger, 1981, p. 3. Author's translation
6. Ibid., p. 22.

7.   Ibid., p. 21
8.   Ibid, p. 4
9.   Aldous Huxley, *The Doors of Perception / Heaven and Hell*, p. 106
10. Ernst Fuchs, *Architectura Cælestis* p. 165
11. Aldous Huxley, *The Doors of Perception / Heaven and Hell*, p. 79
12. Ibid, p. 90.

CH. XIII. THE MYTHOLOGEM OF DEATH AND REBIRTH

1.   'Gospel of Philip' 67:12, *The Nag Hammadi Library*, p. 140.
2.   'Corpus Hermeticum' XI.20, *Hermetica,* p. 41.
3.   C.G. Jung and K. Kerényi, *Essays on a Science of Mythology*, translated by R. F. C. Hull, Bollingen Series XXII, New York, 1969, p. 3.
4.   For an account of this myth and its accompanying mythologem in a multiplicity of cultures, see Joseph L. Henderson and Maud Oakes, *The Wisdom of the Serpent: The Myths of Death, Rebirth, and Resurrection,* Princeton University Press, 1963.
5.   Dante Alighieri, 'Paradiso' Canto XXXI, *The Divine Comedy* translated by Dorothy L. Sayers and Barbara Reynolds, Penguin, 1962, p. 329. NB. Beatrice descended to Limbo to implore Virgil to save Dante from the dark wood. Virgil relates this in the '*Inferno'*, Canto II, l. 82 - 84.
6.   Joseph Campbell, 'The Inspiration of Oriental Art', *Myths to Live By*, Viking Penguin, Bantam, 1972, p. 116.
7.   W. B. Yeats, 'A Dialogue of Self and Soul', *Selected Poetry*, p. 162.
8.   Aldous Huxley, *The Doors of Perception / Heaven and Hell*, Grafton, HarperCollins, 1974, p. 108.
9.   Ibid., p. 107.
10. Stanislav Grof, *LSD Psychotherapy*, Hunter House, 1980. p. 64.
11. Ibid., p. 66.
12. Ibid., p. 54.
13. Ibid., p. 68.
14. Ibid., p. 86.
15. Ibid., pp. 83 - 84.
16. C. G. Jung, (C. W. 5, par. 40) *Symbols of Transformation*, 2nd Ed., translated by R. F. C. Hull, Bollingen Series XX, Princeton University Press, 1956, p. 30.
17. Sigmund Freud, *Introductory Lectures on Psychoanalysis*, translated by James Strachey, Penguin, 1973, p. 445.
18. Ibid., p. 444.
19. Grof, Stanislav, *LSD Psychotherapy*, p. 79.
20. Joseph Campbell, *The Masks of God: Primitive Mythology*, Penguin, 1959, p. 61.
21. Robertson Davies, *What's Bred in the Bone*, Penguin, 1985, p. 74.
22. Robertson Davies, *The Manticore*, Penguin, 1972, p. 87.
23. Robertson Davies, 'Marchbanks' Almanack', 1967 in: Grant, Judith Skelton, *Robertson Davies: Man of Myth*, Penguin, 1994. p. 1.
24. Percy B. Shelley, 'Queen Mab' *Shelley: Poems*, edited by Isabel Quigly, Penguin, 1956,p. 36.
25. Emile Mâle, *The Gothic Image: Religious Art in France of the Thirteenth Century*, translated by Dora Nussey, Harper Torchbooks, 1958, p. 195.
26. Shakespeare, 'As You Like It' Act II, sc. vii.
27. James Frazer, *The New Golden Bough: A New Abridgement of the Classic Work*, edited by Theodore H. Gaster, Criterion Books, 1959, pp. 313 - 314.

CH. XIV. LIFE-THRESHOLD CROSSINGS IN DREAMS

1.   Novalis, 'Heinrich Von Ofterdingen' *The German Mind of the 19th Century: A Literary and Historical Anthology*, edited by Hermann Glaser, Continuum, 1981, p. 35.

2.   Plato, 'Theaetetus' 158d, translated by B. Jowett in *The Theatre of Sleep*, p. 129.

3.   Joseph Campbell, *The Hero with a Thousand Faces*, p. 12.

4.   Gérard de Nerval, *Aurélia ou le Rêve et la Vie*, Pocket, 1994, p. 169.

5.   Baudelaire quoted in *The Theatre of Sleep: An Anthology of Literary Dreams*, edited by Guido Almansi and Claude Beguin, Picador, 1987, p. 67.

6.   Charles Baudelaire, 'lettre à Charles Asselineau' 13 Mars 1856 in *Oeuvres Complètes de Charles Baudelaire*, VOL. IX, Correspondance Générale, Edition Louis Conard 1947 pp. 373 - 377. English translation by J. Romney, in *The Theatre of Sleep*, pp. 67 - 69.

7.   In a letter to his mother, Baudelaire refers to *Histoires extraordinaires*, his translation of Edgar Allan Poe, saying *"The book came out three days ago, and your volume is one of the first three that I've received"*. Histoires extraordinaires was registered by the Bulletin de la Bibliographie de la France on the 12th of April, 1856. Lettre à Mme Aupick, le 15 Mars 1856. In *Oeuvres Complètes de Charles Baudelaire*, VOL. IX, Correspondance Générale, Edition Louis Conard 1947 p. 377.

8.   For more examples of the hero's birth, see Otto Rank, 'The Myth of the Birth of the Hero' *In Quest of the Hero*, introduced by Robert A. Segal, Princeton University Press, 1990. For Jung's psychological analysis of this phenomenon, see his essay C. G. Jung, 'The Psychology of the Child Archetype' in *Psyche and Symbol: A Selection from the Writings of C. G. Jung*, edited by Violet S. de Laszlo, Anchor Doubleday, 1958.

9.   Joseph Campbell, *The Masks of God: Creative Mythology*, p. 678.

10. Mircea Eliade, *Myths, Dreams, and Mysteries*, pp. 51.

CH. XV. NARRATIVE AND THE HERO TASK IN DREAMS

1.   René Descartes, 'Discourse 3' *Discourse on Method and the Meditations*, p. 49

2.   Descartes' dream first appears in A. Baillet, *Vie de Monsieur Descartes*, 1691. The dream was subsequently included in The Complete Works: Descartes, *Oeuvres*, edited by Charles Adam and Paul Tannery, Paris, J. Vrin, 1964 - 1974, volume X, pp. 179 - 188. The following English translation by J. Romney (rendered into the first person) appears in: *The Theatre of Sleep: An Anthology of Literary Dreams*, pp. 264 - 266.

3.   'Later remarks' (also rendered into first person) appear in: Gregor Sebba, *The Dream of Descartes*, edited by Richard A. Watson, Southern Illinois University Press, p. 45.

4.   René Descartes, 'Discourse 2' *Discourse on Method and the Meditations*, p. 35.

5.   Ibid., Discourse 2, p. 41.

6.   Ibid., Meditation 1, p. 100.

7.   Ibid., Meditation 2, p. 103.

8.   Ibid., Discourse 4, p. 53.

9.   Ibid., Meditation 5, p. 145.

10. Ibid., Meditation 6, p. 159.

11. Gregor Sebba, *The Dream of Descartes*, p. 23.

12. Marie-Louise von Franz, *Traüme*, Daimon Verlag, 1985, p. 215. Author's translation

13. René Descartes, 'Discourse 3' *Discourse on Method and the Meditations*, 'Letter from the Author' p. 176.

14. Ibid., Meditation 1, p. 100.

15. Ibid., Meditation 1, p. 96.

16. Ibid., Meditation 1, p. 97.

17. René Descartes, 'Meditation 6' *Discourse on Method and the Meditations*, p. 168.

18. C. G. Jung, *Memories, Dreams, Reflections*, p. 282.

CH. XVI. ONEIRO-MYTHIC ICONOLOGUES

1. Georg Büchner, *Woyzeck*, Sc.viii 'At the Doctor's', translated by Schmidt, Henry, Bard Edition, 1969, p. 38 - 39.

2. Géreard de Nerval, 'Aurelia' *Aurelia followed by Sylvie*, p. 85.

3. Leonard Cohen, 'You Who Pour Mercy into Hell' *Stranger Music*, p. 325

4. August Strindbery, *A Dream Play and Four Chamber Plays*, translated by Walter Gilbert Johnson, W W Norton & Co Inc, 1975. Introduction to A Dream Play.

5. Joseph Campbell, *The Flight of the Wild Gander: Explorations in the Mythical Dimension*, Harper Perennial, 1951, p. 33.

6. For an account of many of the above dream-pioneers, see: Henri Ellenberger, *The Discovery of the Unconscious: The History and Evolution of Dynamic Psychiatry*, Basic Books, 1970.

7. Léon D'Hervey de Saint-Denys, *Les Rêves et les Moyens de les Diriger: Observations Practiques*, Editions Oniros, Ile Saint-Denis cedex. Editions Oniros has also published a companion volume, including his biography, correspondence, and a commentary on his works on Sinology: - *D'Hervey de Saint-Denys 1822 - 1892*, Olivier de Luppé, Angel Pino, Roger Ripert, & Betty Schwartz, Editions Oniros, Ile Saint-Denis cedex. Although 'D'Hervey de Saint-Denys' would be the proper French rendering of his family name, throughout the text I have shortened this to 'Saint-Denys'. All translations from this French edition are by the author, except as noted.

8. Sigmund Freud, *The Interpretation of Dreams*, p.127.

9. Wilhelm Stekel, *Die Sprache des Traumes*, J. F. Bergmann Verlag, Wiesbaden, 1927. All translations from this German edition are by the author.

10. Wilhelm Stekel, *Die Traüme der Dichter*, J. F. Bergmann Verlag, Wiesbaden, 1912. All translations from this German edition are by the author.

11. Sigmund Freud, *The Interpretation of Dreams*, p.466.

12. Sigmund Freud, *The Interpretation of Dreams*, p.302.

13. Wilhelm Stekel, *Die Sprache des Traumes*, p. 354.

14. Ibid., dream 41, p. 52.

15. K. A. Scherner, *Das Leben des Traumes*, Berlin, in Wilhelm Stekel, *Die Sprache des Traumes*, dream 429, p. 227.

16. Wilhelm Stekel, *Die Traüme der Dichter*, p. 207.

17. Hermann Hesse, *Siddhartha*, p. 132.

18. Saint-Denys, *Les Rêves*, p. 160.

19. Ibid., p. 229.

20. Ibid., p. 101.

21. Ibid., p. 235.

22. Ibid., p. 141.

23. Ibid., p. 234.

24. Wilhelm Stekel, *Die Sprache des Traumes*, dream 49, p. 58.

25. Ovid, *Metamorphoses*, Bk. X, translated by Mary M. Innes, Penguin, 1955, p. 231

26. Ibid. p. 232

27. For the myth of Tiresias, see: Robert Graves, *The Greek Myths*, Volume 2, Penguin, 1955, pp. 11 - 14
28. Saint-Denys, *Les Rêves*, p. 243.
29. C. G. Jung, *Memories, Dreams, Reflections*, p. 173.
30. Ibid., p. 172 - 173.
31. Saint-Denys, *Les Rêves*, p. 176.
32. 'The Apocryphon of John' AJn 1:30 in *The Nag Hammadi Library*, p. 105. Amended.

CH. XVII. ONEIRO-ARTISTIC ICONOLOGUES

1. Plato, 'Phaedrus' 275 d, *The Collected Dialogues of Plato*, edited by Edith Hamilton and Huntington Cairns, Bollingen LXXI, Princeton University Press, 1961, p. 521.
2. Friedrich Nietzsche, 'The Dionysian Worldview' part 1 (1871). An unpublished manuscript containing material later used in The Birth of Tragedy, in *Sämtliche Werke: Kritische Studienausgabe*, vol. 1, eds. Giorgio Colli and Mazzino Montinari, de Gruyter, Berlin, 1980, p. 554.
3. Saint-Denys, *Les Rêves*, p. 230 - 231.
4. Ibid. p. 231.
5. Ibid. p. 233 - 234
6. C. G. Jung, *Memories, Dreams, Reflections*, p. 159.
7. William Blake, 'The Marriage of Heaven and Hell' *The Portable Blake*, p. 251.
8. Salvador Dali, *The Secret Life of Salvador Dali*, translated by H. M. Chevalier, Vision Press, 1942, pp. 219 - 220.
9. Friedrich Nietzsche, *Human, All too Human*, § 12, translated by Marion Faher, University of Nebraska Press.
10. Saint-Denys, *Les Rêves*, p. 222.
11. Ibid. p. 236.
12. The expression 'morphological echo' comes from Haim Finkelstein, *Salvador Dali's Art and Writing 1927 - 1942, The Metamorphosis of Narcissus*, Cambridge University Press, 1996, p. 195.
13. Ovid, *Metamorphoses*, Bk. III, l. 14, translated by Mary M. Innes, Penguin, 1955, p. 83
14. Ibid. p. 216. Ovid, *Metamorphoses*, Bk. III, l. 62.
15. Ibid. p. 216. Ovid, *Metamorphoses*, Bk. III, l. 73.
16. Salvador Dali, 'Métamophose de Narcisse' in *Salvador Dali: Retrospective 1920 - 1980*, Centre Georges Pompidou, Musée Nationale d'Art Moderne, 1979, p. 285. Author's translation.
17. Ibid. p. 287. Author's translation.
18. Ibid. p. 288. Author's translation.
19. Ibid. p. 288. Author's translation.
20. Saint-Denys, *Les Rêves*, p. 232
21. Salvador Dali, 'Oui 1', p. 156 in Haim Finkelstein, *Salvador Dali's Art and Writing 1927 - 1942, The Metamorphosis of Narcissus*, Cambridge University Press, 1996, p. 184.
22. Salvador Dali, 'Conquest of the Irrational' in Patrick Walsberg, *Surrealism*, Thames and Hudson, p. 91.
23. Salvador Dali, 'Oui 1', p. 157 in Haim Finkelstein, *Salvador Dali's Art and Writing 1927 - 1942, The Metamorphosis of Narcissus*, Cambridge University Press, 1996, p. 184.

24. Salvador Dali, 'La Femme Visible' in *Salvador Dali: Retrospective 1920 - 1980*, Centre Georges Pompidou, Musée Nationale d'Art Moderne, 1979, p. 245. Author's translation.
25. Salvador Dali in Haim Finkelstein, *Salvador Dali's Art and Writing 1927 - 1942, The Metamorphosis of Narcissus*, Cambridge University Press, 1996, p. 181.
26. Salvador Dali, 'Oui 2', p. 63 in Haim Finkelstein, *Salvador Dali's Art and Writing 1927 - 1942, The Metamorphosis of Narcissus*, Cambridge University Press, 1996, p. 192.
27. Virgil, 'Fourth Eclogue' *Eclogues*, translated by James Laughlin, New Directions. Emile Mâle, *The Gothic Image*, p. 39.
28. Ibid., p. 40.
29. Ibid., p. 40.
30. Ibid., p. 41.
31. Ibid., p. 41.
32. 'Jhasha fish' version of the flood myth in *Satapatha Brahmana*; 'Matsya' version
33. in the *Matsya Purana*. For both versions, see: *Hindu Myths: A Sourcebook Translated from the Sanskrit*, edited by Wendy Doniger O'Flaherty, Penguin, 1975, pp. 179 - 184.

CH. XVIII. CONDENSATION

1. Joseph Campbell, *The Mythic Image*, p. xi.
2. Mircea Eliade, *Myths, Dreams, and Mysteries*, p. 14.
3. Gérard de Nerval, 'Aurélia', in *The Theatre of Sleep,* edited by Guido Almansi and Claude Beguin, p. 280.
4. Joseph Campbell, *The Hero with a Thousand Faces*, p. 19.
5. Sigmund Freud, *The Interpretation of Dreams*, p.400.
6. Ibid. p. 280.
7. Saint-Denys, *Les Rêves*, p. 26.
8. Sigmund Freud, *The Interpretation of Dreams*, p.400.
9. Ibid., p. 218.
10. Ibid., p. 740.
11. Ibid., p. 740.
12. Mircea Eliade, *Shamanism: Archaic Techniques of Ecstasy*, translated by Willard R. Trask, Bollingen LXXVI, Princeton University Press, 1964, p. 94.
13. Stanislav Grof, *LSD Psychotherapy*, p. 86.
14. Wilhelm Stekel, *Die Sprache des Traumes*, dream 95, p. 102.
15. Wilhelm Stekel, *Die Traüme der Dichter*, p. 148 (free translation).
16. Saint-Denys, *Les Rêves,* p. 175.
17. Sigmund Freud, *The Interpretation of Dreams*, p.432.
18. For the complete account of this dream, see: Ibid., p. 182.
19. Ibid., p. 399.
20. Ibid., p. 435.
21. Wilhelm Stekel, *Die Sprache des Traumes*, dream 227, p. 208.
22. Saint-Denys, *Les Rêves*, p. 150.
23. Wilhelm Stekel, *Die Traüme der Dichter*, p. 19.
24. 'Bardo Thödol' or *Tibetan Book of the Dead*, in: Stanislav Grof, *Books of the Dead*, Thames and Hudson, 1994, p. 74, Stanislav and Christian Grof, *Beyond Death*, Thames and Hudson, 1980, p. 81.
25. Wilhelm Stekel, *Die Sprache des Traumes*, dream 88, p. 93.

26. 'Eugnostos the Blessed' 81:21, translated by Douglas M. Parrot in *The Nag Hammadi Library in English*, pp. 232 - 233.
27. 'The Gospel of Philip' 70:14, *The Nag Hammadi Library*, p. 151.
28. C. G. Jung, 'On the Psychology of the Unconscious' C. W. 7i par. 111, *Two Essays on Analytic Psychology,* p. 72.
29. C. G. Jung, 'Gnostic Symbols of the Self', C. W. 9ii, par 307 *The Gnostic Jung,* p. 66.
30. C. G. Jung, *Memories, Dreams, Reflections*, p. 324.
31. Ibid., p. 196.

CH. XIX. DISPLACEMENT

1. Gérard de Nerval, *Aurélia,* p. 98.
2. Sigmund Freud, *The Interpretation of Dreams*, p.353.
3. C. G. Jung, *Memories, Dreams, Reflections*, p. 303.
4. Saint-Denys, *Les Rêves*, pp. 221 - 222.
5. Sigmund Freud, *The Interpretation of Dreams*, p.443.
6. Ibid., p. 414.
7. Sigmund Freud, *Introductory Lectures on Psychoanalysis*, p. 208.
8. Sigmund Freud, *The Interpretation of Dreams*, p.434.
9. 'Thunder, Perfect Mind' 67:17, *The Nag Hammadi Library*, pp. 297 - 303 passim.
10. Sigmund Freud, *The Interpretation of Dreams*, p.427.
11. Sigmund Freud, *A General Introduction to Psycho-analysis*, translated by Joan Riviere, Washington Square Press, 1952, p. 147.
12. Joseph Campbell, *The Masks of God: Occidental Mythology*, p. 157.
13. Ibid., p. 158.
14. Ernst Fuchs, *Phantastiches Leben: Erinnerungen*, Kindler verlag 2001, p. 281. Author's translation.
15. Sigmund Freud, *The Interpretation of Dreams*, p.534.
16. Ibid., p. 439.
17. Ibid., p. 218.
18. Ibid., p. 223.
19. Ibid., p. 440.
20. C. G. Jung, *Memories, Dreams, Reflections*, p. 133.
21. Joseph Campbell, *This Business of the Gods:* Joseph Campbell in conversation with Fraser Boa, Windrose Films Ltd., 1989. pp. 51 - 56.
22. Wilhelm Stekel, *Die Traüme der Dichter*, p. 178.
23. Sigmund Freud, *The Interpretation of Dreams*, p.435.
24. Ibid., p. 435.
25. Saint-Denys, *Les Rêves,* p. 225.
26. Ibid., p.225.
27. C. G. Jung, *Memories, Dreams, Reflections*, p. 323.

CH. XX. THE ETERNAL LABYRINTH

1. Anaximander (1). This is Nietzsche's rendering, which appears in: Friedrich Nietzsche, *Philosophy in the Tragic Age of the Greeks,* translated by Marianne Cowan, Gateway, 1962, p. 45.

APPENDIX I: THE LIFE OF THE BUDDHA

1. 'The First Sermon' or 'Benares Sermon' of the Buddha, in Jean Boisselier, *The Wisdom of the Buddha,* trans. by C. Lovelace, Gallimard / Thames and Hudson 1993, p. 130.
2. The three traditional sources for the life of the Buddha are the *Pali Canon*, the *Lalitavishtara Sutra*, and the *Buddhacharita* of Ashvagosha. Our presentation of the life of the Buddha is drawn from these sources, particularly as presented in Jean Boisselier's *The Wisdom of the Buddha* (Gallimard /Thames and Hudson 1993) and Sherab Chödzin Kohn's *The Awakened One: A Life of the Buddha* (Shambhala 1994)
3. Jean Boisselier, *The Wisdom of the Buddha,* trans. by C. Lovelace, Gallimard / Thames and Hudson 1993, p. 106.

APPENDIX II: LIFE-THRESHOLD CROSSINGS IN DREAMS

1. C. G. Jung, (C. W. 7ii, par 315) 'The Relations between the Ego and the Unconscious' *Two Essays on Analytic Psychology*, p. 197.

*About the
Author*

L. Caruana is an artist and writer living in Paris. He has made his home variously in Toronto, Malta, Vienna, Munich and Monaco. During his wanderings he has actively recorded his visions and expanded their imagery through mythology. His art pursues the creative interplay of different cultural symbols and styles, inspired by memories, dreams and experiments with entheogens. He studied painting in the more traditional manner of apprenticing under Ernst Fuchs, and today he carries on this tradition, teaching classical techniques of painting in the *Visions in the Mischtechnik* seminar. His paintings are regularly exhibited across Europe and throughout America.

From his studio in the Bastille quarter of Paris, L. Caruana continues to paint while writing books, editing the *Visionary Revue*, and giving lectures abroad. See LCaruana.com, VisionaryRevue.com and GnosticQ.com

By the same author:

- *The First Draft of A Manifesto of Visionary Art*
- *The Hidden Passion: A Novel of the Gnostic Christ Based on the Nag Hammadi Texts*